HOW TO SUCCEED AS AN
INDEPENDENT CONSULTANT

HOW TO SUCCEED AS AN INDEPENDENT CONSULTANT

HERMAN HOLTZ

JOHN WILEY & SONS
New York   Chichester   Brisbane   Toronto   Singapore

Library of Congress Cataloging in Publication Data:

Holtz, Herman
    How to succeed as an independent consultant.

    Includes index.
    1. Business consultants.   I. Title.

HD69.C6H63   1982   658.4'6'068   82-13429
ISBN 0-471-86742-X

Printed in the United States of America

20 19 18 17 16 15 14

*To Sherrie, a loving wife,
who started me on a trail
that has led, finally, to
this book*

Preface

The surge of interest in consulting as a profession has been little short of remarkable in recent years, as demonstrated by the increasing number of people who exhibit a desire to join the ranks of professional consultants each year.

One reason for this is the increasing technological development of our society. There is less and less opportunity for the person who "can do anything." Jobs are more and more specialized, and almost all professions today require the individual to specialize within a specialty. For example, there are few general practitioners in law, dentistry, or medicine. There is at least one level of specialization in every engineering field, in computers and data processing, in accounting, in financial management, in other management fields, and even in fields that are at relatively unsophisticated levels of technical complexity. (Even automobile mechanics tend to specialize today).

Another reason is that a much larger proportion of young people have gone to college and acquired special skills and knowledge in one profession or another, and a great number have gone on to acquire graduate degrees as well.

The complexity of society and its technology make it necessary for many people to call upon specialists for various services—to help with job finding and career planning, to solve a data-processing problem, to organize a financial-management plan, to broker a divestiture or acquisition, to prepare a training program, or to handle any of many chores and functions which the individual cannot handle alone. Conditions in general have created the market for consulting services of many kinds, while at the same time there is a growing number of consultants capable of providing those services.

Couple this with the fact that consulting lends itself to self-employment, and it is clear why the activity and interest in consulting have surged. If you have specialized skills and knowledge, it is quite likely that you can begin a free-lance existence as a consultant and prosper—even build a sizable company if you wish.

One of my associates, Steve Lanning, recently launched a quarterly tabloid publication called *Consulting Opportunities Journal.* He mailed 40,000 copies free to a mailing list he had compiled, making a very modest soft-sell appeal for subscriptions. He received nearly 500 subscriptions from that first mailing and by the third edition, the subscriptions had swelled to over 2,000, forcing him to go bi-monthly, with the near certainty that he would have to go monthly in a few months.

For various reasons, a large proportion of those who enter into consulting as a profession do not survive the first year, the chief reason being the failure to market their services effectively. The word "market" is not a synonym for "sell." "Sales" and "marketing" are two different functions, and the failure to recognize the difference is often fatal to a business enterprise like consulting.

A major goal of this book is to teach the marketing of consulting services as well as how to sell such services, for while the two are different functions, sales depend on marketing and cannot be achieved effectively unless the marketing has been done properly. Conversely, if marketing is done well, sales are almost inevitable and are not a cause for major concern. To put it differently, technical and professional skills alone do not a consultant make. To be a successful consultant, you must not only possess the skills, but you must also know how to sell your skills and how to apply them to satisfy the client.

Marketing is the key. Many people who ought to know better confuse "marketing" with "sales." At the risk of oversimplifying, here are thumbnail definitions: "Sales" is getting orders; "marketing" is deciding which to get. That includes analyzing resources and needs and making the proper matches. It includes designing the products or services needed to satisfy the clients' needs, for the consultant is successful only if the client is satisfied.

That's what this book is all about: How to be a *successful* independent consultant. Successful because you understand marketing and know how to prospect, develop leads, close sales, satisfy clients, get recommendations, and grow. That is what you will learn in these pages—not the technical/professional skills which we assume you bring with you—but how to apply your skills, intelligence, common sense, and what you will learn here to the honorable modern profession of consulting. Bring an open mind to your study, for consulting is a much-misunderstood profession, and the truths you are about to learn can make possible a career you never dreamed of.

HERMAN HOLTZ

Silver Spring, Maryland
September 1982

Contents

if so, for what?; do you need an accountant? if so, for what?; accounting is part of management; accounting information is management information; the common mistakes of beginning entrepreneurs; basic rules; basic cost centers and cost definitions; direct and indirect costs; typical indirect costs; fixed versus variable expenses.

ging; the most important thing you can do; first step in analysis; pricing; how to quote prices; where to conduct initial interviews; things that should be settled at first meeting; initial meeting with new client; the kickoff meeting.

ers' bureaus; proposal-writing reminders; proposal do's and don'ts; understanding costs; a handful of terms you'll run into and what they mean; average consulting rates; seminar guidelines; seminar ideas; registration; group consultation ideas and possibilities; custom in-house seminars for extra profits; canned seminars; a few names the consultant ought to know; newsletter ideas and tips for the consultant; where/how to get information input; marketing your newsletter.

HOW TO SUCCEED AS AN INDEPENDENT CONSULTANT

Introduction

Consulting has been a source of controversy around Washington, DC, since 1977 when the Carter Administration first raised strong objections to "excessive" use of consultants by federal agencies. The cause was soon taken up by several Members of Congress, but in Congressional debates, as in the Administration's Office of Management and Budget (OMB), it became apparent that those involved were having great difficulty defining what consulting was. To this day, despite the best efforts of the OMB (via its Office of Federal Procurement Policy—OFPP), nothing approaching consensus has been reached. The OMB/OFPP have finally settled on *their* definition of consulting, but many other federal agencies do not agree with the definition and therefore do not comply fully with Administration directives on what federal agencies ought and ought not to do about contracting for consulting services.

Anyone familiar with consulting or government contracting could have anticipated this problem, given the ill-defined and loosely-used term "consulting" which is the butt of so many jokes, from the allegation that a consultant is someone who borrows your watch to tell you what time it is (Robert Townsend, in *Up the Organization*, New York, Alfred A. Knopf, 1970) to the general observation in and around Washington, DC, that a consultant is anyone who is out of work but has a briefcase. A consultant, however, can be properly defined as anyone who can and does render advice and/or related services in any skill area of at least a quasi-professional nature, at some fixed fee or rate, on a contractual basis. Ordinarily the services and skills/knowledge required are somewhat specialized and not commonly available. Only rarely, however, can consultants command substantial fees for advice alone; most clients want work done.

In the medical profession, a specialist becomes a consultant usually by virtue of the fact that the physician directly responsible for the patient has called the specialist in to "consult." Had the patient visited that specialist directly, the specialist would not have been a consultant.

In the defense and aerospace industries, many engineers and other technical specialists are hired as temporary employees under contract rather than as direct staff. But many such short-term contract specialists call themselves consultants, and the firms who supply such help often refer to themselves as consulting firms.

One definition given to distinguish consulting as a profession is that the consultant is a specialist who is retained to solve a problem. But offer such specialist a contract which requires the consultant's special skills and abilities but entails no problem-solving requirement, and see whether the consultant then refuses to accept the assignment!

The fact is that any specialist may call himself or herself a consultant and is likely to do so, unless another title appears better suited to the needs of one's practice. A lawyer is not likely to offer services as a "legal consultant" although it would be perfectly legitimate to do so. On the other hand, firms originally founded as engineering or accounting firms have sometimes found it advantageous to shift their identities somewhat and build reputations as consulting organizations. Witness such as Booz Allen; Arthur Young & Co.; Peat, Marwick, & Mitchell; and Price Waterhouse, to name only a few.

The self-employed independent consultant is likely to undertake short-term assignments almost exclusively. However, even that does not distinguish the consultant from another technical or professional specialist contractor, for many of the larger consulting firms undertake major projects running for several years.

Defining what you do as an independent consultant, then, depends primarily on what you are willing to do, on what kinds of assignments or contracts you wish to accept. If you wish to reject any contract that does not include a problem-solving element, you are of course free to do so, as you are free to refuse to accept a requirement that includes writing a final report or making a presentation to the client's staff. You and you alone may determine just what that term "consultant" means when it is applied to you.

One the other hand, you don't have that control over what the prospective client perceives the consultant and the consulting service to be. Is that important? It certainly is, if you are to stand a chance of closing the sale. You must know what the client expects and wants to see—that is, the image you must project. That could be troubleshooter and problem solver, father confessor, extra hands and feet, resident sage, guidance counselor, or anything else. Your success in marketing depends almost exclusively on two factors:

1. How accurately you have evaluated the image you must project and succeeded in projecting it.
2. How effectively you have convinced the prospective client that you are exactly what he or she is looking for.

The importance of this is not confined to the marketing function alone, however. You will find that these same principles apply almost equally to satisfying your client that you have performed faithfully and well, for to a great degree the quality of the services you provide depends on the client's perception of how well you have performed. In fact, in a great many consulting situations, the quality of the services you provide is entirely a factor of the client's perception of that quality.

The typical client looks upon you, the consultant, as someone who has all the answers in your field. My clients expect me to be able to answer any question across the entire range of situations, forms, formats, regulations, and other matters bearing on marketing to and purchasing by the federal government. Neither I nor anyone else, of course, has all that vast array of information and wisdom available on instantaneous call. At the same time, to say bluntly, "I don't know," when asked a question by a client is to throw cold water on the client who believes that, as a consultant, you *must* know. Why are you collecting that $500/day fee if you don't know all the answers? (Or even $200/day?) How dare you not know?

That the consultant is only a human, after all, must never be revealed. The consultant must be an expert in all things pertaining to the field of specialization and even more—the consultant must be able to speak publicly, write well, debate, present, persuade, devise strategy and otherwise do whatever must be done to satisfy the client's need. Here we encounter the great paradox of consulting: The consultant must somehow be both the specialist and the generalist! The technical or professional specialist in whatever the disciplines of the field are, and yet a troubleshooter, lecturer, writer, advisor, and whatever else the typical consulting situation requires. If the consultant operates an independent practice, it is also essential that the consultant be an effective marketer and businessperson. Fortunately, it is rare that a consultant must be all of these things in connection with a single assignment or project. However, over the course of many assignments and projects the consultant will find most of these skills a great asset.

All of this is considered in the many pages that follow. The assumption upon which I base this book is that the reader approaches it in possession of some set of skills, training, experience, and/or specialized knowledge which is a sound basis for establishing a consulting practice, but needs some guidance in related fields necessary to establishing and operating a successful, independent consulting practice. That is the end to which this book is addressed: Assisting the reader in putting his or her special abilities to work in building and operating a profitable and satisfying practice of the type which has come to to be called "consulting."

It may also be that the employer needs a
ized skill which is especially difficult to fin
case of a need tailor-made for consulting, l
quired for a limited period of time, to solv

THE AEROSPACE INDUSTRIES

The kind of situation just described, wher
limited time periods and either cannot or p
staff, existed long before computers came
World War II, when our government becam
in what soon became known as the Cold Wa
the U.S. Government were given large buc
equipped with modern arms under virtually
existed during the hot war with the Axis p
awarded to such companies as RCA, Gen
Electric, North American, and Boeing.

A new phenomenon appeared concu
procuring huge complexes of equipment, c
tional entities. A fighter airplane, for exampl
an airplane equipped with guns, radar, radic
was now a complete defense system with
were no longer radar sets; they were part of
tems, detection systems, early warning sys
tems, and so forth. We had entered an era of
the new complexities of that concept. An enti
sion of a large corporation might be dedicate
ment of a single system, and the team of tech
could easily involve thousands of different k

The need for trained specialists with releva
overnight, and companies with huge defen
gaps in the technical teams they assembled
many qualified new-hires as they could man
some of their problems, they began to hire
were offered to them on a contract basis, to be
rate and, in many cases, with a per diem exp
an in-house staff engineer might earn $8,500 a
gineers supplied by the firms that soon bec
might be billed to the company at nine dollars
would pay the engineer perhaps six dollars a
ance, and other costs, and getting their profit o

1

What Does (Should) a Consultant Do?

Better be proficient in one art than a smatterer in a hundred
Japanese proverb

It becomes more and more difficult t[...]
ify as "consulting" from any other set [...]
professional specialist of any kind. P[...]
title itself or in the self-image of that p[...]
self a consultant, for it is difficult to p[...]
tic in the services provided. Perhaps [...]
and complex society a great many ser[...]
ized as consulting contracts. Let's tal[...]

COMPUTERS AND DATA PROCESS[...]

When decades or even centuries from [...]
spective, there is no doubt that compu[...]
decisive, shaping influences of the era[...]
ically to include the entire family tr[...]
ENIAC) are almost everywhere—in ou[...]
tiny electronic calculators; in desk dr[...]
tors, super-calculators, mini-compute[...]
other spin-off devices; under the hooc[...]
our homes and classrooms. The help-[...]
jor newspaper in every population ce[...]
help under such headings as *compute[...]
formation analysts, systems analysts. '*[...]
in response to any of these advertise[...]
people who accept contracts to do th[...]
but at daily consulting fees rather tha[...]
for the difference between earning a p[...]
fits the job provides, and charging a d[...]
your own costs for other benefits, you[...]
the employee does. What is the diff[...]
should an employer favor one arran[...]
should you as the technical/profession[...]
over the other?

Because qualified people are not ea[...]
fessions, sometimes hiring a specialist [...]
way the employer can get the work d[...]
employer needs to have done is a te[...]
workload and not a permanent requir[...]
an economy to hire a consultant and [...]
terminating an employee. No employ[...]
employees if it can be avoided.

will also get extra per diem pay ranging to an additional $100 or $150 per week. The job shopper usually gives up the stability of staying in one place, facing the need to accept jobs all over the U.S. in order to work steadily and many have accepted assignments to foreign countries as well. To those who prefer the nomadic existence of a modern-day itinerant worker, this is an advantage.

THE TRUE CONSULTANT COMPANY

Although job shops often list themselves as consulting organizations, they are not truly consulting organizations in the sense that they undertake true consultant-type projects. Rather, they are suppliers of contract labor. Organizations that are truly consulting companies are quite different. They employ people on a permanent basis to work in the company's own facilities on a project managed by the company and for which the company is responsible.

There are many such companies. Some list themselves as "consulting engineers," while many others announce that they are "management consultants" or "management services" companies. And a large percentage of these, especially the management consultants, specialize in handling government projects.

Some of these companies have many branch offices. Some of the branch offices are permanent offices in areas where the company can get new business on a regular basis, while other "branch offices" are really only "project offices," organized strictly for a single project contracted for and where there is little likelihood of getting additional contracts. For example, a consulting firm might win a contract with an Army base in the Arizona desert and find it necessary to have an office near the base. The company will, for at least the life of the project, list that project office as a branch office to enhance its own image as a large organization.

HYBRIDS

It's not a black and white world, and making these black and white distinctions is helpful in perceiving the basic nature of things, but it is also necessary to see that few of these companies conform completely to the basic characterizations. For example, the job shop may very well have some in-house facilities to do some drafting, technical writing, engineering, or other tasks, and may therefore take on some projects as projects rather than as suppliers of contract workers. Or the management consulting organization may very well accept a contract to supply workers to work on the client's premises, and this is not an unusual case at all.

But even here there are exceptions to what were presented earlier as basic situations and conditions. Temporary or contract workers assigned to work on a client's facilities in private industry are usually under the supervision of the client's managers and supervisors. The U.S. Government, however, often has such contract personnel working on federal facilities, and the law forbids civil service personnel from supervising contract workers or being supervised by contract workers. Therefore, when the federal government awards a contract in which the contractor's staff will work on federal premises—even when the people are operating government facilities such as laboratories and data-processing centers—the contractor must provide supervisors and managers, who can get only technical direction from civil service personnel.

There are also many organizations and individuals who do not list themselves as consultants, but who provide the same services as others who do list themselves as consultants. The term "consultant" really makes no difference in identifying or defining what the organization or individual actually does. It is my view, however, that anyone who provides a technical or professional service, or who undertakes work which is essentially a technical or professional service (even though it may involve other activities), is consulting. Therefore, while President Carter's Office of Management and Budget wound up in the position of appearing to say, "We are not at all sure just what 'consulting' is, but whatever it is, we're against it," I say "No matter what others mean by the term 'consulting,' I know that *I* mean by it, and I'll discuss whatever *I* think consulting is and what consultants do or ought to do." However, let me stress that the main focus of this book is on the self-employed, independent consultant, or at least on the small consulting organization rather than on the larger companies.

THE CONSULTANT AS A SELF-EMPLOYED, INDEPENDENT INDIVIDUAL

By and large, the self-employed and independent consultant has all the options already described—accepting projects, with responsibility for producing some specified result or product; hiring out as temporary labor on contract, to be paid some hourly, daily, or weekly rate; some hybrid of these two basic approaches to selling technical and professional services; or almost any other arrangement desired which appears practicable and reasonable. The independent consultant has almost unlimited freedom within whatever the consultant believes possible and acceptable. Few other independent, self-employment careers offer this degree of freedom and flexibility. Many entail licensing of some sort, which establishes certain constraints; some place the practitioner under professional ethical codes which have almost the force of law; and some require that clients be received at the practitioner's office, which creates an obligation and an overhead expense that may determine what the practitioner can and cannot do.

For most consultants there is complete freedom from these restraints. No formal licensing, no control or heavy influence by any association, and infrequent need to have clients visit us means that most of us have no practical restriction on working from our own homes except for personal considerations.

A FEW EXCEPTIONS

There are, of course, some exceptions. Sometimes the nature of the consulting practice is such that clients must visit the consultant and, therefore, the consultant must establish and maintain professional offices. Also the consultant may find it more comfortable or personally preferable to have offices away from home. This entails the expense of rent, telephone, secretary or answering service, and perhaps a few incidentals. This is all overhead which must be reflected in the fees charged.

A few consulting professions require licenses of some sort. For some, the mere existence of an office away from home requires a license as well as creating additional tax burdens. All of this should be considered when making the basic decision as to where and how to establish the operating center for your consulting practice.

WHAT FIELDS ARE SUITABLE FOR CONSULTING?

Many of us have a tendency to assume that what we ourselves know well is common knowledge. The first time I conducted a seminar on how to write proposals for government contracts, I stipulated in my advertising that it was a graduate course and not at all suitable for beginners at proposal writing. Nevertheless, a generous proportion of the 54 attendees who registered for that first session were beginners, lured by my promises to reveal a number of inside tips I had learned over the years. However, there were also a number of thoroughly experienced people, including two senior executives who were in the process of forming a new division in their large corporation. They had come to the seminar to see if they could pick up even a handful of useful ideas.

Until I conducted that session, I had doubts that I could reveal enough little-known information to justify the cost and the full day's time spent by each attendee. I was amazed to discover that even senior, experienced people were unaware of many basic facts I would have expected them to know as well as I did.

One example was the topic of costs—the cost analyses and presentations required in most proposals. I had expected to do little more than mention these briefly in passing, but, to my amazement, that portion of my presentation proved to be one of the areas of greatest interest to the attendees. Even senior people tend to be somewhat confused and uncertain about "direct" and "indirect" costs, overhead, "other direct," and many other *basic* cost elements and concepts, let alone the more esoteric jargon and concepts such as "G&A" and "expense pools."

This has been an experience repeated in almost every seminar I have conducted, and I am always at least slightly surprised by it. I can never believe that experienced proposal writers in contracting companies have so little understanding of what costs are, how they are generated, how they proliferate, how they must be presented—that is because I myself found the matter of costs a fascinating one many years ago when I first became involved in proposal writing and pursuing contracts. Unlike many, I was not content to turn this portion of the effort over to the company's accountants; I insisted that I would work out the costs and let the accountants review them. I insisted that I would not submit a proposal until and unless I personally approved of everything in that proposal. In the course of time, I became so knowledgeable about the cost side of the business that I took such knowledge for granted and assumed that everyone writing proposals was equally knowledgeable. Therefore, I was too modest about what I had to offer listeners in this respect.

It's a common enough error. Most of us assume that we have special knowledge or abilities to offer to those who are unfamiliar with our fields. Not so: You can probably sell your services to your technical/professional peers once you take the trouble to learn in what areas they most need help, or what special knowledge or skills you have in your field that is helpful, yet not widely known or available in your profession.

That applies to virtually all professions and fields. Following is a list of just some of the fields/areas in which consulting services are offered. Even these are, for the most part, *generalized* items, with various specializations possible within each. Study this list to gain an appreciation of the diversity. You may well find yourself qualified to consult in more than one field.

Engineering	Personnel
Accounting	Public relations
Management	Marketing
Office design	Security
Interior decorating	Mergers and divestitures
Data processing	Psychology
Industrial methods	Food preparation
Municipal services	Grantsmanship
Education	Health care
Design	Communications
Organizational development	Project organization
Executive search	Real estate
Publishing, general	Publishing, technical
Convention management	Drug and alcohol abuse
Business writing	Project management
Training	Medicine
Advertising	Office procedures
Sales	Graphics design
New ventures	Auditing
Financial management	Restaurant operation
Testing	Public health service
Hotel management	Audiovisual presentation
Club management	

A few years ago the Administrator of the General Services Administration was Jay Solomon, a businessman who had a great deal of experience in having buildings erected. He had concluded that the most common trouble found in new and old buildings was leaking roofs. He therefore decided to develop advanced roofing designs and procedures and began a search for roofing consultants, placing a great many under contract to the federal government's Public Buildings Service.

A number of federal agencies have become devoted to the practice of value engineering or value management, as it is also called, and especially to the offshoot disciplines known as "Life Cycle Costing" and "Design to Cost." A great many consultants have sprung up around these areas, with some certified by a professional association, SAVE (Society of American

Value Engineers), as "Certified Value Specialists" and others simply "hanging out their shingles" as consultants in the various disciplines.

A Chicago woman ran a small classified advertisement, offering to write letters for people who had difficulty writing letters, letters of complaint, love letters, letters of inquiry, and so forth. To her surprise, she was inundated with orders for many weeks from that one small advertisement.

Many people run resume services from their homes, helping others organize their working experience into the best possible resumes and letters. Some go beyond that to offer career counseling, and some offer to help clients prepare Form 171, the U.S. Government's form for applying for a civil service job.

One woman who discovered that she had a marked talent for organizing office routine and office procedures ventured into supplying that service to clients as an independent consultant. She was so successful at it that she won long-term consulting assignments from the U.S. Government as well as from private clients.

Quite a few people got into consulting specialties connected with training hard-core-unemployed people as a result of Lyndon Johnson's War on Poverty and related programs. There are a number of consultants in this and related fields of training, education, and social services.

There are many individuals throughout the country who offer services as financial consultants. In that role they assist clients in finding capital for business ventures, and many of them are experts at drawing up the complicated applications—called loan packages in the trade—which are vital to winning approval of loans and equity funding.

There are also "consultants' consultants." At least two who have been so characterized conduct regular seminars in the art and procedures of organizing and operating a consulting practice.

One man who was a bookstore manager for 10 years lost his job and became a successful consultant to publishers and to associations who wished to be guided in publishing one or more books as publications of their own associations. He also has presented seminars on the subject and self-published several books of his own.

In a number of cases, engineers and other specialists who were employed as job shoppers decided to cut out the middle man, that is, the job shop that employed them, and contract directly with the client company. In many cases a lower billing rate was not an inducement since the client company could pass the cost on to the government under their cost-plus contracts. As an inducement, some of these entrepreneurs simply studied the market continuously and "specialized" in whatever was the current greatest need.

THE MARKET

Needs change constantly, and markets change as a reflection of this. A good example is the computer-engineering field as it evolved. One had only to read the engineering help-wanted advertisements to identify the needs and markets in computer engineering, hence consulting opportunities in that field. At first, the great need was for engineers familiar with logical circuitry—flip-flops and gates of various kinds. As that technology became well established, the need for better memory (data storage) devices grew, and there was a period when engineers with knowledge of or experience in magnetic drums were in great demand. But drums became obsolete eventually, and storage was better handled by the new ferrite cores.

It never stops. As the technology progresses, the needs and the market for special knowledge and skills change. The successful consultant must stay in touch with the market; otherwise, you find yourself offering something for which there is no longer a demand. Making it your business to know what there is a current market for and shaping your offers to coincide with current needs is an integral part of marketing. Marketing cannot sell that for which there is no demand. (We'll discuss this in greater depth later, when we address marketing per se.)

THE SETS OF SKILLS NEEDED

One of the critical matters we will expand on later is the breadth and types of services necessary to make a success of your enterprise. It is as much a mistake to permit yourself to become overspecialized as it is to be too generalized. The consultant is necessarily something of a specialist, but the independent, self-employed entrepreneur is necessarily something of a generalist. The successful consultant must bring to bear a variety of skills in addition to the main skill upon which the practice is predicated. And these ancillary skills fall into two broad categories:

1. That set of skills necessary for the successful conduct of any enterprise (marketing, selling, accounting, managing, etc.)
2. That set of skills necessary to the support of the basic consulting skill supplied to the client (writing, analyzing, listening, presenting, etc.)

Even this is something of an oversimplification. That set of skills listed above as item (2) represents skills needed to make the effective delivery of the basic skill possible, but those ancillary skills are also necessary to broaden the base of income-producing activities. This will become clearer later, as we examine each of these ancillary-skill areas and how to employ the skills in your consulting practice. Be assured, however, that to a very large degree your success as a consultant is geared closely to the number of related skills you can marshal and how well you employ them. That success refers to both the degree to which you please your clients and the profits you enjoy from your practice, both essential to giving you personal satisfaction from your practice.

Let's take a typical case out of my own consulting experience to illustrate this more precisely.

One client of mine is a corporation made up of about 20 separate companies. I provide services to both the corporate director of marketing and to several of the companies. I am retained because I have specialized knowledge of federal government procurement and means of marketing to federal agencies. Here is a brief account of how this evolved:

1. The corporate headquarters of this company was included in a mailing I made, inviting prospects to attend a seminar on government marketing.

2. The corporation decided to pursue government contracts aggressively though they had previously made no special efforts to get government business. They sent two people to attend the seminar.

3. The newly appointed corporate director of government marketing called, invited me to have lunch and discuss consulting services.

4. I was retained to help prepare a "capabilities brochure."

5. I was retained by one of their companies to help write a proposal.

6. I was retained to prepare and deliver an in-house seminar to representatives of all the companies.

All of this means that I had to be a good listener, to gather the facts of their needs and desires. I had to be an analyst, to determine what services I should offer and what I should recommend. I had to be a writer, to provide several specific services, as well as to make written submittals to persuade them to retain me. I had also to negotiate contracts with them and to work closely with their own staff, both junior and senior people in the organization.

Note that while the main basis for my retention by this client is my knowledge of government marketing, what I am required to provide requires listening, analyzing, speaking, presenting, reporting, and writing. But I have also gotten involved in preparing protests (appeals) and in negotiating with the customer in their behalf. Moreover, I have frequently had to lead a team in conducting an overall marketing effort.

I cite this particular client because I have provided such a range of services and skills, but I have had to do some of these things for each of many other clients, just as you will. You will always have to be a good listener—as a first order of business. You will often have to be an analyst, to help the client translate the symptoms into a problem definition and decide what the specific need is. You will sometimes have to be a good explainer, sometimes a good presenter, to lead the client (sometimes explaining what you propose to a sizable staff) into complete understanding and agreement. You often must prepare a proposal to win final approval and a signed contract. You may have to submit a final report, or even a thick manual, as an end-product, and you may have to make a final presentation to an assembled staff. The following is an example of that.

A contract which I had won by submitting a successful proposal called for developing an evaluation model for certain auto-instructional systems in the Postal Service training establishment. Later, when the model was complete and presented in a final report, documented in detail and providing all the necessary data for implementing it, I was asked to make a formal presentation to the assembled staff. This proved to be about 20 people, eager to learn about the new system but quite skeptical about its practicality. It taxed my presentation skills because the staff included so many who were highly skeptical and challenged what I said more or less continuously. Fortunately, the director was pleased, and I continued to win new contracts from the organization. But the presentation was a critical factor in satisfying the client, as important to the final success of the project as the written report and the model itself.

One skill required for this particular project was research, and this was quite important because the client had to be shown that I had made a thorough survey of the literature available on the subject of modeling training programs, and was not reinventing the wheel nor going against any demonstrated experience in this field.

THE AVENUES OF SPECIALIZATION

A consultant's main specialty may be a subject area, skill, or some combination thereof. Engineering has been listed as an example of a consulting field. There are, however, many kinds of engineers—electrical/electronic, chemical, mechanical, and civil, to name just a few. There are specialties within each of these general engineering fields, and virtually all engineers eventually specialize. An electrical engineer, for example, may specialize in power systems, and an electronics engineer may specialize in radar or test instruments. A civil engineer may specialize in tunneling or bridges or even high-rise construction or road building. A mechanical engineer may work in rockets and propulsion systems or in automation.

Engineers specialize still further, so that an engineer specializing in test equipment may restrict even that to signal-generating equipment or ultra-sensitive detection equipment.

This is equally true in many other fields. I am somewhat of a generalist in proposal writing and government marketing, but there are many who specialize in marketing to the military agencies only or to the social service agencies only. There are some who work on grant applications only, and even here some specialize in the arts and humanities, in health care, or in occupational safety. For that reason, even that relatively long list supplied earlier, containing 45 descriptors of general fields in which individuals consult, can be multiplied by a factor of at least four or five and still represent only a small portion of all the specialties in which consulting is a viable possibility.

That list was compiled to illustrate fields of knowledge primarily, with the specific skill a secondary consideration. For example, civil engineering is a technological field, and the consultant in that field supplies both knowledge of civil engineering and the skill to carry out engineering tasks in that field.

Another list might be drawn up in which the individual skill is stressed, rather than the subject-matter field in which the skill can be used most effectively. Here, for example, is a brief list of some skills to illustrate that point:

General writer	General illustrator
Instructor	Researcher
Reporter	Editor
Technical illustrator	Draftsperson
System analyst	Business programmer
Tax specialist	Copywriter
Auditor	Computer operator
Appraiser	Chef
Photographer	Scientific programmer
Investigator	Typographer
Technical writer	Recruiter
Mathematician	Grants writer

In almost every case above, there is ample room for further specialization without becoming overspecialized. Even among technical writers, for example, there are those who declare themselves to be "radar writers," specialists in "documenting" computer software, writers of manuals on missile systems, and specialists along the lines of various kinds of systems and equipment. Writers may be general writers of many things, but some fields of writing require special knowledge. The general writer, for example, would find it impractical to attempt to write a technical manual without having the technical knowledge usually considered necessary.

You may choose to specialize, then, as the expert in knowledge of some field or as the expert practitioner of some identifiable skill. In either case, it is necessary to determine just how specialized the offered service is to be. It is fatal to make it so narrow that most of the potential market has been excluded, but it is also necessary to avoid making it so wide that you undertake projects that you cannot carry out successfully or find yourself pursuing contracts for projects that really do not require or justify specialist skills.

You may not always have a free choice in this; the specialty you are able to offer may itself dictate how you offer yourself. A technical writer who happens also to be an engineer may choose to offer engineering as the prime service/capability, with technical writing as one of several engineering services. The technical writer who is not an engineer does not have that option. However, a technical writer may have enough experience and know-how in the field of technical writing to offer services as a leader/manager/designer or other functionary in technical publications, perhaps even to offer services to create and develop a technical-publications function or department in a company as a turnkey project. Or the technical writer may also be a competent technical editor, draftsperson, or illustrator.

As you can see from this, deciding what to offer clients is not a decision to be made hastily or without a great deal of analysis and deliberation. Whether you are a writer who has certain technical abilities or an engineer who writes may make a great deal of difference in how successful you are in finding clients for your services. I, for example, happen to have had an engineering education and a reasonable amount of experience in that field. I personally identify as a writer. Clients perceive me as a marketing specialist, with special emphasis on government marketing, who can write proposals and lecture on the subject. For purely business reasons, I promote the clients' image of me rather than my own. As you can see, I have at least three choices of image I can opt for in selling my own services, and I choose that image which is best for marketing purposes, rather than one to suit my own prejudices about what I am and what I offer. For one of the keys to successful marketing is discovering what it is that the client believes you are or wishes you to be. Or, to put it differently, what the client wishes to buy from you or believes you are selling. Until you have determined what the client really wishes to buy, you can't be sure of what you should sell.

That is not as cynical an observation as it may appear to be. I am not saying that you must deceive your clients. But a cup that is half full is also a cup that is half empty, and most people would prefer a half-full cup to a half-empty one!

In my own field, I am faced with the problem that many, if not most, of the people I encounter want to believe that since they have an education—almost all are college graduates, and many have advanced degrees—they can write a report or proposal as well as the next person. They somehow think it demeaning to be less than totally proficient in the arts of writing. Therefore, they are not impressed with the fact that I am a professional writer, nor do they wish to believe that I can write a proposal better than they. For that reason, offering my services as an expert proposal writer evokes little real enthusiasm and may even evoke a bit of hostility because of the implication that they are not fully expert proposal writers.

On the other hand, no one finds pride or ego threatened by my professed expertness in government marketing. They are perfectly willing to concede that I have superior credentials in that field and that they can therefore retain me to write their proposals without even a tacit admission that they lack any skills they believe they ought to be able to boast of.

For that reason alone (although there are other reasons) my services as a government-marketing consultant are far more attractive than would be my services as a writing or proposal-writing consultant. The clients do not wish to buy my writing skills as much as they wish to buy my government-marketing know-how. And even that does not define or identify precisely what result the client is seeking to enjoy as a direct result of my services. Note the adjective *direct*. It's a highly significant point to make, for the following reason:

We've already established that no one wants to buy my services for the sake of having the services per se; if they buy my services at all, it's because they hope and expect to get a beneficial result. And in my case, that result is government business—contracts. The client is either seeking to begin winning government contracts for the first time, or to increase the ratio of success in winning government contracts if the firm is already doing some business with the government. That is the long-term, ultimate benefit sought.

But the client is neither stupid nor naive. To close a sale, I must show the prospective client some chain of promised events which will lead to that end-result of government contracts or more government contracts. I must, in short, show what the immediate or direct result of my services will be, so that my client can believe that over the long term, the promised benefit will result. In my case, the direct result may be proposal-writing knowledge resulting from a seminar, or it may be a more effective proposal resulting from my efforts applied directly to a specific proposal-writing project.

Later, in discussions of marketing, sales, and advertising, we'll probe this topic again and in greater detail. It's the key to successful marketing, and successful marketing is the key to entrepreneurial success.

2

Why Do So Many Consultants Fail? How To Succeed

All you need in this life is ignorance and confidence, and then Success is sure

Samuel Clemens (Mark Twain), 1887

Periodically, I hear from a friend or acquaintance who tells me that he or she has established a consulting practice. I am invited to recommend clients to the new consultant and to call on him or her for backup when I undertake projects in which I need help. Almost without exception, within the year the new consultant is once again busily employed on someone's payroll as a permanent employee. Frequently the employment is with a company that has used the individual's consulting services during that year.

There are many reasons for such failures. The Small Business Administration and almost anyone with business experience will tell you quickly enough that the first year is almost invariably a critical one, and by far the overwhelming majority of enterprises that fail, do so in the first year. The odds against ultimate success drop sharply in the second year. That is, surviving that critical first year greatly improves the chances for success.

That is not an accidental circumstance, but an entirely logical and fundamental truth of business. That first year is not only a kind of "shakedown cruise," where the new entrepreneur tries out ideas and hones them against the wheel of experience, but it is in general a time of learning. As Howard Shenson reports in one of his books about consulting, a client who was making a fourth effort to launch a successful enterprise after three failed efforts confessed to having made many mistakes. He observed that he had had to learn, in those three failures, the lesson of accounts receivable (too much credit extended to customers), the lesson of accounts payable (too many bills piled up), and the lesson of overhead (too much of it!).

The fact is that for any new entrepreneur to succeed the first time in a new enterprise is almost a miracle. No amount of reading, study, listening to lectures, and other forms of learning can approach experience as a teacher. Even the top executives, with many years of successful experience building and operating important corporations, make major mistakes. (Witness Chrysler, Korvette's, Grant's, Robert Hall, and other large companies who made major blunders and paid dearly.) And if you research sufficiently, you will find that by far the majority of successful entrepreneurs had a failure or two—many had more than the traditional three failures—before finally succeeding.

For most, that first year is a year of mistakes that are almost inevitable for the entrepreneur who has no prior experience in establishing and building a successful business. Most beginning consultants have no models except the companies for which they have worked, but those are models of *established* success, not of successful struggles to surmount the obstacles and achieve the success. Those are not the models that teach the neophyte consultants what the basic initial mistakes most commonly are, and how to avoid or overcome them.

In a more positive approach to this initial phase, the so-called mistakes are best not regarded as mistakes at all, but as learning experiences. The consultant is an entrepreneur, and entrepreneurship must be learned as anything else must be learned. A basic truth is, however, that entrepreneurship must, almost without exception, be learned in the school of experience. Even those who do not fail the first time they make a try at consulting or any other kind of enterprise make their share of mistakes and do their share of learning. They are blessed by managing somehow to avoid making any *fatal* mistakes or being somehow in a position to survive the mistakes and apply the newly won education directly and immediately to the enterprise in hand.

As Oscar Wilde observed in *Lady Windermere's Fan*, "Experience is the name everyone gives to his mistakes." One should *expect* to undergo these learning experiences, whether we call them mistakes or not. In fact, for those who are alert enough and wise enough to learn immediately and to avoid making *disastrous* mistakes, the education is well-bought, a bargain, an indispensable asset, and virtual insurance against future failure.

WHAT IS FAILURE?

England is alleged to lose every battle in a war except the last one. Pundits have coined many *bon mots* to jeer at winning the battles and losing the war. More than one business entrepreneur has observed that you can't beat a person who refuses to quit. All of this, translated into terms of business entrepreneurship, means that you haven't failed unless you admit failure, quit, and try no more.

It is a rare person who has not tasted temporary setbacks. The success stories of almost every successful person form a saga of courage to get up again after being floored, to try once again, and of steadfastly repeating this comeback series, refusing to be beaten. For when you refuse to be beaten, you must eventually succeed. It's all but inevitable. The true failures are those who lose heart at the first setback, those who become discouraged too readily, those who believe that the prize is not worth the struggle, even if it can be attained.

Perhaps you will be the exception, one of those fortunate ones who manages to avoid all but the minor mistakes, and succeeds almost without trying. For it seems that like the cliche about greatness, some individuals are virtually born to success, some achieve success, and some have success thrust upon them. But it is far more likely that you will have to achieve success than to be born to it or have it thrust upon you. Be prepared to experience many lessons, if you wish to achieve success, for each setback is a lesson, not a failure. It is a failure only if you permit it to be a failure, only if you permit it to defeat you.

THE COMMON MISTAKES OF NEOPHYTE CONSULTANTS

Consultants must be eternal optimists, for most new consultants I have known have started on an unacceptably narrow base, with cheerful confidence that they would somehow manage to survive and prosper despite an inadequate business base. The base on which far too many consultants begin is too narrow in two ways:

1.   Most consultants start a practice based on only one or two established clients, and some with no established clients.
2.   Most new consultants start a practice based on only one or, at most, two services, and a much too highly specialized arena of operations.

The first error is not always one of commission because most independent consultants do not make a deliberate, premeditated decision to become consultants. Rather, in many cases, the individual is all but forced into the consulting life by economic circumstance, usually because the end of a contract or some other factor has made the consultant jobless. When such a skilled technical or professional specialist has many "contacts" in the business or industry, it seems certain that a few telephone calls, a personal visit or two, and the mailing of a few resumes will enable him or her to get a new consulting practice off the ground quickly. It seems logical enough, especially when the new consultant manages to line up one client almost immediately.

That one client is the cause of the trouble. The new consultant is deceived into believing that it's easy for such a highly specialized and competent specialist to get all the work he or she can handle. So immediately there is a frenzy of activity setting up all the apparatus of the new consultancy—an office, typewriter, filing cabinets, business cards, letterheads and envelopes, brochures, telephone, and resumes—and all the very best and most expensive.

Then the first consulting assignments are complete and business dries up. Maybe it's a seasonal slump and maybe it's just not enough or not very effective marketing. Maybe the consultant dosen't know how to analyze the market and work out an effective marketing plan.

One problem with independent entrepreneurship, whether it's in consulting or anything else, is that all businesses are seasonal to some extent. Even in those businesses which are not particularly seasonal, however, there are unpredictable ups and downs which reflect economic conditions of the moment or other uncontrollable and unpredictable factors. (In fact, any given enterprise often bucks the tide, busy when competitors are slow and vice versa.) The independent entrepreneur is at a decided disadvantage in this because there is little the independent can do to retrench. The consultancy has only one employee, so lay-offs are not possible. Independents don't do much advertising, so economies there are not possible, and it is difficult for the independent, one-person enterprise to build reserves when business is brisk, so there is little "fat" to subsist on until business picks up again.

This is not to say that there are no answers to these problems. There obviously must be or there would be no independent entrepreneurs. But before we talk about remedies and preventive measures, let's look at that other problem mentioned earlier, the over-specialized or too narrow arena of operations.

Let's take the typical case of John, a specialist in computer-related activities. A Ph. D., he is really *Dr. John.* Dr. John is one of those relatively rare technical/professional specialists who happens to write really well. He is an exceptionally able proposal writer who thinks clearly, and knows how to devise strategies and implement them in written presentation. Therefore, when John's employers found business was slow and let him go, he made a few telephone calls and soon had several proposal-writing projects lined up at excellent daily rates. That kept him so busy for the next few months that he was compelled to take on a partner to help him handle it all.

Proposal writing has its peak seasons, but it never is in a true slump; there is a need for proposal writing the year around. But in the off-peak season, many companies can handle their proposal writing without outside help. Hence, as far as a proposal consultant is concerned, there are busy seasons and slump seasons.

John offered proposal-writing services only. He thought that since there was such demand for his services those first few months that even in the slow season he could keep reasonably busy. He was mistaken. When the peak season ended, he had absolutely no work, and it wasn't long before he was in quest of a permanent job on someone's payroll again.

John's is not an unusual case. It is, in fact, common for new consultants to deceive themselves as to the demand for the services they provide.

Many consultants think that the more highly specialized the service they offer, the more in demand they will be. Unfortunately, the contrary is true; the more highly specialized the service, the smaller the market potential. For example, if you are a civil engineer and will undertake any kind of earth-moving project, you will certainly have a greater number of prospects than if you will undertake only road-building projects or only mining excavations.

THE BASIC TRADE-OFFS

Everything in life is a trade-off. A big automobile is more comfortable and, presumably, safer in an accident, but a small car is more economical to buy and to operate. This is a trade-off in economy versus comfort. An engine can be designed to operate most efficiently at 25 mph or at 50 mph, a trade-off between greatest efficiency in city driving or highway driving. You can trade off between durability and style in buying clothes; or between initial investment and upkeep in buying a house. In all things you can gain more of one thing only at the cost of less of something else. You must pay, somehow, for everything you gain.

So it is in deciding what services you will offer. The more highly specialized they are, the more sharply targeted your advertising can be, the more desirable a specialist you may appear to be, and the more you may charge (presumably). But, on the other hand, the more specialized you are, the more difficult it will be for you to find clients.

At the other end of this spectrum, the more generalized your services are, the less credible you are as a consultant because clients expect consultants to be specialists, not generalists, and this is likely to affect your ability to command an adequate fee. But it will definitely broaden your market base, offering a wider range of prospective clients.

Recently, in my own field as a marketing consultant, I had an experience which illustrates this. My real specialty is intimate knowledge of the federal government market and a well-developed ability to devise successful strategies for proposals. However, I am a writer, and many of my clients engage me to write their proposals for them as well as to devise strategies. A new client recently could not understand that I am primarily a consultant with highly specialized knowledge of the government market and basically a strategist. He insisted that I was too high-priced as a writer, and I was unable to make him understand that writing was incidental, and that he was being asked to pay me, not for writing per se, but (in effect) for knowing *what* to write. I did not succeed in making my point, possibly because he could not erase from his mind the image of a writer commanding far more money than writers normally command.

Still, as far as I am concerned, the trade-off is a good one. If I did not offer a variety of services—consulting per se, writing, lecturing, seminars, training, market research, requirements analysis, and other related functions—I could not possibly stay busy enough the year around to survive as a consultant. And, in fact, I did fail in my early efforts at consulting for that very reason. I had to learn my lessons, too, and I don't enjoy everything I do as a consultant, but some of it is necessary so that I can be free to do those things I do enjoy as a consultant.

One major mistake you must not make is this: Do not indulge yourself simply because you are an independent entrepreneur and in control of your own activities. One indispensable characteristic you need is self-discipline. You must be a stern employer of yourself if you are to succeed, and business decisions must be based on economic need and business considerations, not on personal preference.

MARKETING

If one basic mistake the neophyte makes is offering too narrow a range of services, the other mistake is offering services to too narrow a range or array of clients. Typically, the beginner initiates a practice with one or two good clients—and assumes that this will constitute an adequate launching pad and that later, if and when things slow down a bit, there will be ample time to worry about marketing and finding additional clients. Many beginners don't even think about the matter until the day arrives when there is no work.

A common basic mistake is to assume that the time to begin marketing is when you need new business, not before. After all, is it not a waste of money to advertise and otherwise seek business when you already have plenty of business? The fact is that in every business there is some time lag between the marketing or sales effort and the sales. In a typical retail business, the time lag may be so short as to be almost non-existent; perhaps advertising in the morning newspaper will bring customers through your doors before the day is over. But in many enterprises, and especially in consulting, there is a considerable time lag between the marketing effort and the actual sale or signed contracts. In fact, even highly effective marketing may not result in actual sales for many weeks or even months after the marketing campaign has been launched. And the small consulting practice is often not well-funded and can't survive many months of zero income.

Marketing, therefore, is something that should be planned and initiated almost from the first day, and perhaps even before the consultant's doors are open. In a later chapter, we will discuss some methods for marketing consulting services effectively, and you will find that it is in the nature of the work that ordinarily marketing does not have next-day results.

SURVIVAL TIPS

In the next chapter we are going to discuss many start-up considerations in highly specific terms. Philosophically, however, you must be aware of certain facts of life, even some which are ironic. One of these is popularly known as "Murphy's Law," and it states that "Anything that can go wrong will." Truer words have probably never been written. That "piece of cake" first contract turned out to be seven times more troublesome than you expected, and you wound up biting your tongue to avoid offending your first client. The guy you hired to help with the second job laid an egg, and you paid him off, doing the work over yourself. The next job turned out to be only one fourth the size you were promised, and the fifth contract somehow never materialized at all. Meanwhile, your telephone-answering machine gave you a lot of trouble, and that cost you some business. The accountant charged you more than twice as much as you expected to set your books up, and the bill from the printer for your office stationery and brochures—whew! Then there were a few personal problems that cost a lot of money and ate into your reserves.

All in all, Murphy was right, and you're off to a less auspicious start than you had hoped for. More things went wrong than went right, and maybe you should not have been quite so optimistic and expansive in buying that expensive furniture and ordering all that fancy literature made up, not to mention having an accountant set up such an elaborate accounting/bookkeeping system.

From all this you learn one basic survival tip a bit late, and it's this: *expect* "everything to go wrong," and plan for it. Make $50 mistakes, not $500 mistakes. Put off every expenditure you can put off. Don't count on any sale or income that isn't guaranteed by being actually in hand or under firm commitment of some sort. Don't turn down the $300 contract offered you today because you expect a $1,000 contract tomorrow. Take what you can get *now, today*. If that $1,000 contract does materialize tomorrow (and Murphy's Law bets that it won't), time enough then to worry about it.

Do those first two or three contracts keep you too busy for marketing? Find the time. *Make* the time. The business you save may be your own! Never permit yourself to be too busy for marketing. Today's contract is important, of course, but so is tomorrow's contract. If you're too busy to market today, tomorrow's contract may just never materialize at all. It's not a 40-hour business, at least not in the first year, when you're trying to build something. If you really mean to be successful, you'll have to work 60, 70, even 80 hours a week. Success rarely comes easily; you have to work for it.

Don't be too much the specialist. That is, don't expect the client to tailor needs to your services; you tailor your services to the client's needs. In my own practice, I do many things that are not part of what I consider my basic services, but they are what clients require, and I can do them; therefore, I do. In this connection, bear this in mind: perhaps you are in fact necessarily highly specialized by the very nature of your field; perhaps you're a brain surgeon or a tax expert. But most consultants are not that highly specialized, and rarely are clients' needs that highly specialized. A great many neophytes defeat their own marketing efforts by either overspecializing or by appearing to overspecialize through failure to define fully what they do or offer to do. Here's an example of how that can happen.

One company which was fairly prominent in the training and education field manufactured and marketed a teaching machine, a device for presenting the learning programs written by the company. These programs were produced by being typed onto camera copy, which was then photographed and produced on reels of 35mm film, the latter being the actual product that went into the teaching machine, to be projected onto a screen for the learner. However, the company also developed training programs which were produced as printed manuals, sometimes referred to in that industry as "paper programs."

One day the marketing manager learned that a good customer of the company had awarded a large contract to a competitor for the development of a paper program. "Why didn't you invite us to submit a bid for that?" he asked. The answer came as a surprise: "Why, I had no idea you fellows did paper programs too. Why didn't you tell us?"

That's what is sometimes known as a breakdown in communications. It wasn't that the training developer had misrepresented what they did, but that they had failed to be entirely specific, and the customer had made what appeared to be a perfectly reasonable assumption.

There is always a tendency to assume that the other fellow is a specialist. Everyone wants to "tag" you in some manner, especially today, when there is such an enormous tendency to specialization. Physicians, for example, are almost never general practitioners anymore; they are internists, surgeons, obstetricians, orthopedists, and other kinds of specialists. Others will "tag" you, probably as some much narrower kind of specialist than you wish to appear, if you don't take steps to counter this. You must constantly stress *all* the kinds of services you perform if you do not wish to miss sales opportunities.

A client called me one day, a government executive calling in his official capacity. He wished to know whether I knew of anyone who could handle a specific writing assignment for his agency. I certainly did—*me*. He thought I would direct him to someone else, but it was a nice $6,000 contract I could very well handle myself.

I generally provide my services by the day, at a daily rate, but sometimes a client wishes to utilize my services for less than a full day. I therefore offer an hourly rate, too, and that has produced some lucrative tasks I might otherwise not have gotten.

What I usually write for clients, in my capacity as a government marketing consultant, are proposals. But that has not prevented me from writing newsletters, term papers, theses, and whatever else clients want written and are willing to pay me for.

Even if you have the goal of being highly specialized, it may be necessary, for purely economic reasons to be somewhat less specialized during the first year of your enterprise unless your financial condition permits you to hold out that first year in spite of sparse sales. However, if yours is the more typical case and you must keep busy to survive that first year, you are probably forced to accept whatever work you can get. Later, when you have built the practice and can afford to turn away some work, will be time enough to restrict yourself to that narrow field of specialization. But it is unlikely that you shall be able to do that in your first year.

For the same reasons, it is always advisable to keep costs down that first year. If it is impossible or impractical for you to have an office in your own home, it does not follow that you must set up your office in the most expensive location in town, nor even that you must necessarily be "in town." In these times, metropolitan suburbs are often much less expensive and even more prestigious than in-town locations.

The same considerations apply to business cards, stationery, brochures, office furniture, and other appurtenances of your practice. While image has some importance, it is not necessary to go to extremes to achieve it. In fact, going too far may have the opposite effect and create an adverse impression. (More details about this in the next chapter.) In general, the impression you ought to strive for is that you are professional and businesslike, but at the same time level-headed and practical. It's easy to go overboard and give the impression to prospective clients that you are far too high-priced. Therefore, in doing whatever is necessary to create that businesslike and professional image, don't fall into the error of "too much of a good thing."

THE PERSON YOU NEED TO BE

By now it should be apparent that in virtually everything you must see things from the customer's perspective. You must worry about your image because consulting is generally a highly personalized service, and in a great many cases the client feels that he or she is hiring you temporarily rather than buying something from you. That means that as far as the client's perspective is concerned, the two of you will have a continuing, close relationship, rather than a brief business exchange. The compatibility of your two personalities therefore becomes a factor. Where the client might buy something from someone he or she didn't especially "take to" because the entire exchange brings them into direct contact for a very short time only, that client is not likely to want a close and continuing relationship with someone not especially compatible. So, if your service requires a great deal of personal contact and a close working relationship, your personal characteristics become important. That means that it is probably essential that you don't "come on too strongly," aren't one of those back-slapping, too jovial types, don't guffaw loudly, don't tell racy stories, and aren't guilty of many other practices that many men and women find offensive. Far better to be completely bland, even humorless, almost to the point where you fade into the wallpaper and become virtually invisible. Ideally, of course, you should fall somewhere between the extremes and be the dignified, quiet type, with a ready smile, a soft voice, and a great capability for listening attentively and patiently.

One mistake of the beginner is to go to extremes in being "Mister (or Ms.) Personality," with a store of jokes, a loud voice, ultra self-assurance, and a capability for dominating the conversation, even for appearing to know the answer before hearing the question. As one prospect told me after he had become my customer and I had done several tasks for him, "I liked you right away because you didn't come on too strong, and yet you showed me that you had self-confidence." It's easier to achieve that image with a quiet approach than an over-eager one.

THE ART OF LISTENING

Nowhere is this image and the ability to listen attentively and patiently more important than in the first contact or initial meeting. Whether you have made a "cold call" and been invited in to discuss what you wish to offer or have been invited in as a result of a casual meeting with the prospective client at an earlier time, the proper approach is the same. You are acting as a salesperson about to make an initial presentation, in the hope of negotiating a contract for your services. Nevertheless, your entire orientation ought to be that of the consultant, despite the fact that you are not yet hired. Here is an example of how that ought to work:

I once made a cold call on a government executive, after a brief introduction by another government executive whom I had met only a few minutes earlier. I had explained that I was a consultant who specialized in writing assignments, particularly in technological areas, and the man who introduced me to this gentleman—I later became friendly enough to call him Stan—thought that Stan might be interested in what I could offer.

I first gave Stan the opportunity to question me about what I could do and kept my answers as brief and to the point as possible. No superlatives, no hyperbole, no extravagant claims, but just factual reporting.

I then proceeded to question Stan quietly and tactfully about his work and his problems. When he described the problem which concerned him most at the moment, I suggested a problem-solving approach which I could implement for him. We discussed cost, and I suggested about $2,400. Stan then invited me to put my offer in writing, an informal letter proposal, and send it to him. It resulted in a purchase order and a continuing relationship with additional business. Ultimately, it led to $65,000 worth of business.

The key here was simply that I focused all my attention on Stan's needs, his problem(s) and what I could offer in the way of help. Not once did I focus on what *I* wanted. I knew that I could get what I wanted only by somehow giving my prospect what *he* wanted.

That, in a nutshell, is the entire art of marketing and selling: giving the prospects what they want. Do that, and sales are inevitable. You will find that marketing is, among other things, the art of discovering what the customers want and giving it to them. However, that is not the only point made here and isn't even the main point. Let me add a little more information about this experience, and you will probably perceive that main point before I make it.

My original idea in approaching the federal agency which employed Stan was to offer my help in developing safety standards, for it is an agency which is in the business of creating safety standards, among other things, and my engineering background qualifies me to develop safety standards in a number of areas. It turned out, however, that Stan's most urgent immediate problem concerned the development of an educational curriculum for use in junior colleges. He had a two-volume safety-training program in hand, recently delivered by a contractor who had developed what purported to be an instructor guide and a student guide. Stan felt that these were adequate, substantively, to furnish the data base for the desired curriculum, but someone had to prepare a plan specifically for the use of these two volumes. The contractor had not provided anything which would furnish direct guidance in using these as the basis for education and training programs, and Stan did not have the time to devote to preparing such a plan.

It was this problem and need to which I responded, despite the fact that I had not come there seeking work in the training and education field (although I did have some earlier experience in that field and was thus able to propose an approach to the problem). Had I decided that this was not the work I wished to do, I could have excused myself gracefully and gone on my way. And I would have lost $65,000 worth of future business.

The point, then, is that not only must the consultant resist wearing blinders which prevent him from perceiving unexpected opportunities such as this, but the consultant must also *permit the client to decide what the client needs and what the consultant will furnish.* Every initial meeting and discussion with a prospective client must be in pursuit of inducing the prospective client to tell you what to offer, what to propose. That is the proper attitude for the consultant, unlike that of the salesperson who is limited to and restricted by whatever he or she has to sell. These are two basically different selling situations, and it is of critical importance that you understand the basic difference between these two situations.

THE TWO BASIC SELLING SITUATIONS

Wise heads have pointed out that every business is a service business. A much-respected management consultant and author, Peter Drucker, made the point that a great many executives do not know what business they are in, and are therefore severely handicapped in running their companies successfully. Let's explore these ideas first.

The point has already been made that you can only get a realistic look at your business from the customer's viewpoint, and that marketing means giving the customer what the customer wants. What those who say that every business is a service business mean is just this: No one wants to buy the things or services offered per se; they want what those things or services *do* for them. That's why brewers do not sell you on how good their product is, but suggest that drinking their product is fun—laughing it up at the local tavern and sporting with the opposite sex on a sunny beach. Cologne means being adored by the girls, men, and our shampoo means your man will run his fingers lovingly through your hair, girls. Insurance means protecting your loved ones and having peace of mind (that is, having freedom from guilt, a powerful sales motivator). Some automobiles mean economy; others mean a macho image or a feeling of POWER.

Most effective advertising concentrates on what the product or service will do for the prospect—the much-to-be-desired results that will follow the purchase. No more embarrassment from those dirty rings around the collar of your husband's shirts. Admiring praises from friends and relatives who dine from your see-your-own-face-in-it dishes. Swift and easy waxing of your kitchen floor. Fast promotions on the job. It is true that people will believe what they devoutly wish to believe. They are able to suspend logic and reason when they want badly enough to believe and you give them the grounds for the necessary rationalization. So, if you sell Volkswagens you're in the money-saving-transportation business. If you sell Fiats you're in the macho, man about town, jet set, image-making business. If you sell laundry detergents you're in the less-work-for-mother business, or maybe in the great-housewife image-maker business.

Customers buy love, prestige, ego-gratification, security, success, self-image, recognition, and a dozen other emotional satisfactions we all need. We need to feel worthy, appreciated, respected, loved. We'll spend our money to get it. We'll break down walls to get it. And we'll make those who provide it successful beyond mere wealth.

The only way to discover what business you are in is to ask the customer. For consultants are not in "the consulting business." Far from it. Consultants are in the problem-solving business. In the final analysis, every custom service is a problem-solving service. But that does not necessarily mean that your client has a problem he or she does not know how to solve. Never make the mistake of assuming that your client knows less than you about how to solve the problem. That may or may not be the case, but it's most risky to operate on that assumption unless you (1) know it to be fact and (2) the client is willing to operate on that premise. Ordinary diplomacy mandates that you do not flaunt superior knowledge even if you have it; an amazingly large number of clients prefer to believe that they know what to do but are simply too busy to do it.

For example, there are countless cases where a client calls in a freelance writer, offers a hopelessly inept manuscript, and asks for a quote to edit it and "clean it up a bit." The client does not wish to admit, even to himself or herself, that the writing is inadequate and the manuscript ought to be trashed in favor of an entirely fresh writing effort. The smart consultant agrees that a "heavy edit" is in order, quotes for a total rewrite, and winds up with the job.

What's the difference whether your purchase order and invoice reads "writing" or "editing" as the service performed? As long as you have done what had to be done, the client is satisfied, you have been paid for what you actually did, you have carried out your mission and given value for your fees.

Of course, there are other situations in which the problem is not something requiring extensive analysis to solve. In many cases, the client simply does not have anyone on staff with skills such as yours because the need for them is only occasional. In such cases, the client simply wants some additional hands and feet to bring the needed skills to bear. Retaining a consultant who can do the work is the whole solution to the problem. Do not make the mistake of assuming that your work is so mysterious that the client does not know where else to turn for help. The fact that you are a data-processing expert and the client knows almost nothing about the subject, for example, does not place the client at your mercy, to be exploited as you see fit. In this kind of selling situation, what the client wants is simply relief from what could be a headache, a need for something that cannot be done in-house except by retaining a consultant. As far as the client knows, one EDP consultant is as expert and capable as the next one. That suggests that the selection of a consultant ought to be on the basis of price primarily. However, some clients may have reason to appreciate the fact that any given consultant may very well be far more capable and perhaps more efficient than the next one. Or you may be able to persuade the client to perceive that. In that case, price may become a secondary consideration. Or you may be able to show that even if your daily rate is higher than others, your greater efficiency results in a lower total price for the job.

In any case, all these are situations in which the client seeks or considers the services of a consultant because the client has a recognized problem of some kind, for which consulting services may be a good solution. The selling effort here is necessarily that of trying to persuade the client that you are the best possible candidate for the job, on the general argument that your services are the best possible solution. (We'll discuss later the specific sales arguments most effectively used in such cases.)

There is another kind of selling situation in which the prospective client is not aware of or does not recognize the existence of a problem. To sell this prospect it is necessary to get the prospect to agree that there is a problem or need for what you offer.

For example, let us suppose that you are an EDP expert and you find yourself discussing what you do with a prospect who has a computer system in-house and appears to be well satisfied with it. It's quite possible, of course, that the system is far from being as swift (which means economical, in most cases) or as dependable as it ought to be. But it's also quite possible that the prospect has no way of even suspecting that the system is not A-OK in all respects. To have any chance of making a sale here, you are going to have to find the problem and build a sales argument around it. To do this, you will have to gather information from the prospect through tactful questioning and discussion. Once you get a few basic facts, your own expert knowledge will probably guide you to the most likely areas in which you can uncover a problem.

The term "problem" is used in a special sense here, especially inasmuch as we are talking about conditions and needs which the prospect will not have recognized. So, very much like the question of whether a falling tree makes noise if no one hears it, the question here might be: Is there a problem if the prospective client does not recognize it? The term as used here then, refers really to any condition that provides you an opportunity to offer a prospect some benefit. Even if the prospect's computer system were working at the highest efficiency commonly known, but you had some new idea or new item that would raise that efficiency still further, you can "give" the prospect a "problem" in the sense we use the term here: The problem is that the prospect's system is less efficient (hence, more costly) than it could be.

That is exactly how a great many salespeople must handle each presentation because that is their basic selling situation if they offer something new. Their selling job is to create a need, which really means to make prospects aware of what benefits their offer can bring and make them want the product or service.

A consultant may be in either kind of selling situation, depending partly on what kind of services the consultant offers, and partly on how diverse the consultant's activities are. If your basic service is a troubleshooting one, you're probably mostly in the first situation discussed here, where you are talking to a prospect who has a recognized problem. But if you also conduct seminars or publish a newsletter, you are in the other kind of selling situation, where you must convince prospects that certain benefits will be derived and that the failure to gain those benefits constitutes a problem.

Whichever selling situation you find yourself in, you are far more likely to close the sale by inducing the client to define what he or she is buying, and by making it quite apparent to the client that you understand what the client perceives as the need which must be satisfied. In fact, that itself is almost always a major consideration in competing for government contracts; government agencies always study contractors' proposals for a number of factors, but two of the principal factors studied are these:

1. Evidence that the proposer fully understands the requirement—*what the client wants.*
2. A proposal that is fully *responsive* to the requirement.

Again and again, proposals (even from major corporations) are rejected because they fail to satisy both the above conditions. In one case, a growing disregard for what the client defined as the requirement cost one man his company. This man—we'll call him Sam here—was an experienced engineer who had worked on many U.S. Navy programs and had ultimately launched his own engineering-services company in suburban Washington, DC. Through his many contacts in the Navy offices (the Navy's major procurements are made almost entirely in Washington, DC and environs) Sam built a successful engineering company. Since he was really an exceptionally competent engineer with a thorough knowledge of the Navy's programs and needs, Sam became so successful that he soon was having contracts handed to him by the Navy instead of being forced to compete for all of his work. This was unfortunate because Sam became overconfident. He soon began to brush the Navy executives' opinions aside and insist that he knew better than any of them what the Navy needed. The result was, of course, inevitable; his customers soon began to seek out more pliable and cooperative engineering firms to let contracts to. Before long, Sam's company was forced to close its doors, victim of its failure to listen to what the client wished to buy.

HOW DIVERSE SHOULD YOUR SKILLS BE?

It is an irony of the consulting profession that the consultant—the self-employed, independent consultant, at least—must be both specialist and generalist. Specialist because consultants are retained for their specialized capabilities; generalist because the independent consultant must carry out a multitude of functions connected with both sides of consulting, the technical side and the business or management side. Both sides of consulting require some diversity of skills, and the consultant who would succeed in an individual enterprise must be the master of at least some of these, although it is possible to handle others without doing them personally.

As in most things, it is not black-and-white distinction entirely. Some of the skills we will discuss here are definitely those concerned only with the services themselves, some are entirely concerned with the business side or management of the enterprise, and some are in a gray area, straddling the two sides of the enterprise. Let's look first at some of the business skills required, and how they can best be provided.

THE CONSULTANT AS A BUSINESSPERSON

Skills that are usually essential to and associated with operating and managing a business enterprise, no matter what kind of enterprise, are these:

Accounting and related record-keeping
Cost estimating and pricing
Scheduling and time management
Financial management

There are other skills which are, in some enterprises, definitely part of the general business and management side. For consulting enterprises, however, this is not always the case. Marketing, for example, is a special consideration in the consulting enterprise, and falls into that gray area referred to earlier. That will become clearer as we probe the marketing functions later.

Accounting and related record-keeping may be done by the consultant, or it may be handled by engaging the contract services of a public accounting firm. Many small businesses prefer to retain a public accountant to handle this work.Essentially,this can be done in either of two ways:

1.   The accountant sets up the books and a system for you to file things, so that the accountant can come in periodically—once a week or once a month, as necessary—and do all the postings and balancings and make up any necessary records and reports.

2.   The accountant sets up the system and instructs the client in how to post various items and "keep the books." In such arrangements, the accountant generally handles the tax work every quarter and at the end of the year.

On the other hand, it is not difficult for the small entrepreneur to handle the accounting problems by using one of the several off-the-shelf systems available in any good office-supplies emporium. These are simple systems, easy to handle and entirely suitable to the small enterprise. In fact, they offer the small businessperson a decided advantage in that keeping your own books keeps you informed continuously, whereas the public accountant sometimes has unpleasant surprises for you every three months.

Bear in mind that accounting has the keeping of records for tax purposes as only one of its objectives, and that not the main objective. This is not to derogate the importance of tax records, but the main importance of accounting is to furnish information for the judicious management of the enterprise. In not a few cases, lack of proper accounting or, more likely, lack of proper use of accounting information, has been given as the principal reason for business failure. Accounting is what tells the manager whether the enterprise is making or losing money, and, if the accounting function is properly designed for the enterprise, it also tells management why and where the troubles are.

This is one argument for doing your own books when you are small. The larger organization usually has a comptroller whose functions include that of monitoring all accounting information and alerting management to problems. But it is unlikely that a public accountant can do that for you on a timely basis. In most cases, by the time the public accountant has advised you that you are losing money or have other troubles, the troubles are so well advanced that you are likely to have great problems rescuing your business if you are able to do so at all. It is far more advantageous to keep the books yourself and know every day how you are doing.

One other point: The public accountant is not familiar with your business or, very likely, with your industry in general. It is unlikely that the public accountant has designed an accounting system best suited to your needs. In fact, it has been my experience that the typical public accountant will assume that you plan to grow considerably, and believes that you are well-served by an accounting system for a fairly large company, such as is assumed to be your goal. Unfortunately, the more elaborate the accounting system, the more difficult it is for non-accountants to perceive and grasp the salient facts quickly. It is far better, in my opinion, to employ the simplest accounting system possible and stay away from overdeveloped systems which are far in excess of what you are ever likely to need.

Financial management is often considered to be a proper function of the accountants. That, I believe, is a mistake. There are certain functions of financial management which are usually carried out in the accounting department, but they are not the management of the company's finances. Here is what financial management ordinarily entails:

Cost analyses, to ensure that work is estimated and priced properly

Invoicing promptly, and following up to maximize cash flow

Taking advantage of all discounts

Cost control, including cost reduction and cost avoidance

Funding, including equity financing, bank loans, and other means of funding

Even with outside help, such as a public accountant to perform some of these chores, the entrepreneur has to do the managing and make the decisions.

Scheduling and time management are, of course, executive management functions in the small enterprise. In the case of the independent consultant, it is scheduling work and managing the time of the consultant. That includes both work done under contract for clients (billable time) and other functions which must be carried out (overhead time).

THE CONSULTANT AS A TECHNICAL/PROFESSIONAL SPECIALIST

The skills and abilities you sell to clients are not as easy to specify because they vary greatly from one profession or field to another. However, they can be generalized along the following lines:

Analysis and problem identification

Problem solving

Public speaking

Writing

Listening

Doing

Of course, not all of these skills are required on every assignment or project. Not every assignment, for example, entails a need to analyze symptoms and identify a problem or develop a solution. Still, the skills must be available when needed, for they are generally assumed to be at the heart of the consulting idea; the typical client believes that a competent consultant is one who can provide analysis and problem solving.

On the other hand, listening is always a required skill, and the art of listening is indeed a skill. Listening is probably the most important part of analysis and problem solving.

Doing whatever it is that the consultant's special field involves whether it be engineering, marketing, training, computer systems design, or something else, is a frequent requirement. The consultant must actually be able to do that about which he or she advises.

Public speaking is often required, especially when the client is a large organization and the consultant must address fairly large groups of staff personnel.

Writing falls into that same category. Consulting requires the writing of proposals and reports as a minimum, although there are numerous other uses of writing skills in the consulting field.

THE GRAY AREAS

One skill area reserved for the "gray area" is marketing. This is because consulting services cannot be sold in the same manner as one might sell photographic services or roofing repair. Many consultants have employed traditional advertising and sales-promotional methods and been puzzled when they failed to produce consulting contracts.

To some extent this is due to a failure to perform one of the first chores of marketing: deciding who your proper prospects are as well as what you propose to sell. Far too often, the beginning consultant appears to believe that the mere announcement of his availability and willingness to undertake certain kinds of tasks is sufficient to bring in projects. Not so. Clients must be acquired through sound marketing and selling achievements, and the marketing entails doing some things that involve the consultant's technical/professional skills. That's why I have listed this here.

Very much the same consideration applies to writing and speaking skills, as you will see when we discuss marketing in greater depth, as well as the various profit centers the "compleat consultant" enjoys. And that strikes at the heart of this chapter: how to survive that first year.

DO'S AND DON'TS, ESPECIALLY FOR THE FIRST YEAR

Because the first year is probably the most critical one of your consulting enterprise, it is also the one in which you should be most conservative. Undertake absolutely no expenses which are not absolutely necessary, and particularly do not undertake long-term commitments like expensive advertising in the Yellow Pages. (Once you agree to a Yellow Pages advertisement, you are obliged to pay for it every month for a year.) Don't sign a long-term lease on an office or suite of offices. If you must rent office space, be modest in your demands. Rent a single office, not a suite, and try to select an area where the rents are not excessive and where you do not have to pay a monthly fee to park your automobile. Buy your business cards and letterheads in modest quantity. Sure, they're considerably cheaper when bought in large quantity, but that requires a much larger cash outlay, and you'll probably be better able to afford that later, after you're established. Besides, you may have a change of address after the first year.

Be equally modest in furnishing your office. You can buy a desk for about $150 as well as for $1,000 or more. And in many cities you can buy used office furniture in good condition for less than one half of new furniture prices. (I bought out most of the office furniture of a small company discontinuing business at about 30¢ on the dollar compared with the cost of new furniture.) Time enough to buy more things later, when money is coming in.

In short, be modest in making the initial investment, for that is what all of this is. Presumably, you have at this point not yet taken in ten cents, and every dollar you spend now is a dollar less you have to finance operations and carry yourself until you begin to get paying projects in.

There is a way to avoid even this modest cost, even if you have to rent office space away from home. Most cities of size have office buildings where you may rent desk-space rather than office space, and it isn't even your desk. For a modest monthly sum, often less than $100, you can have a desk assigned to you in a good business address, with telephone-answering, copying, secretarial, and conference-room services (if you receive clients at your office address). If you are concerned with the probability that the address is a temporary one that will change soon, you can rent a post office box quite reasonably and use that for your stationery. (I work at home and use a post office box without problems.)

In other words, it is possible to hang out your shingle and open your doors with an extremely small investment. In most cases, consulting is an enterprise that does not require much capital for anything except paying yourself a suitable salary while you are getting established in your new practice. And on that point, let's talk about some more do's and don'ts:

Do hang on to any income-producing activities as long as possible while you are setting up your new consulting practice. It is possible to do some consulting on a part-time basis, and if that is possible for you, do so while you keep your job. If you can manage to do this for the first year, you will have far better prospects the second year because you won't be starting out cold.

The same consideration applies if you are in some other business which you plan to abandon in favor of consulting. In fact, you may be in an even better position to keep your income coming in if this is the case, because you are more the master of your own time. No matter how eager you are to get out of whatever business you are in, don't be hasty about it. Give your consulting practice a fair chance to get started.

Don't be too narrow or too specialized in what you do as a consultant. Even medical people and lawyers often begin their practices as generalists and turn to specialization later, when they have become somewhat established and can afford to turn away work they prefer not to do. In any case, it is likely that in the beginning you won't actually know which are the best services to offer in terms of the market and the profitability. One thing you can be sure of is that there are few things you can be sure of at first. The first year is likely to produce many surprises. (Remember Murphy's Law?) The services you thought would be eagerly bought by clients turn out to be a drug on the market, and those you thought would not sell well at all often turn out to be those most in demand and the mainstay of your work.

Once I thought that there would be a hungry market for news I could provide about government procurement. After all, I was in Washington, DC, the heart of the system. To my surprise, there was little demand for it, but there was a brisk demand for how-to information on government marketing generally and proposal writing especially. And I also found a far greater demand than I had anticipated for information as to *where* the various government purchasing offices are.

I thought the market had a surfeit of seminars, but I found many eager to attend seminars that were marketed with a sharp focus on commonly recognized problems and their solution. And I once thought that pursuing contracts with the government agencies as a one-man enterprise was doomed to failure, but I subsequently won many thousands of dollars worth of small contracts from government agencies and even found certain distinct advantages in being an independent entrepreneur.

Therefore, begin your practice on the assumption that you do not know exactly what the market is, what prospective clients want and, perhaps, not even exactly who the best prospects are for your services. Expect the first year to be your major education period (although you go on learning forever, if you are wise). If you want the greatest benefit from it, give yourself the maximum exposure by offering and undertaking just about every service you can relative to your main technical/professional field. I can recall an almost countless number of profitable consulting assignments that came to me unexpectedly, assignments for services I had never anticipated a market for.

There is an excellent possibility that the consulting practice you will be pursuing after the first year will be considerably different from the one you originally conceived and projected. As we progress through these pages, you will learn of many different kinds of profit centers that are available to you as a consultant if you are truly an enterprising individual who is alert for and willing to exploit opportunities. In fact, few enterprises offer the flexibility that enables you to take advantage of opportunities as consulting generally does.

TIPS ON KEEPING EXPENSES DOWN

I am continually amazed at the typical American's inability to fully undertstand that any free-enterprise system such as ours is also, necessarily, a *competitive* system. Despite our inflation, which is defined by some economists as "too many dollars chasing too few goods," in most things you still have a choice because you still have vendors and business people competing with each other for your business. Nevertheless, many entrepreneurs as well as consumers simply groan at high prices, then sign and pay the bill without even making an effort to see if they can do better. This probably is a factor in our inflation, since there is absolutely no doubt that most businesses, large and small, will set prices based primarily on what the traffic will bear.

Several years ago, when I decided that I could not tolerate further increases in the already too costly rent for my downtown offices and parking space for my car, I did away with all this cost by setting up an office in my own home in the suburbs. I fully expected this move to cost me a good bit of business for at least the first year after my move; to my delight, I saved far more money than that represented by the small amount of business lost.

Having moved, I needed new suppliers, and one of the things I used in fairly extensive quantity was short-run printing, usually sales letters and other such material, in runs of a few hundred to a few thousand, both of which are "short runs" in printing. Almost immediately after moving, then, I searched out a few local printers and began to call them for quotations. I was shocked at the prices. I was being quoted prices which were even higher than I had been paying in downtown Washington, DC, and those had been far from cheap. And it seemed as if every printer I called quoted me a higher price than the previous one.

I rebelled at paying these prices which I deemed to be exorbitant and simply a reflection of the merchants' greed in what is alleged to be a depression-proof area. And then I was struck with an idea: Every printer I had called was one with a prominent advertisement in the Yellow Pages. What would happen if I called a printer who had no advertisement, but simply a listing as a printer?

In no time at all, I began to get quotations I found entirely acceptable, quotations that were not only half of what I had been getting, but were even well under the prices I had been paying in town. As I tried out one of these shops that didn't run a large advertisement, I soon learned I wasn't paying a low price for poor work, either. The work I was getting was easily the equal of anything I had ever gotten in town, and the service was outstandingly good.

I have since used exactly the same idea in finding typewriter-repair service, office supplies, and whatever else I must find a vendor or supplier for. Perhaps advertising pays, but it also costs, and those costs are inevitably reflected in the supplier's prices!

One area which has proved disastrous for many independent consultants is that of help when the consultant can't handle the job alone. I do not refer to services such as typesetting, accounting, or routine computer data processing, for these can usually be bought economically by following the principles just expressed of seeking the advantage of competition. But projects arise in which the consultant needs the help of a specialist to do something which is integral to the project and requires some creative or professional skill. For example, you may need someone to design a logo for a client or to create some new computer software or to write something or other. Sometimes it is necessary to call on help because there is just too much work for you to handle alone within the schedule, and sometimes you need to apply some skills you don't possess personally, which are not a major part of the project, but are nonetheless important and must be done properly. The independent entrepreneur has no choice but to get help for these chores. Typically, this help is for a short time only.

Some consultants will hire part-time or temporary help to handle such problems, as employees. That may be a satisfactory solution when you know the capabilities of that temporary help and can be sure that you will get what you need within the budget you have established. But what if you do not know anyone on whom you are absolutely sure you can rely? Here are things that can happen (and have happened to me, unfortunately):

The person(s) you hire say they are eager to do the work and sometimes start off well, but as the job progresses, they seem to lose some of their enthusiasm and may begin letting you down by not showing up when promised or not delivering when promised. Or even what was promised. They may deliver work of dubious quality which either you, your client, or both of you find unacceptable. They may take twice as many hours as originally estimated.

If you have hired the individual(s) as your employee(s), you are going to have to pay whatever salary you agreed on, even if the work is unsatisfactory. If the job takes far longer than whatever original estimate you worked on, you are stuck for it; you've no choice but to pay. And pay. And pay.

SUBCONTRACTING: A FAR BETTER ANSWER

I found it far smarter to subcontract work. This enabled me to pay for results only. I was not compelled to pay for mere effort. That is, I contracted whatever I wanted done on the clear provision that payment would not be made unless and until the work was inspected and found acceptable, either by me or by my client. Sometimes I was more demanding than my client, and would reject work my client might have accepted.

Exactly the same safeguard against excessive cost is available to you if you insist on negotiating a fixed price agreement with your subcontractor. Here is the danger: Typically, craftsmen and artisans, such as illustrators and even computer programmers, will offer to work at some hourly rate and prefer to negotiate a contract guaranteeing only that hourly rate but not fixing any maximum number of hours. What's wrong with this is obviously that you've no protection against the vendor who estimates low, deliberately or otherwise, and then takes far more time than originally estimated.

Not only can you be "burned" on total price this way, but you may also find that you can't enforce a provision about paying only when the work has been found acceptable, because the agreement to pay an hourly rate may very well be interpreted as binding on you for hours worked regardless of the quality of the result. That would be especially true if you had decided in the middle of the job that you were not getting the quality you wanted and decided to terminate the contract. The other party might very well argue that you couldn't really judge the quality and acceptability until the work was completed!

I object to subcontracting on the basis of hourly rates, even with a contract provision guaranteeing a maximum number of hours because it builds such traps and hazards into the arrangement. Moreover, I reject the principle that inevitably means I must pay for effort rather than results. Someone who is slow benefits from being slow, while a fast worker is penalized for being efficient. It's a nonsensical arrangement for this reason. Here is how I handle this problem:

I sit down with the other party, my prospective subcontractor, and discuss the requirement. We reach agreement on how many hours such a task ought to take, and what an adequate hourly rate is for such work, in short, what the job ought to cost with a competent individual doing the work at a reasonable rate. That becomes the fixed price, payable on delivery of an acceptable result. (If the contract is for a fairly long term, and the contractor wants progress payments, they are made for partial deliveries of acceptable work.)

In short, a contractor who is slow at whatever the work is should not penalize me for slowness; that's asking me to subsidize incompetence. On the other hand, the efficient contractor ought to be able to benefit from that efficiency. If the contractor has invested in equipment to increase efficiency, the contractor is entitled to have that equipment earning more money by increasing efficiency. Don't expect a contractor to work cheaply, however; it's when you seek a bargain at someone else's expense, or when motivated by greed rather than good business judgment, that you are asking for trouble. Be prepared to pay a fair price for what you need, but also be an alert businessperson and buy *results*, not *effort*. Before I learned all the bitter truths listed here, I labored a great many evenings into the small hours repairing or redoing work for which I had already paid. Be aware, if you are not already, that in every profession and trade there are a great many individuals who are far less capable than they ought to be. It's a great mistake to simply accept everyone at face value. Experience has shown me clearly that there are successful printers who turn out shoddy work, successful illustrators who have no talent, successful computer programmers who write poor programs, and inept people generally everywhere. Even commercial success is no guarantee of quality or dependability. Ironically, sometimes the most competent individuals were the lowest priced: even semi-competent people demand high prices and often appear to be totally unaware of the quality of their work or their relative incompetence.

My own experience suggests to me that in all trades, crafts, and professions, not more than 10 percent of the practitioners are really at the top of their field, the really outstanding performers; not more than 20 percent are really fully competent; and the rest are scattered along the spectrum from mediocrity to abysmal incompetence. I find, in practice, that it is not incompetence that we must guard against, for it is easy to spot true incompetence. What is really the hazard is semi-competence. The semi-competent individual often *talks* a good game—*appears* to know what to do and how to do it well, but is far better at talking about it than doing it. Again and again I have encountered people like this, and the hazard is that it takes so long to determine that they are not really fully competent. They tend to be dilettantes; they know how to talk knowledgeably, use the right "buzz words," dropping names, dropping phrases and terms that suggest a far greater competence than they have.

I have found this disease of semi-competence in many places; for example, an accountant who could discuss accounting intelligently, but couldn't do it at all well (as witness a continuing stream of invoices returned with caustic comments about their inaccuracy and the embarrassment of almost invariably defective cost estimates), and technical writers who talked the jargon of the profession but could not write and had inadequate technical knowledge as well.

As in paying for results rather than effort, judge others by the results of their work, by what they do, not by what they say. It pays to be a skeptic in this matter.

One final word of caution about hiring subcontractors: I reached a point of frustration with moonlighters where I flatly refused to hire a moonlighter to do anything I needed on some definite schedule unless I personally knew the moonlighter to be entirely dependable. I still do not really understand this, but experience has taught me that a great many people who hold down regular jobs want to earn extra money and will promise almost anything to earn it until they discover that they are going to have to make a few sacrifices, such as not seeing their favorite TV shows or passing up a dinner invitation. Typically, they respond well to an offer to subcontract work to them or to work on a part-time payroll in your office. But far too often, after an enthusiastic beginning moonlighters will begin to weary of working two jobs and making a few sacrifices, even minor ones. Perhaps they simply forget how badly they wanted to earn some extra money, as soon as they have earned a little money. Whatever the reasons, I learned that moonlighters were far less dependable than independent freelancers, who depended on those small contracts. (Moonlighters can afford to be relatively independent.) Once I had been victimized in this manner often enough, I simply refused to contract with moonlighters except as noted. I found it easy enough to find freelancers in most fields where I needed help or other consultants who could give me some time and help me with a project. I recommend, therefore, that you consider this when hiring extra help or letting subcontracts.

3

Founding the Consulting Practice

Well begun is half done.

Horace

GENERAL CONSIDERATIONS, SUCH AS LICENSING

Consulting is a business as well as a profession; therefore you need to consider what your business needs are as well as what your professional needs are. Some of these needs depend on local laws, that is, they vary according to where you choose to establish your practice. Other needs are independent of local conditions and apply wherever you are.

In general, the consultant requires no special license nor the passing of any kinds of examinations, but there are exceptions. Some jurisdictions require a mercantile license or occupational license for anyone offering goods or services for sale. Some require licensing of certain professions, such as engineering. It is necessary to check this out in your own state, county, and city. If you live in a city, someone at city hall can usually guide you in this. If you live in some unincorporated jurisdiction, you'll probably have to visit the county seat to get the information you need. In either case, you can probably find out about state requirements there also.

In this connection, note that there may be a difference between operating from an office location and operating from your own home as far as licensing is concerned. You'll want to check into this. You should also check into the possibility of any special provisions. For example, in some places, veterans are licensed without charge or at a reduced fee. In one case in my own experience, when I checked into the city hall for a license, I was advised that as a veteran I was entitled to special considerations (reduced fee), but that since we were near the end of a license year, I would be wise to wait until the new year started. In the meanwhile, the official told me, it would be all right for me to operate my business without a license. A competitor made a complaint against me, charging that I was unlicensed, and this could have meant serious trouble for me if I had not had the written authorization of the aforementioned official to operate without a license for a few weeks.

A NAME FOR YOUR BUSINESS

Most independent consultants trade under their own names, so that their business cards and letterheads read somewhat along the lines

Robert W. Higgins
Environmental Consultant

along with an address, telephone, and perhaps another term or two such as "Impact Statements Prepared" or "Studies and Surveys."

Some consultants, however, prefer to adopt what they believe to be a more impressive name, such as "Higgins Environmentalists," with the hope that this will bring in more business or with the expectation that the practice will grow and ultimately employ a number of environmental consultants. A common preference is a name that includes the word "associates," such as "Higgins Environmental Associates" or "Environmental Consulting Associates," or any of many possible variants on that theme. In most jurisdictions this is known as trading under a "fictitious name" and comes under an act such as the Fictitious Names Act. Although the legislation may be known by another name, the overall intent of such laws is the same. They are designed to protect the public from illegal business tactics hidden under "straw" names. All such acts require you to tell the world under what name you are doing business and what your real name is. If Environmental Consultant Associates accepts a retainer to do a job for a client and then fails to do anything, the client can find out who Environmental Consultant Associates really is and take whatever legal action is necessary.

To accomplish this, it is generally provided that you fill out some forms and pay a fee (sometimes you need to register with both the state and the local jurisdiction and pay fees to both), and then you must announce what you are doing by running an advertisement in a local newspaper or a special legal paper used widely for that purpose (*The Legal Intelligencer*).

You can retain a local lawyer to do this work for you or you can do it yourself. When setting up a business practice once in Philadelphia, Pennsylvania, I found a clerk at City Hall could provide me with complete instructions, including even the suggested wording for the advertisement. In those days, a typical legal fee for this work was about $50 plus whatever the fees and advertising came to. Today I would expect the legal fee to be probably two or three times that amount.

Of course, you can avoid all of this by trading under your own name, and you can add anything you want as long as the entire title includes and is basically your personal name: "Paul Jones," "Paul Jones, Consultant," "Paul Jones Consulting Services." "Paul Jones and Associates," or anything else along those lines. Bear in mind that there are some very large and successful consulting firms named after their founders, such as "Arthur Young and Company."

Note, too, that if you incorporate, the incorporation covers the matter of a fictitious name, since the name of the corporation is duly registered, along with all the details of ownership. It is never necessary to register a corporation under a fictitious names law.

WHAT TYPE OF BUSINESS ORGANIZATION IS RIGHT FOR YOU?

I am constantly amazed at how many fledgling, one-person enterprises start life as corporations, frequently on the advice of the entrepreneur's accountant. Let's consider the several possible alternatives:

If you own the business and all its assets, whether you work alone or have assistance, you can be a "sole proprietorship," which means simply that you own the business and are not incorporated. It's the simplest possible way of organizing, for all purposes, accounting, taxes, deeds, and anything else. That does not mean that it's the best way or the right way. Depending on various considerations which we will discuss here , it may or may not be the best or right way for you.

If you have a partner or two, you are obviously in a partnership and should have a partnership agreement. You would probably be wise to retain an attorney to draw up the partnership agreement. In fact, it would probably be wise for each partner to be represented by an attorney so that each individual's interests are properly represented and properly protected. One thing that destroys partnerships is unpleasant surprises when the partners have different understandings and shares than they originally thought.

It may also be wise to consider having your spouse named a partner, even if he or she is not especially active in the enterprise. Again, an attorney can advise you on the pros and cons, especially as regards taxes and survivor benefits.

Finally, you may wish to incorporate. A corporation may be the right vehicle in which to conduct your business or it may not be. Even if it is, there are a number of corporate arrangements, and it is important to select the one which is best for you. Here are the major types:

For a small, individually-owned enterprise, should you decide to incorporate, probably the close corporation is most suitable. You, you and your partner(s), or you and whoever you wish to assign it to, own all the stock. You can't offer stock on the open market, but you can sell it privately to the limits prescribed.

It is possible to "go public", that is, set up a public corporation and offer stock for sale. It is unlikely that you would wish to do this while you are a small, independent enterprise. It generally requires considerable capital to do this and an abundance of legal services, with an ample supply of financial/stock expertise and services. This is far beyond the scope of the small, independent consultancy.

It is possible, also, to set up a non-profit corporation, and there are certain benefits in so doing, although, again, the idea is not usually suitable for a small, independent enterprise. With a non-profit corporation, you can draw a salary and expenses and perhaps fringe benefits, but you cannot accumulate a reserve of profits and you do not have a personally owned asset, that is, you can never hold an equity position in a non-profit corporation.

For our purposes, let us assume that when we speak of corporations and incorporating, we are referring to the small, close corporation.

PROS AND CONS OF INCORPORATING

Many laymen have an idea that if they incorporate their small businesses, they will immediately benefit by being taxed at a lower rate or having a greater allowance for business deductions. This is partly true, but for most practical purposes it is a myth. The tax benefits are principally only the lower rate you can get on what you leave "in the corporation" (as distinct from drawing a salary or bonuses for your personal use), and that only when your corporate profits are at least well in excess of $40–50,000 annually. If, for example, the corporation shows $100,000 annual profit and you draw $50,000 in salary and leave the rest in corporate bank accounts, what is left in the corporate bank accounts is taxed at a lower rate than the money you drew as salary.

Corporations are "entities," in a legal sense, just as every human is an entity. The corporation is treated as though it were a person in a number of ways but not in all ways. However, contrary to popular beliefs, the corporation does not have greater freedom in taking business deductions than you do as a sole proprietor. Any deduction allowable as a legitimate business expense of the corporation—rent, light, licenses, insurance, taxes, repairs, travel, entertainment, or other—is equally deductible as an expense of the sole proprietor or self-employed entrepreneur. Taxes are levied on profits, not on income (business income, that is) or net sales. Don't incorporate for tax breaks unless the corporation is likely to be left with a substantial amount of profit after your personal draw or salary.

One major advantage of the corporation is that it isolates your business assets and obligations from your personal assets and obligations. A creditor cannot seize your personal automobile or other property in payment of debts owed by the corporation. That is the reason a great many people incorporate, but it is only a legitimate consideration if there is the possibility that you will need such protection, that is, if you expect to have significant liabilities and, therefore, are running a serious risk that if the business fails, you would be personally liable for large sums. In such case it is probably wise to give serious thought to incorporating.

On the other hand, most consultants don't undertake large obligations because consulting usually does not require extensive investment, but depends primarily on the sale of labor to produce income. For most consultants the typical investment is in office furniture, a typewriter, a calculator, a few books, and some printing. It's only rarely that a consultant needs to invest in a computer or some other capital equipment.

It is necessary to consider the possibility of lawsuits, which could result in judgments and be as devastating as judgments rendered for any other reason. If there is a serious possibility that whatever you do could result in a lawsuit and judgment against you or amounts beyond the protection of the insurance you carry, that may well be justification for incorporating. For example, a hypnotist might conceivably be sued by a client who claims ill effects from the hypnotic treatments, or a business client may claim damages resulting from your work. You can usually get insurance coverage to protect you from such claims, but it is possible that incorporating might be better. It would be best to consult an attorney.

If you have any question about whether you need the protection of a corporation, it is your lawyer, not your accountant, who can best advise you on this. The accountant can advise you on the tax aspects of incorporating, but remember that the accountant has a conflict of interest here; it is in the accountant's interest to have you incorporate because the corporation then requires additional, more complex, and more expensive accounting work. Of course, your lawyer has the same problem; incorporating you usually means a a legal fee. Therefore, it is best to question both your accountant and your lawyer if you wish to consider incorporation, and ask them to list for you all the pros and cons they can think of. Then you make the decision.

A wrong reason for incorporating is the belief held by many companies that the term "Inc." after their trade name adds prestige and makes their business ventures more credible. Not so. Anyone can be incorporated for as little as $50, so it isn't more than $50 worth of prestige! It's entirely the wrong reason for forming a corporation.

Another consideration which may affect your decision about incorporating is that partnerships are notoriously difficult to sustain, and relatively few last through the years. Even those that retain the names, such as "Jones & Smith," are often *sans* Jones or Smith after the first few years. For example, "Revlon" is a coinage of the names of two partners, but actual founder Charles Revson found the partnership almost unmanageable and paid his partner to keep out of the way and leave everything to Revson. Sometimes, partnerships have a better chance of survival in a close corporation, in which each partner has an equal share of stock.

Bear in mind that operating a corporation adds expense. There is more accounting work, more tax work, reports to file, and a miscellany of tasks. It is not a great expense, it's true, but it is an expense nevertheless.

In the end, how you choose to organize and operate your consulting practice is a decision that must be made with due consideration to your own circumstances and needs. A few of the pros and cons have been given here, but they are by no means all the factors to consider or all the situations in which you might find yourself.

Don't be misled, either. I have met individuals who felt they could not incorporate their businesses because they worked from their homes, and they thought that incorporating would compel them to establish formal offices in commercial locations. This is not so; the state does not care where your corporation does its business, as far as a legal address is concerned. (That's a matter that concerns the zoning commission in most localities.)

Consider, then, your own needs, your own problems, your local laws, and whatever else applies to you, and be governed accordingly. And remember, too, that you can always incorporate later.

DO YOU NEED A LAWYER? IF SO, FOR WHAT?

It has always been rather easy to incorporate a business in Delaware, which traditionally had modest fees and simple processes for incorporation. Therefore, a great many corporations chose to incorporate in that state, among them many of the largest corporations in the country. However, in recent years, most other states have made it equally easy to incorporate so you can probably incorporate today in your own state as easily as you can in Delaware. And if you incorporate in your own state, you won't have the expense of maintaining a corporate address in Delaware and of registering as a foreign corporation in your own state.

If you choose to do it yourself, you can get a book which will provide instructions in simple language and all the forms you need, including a suitable set of bylaws. (See The Reference File, Chapter 15.) These books will also provide an abundance of information about the advantages of incorporating, the several types of corporation, and how to operate the corporation—how to draw up a resolution, for example, which you must do to open a corporate bank account and to carry out many other functions of the corporation.

Strictly speaking, you do not need a lawyer to set up a corporation, to draw up contracts, and to carry out most other business functions. That is not to say that you should not have a lawyer; for many, it is far better to retain a lawyer than to chance it alone, but the choice is yours. However, if you do use a lawyer to handle all your legal chores, even the minor ones, I recommend that you do not make the mistake of asking or permitting your lawyer to make your business decisions. That is not your lawyer's function. Use your lawyer to provide information to you, to explain pros and cons as they apply to your situation, and possibly to make recommendations. But the decision is always yours and only yours to make; no one else can make it for you.

DO YOU NEED AN ACCOUNTANT? IF SO, FOR WHAT?

Very much the same considerations expressed with regard to your need for a lawyer apply to your need for an accountant. Strictly speaking, you do not need an accountant, but you may prefer to have one. However, "having an accountant" is different from having a lawyer. You turn to your lawyer intermittently as things arise in which you need legal advice or legal service, and sometimes you have no need of your lawyer's services for many months at a time. Accounting, however, is a regular and necessary function of a business which must go on every day. If you use an accountant's services, you generally use them on some regular basis. However, you have more choices here than you may have thought possible.

Here are some of the accounting functions that must be performed in the typical accounting system, whether for a small or large business:

Journalizing.   Entering bills, receivables, and other items into the daily journals as they happen. (A small system may have only a single journal; a large system may have several.)

Posting.   Transferring the journal entries to their proper columns on the ledgers. (The size or number of ledgers depends primarily on the size of the system, but also on its complexity.)

Balancing and Auditing.   Verifying the correctness of the entries through striking various mathematical balances and checking specific items.

Calculating Overhead.   Determining the cost of doing business as a mathematical rate—percentage of direct labor, percentage of sales, or whatever is most convenient and useful.

Generating Various Reports and Statements.   Preparing such things as the Profit & Loss Statement, the Balance Sheet, and various monthly, quarterly, semi-annual, and annual reports.

Tax Work. Making out tax returns for the various government agencies to which taxes must be remitted, along with whatever reports and statements are required.

Scheduling Payables. Listing payables, with schedules for paying them, usually with an eye to prompt-payment discounts.

Invoicing Receivables. Sending out invoices for receivables.

Miscellaneous. Following up on receivables which are overdue, preparing special reports, preparing estimates, and sundry tasks peculiar to the business and its needs, such as making up payrolls or handling work contracted out to a data-processing firm.

These are general and vary considerably from company to company. Where the company has a full-time accountant on staff, the accountant and assistants do all the tasks listed plus actually drawing checks up and making up the payroll. Here, however, we are envisioning the self-employed professional, who is most likely to retain a public accountant to do whatever a self-employed professional needs to do as regards accounting. Even here there are several alternatives available.

There was a time when I retained a public accountant to look after all my accounting needs. Once a month I bundled up all my payables and receivables, my bank statements and cancelled checks, and sent them off to him. Usually two to three months later, the accountant sent me a statement showing me the state of my business, and how much money I made or lost two or three months ago. Once a year the accountant made up my taxes.

I grew more and more unhappy with this arrangement. For one thing, I felt that I was too small a business to wait two to three months to learn that I was losing money. I could easily lose far more money than I could afford to lose. I needed to know immediately if my operations began to lose money. Also, what the accountant was doing for me, and what I was paying him every month for, was really not very much. I did the billing, the dunning of overdue accounts, paying of all accounts due, with proper aging of payables. What he did was primarily a recapitulation of what I had already done, and drawing a balance to show profit or loss. The most valuable service he provided was the tax work, which I found burdensome and was quite happy to have done by someone else. I decided to make a change.

I decided to resort to a proprietary system, available in most good office-supply emporiums for only a few dollars, and quite suitable for the very small business. There are several such systems available, and I chose the Dome system. This is contained in a single volume, with standard forms in which you journalize the daily transactions, assigning each a number supplied for that category of expense (if it's a payable or a payout), and entering also your sales (receipts) in a journal entry. Once a week you add up the items in each category and post the total on another sheet which serves as the ledger sheet, and run the totals. Payroll forms are provided, also, if you have a payroll to make up. The forms in which you post receipts and payouts carry for both types of entries "Total as of last week," "Total this week," and "Total to date." Therefore, you always know at a glance how much you've taken in and how much you've paid out this week, prior to this week, and year to date. If you think your expenses are running too high, you can check each category of expense almost at a glance to determine where and for what you are spending money, whether there has been a surge of one kind of expense, or other such factors. Simplicity itself, but the principal advantage is that you always have up-to-date information. If you have problems developing, you know about them immediately, and it's relatively easy to track them down and find out exactly what the causes are.

Having severed relations with my earlier accountant and gone over to this peerless do-it-yourself system, I looked for an accountant to do my taxes. That was something I didn't care to do myself despite the provisions made for doing it in my Dome system. When I consulted a public accountant who had been recommended to me, I found myself fighting off his insistence that he had to set up books for me. He wanted to "do his thing" and saddle me with an accounting system suitable for General Motors or IBM! He also looked at the kinds of things I did and began to counsel me to charge higher rates for my consulting services, to set up special bank accounts and to do many other things dear to his heart as a Certified Public Accountant. We argued the merits of his proposed system versus my modest little Dome system until he either saw that it was futile to argue with me, or was genuinely convinced that I was right in asserting that my system was far better suited to my needs. (I've never been sure which was the case.) To this day, I send him my Dome book at tax time, and he prepares my returns. It's eminently satisfactory to me, and it's one way in which you can have an accountant, yet not incur a heavy cost burden.

There are other ways than the two described here to "have an accountant." There are accountants who will call on you at your own office once a week, once a month, or as often as you wish, and do the work of posting and whatever else has to be done in your own office. Accountants will draw up checks for you, reconcile your bank statements, organize your corporation and write corporate resolutions, or whatever you want. It's entirely up to you. As in the case of your lawyer, use your accountant to perform chores that require the accountant's special knowledge, discuss problems and solicit advice if you wish, but don't expect or permit your accountant to make decisions for you. You must make all decisions, after you have gathered the information and recommendations you need.

However, you will not be ready to decide what kinds of accounting services you need until you have a clear understanding of what accounting is and what it should do for you. Let's discuss that next.

ACCOUNTING IS PART OF MANAGEMENT

Far too many businesspeople regard accounting as an administrative chore and a necessary evil. That is one reason for confusion in accounting for business failures; sometimes SBA and others who claim to be business experts list weaknesses in accounting as a chief cause of the high rate of bankruptcies; at other times poor management is the cause assigned. Both observations are correct, because accounting is an indispensable element of management and the source of critical information.

Few human activities have been the subject of more books, articles, speeches, conventions, conferences, and formal courses of instruction than has management. Yet, with all this enormous outpouring of information and opinion, there is little agreement on what management is. Go to a well-stocked bookstore, especially one on or near a college campus, and look at the titles. You'll find millions of words purporting to teach all the latest management miracles—management by objectives, zero-based budgeting, Program Evaluation and Review Technique (PERT), Critical Path Method (CPM), management grid, cost-effectiveness, and literally dozens of other works offering management wisdom, even the Theory X and Theory Y conjectures and, more recently, even Theory Z! One recent title offers to teach "management through people," although some earlier experts have insisted that management has always been "through people" by its very nature, in fact, that a proper definition of management is getting things done through other people.

I suspect that at least some of the management experts cared less about a helpful definition of management than they did about creating some clever aphorism, such as, "Management is the art of getting others to do what you want them to do." The hazard lies in trying to capture the essence of management in a brief phrase or to mechanize it by such a device as PERT or cost-effectiveness. Helpful as these devices may be, they apply in only some of the cases, and they are not definitions of management, but mechanical tools that may help a manager. Let us consider what management is without worrying about how many words or sentences we need to get a clear understanding.

Let's consider first the one-person enterprise. Since there is only one person involved, how can management be the art of getting things done through others? Still, would anyone say that no management is necessary if there is only one employee? Obviously not. So that tends to invalidate the idea that management necessarily means getting things done through other people.

Let's consider what every enterprise has, whether it employs one person or a thousand people.

1. Every enterprise has a mission or objective of some sort, a purpose for existing.

2. Every enterprise has resources of some sort—if not employees, then money and other things such as materials, goods, and facilities.

3. Every enterprise has a need to produce more than it consumes, take in more money than it pays out, or turn a profit if it is a for-profit enterprise. Even non-profit organizations must carry out their missions with the resources they have.

4. Every enterprise has some sort of operating plan, perhaps a highly detailed one with published procedures and well-established methods of operation, perhaps a generalized plan existing only in the head of the lone entrepreneur.

Management is the final common denominator. Every enterprise must be managed if it is to survive and prosper. Recognizing that, we can begin to approach a definition and understanding of management. My own definition of management is that management is the process of carrying out the mission or meeting the objectives with the available resources, whatever they are. If you noticed that item 3 above already provided this definition, you get an "A".

The quality of management may be measured by how effectively the manager uses the resources to carry out the mission and satisfy the purposes of the organization. And the difference between good and bad management is essentially the degree to which management carries out the mission of the organization with the available resources. Anyone can accomplish anything, in theory at least, with unlimited resources. In real life, however, there are rarely enough resources, and the usual problem of management is to find a means for meeting all objectives in spite of inadequate resources. Really good managers always find ways to do just that.

How does accounting fit into this? The accounting function does not have as its prime objective satisfying the tax collectors, despite the need to do that. The prime objective of accounting should be the provision of accurate and reliable information to managers so that managers can make good decisions. Decisions are not likely to be better than the information upon which they are based; hence, the need for accurate and timely information from the accounting department. And hence the crippling effects of accounting information that reports two or three months after the fact.

Let us suppose, for example, that you have launched an advertising campaign, ordinarily a major expense. Can you afford to wait three months to discover that it is laying an egg and you are losing money? Or that one advertisement is doing well while all the others are doing poorly? Or that you are doing a brisk business but are carrying a steadily increasing load of delinquent accounts?

These factors, among others, can spell the difference between success and failure for any business, but especially for a fledgling business. In many cases of small business failure, the facts come to light too late for the entrepreneur to salvage the situation. By the time the facts are revealed, the burden of debt and losses is fatal. The large corporation may be able to wait a month or two to learn the bad news, but the small business usually cannot. Most small businesses need information on an almost daily basis.

ACCOUNTING INFORMATION IS MANAGEMENT INFORMATION

The mistake many managers make is that they fail to recognize that the information coming out of the accounting function is information for managers, information that reports what is happening. Here are some of the kinds of information you need to have if you are to be in full command of your enterprise:

Overhead Costs. Rent, heat, light, telephone, etc.—what they are, specifically, and whether they are going up or down.

Sales Figure. Dollar volume and trends.

Cost of Sales. Total cost of getting and carrying out every project or task.

Markup. How much you are adding to your own costs so that you can meet all expenses and turn a profit.

This basic data, if you study it carefully, will alert you to problems such as slipping sales or profits, whereupon you begin to search for causes so that you can correct the problems.

Don't wait for the accountant to tell you that you are in the red; you should not only know that as soon as the accountant does, but you should probably have been able to see the trend in that direction in time to take corrective action.

For example, when I required a rather substantial amount of printing work, I watched the printing costs closely. If they began to climb more steeply than I thought inflation should cause, I checked into this and sometimes I changed printers. Although friends who had more experience than I in certain of my activities advised me about seasonal peaks and valleys, I found that my own accounting reports did not bear out their forecasts at all. I was doing well when, according to them, I should have been wasting my money in advertising, and doing poorly in months they claimed were ordinarily good months. What friends advised represented their opinions. What my account ledgers reported were facts. I respect and weigh opinions, but act in response to facts.

I found that doing my own bookkeeping did far more for me than save me a monthly accountant's fee. Far more beneficial was the timeliness of the information I derived from doing my own postings and correlations. This is particularly helpful when the enterprise is young, and the entrepreneur is working with virtually every factor an unknown and perhaps making many classical mistakes.

THE COMMON MISTAKES OF BEGINNING ENTREPRENEURS

Financial reporting services and other experts report with obvious horror the high rate of small business failures, sometimes as high as 70 percent. But perhaps even more striking than the 70-percent failure rate is the 30-percent success rate. That is, given the enormous range of "opportunities" to make fatal mistakes, and given the complete business naivete of new entrepreneurs, it is perhaps marvelous that 30 percent or more of them survive! Here are a few of the mistakes I have found many beginners guilty of:

Failing to understand the meaning of "profit." A surprising number of individuals new to self-employment tend to regard anything left after expenses as their income and the profit of their enterpreise.

Assuming that successful marketing results from being the low bidder, and therefore underpricing everything they bid on.

Going to the opposite extreme and overpricing everything they bid on.

Failing to charge their enterprises for facilities they provide, such as an

automobile, office space at home, and telephone service, under the naive assumption that since these have always been personal investments
and expenses, they are free as far as the business is concerned!

It is with such reasoning as this that self-employed individuals often continue for years to eke out a living, but never manage to grow or to do more
than earn a rather meager income.

BASIC RULES

Here are some basic rules which ought to be inviolate except under the
most extraordinary circumstances:

1. You must know and charge each and every cost incurred for your
    venture.
2. Your personal draw or salary is a cost, chargeable to the venture. (It
    is not profit.)
3. Anything you supply in kind, such as office space, must be evalu-
    ated and charged at its fair value.
4. All costs must be recovered by your venture, and your prices must
    reflect all costs plus some margin of profit.
5. With all of this in mind, you must yet be reasonably competitive in
    price.

BASIC COST CENTERS AND COST DEFINITIONS

It is not my purpose to teach you accounting nor am I qualified to do so.
But it is important for businesspeople to understand the basics of costs.
Far too many entrepreneurs and managers do not take the trouble to learn
accounting basics under the mistaken idea that accounting is of no concern to them in their main functions. That's tantamount to saying that
business success is not concerned with profit, which of course is nonsense. It is essential for the entrepreneur to understand costs, especially
in these complex times.

Were this a formal course in accounting, you would be learning a great
many technical terms, and you would learn that there are many labels
used by accountants to define or describe what has happened to the
money invested in and resulting from sales. The layman soon becomes ut-

terly confused by all of this, and many simply throw up their hands in despair and reason that it should be left to the accountants as technical experts. To do this is to put much more of your business control into the hands of the accountants than you realize and deny yourself ready access to the information you need in order to make wise business decisions. You are then running your business blindfolded.

It is essential that you understand the underlying basics of accounting, but without getting bogged down in extraneous and confusing jargon. It is really not that complex or difficult to understand if we talk about basics only, concerning ourselves with the general and broad discriminations and not with the minute ones.

First of all, there are various "kinds" of costs—payroll, taxes, insurance, rent, utilities, advertising, leasehold improvements, and others. The list probably runs to 20, 30, 50, even 100 items, depending on the size and complexity of your enterprise. However, for purposes of general management the costs are generally lumped under broad headings such as *fixed* costs and *variable* costs, *overhead* costs, *labor* costs, *material* costs, and other such catchall categories. For our purposes let's start with only two broad cost categories common to all businesses and then go on from those basics to a few deeper investigations into the financial side of business management.

DIRECT AND INDIRECT COSTS

Although it's true enough that it costs money to run any kind of business, the ratio between direct and indirect costs is quite different for different kinds of enterprises. Some kinds of business require a heavy proportion of indirect cost, whereas in other types of business costs tend to peak on the direct-cost side. The definitions of direct and indirect costs are often quite different in different types of businesses; what may be listed as an indirect cost in one business may be found to be included in a list of direct costs for another. This discussion must necessarily concern only the typical small consulting venture.

In any business enterprise, such items as rent, heat, light, advertising, insurance, and taxes are almost invariably indirect cost items, also called *overhead*. Indirect costs and overhead are not identical terms, however. *Indirect* is the more inclusive term, and *overhead* is a subgrouping of indirect costs. Before defining these, however, let's introduce and define direct costs.

The direct costs of an enterprise are those costs which can be clearly and specifically identified for each sale. For instance, if you sell calculators that cost you $3 each, the actual $3 cost to you of the item you are selling is direct cost. Or if you accept a contract to do something for a client, the cost of the labor and anything else that you can assign quantitatively to the sale is direct cost.

There are many other costs in conducting your enterprise—those typical overhead items mentioned above, which go on whether you are doing business or not, and any other expense that you cannot apportion to individual sales. For example, if a consulting project requires you to have a report printed, that should be counted a direct cost, because you can identify it and post it in your books as an expense incurred entirely for that specific project. On the other hand, the cost of printing business cards, letterheads, and brochures is a different matter entirely, since it is impossible to connect the cost of these directly with any particular sale or contract, just as it is impossible to assign some specific portion of your rent or maintenance costs to a given sale. These costs therefore must be indirect costs.

That does not mean that such costs will not be reflected in your selling prices, however; they certainly must be, if you are to stay in business. But they will be handled in another way, as part of your general overhead, by adding some factor to your direct costs. The two together reflect your total cost for that sale, and that total cost, along with whatever profit you choose to add, is the selling price.

The factor is a *rate* of overhead which, in labor-intensive businesses, is generally a percentage of direct labor. That is, in estimating a project you estimate the amount and cost of the direct labor required, then add some fixed percentage of that direct-labor cost to cover the overhead expenses. To the resulting figure you add other direct expenses you anticipate, such as printing a report, long-distance telephone calls, computer time, or any other cost you expect to incur for this project alone. Finally, having added up all these costs, and remembering that if the direct-labor cost is for your own personal labor, the compensation to you is part of business costs and not profits, you add a figure to cover profit or fee.

Typically, you determine what your overhead rate is by looking at last year's figures and basing your calculations on that. If, for example, you learn from last year's figures that you charged out to clients $65,000 worth of direct labor and incurred $34,000 worth of indirect costs during the year, your overhead rate was

$$34,000/65,000 = 0.52$$
$$0.52 = 52\%$$

What this means is simply that for every dollar of direct-labor cost (that is, for every dollar you paid yourself or anyone else working directly on consulting projects), you had to pay out 52¢ in rent, heat, light, stationery, and other such costs. Therefore, on the reasonable assumption that your ratio of direct to indirect costs is about the same this year, you add 52 percent of all direct labor in pricing projects this year.

The first year is a problem because there is no history to base rates on. The best you can do is to guess at what your overhead rate is to be. Let's look at how you do this.

Let us suppose that you anticipate spending at least one half your time (and because you are self-employed and can't afford the luxury of 40-hour weeks in your first year of business, we'll consider half-time to mean 25 hours per week) on projects for which you are being paid, and plan to pay yourself $25,000 year until you are established and can pay yourself more. That works out to $19.23 per hour, for the 25 hours per week you plan to be on chargeable time. That is the hourly direct-labor rate.

To that you must add the overhead percentage. If you estimate the cost of overhead items to be, let us say, $15,000 for the year, the rate would be
$$15{,}000/25{,}000 = 0.60 = 60\%$$
The hourly rate you charge, with overhead, is then
$$19.23 + [19.23 \times 0.60] = 19.23 + 11.53 = 30.76$$
Working approximately 25 hours per week at an hourly rate of $30.76 will bring you back your estimated costs, including your salary. But that figure does not include profit, so you must add a profit figure, and if that is to be 10 percent, for example, your hourly billing rate becomes $33.84. If there are other expenses associated with the job, they are added usually before the 10-percent profit is calculated if you are quoting a fixed-price project, but usually as a separate item if you are billing the client on a fixed hourly or daily rate. The above explains how you calculate rates so as to recover all expenses.

However, it does not take into account what the market is, normally, for the services you provide. That is, $33.84 may well be far below what most consultants in your professional field charge. If so, the rate should be raised to be reasonably competitive but not to lag far behind what clients ought to pay. If the reverse is true and your rate is far in excess of the normal market for such services, this could prove to be a serious handicap in winning business.

The reasons for guarding against carelessness in permitting expenses to grow should be apparent now. If you treat yourself too well, with luxurious first-class accommodations when you travel on business, unduly expensive office furnishings and other extravagances, it is quite easy to allow your overhead rate to soar to 150 percent and even more, so that you then (using our earlier figures) would have to persuade clients to pay you $52.88 so that you could make your own modest $25,000 per year. And if you wished to give yourself a raise to a perhaps more appropriate and more just $40,000 a year, your hourly billing rate would soar to $84.59 an hour, or $676.72 per day, which some clients might find excessive. On the other hand, if you manage to keep your overhead rate down to a reasonable 60 percent, as suggested, you can realize a $40,000 salary while billing clients only about $55 per hour, which is competitive in most circumstances.

TYPICAL INDIRECT COSTS

Those who have not yet had the experience of meeting all the obligations of a business enterprise often fail to realize just how many indirect expenses there are. Here are the major categories of indirect expenses you will encounter in most enterprises, even if you have no other employees than yourself:

Rent (which may or may not include heat and light)

Parking (a substantial expense in many urban areas)

Insurance (usually several kinds, some required by law, others by good sense)

Taxes (depending on locale, sales, unemployment, personal property, inventory)

Licenses (as in the case of taxes, varies considerably)

Depreciation (recovering the cost of major items—furniture and equipment, for example)

Stationery (cards, letterheads, envelopes, at least)

Advertising (any expense incurred for the purpose, even mailing out literature)

Telephone (including such things as answering services or answering machines)

Travel (auto expense, air travel, other)

Printing and copying (copying, especially, but there will be printing, too)

Contributions (you'll be approached and solicited)

Subscriptions (consultants must read widely)

Memberships (most consultants need to belong to several organizations)

Entertainment (taking prospects to lunch, for example)

Some of these items may appear as "other direct cost" in some projects. It is not unusual for projects to require printing, copying, travel, and other such items, but these should be charged directly to the client, not to the general overhead. Reason? Charging such items to the general overhead inflates it falsely, adding a burden to other jobs you quote. Unless you are doing government cost-plus work exclusively (and hardly anyone is, today), inflated overhead is not an asset. Normally, the lower your overhead rate is, the more competitive and the more profitable you are.

FIXED VERSUS VARIABLE EXPENSES

Certain kinds of expenses are fixed. Rent is one. Although most of today's leases have escalation clauses and even provide that you can be billed at the end of each year for such unanticipated costs as an increase in real estate taxes, rent is relatively stable and is generally carried as a fixed cost on the books. Yellow-page advertising is also a fixed cost because it will not vary for the year, and you have committed yourself to paying for it for the year.

On the other hand, telephone expenses are both fixed and variable—fixed as far as the cost of the basic service is concerned, but variable as far as toll calls and other "extras" are concerned. "Variable" simply means that you can't anticipate exactly what the costs will be every month. But it also means that you have (in most cases) a degree of control over the costs; you can take steps to minimize long-distance calls, for example.

This is an important consideration when you are establishing your enterprise. Unwise decisions here can saddle you with fixed expenses that will overburden your fledgling business and sink it if you don't meet with instant success in the marketplace. If you buy $10,000 worth of furniture and equipment and commit yourself to five years of burdensome payments, you will probably not be able to get out from under the burden, should business be slow in coming in the first year or two. Hence, it is wise to consider carefully each thing you believe you need to invest in, to determine whether the investment represents a long-term burden or whether it is something you can cut if you need to. Many a successful business has been started at the entrepreneur's kitchen table, and sometimes the success was due in great measure to the fact that it started that way, with minimal demands for income. It is difficult enough, under the best of circumstances, to make an early success of any business enterprise. Wisdom in avoiding or minimizing the burden at the outset means that the enterprise has a far greater chance of success.

Marketing and Sales: Finding Leads and Closing Them

There are several ways to judge the health of an enterprise, and a close study of the sales log is a good place to start.

SUCCESS IN MARKETING IS ALWAYS A TONIC FOR AN AILING BUSINESS

According to the Small Business Administration and numerous other sources, a major cause of the many small-business failures every year is what is referred to as "undercapitalization." That means not having enough money to survive the early months of getting started and perhaps not enough money to undertake proper marketing and sales promotion. Too many new small-business ventures cannot afford the many mistakes which virtually every entrepreneur makes in the early months, before the venture is well-established and has developed successful operating methods.

Whenever a business is undercapitalized, or perishes for any of the other standard reasons offered—poor accounting systems, poor management, poor inventory control, for example—it also suffers from a lack of sales. Somehow, no matter what kinds of problems a venture has, nor how severe the problems of undercapitalization and poor management, the firm that is *doing business* and enjoying an adequate sales volume always manages to survive. It seems that it is only when sales are far short of the mark that the other problems overwhelm the enterprise and put it under.

There is nothing wrong with most enterprises, then, that adequate sales volume wouldn't cure. When I presented this idea to a large number of practicing consultants and small service firms for their reactions, I discovered that, without exception, all those individuals and small companies—some of which were of fair size and had been in operation a number of years—agreed that their greatest need was always more sales.

We have, therefore, justification for making marketing a prime priority in getting a venture established. If someone were to ask you what the main objective of a business is, you might say "to turn a profit" or "to give me a living income." That would be a direct, personal reaction. Peter Drucker has said that the main objective of business is to create a customer. Others have said that the main purpose of an enterprise is to grow, and some have even said that their purpose in business was to survive. All of which is getting to the same point: success. Businesses with enough customers are successful businesses, and successful businesses survive, grow, show profits, and provide income. The very term "doing business" means selling whatever you sell—having customers—so it seems fair to say that customers = business. Certainly, if you do not have customers you are not doing business, and if you are not doing business there seems to be little point in running excellent accounting systems, establishing enlightened management, and installing top-notch inventory control. For what is there to account for and manage if you are not doing business?

It is true that there have been cases of businesses doing enough trading and having enough customers which still went under. Probably the AutoTrain fiasco was such a case, because the failure appears to have been reckless and irresponsible dissipation of corporate assets by a Chief Executive Officer (CEO) who had somehow lost his sense of values and was running out of control. But that is an exception which proves nothing except that there are always exceptions. In almost every case of business failure it can be shown that it was also a case of marketing failure.

On the other hand, effective marketing can overcome almost any problem, even that of an unexciting product or only average quality. Marketing sold beach pebbles ("Pet Rocks") and created a millionaire almost literally overnight, and effective marketing has created many major corporations—Sears-Roebuck, Montgomery Ward, Singer Sewing Machines, and IBM are prime examples of what good marketing can create.

Because of the importance of marketing, I believe that this is the most important chapter in this book. You will make mistakes—a few even if you are already experienced, a great many if you are starting out in your first independent business venture. They are part of the learning process. I believe, however, that there is one mistake you can't afford to make. You can't afford to miss out completely on marketing. You must learn how to market your services effectively if you learn nothing else. You can hire specialists or contract for accounting, report writing, and many other functions—even sales—but you cannot afford to lose control of marketing.

WHAT ARE "MARKETING" AND "SALES"? ARE THEY DIFFERENT?

The business world tends to use the terms *marketing* and *sales* interchangeably, and there is a tendency to believe that they are synonymous. They are not, and the difference is functional, not merely semantic. It may easily mean the difference between success and failure of the enterprise. Hence, the importance of understanding what each term means.

In general, *marketing* is broader in scope. That is, while *sales* is the function or set of functions necessary to get orders, a great deal of earlier work was necessary to get into a position for pursuing and closing sales. You had to do at least the following:

Decide what you would sell. (Clearly identify products/services.)

Decide to whom you would sell. (Define best prospects for what you sell.)

Determine how to reach them. (Design advertising and sales promotion campaigns.)

Decide what your specific offer would be.

We've already covered, at least to some degree, deciding what you will sell (basically), and we'll go further into that as we progress.

Deciding on your prospects is a serious matter. Many business failures are traceable to thoughtless and irresponsible sales efforts, made without considering who were the proper prospects for whatever the entrepreneur wished to offer.

Deciding how you will reach them—how you will make your sales presentation and get them to consider your offer—is another serious matter. Sales campaigns have broken down because the seller was unable to reach the prospects decided on. It's of little use to select the best prospects for what you wish to sell if you are unable to reach these prospects effectively.

Finally, deciding what the specific offer is to be is a marketing matter. Our English language, rich though it is, does not make a clear distinction between what you wish to sell and the offer you wish to make, yet the distinction is a most important one for our purposes, and we'll discuss it in some depth shortly. But for the moment let's make this point for you to consider. You have to do two things in your sales efforts: Make the prospect want what you are selling, and provide some additional incentive to the prospect to act now and buy what you are selling. The latter element of the sales effort is what I refer to as the "offer." Since the movie *The Godfather*, "an offer you can't refuse" has come into the vernacular, to identify an offer of overpowering persuasion, and it's appropriate to this discussion. Consider what many magazines do to win subscription sales: first the advertising describes all the reasons you ought to read the magazine and then it offers you a trial subscription, a special discounted rate, a bonus publication of some sort, and sometimes even more inducements. That last set of inducements is "the offer," and it is designed to accomplish at least these things:

Add the final bits of persuasion to the hesitant and undecided prospects.

Persuade prospects to act *now,* rather than "think about it."

Appeal to the greed that lurks in so many of us.

Exploit the widespread appeal of such words as *free, sale, special offer, bonus, new, money-back guarantee.* Make no mistake about it—these terms simply do not "wear out", they never lose their appeal. People go on believing these words for the simplest of reasons: they *want* to believe in Santa Claus. It's easy to believe that something is free or a great bargain if you want to believe it.

How does all this apply to selling consulting services, which can't be huckstered like fish or shoes? Let's look at the marketing of professional services in greater depth.

THE LINE OF DEPARTURE

A function of marketing is deciding who your best prospects are and how you can best reach them. That assumes that you are starting with a firm idea of precisely what you wish to sell. It is possible, however, that you have some degree of flexibility in deciding what you wish to sell—that you have options or can somehow modify your basic service so as to appeal to different prospects.

The two factors, what you wish to sell and to whom you must offer it, are definitely related. If your chosen field of consulting services is office systems, that dictates that your prospects must be organizations operating in offices, rather than individual consumers. On the other hand, if you are a physical fitness specialist, you are most likely to find your best prospects among individuals, although it is possible that you might make arrangements with or through organizations.

If you have access to a special audience that gives you an advantage in selling to them, you may find it a good plan to consider what you can offer to this special audience that would have great appeal and take advantage of your special situation. If they were a group of medical specialists, for example, and you were qualified, you might wish to offer these people investment counseling since medical specialists often look for sound investment opportunities.

A consultant is far more likely, however, to operate in a general area of technical/professional capability than in some specific skill. It is rare that circumstances dictate absolutely what the consultant must offer to sell; usually the consultant has at least some degree of flexibility in what he identifies as the service offered. Or, more significantly, the *main* service offered, for it is important that the prospect's attention and the entire sales effort be sharply focused. One of the most common mistakes neophytes in advertising and selling make is trying to sell everything. The result is confusion and indecision, the opposite of what sales and advertising efforts are trying to accomplish.

It is therefore urgent that you decide what is to be the focus of your marketing and sales effort and build around that. One consultant, for example, is a hypnotist who specializes in aiding people overcome such problems as phobias and inability to quit smoking even when they wish to quit. He identifies his services rather loosely as being indirectly connected with medical problems, and he advertises in local newspapers for clients. This gentleman could also offer to provide demonstrations of hypnosis for entertainment or for more serious purposes. Presumably, he could also teach others the art of hypnosis or self-hypnosis through seminars, formal classes, or by other vehicles. I learned self-hypnosis to relieve insomnia, a common problem and another focal point on which a sales appeal might be made.

The point is that this gentleman has many possible services or objectives on which to focus his sales effort, but the temptation to try to appeal to all possible markets would only dissipate the entire marketing and sales program effort.

WHAT IS A MARKET?

"Market" is a rather vague term, susceptible to so many definitions and shades of meaning that it becomes almost meaningless. For example, there is a computer market—those who have a need for and will buy computers. There is a hospital market. Here we have defined "market" in terms of what is sold—computers—and in terms of type of establishment—hospitals (who buy hospital supplies, but who might buy computers, too). The word is sometimes used to refer to demand, as in "There is not much of a market for horseshoes these days," or "We're having a bull market on Wall Street this month." We also refer to "the marketplace" as if it were a physical location although we really refer to the demand as in, "The final test is what happens to it in the marketplace." It is used to refer to demand also when we talk about stimulating or creating demand, as in the expression, "making a market."

If the word *market* means all these things, it is small wonder that the other form of that word, *marketing*, means a great many different things also. But for this discussion, *market* refers primarily to who the buyers are. The context in which it is used will make the intent clear enough.

In defining the market(s) of interest to you, refine the definition to a point which enables you to make operating decisions about whom you must reach, how you must reach them, and with what you must reach them. Consider the several steps:

1. In the broadest terms, identify market(s) as individual consumers or organizations of some kinds or both. (If both, is one the major target or are they equally important? Decide.)

2. Break down and refine definition(s):

    (a)   If individuals, define in terms of which *role* they occupy as buyers—for example, housewives, business executives, fathers and mothers, automobile owners, home owners, city dwellers, suburban dwellers.

    (b)   If organizations, break down in two steps: For-profit businesses and/or nonprofit organizations, then types— large/small, type of organization/type of business, privately held/public corporation, or other term helpful to determining how to reach and with what.

The process usually goes even further, until it reaches the point where it produces definitions or identities that enable you to evaluate the viability of what you wish to sell, the practicality of being able to reach the prospects, the size of the potential market, and other matters bearing on your prospects for success. In fact, you must pursue the process until you reach the point of being able to make a sensible evaluation of these other matters and can modify other plans you have drawn up, such as what you wish to sell.

This is marketing: defining the market, examining it, designing it, getting it all together, evaluating the result, going back to make changes which will fine-tune it—but also throwing the whole thing out and starting over, if it dosen't work when it is put all together.

The marketing entity resulting from all the analytical and planning decisions that lead to the sales effort is made up of mutually dependent elements which must be matched, like the parts of a complex precision machine, so that all work together smoothly and effectively. It is not a matter of artistry, as in combining musical notes or elements in a painting, but a functional matter as in a fine automobile engine where, if one part is improperly designed or faulty in its function, the entire engine functions poorly or not at all.

So it is with marketing. The finest service will not furnish the basis for a successful practice if there are only a few hundred people in the whole country who have need of or use for the service you offer. It is futile to identify several million prospects for your service if you cannot find a way to reach them and present your offer. You can't build a successful enterprise if your prospects want what you offer but can't afford it.

There is also the matter of delivery. You must not only appeal to your chosen prospects with your offer and have the means to reach them, but you must also reach them with your service or product, be able to deliver and do so in an economically viable way. That is, if your prospects are all located several thousands of miles away and what you offer does not justify the travel expense and travel time, it is futile to get the orders, is it not? It is not unusual for neophyte entrepreneurs to win orders they find themselves unable to satisfy for one reason or another.

Therefore, all the decisions you make with regard to what you will sell, what you will offer, to whom, how, and other related matters, should be *tentative* decisions, to be compiled into an experimental marketing plan which is then subject to revision, redesign, discard, or whatever final decisions come out of examining the total marketing picture for its validity and practicality.

SOME BASIC PRINCIPLES

It's a mistake to believe that anyone makes buying decisions rationally, although we all want to believe that we do. Even when we are making the buying decision as a routine matter in the course of doing business, emotional influences inevitably enter into the decision, unconscious though they may be. To see the truth in this, let's examine the simple purchase of a paste pot.

Once there was little choice. You were all but forced to buy what was literally a "paste pot"—a container with a lid, in which was embedded a brush or applicator of some sort. These are still available, with paste, rubber cement, or other mucilage. However, today there are many options to that messy paste pot. ("Messy" is itself an emotion-laden word.) Today, you can get mucilage in spray cans, tubes, and glue sticks. Once, rubber cement in pots with brushes was the universal mucilage of artists and anyone else doing cut-and-paste operations for offset printing. Today, a great many former daubers of rubber cement (users of rubber cement paste pots) are now sprayers of rubber cement (users of rubber cement in spray cans).

The reasons for preferring the spray can to the paste pot are not rational ones, for rubber cement is much cheaper in pots than it is in spray cans. But it is much less messy to use in spray cans and much more *convenient*. (Convenience is a powerful emotional motivation.) Because no one wishes to admit even to oneself an irrational motivation for anything, we work at persuading ourselves that spraying rubber cement is actually more efficient and more economical than painting it on with a brush, and that this justifies paying the higher price. But it is, in fact, a rationalization our self-esteem demands.

That is the basic clue to all marketing and selling—find the right emotional appeal (make the prospect *want* the item), and furnish the prospect the logic necessary to rationalize that emotional buying decision. Show the prospect, somehow, that the $19,000 red sports car or huge super-equipped luxury car is actually a "good buy" or a "smart buy." If you fail to do this, the prospect is likely to draw back from the brink of a sale with a feeling of guilt at this foolish indulgence.

The reverse of this is true also. Suppose that what you are selling is eminently practical—is efficient, economical, the best way to solve some given problem, and unquestionably the "smart" way to go. Those terms—economical, efficient, effective—won't do the job. Logically, they ought to motivate, but we are not dealing with logic here; we are dealing with emotion. Some competitor, whose service may not be nearly as effective or efficient as yours is, will win the contract because of a socko emotional sales message. If you want to win that sale, use all the above logic as the backup motivators but never as the primary motivators. For the primary motivation, you have to find the right emotional appeal and use it effectively.

Let's go back to that hypnotist who is going to help people quit smoking through hypnosis. Suppose he can summon up a bushel-basketful of logic and sound evidence that hypnosis is the most effective, most reliable, and swiftest way to quit smoking. Will those arguments win sales? The answer is yes, they will win *some* sales, especially if our friend the hypnotist has no immediate competition. But suppose he has a competitor who advertises that his clients will quit smoking painlessly, without withdrawal agonies, practically overnight, through an experience so pleasant that it also leaves them with a feeling of well-being such as they have never before experienced. And *then* introduces the logic and evidence. What do you suppose will happen?

There is another way to look at this. The basic appeal consists of a promise of some benefit to result from utilizing the service you offer to sell. The logic or evidence that follows the promise must convince the prospect that your service can and does produce the result promised, that you are qualified and capable of producing the results, and/or that you are reliable and dependable as a source of said services and promised results. Examine any effective sales promotion and advertising, and you will find these elements present.

Where logical evidence is not available, as in convincing prospects that the beer being advertised is all but guaranteed to produce good fellowship and fun times, or the cigarettes advertised will make you a "macho" man, other kinds of evidence are used, such as a prominent show-business figure smiling or offering a testimonial (would John Wayne lie to you?) or the white coat of a scientist in a laboratory. The intent is the same—to persuade the prospect that the promise is valid and the benefits will be delivered, even if the evidence is largely manufactured or merely additional claims. Note, however, that even when the alleged evidence is merely more unsupported claims, a distinct effort is made to make that additional, backup argument *appear* objective, logical, and scientific.

So the first step is always the same—promising some much-to-be-desired result that has great emotional appeal, followed by rationales that have the dual purposes of validating the promises and proving that they will be made good if the prospect makes the purchase, and convincng the skeptical or still-undecided prospect who wants more proof that the advertiser will do what he or she says.

Does it work? The multibillion-dollar advertising industry in the United States furnishes its own kind of evidence that it works, even when it's not done as well as it ought to be. Many rather dreadful commercials still manage to produce enough sales to justify their high costs.

TYPICAL MOTIVATORS

Although there are approximately four billion individuals in this world, and each of us is unique, we share many common needs and drives. All of us need love, warmth, security, prestige, respect, success, ego gratification, and many other emotional satisfactions, all of which might be lumped under a general label of "security," both physical and psychological. All successful sales appeals are based on these needs and drives. Let's look at a few examples:

Insurance. The arguments used to sell insurance are based on love of family and the need to protect them and safeguard their future; on self-security, creating a fund or financial resource for the future; on ego—being an important person who cannot afford to leave this existence without compensating for the great loss with a large sum of money; and on guilt—safeguarding family, partners, children, or others is a must that only a blackguard would fail in.

Automobiles. Automobiles are often sold on the basis of the prospect's self-image—macho man, man about town, beautiful and independent career woman, successful executive, and other such fantasies or realities.

Cosmetics. Almost without exception, sex appeal is the motivator—the need to be attractive and to be loved, and the suggestion that the glamorous stars of show business use these same products not only supports the emotional reason with rationale but also adds directly to the emotional appeal—sharing something with such beautiful and successful people and being as good as they are.

Clothes.   See cosmetics, for the situation is quite similar, and the reasoning is very much along the same lines.

But let's see how you might use emotional motivators in selling consulting services, for that is a different proposition. Or is it?

Time Management.   Management consultants who teach or devise systems for better time management often focus on reducing stress and enabling the manager to operate in a more relaxed and more efficient manner, often with the implication that a result will be a far better image in the company for the manager who is now much more in command of the situation. In general, management consultants tend to focus on whatever is "in" at the moment—such as MBO (Management by Objectives)—for its almost automatic appeal to the need to be up to date in everything. Sometimes it is most helpful to stress, in presentation, that whatever is being offered is new and very much the latest development in the field.

Computer Systems/Services.   Aside from being "the only way to go" for the modern, aggressive, and successful company (and, of course, every executive wants to think of his or her company in those terms, so the premise is acceptable!), the able computer consultant helps the company save time and money, commands the respect of contemporaries and customers by having the most up-to-date and most efficient systems, and otherwise develops a much-to-be-desired image in the business world. And everyone in business wants a good image!

Marketing Services.   Here the carrot is obvious. The promise is one of far more success at winning those profitable and prestigious contracts or sales that make a CEO's mouth water or, in some cases, getting into an adjacent field that is most tempting. In personal terms, the company's marketing executive wants the help which may, he hopes, make him or her a hero in the company.

Bear in mind always that even when you are appealing to organizations, you are still appealing to and dealing with individual humans. The proprietor, if it is a small company and you are dealing directly with the proprietor, wants sales, profits, and growth, with growth probably being the most motivating factor and the one which ought to be stressed as a promised result if it fits what you offer. It is a rare business owner who is not, consciously or unconsciously, dedicated to growing and becoming more of a force, more prominent, more important, more respected within the business community. Those are ambitions to be considered in fashioning a presentation and determining what the promised benefits are to be.

When you are dealing with a larger organization where your presentation is being made to people on staff, no matter their roles or their levels they have the same ambitions to grow as individuals. Offer them help in accomplishing important things that will bring them local, in-house renown.

These are what I think of as *positive motivators*—promises of much-to-be-desired blessings. But there are also some highly effective motivators I think of as *negative motivators*. These are promises of avoiding disastrous things that are likely to occur. Using guilt to sell insurance is an excellent example. The motivator is based on the undeniable truth that no one knows how much time he or she has on Earth, and one day it will be too late to take those all-important steps of taking out insurance to protect one's loved ones, overcome the tragedy of having a house burn down or wash away in storm or flood, and otherwise take the proper steps before disaster strikes.

Security devices such as locks and burglar alarms are generally sold on that same basis of negative motivation. So, too, although with less drama, are sold chimney cleaning, furnace checkover before the winter snows fly, storm windows and insulation, and numerous other products and services. All that is necessary is that the threat be a commonly recognized one that is serious enough to compel consideration of preventive or corrective measures. The appeal is still emotional, of course, with the main stress on what can happen—a huge tree falling on the home and crushing it, a family huddled outside a burned-out house in their nightclothes, an almost-demolished automobile, and other such images.

One commonly used and effective motivator with both negative and positive elements is the problem-solving appeal. Find a common enough problem for which most solutions are less than completely satisfactory and build your appeal around your better solution. A great many things which can be sold by other means as well can be sold effectively in this way. Let's look at a few examples:

Computer Services.   A rich field for this approach because computers offer numerous benefits in solving such problems as too much help, capable help difficult to find, or too slow a turnaround time. (Let the computer do the job, at less expense and with greater speed and dependability.)

Office Systems.   No more problems of misplaced files or lost correspondence and the resulting embarrassment with customers and superiors, faster follow-up on delinquent accounts receivable and consequent help in solving the pervasive cash-flow problem. An easy area to find common problems that need better solutions.

Marketing Services. No more getting bids or proposals in too late, failing to learn about bid and proposal opportunities, poor advertising copy, and a myriad of other such problems crying to be solved. Another area rich in opportunities for problem-solving motivation.

The fact is that almost anything can be sold as a solution for problems. If we look back at some of the examples we used earlier, here is how we might have used the problem-solving approach with some of them:

Insurance. Solves many problems, such as how to protect your family's equity in your house (mortgage insurance) should something happen to the major wage earner; how to protect a business partner (partnership/survivor insurance); and many other kinds of presentations, in which the prospect is educated to the many varieties of insurance he probably never dreamed existed.

Automobiles. Another rich area. Problems of vehicle dependability, for one. A recent sales promotion featured the ability of the vehicle to shift to four-wheel drive, with an illustration of how this overcomes the problems of driving in mud, snow, and ice. Problems of transporting many children—solving it helped sell many station wagons.

Cosmetics. Easy to find problems here since many cosmetic items are designed expressly to solve problems, for example, broken nails, hard-to-manage hair, and skin flaws.

Clothes. Easy area again, with so many prospects requiring clothes to fit individual characteristics—hence, "husky," "tall," and "slim" specialties. Also business suits to make the too-young-looking executive a bit more professional- or mature-looking, clothes better suited to the needs of those who travel a great deal (e.g., wrinkle-proof), and other needs an imaginative marketer can create.

Time Management. An absolute "natural," of course, no one ever has enough time to get everything done, especially the busy executive. Easy to think up problems that time management can solve.

As you can see, the problem-solving motivator can be either negative or positive—either solving problems that threaten disaster if not solved, or solving problems that greatly improve operations, bring new benefits, and are better solutions than those available heretofore.

In this positive-thinking world, you might suppose that wherever you have a choice you would be well-advised to use the most positive motivators you can fix your sights on. Not so. Negative motivators are often the most effective ones. Fear is a most effective motivator in a great many circumstances. There seems to be general agreement among psychiatrists and psychologists that none of us is completely free of insecurity, which can only mean that all of us experience some fear. Perhaps in many of us it is buried to some fair depth below the conscious level, but we do live in a stressful society and we manage to dredge that fear up readily under the right stimulus. There are many of us in whom the fear is barely below the conscious level, and there are some in whom fear appears to be a permanent consciousness. Never write fear off as second- or third-priority choice for sales motivation. It is often the first choice, the most effective sales motivator.

The recent spate of best-seller books on the impending doom of our financial system and all its works is an excellent testimonial to the salubrious effect of fear as a sales motivator. The gloomier and doomier the gloom-and-doom opus was, the more copies it sold. Not only were readers trying to discover the escape hatches they should know about when the financial Armageddon arrives, but they appeared to be fascinated by fear and disaster itself. The tremendous surge of interest and activity in collector's items—everything from stamps and coins to plates and memorabilia—is further testimonial to the fear that money is rapidly becoming worthless and that other physical items represent greater security than do figures inscribed in bank books or on government bonds.

Pick up a magazine at random and leaf through it. Stop and look at the advertisements and analyze what they are attempting to do and how. I happen to have near at hand a news magazine, *U.S. News & World Report.* I'm going to follow my own suggestion here, and share with you what I find:

1. Inside the cover is a full-page color advertisement for an automobile. It stresses front-wheel drive, four-cylinder engine for economy, and a few minor luxury features. It's pictured in the driveway of an impressive house, with the handsome owner-couple admiring it. Main message: Style. The couple are all but carried away with their admiration of this smart-looking, modern luxury.

2. Next is a whiskey advertisement in which the advertiser claims that taste tests prove that the advertised whiskey tastes better than a famous, higher-priced competitor. The copy trades on the name of the famous competitor, has pocketbook appeal, but the main message is based on the alleged "nationwide taste tests."

3.   Another page extols the virtues of "telemarketing," stresses that it delivers great benefits by producing sales, but makes its stand primarily as a problem solver—beats the high cost of doing business today. The copy uses such emotional words as "dramatic new way" and "soaring costs." It enumerates benefits, too, such as better customer service.

4.   A vodka advertisement features a famous lawyer seated in an easy chair (his photo dominates the page), endorsing the brand. The "evidence" for the claim of superiority is the "authority" figure.

5.   An airline uses a slightly different kind of "evidence" to support its claim, taking a two-page spread to present a line of airline pilots and flight attendants, who presumably testify that more people use that airline than any other; hence, it's a better airline.

6.   An insurance advertisement in a business magazine illustrates clearly how advertising can be based on fear. Pictured is a desperate store owner who is cornered in an empty store with signs promising a giant sale, with customers crowding the front door and glaring at him accusingly because it is obvious that he has nothing to sell. The advertiser is selling something they call "contingent business interruption" insurance to people who have such problems as a supplier failing to deliver ordered merchandise. Based on fear, but with reference to problems that interrupt normal business operation.

7.   The manufacturer of warehouse material-handling equipment advertises with studied cleverness, "NO. ONE MAKES IT BETTER." The pun intended here is that it can be read as both *Number one makes it better* and *No one makes it better.* Another of many cases of copywriters being clever instead of good. Cute copy is lost on advertisers, and even if readers get the double meaning of the above cleverness, it does nothing for the sale. Cleverness does not sell anything. What is wrong with the above headline, and with most other headlines and copy that is cute and clever is simple enough—it does not give the reader a reason to buy or even to become interested. Whether you say that number one makes it better or no one makes it better, you are merely patting yourself on the back and making unsupported claims. The advertising business is full of examples of clever advertising copy that failed to sell the merchandise or service, and the cleverness often cost the agency the account. Two examples: An early Volkswagen TV commercial and the now-famous Alka Seltzer "stomachs" commercial. Both were lauded within the advertising-agency industry for excellence. Unfortunately, neither commercial sold the product: the copywriters were so preoccupied with being clever that they apparently forgot to sell the product.

All of this is with reference to advertising copy, not because I advocate that the consultant become a skilled advertising copywriter. Quite the contrary, media advertising is of most limited usefulness in marketing consulting services. But the principles of marketing and selling are most easily pointed out and explained by using TV and print-media advertising as examples, and these principles translate directly into the methods that market consulting services effectively, as will soon be shown here.

EVIDENCE AND RATIONALE

We have been looking primarily at emotional motivators and analyzing what they are, what they do, how they work, and how they are applied to specific needs. In so doing, we looked briefly at some of the kinds of material used as "evidence" or "proof" that the claims and promises made in the initial motivator were valid and would be made good. And that is not to overlook the other functions of such material—to help the hesitant or still-skeptical prospect decide to buy, and to help the prospect reassure himself or herself that the buying decision makes good sense and is entirely logical. Let us look now at some examples of how such material is developed, introduced, or used.

One way that has been mentioned already is the testimonial, especially one from a public figure whose face is familiar, or someone in a prominent job, such as the famous lawyer used in an advertisement described earlier. However, testimonials by ordinary consumers, as used frequently by advertisers of household cleansers and detergents, are also effective. Written testimonials help, too, even if the author's name is withheld, with the notation that the letter is on file and available on demand.

The names of other clients, especially if they are well-known individuals or well-known companies, are good evidence of the worth of what you sell.

Technical jargon is sometimes used. "Rack and pinion steering" and "MacPherson strut suspension" are phrases that are intended to demonstrate the validity of claims even if the reader hasn't the faintest idea what they are. Somehow, that lends the claim an air of authority and authenticity.

Take note here of an important point: The difference between objective reality and prospects' perceptions. There may very well be quite a gulf here. For example, there is absolutely no logic in the concept that because Norm Crosby claims to like _____ beer and appears to be drinking it, you or I will like it. But that is beside the point as far as most prospects are concerned. The fact that Norm Crosby is a prominent and successful entertainer lends him an air of authority in other matters, and a great many people will have instant faith in anything he says. He's far too nice and sincere a guy to lie to the viewers, goes the unconscious reasoning, and he's having such a good time drinking _____ beer with his friends. Therefore, it must be fun to drink _____ beer.

The simple fact is that it is quite easy to persuade people of what they want to believe. If the emotional motivator is appealing enough and the prospect wants badly enough to believe it, and if the proof is not too far-fetched to swallow, and especially if the famous figure testifying for the product or service is likable enough, it's quite easy to suspend our skepticism.

Being likable is important if the evidence relies on anyone's testimony. Who wants to believe anything from someone we dislike intensely? And who wants to have doubts about representations made by someone we like or admire? (Note that TV commercials that use celebrity figures for testimonials never use "heavies," but always someone who is popular and has an image of joviality or, at least, sincerity.) The owner of a TV-service firm once remarked to me that there were noticeably fewer complaints from customers whose sets had been serviced by the more jovial and friendly servicemen on his staff than from other customers whose sets had been serviced by those of his staff who were less outgoing and more closemouthed.

THE CUSTOMER'S PERCEPTION

There are few tinkerer-inventors any longer. Modern technology is such that most technological advances are made in costly laboratories by large teams of specialists. However, there is at least one modern-day Edison who turns out a stream of new inventions in his own, private laboratory-workshop. And he has done so since his school days. He says he has never worked for someone else, but has always managed to earn his living by selling his inventions, some of which are technologically quite sophisticated, others of which are almost frivolous, like the gadget that scrambles an egg in its shell.

One of this gentleman's early inventions was a device to persuade ketchup to pour less reluctantly from its narrow-necked bottle. Our inventor friend had realized that the chief problem is one of enabling air to replace the space occupied by ketchup in the neck of the bottle, and he created a simple device to do just that. Voilà! The ketchup poured out of a fresh bottle with much greater enthusiasm. So our hero trotted off to the chief maker and seller of ketchup with his marvelous development, with visions of dollar bills dancing in his head. He was sure that his fortune would be made as soon as he had explained how he had solved this important problem. To his dismay, his invention was greeted by the ketchup makers with horror. The ketchup kings shuddered as they shrank back from this man who threatened destruction. "Free-running ketchup is the last thing in the world we want," they fairly shrieked. "Our whole reputation is based on how thick our ketchup is. Are you trying to destroy that?"

The inventor learned something from that early experience. He says that he made the mistake of offering the company something they needed rather than something they wanted. He was only partly right. He should have offered them something they wanted, true enough, but he was wrong about their needing his invention. They did not need it and they were entirely right in their assessment of it as it related to them. The concept having been built that ketchup should be thick and difficult to pour, thickness and slowness of pouring became the standards of quality in the public mind. Anything that poured easily would therefore be a poor grade of ketchup. The invention could easily have destroyed their top position in the ketchup trade.

In all marketing activities it is necessary to view the situation always from the customer's perception. Your perception, as the seller, counts for nothing; it is not you but the customer who must be persuaded. You cannot possibly market effectively unless you understand the customer's perspective, biases, and opinions. That is, unless you understand the true meaning of "needs," as the term is relevant to marketing.

NEEDS: WHAT ARE THEY?

Need has a different meaning in general usage than it does in sales and marketing. When the average individual says, "I need new shoes," the meaning is that the old shoes are worn out or that some special occasion makes it absolutely necessary to have new shoes. As used ordinarily, therefore *need* refers to a requirement brought about by something other than mere whim or desire, such as the old one having worn out and failed.

It is not too surprising that when we *want* something and acquiring that something means spending money we can't afford or shouldn't spend for the purpose, we decide that we *need* it. Perhaps those old shoes are in good condition, perfectly serviceable and unmarred, but they are old and "it's time" for a new pair, so it isn't too difficult to rationalize and decide that they're terribly out of style, never were comfortable anyhow, and really have served so long that they don't owe you anything. Ergo, it's perfectly justifiable to throw them out and get a new pair. (The inevitable manufactured evidence to justify the emotional buying decision.)

Need, then, for marketing purposes, is identical with *desire.* A need is whatever a prospective customer decides to want. But marketers talk about two classes of need, *felt* needs and *created* needs.

THE FELT NEED

In general terms, a felt need is one the prospect has decided to experience without any prompting or suggestion from anyone else. The customer who walks into the shoe store to buy a pair of shoes has a felt need for new shoes, perhaps even for some specific type or style already conceived as what is needed. But if the shoe clerk can persuade the customer to decide that he or she has also a need of shoelaces, polish, or other items, the clerk has "created" a need—stimulated a desire, that is, which is the same thing in terms of practical results. Creating a need, then, means somehow persuading a prospect to feel a want for something, as compared with the prospect feeling the want spontaneously.

CREATING NEEDS

New needs are created almost continuously, partly through advertising and sales promotion, partly through the development of new products of various kinds. In a great many cases, creating a new need soon results in many people having a new felt need. New products often do that. There was, for example, no felt need for TV in 1940 or before that, simply because no one except those engaged in research and development or readers of science fiction was even aware that it was a serious possibility. Once available, however, its acceptance was spectacular and immediate, and the need for it spread rapidly.

That's the story with every new product or service. If it catches on with the public, it creates a new need and often several new needs, just as TV and computers have created needs for programs and service as well as for the equipment itself.

Of course, not everything new does catch on immediately, and some things never do. Many new products and services linger on for a while and then disappear from view, having either failed to stir the fancy of prospective customers or been rapidly outdated by even newer products or services. Transistors, for example, have made vacuum tubes used in radio and TV almost obsolete, and buggy whips and horse shoes are the subject of so many jests used to stress obsolescence that they have become its symbols.

Created need, then, is tantamount to acceptance by consumers. To paraphrase an old saying, some new products or services are born to acceptance, some achieve acceptance, and some have acceptance thrust upon them. Some things, such as TV, are born to acceptance, the public embraces them immediately, and it takes little selling to put them over. Some, such as airplanes, have acceptance thrust upon them. In this case, World War I forced the rapid development of airplanes, and World War II resulted in the evolution of helicopters and jet aircraft. Some, such as ballpoint pens, achieved acceptance as users were gradually weaned away from their familiar fountain pens by massive sales promotions and advertising. (The first ballpoint pens introduced retailed for $15, more than the price of a good fountain pen at the time.)

Most of us in the consulting field have to *achieve* acceptance of our services. It is rare that a consultant is an instant success. In most cases, success is achieved by unremitting marketing effort, gradually and on a slowly rising curve. That means that the consultant almost invariably must create the need for his or her services, must market aggressively.

THE TWO MARKETING PROBLEMS

There are two basic situations, representing two kinds of problems:

1. The new product/service genre.
2. The new product/service "brand."

The introduction of TV receivers into the marketplace created an immediate need for related services—receiver and antenna installation and maintenance services, for example. In the beginning, selling TV service required little more than the bare announcement that it was available. There were so few independent TV service dealers—initially, all the major manufacturers provided their own service, to back up their sales programs—that little real selling was needed.

However, not everything meets with immediate acceptance. Sometimes the public resists new products and services simply because they are new and alien; most of us are reluctant to shed what is familiar and comfortable. It often takes determined and aggressive marketing to sell something that is new and different, that is, to achieve acceptance.

Sometimes, the new item achieves acceptance as it begins to become familiar, but not always. Some items never become widely-felt needs, but must always be pressed hard. Encyclopedias are a good example of this.

The first selling problem, then, is one of selling something new and different—not a new brand of lipstick, for example, but a new genre, such as fake fingernails—which does not become an immediate success on its own. Most new products and services must be sold aggressively for a long time before achieving wide acceptance. Many consulting services are in this category, and a great many never become felt needs on a wide scale, but must always be sold aggressively.

The other problem stems largely from the opposite situation, the wide and enthusiastic acceptance of a new genre of product or service. Because the product or idea catches on and becomes a felt need, as in the case of TV, a great many sellers get into the marketplace quickly. Now the marketing problem is not one of acceptance, but one of selling your own brand or model.

TV is an excellent example. Because it became so popular so rapidly, there were soon dozens of makes on the market. In addition to the well-known major brands—for example, RCA, Philco, Zenith, GE—there were Packard-Bell, Natalie Kalmus, Warwick, and the private brand of every major department-store chain as well.

It happened with automobiles earlier, after Henry Ford had demonstrated that there was a major market for automobiles. Many of us can remember now-extinct species such as DeSoto, Packard, and Studebaker, but how many remember the prehistoric dinosaurs of the automobile industry: Moon, Star, Jewett, Locomobile, White, Stanley, Reo, Cord, Willys, Overland, and as many as 30 or 40 others?

It happened even in computers. Once there were Philco, RCA, GE, and a few other computers that no longer are being manufactured.

The point of all this is that to market your consulting services, as well as any products you may develop, effectively, you must determine which kind of marketing problem you are facing. Are you persuading prospects that they have need for the *kind* of service you offer, or are you selling a customer who has a felt need for your kind of service but is considering other suppliers?

It is also possible that you have both problems, that you must first convince the prospect of the need for what you offer, and then that you are the right choice for the job. Unless you recognize this dual problem and act in response to it, you may very well be selling for your competitors.

TWO-STEP SELLING

A variety of marketing situations exists in addition to the two just discussed. Many items and services can be sold spontaneously. House-to-house salespeople, such as Avon saleswomen, operate on the reasonable assumption that all women use cosmetics and are therefore good prospects for Avon products. This makes house-to-house selling feasible; every household normally has women, and all are good prospects.

Not everyone drinks beer, but enough people do to make general advertising on TV and in newspapers and magazines feasible and worthwhile. A large percentage of those to whom the presentations are directed are good prospects.

For a great many items, the sale is spontaneous, following the sales presentation immediately. The TV viewer may pop into the drug store the next day to buy items huckstered on TV the previous evening, and will probably pick up a few items as impulse purchases.

Not so the automobile buyer. No one expects the TV viewer to rush to the dealer next day and say, "Give me one of those Super-Horsepower Steamboats I saw on TV last night." The purpose of these commercials is to persuade the viewer to stop at the dealer's showroom as soon as convenient, just to browse around and look at the new models, so the dealer's salespeople can go to work. To put it another way, this kind of TV commercial or print advertisement is designed to develop sales leads—individuals showing enough interest to be worth working on, in the hopes of making a sale.

Consulting services fits into this last category in most cases. The sale requires two steps, finding leads and closing them. That is, finding prospects or potential customers—those displaying some interest and the possibility that a need can be generated—and persuading them to give you the order. It's rare that a consultant's client buys the services casually, with only a moment's reflection, as though it were a manicure or shoe shine.

The marketing of your services, therefore, should be designed to do exactly those two things, each as a distinct function. But there are a few things you must do even before you begin to seek out and develop leads.

IDENTIFYING YOUR MARKETS

As a specialist in selling to the federal government, I started offering my consulting services to very small businesses, helping clients write proposals. I assumed that the larger companies, especially the major corporations, had their own on-staff experts who were probably far better qualified than I to handle all their marketing to the government.

That proved to be about as wrong an idea as I could have had, and it was wrong in two ways: Not only did I eventually do work for some of the largest and most important corporations in the United States, but writing proposals was only one of several consulting services needed. I was guilty of "assuming facts not in evidence," based on what I thought was logical. But what I thought was not logic at all; it was prejudice, bias, and a belief in mythology.

Business mythology leads many of us to believe that the bigger the corporation, the more able and wise its leaders, and the more capable—perhaps even infallible—its in-house staffs of experts. What rot! Disillusioning experience demonstrates plainly that even in the supercorporation there are fools and incompetents or semi-competents at the top as at the bottom. At one time when I was division executive in a corporation which now enjoys gross sales annually in more than 10 figures, the comptroller of this multi-division industrial behemoth was a thoroughly likable, jovial semi-competent who had become a "hero" in the company by finding ten-percent money at a time when prime was well under five percent. The company's chief attorney got the company into difficulties with a federal agency because he couldn't read a contract accurately. There must also be many unsteady hands at the helms of major organizations such as E.J. Korvette, Robert Hall, W.T. Grant, and others. At this writing, the fate of Chrysler Corporation is not yet certain.

I also found that my clientele were not all individuals or organizations who needed help in writing proposals, or even those who were already into contracting with the government. Some were individuals and organizations who thought they ought to be selling to government agencies, but had no idea of how to get started or who in the government might be interested in whatever goods or services they had to offer. They wanted the most basic marketing guidance or market studies, some of which I could do without leaving my desk. I found also that there were clients who needed only some personal orientation in the federal markets, but who could not afford to pay my standard daily fees. (More on coping with that problem later.)

In short, I started out by assuming certain things to be facts, with absolutely no basis for the assumptions, except some vague notions I had gathered somewhere, somehow. And the longer I worked at consulting and related activities, the more markets I discovered. Since that time I have come to realize that mine was a most common failing. Others commit the same follies of making unwarranted assumptions, underestimating the importance of what they know and can do, and taking far too narrow a view of the market possibilities.

MARKETS ARE NOT ABSOLUTES

Markets are neither constants nor independent variables. They are usually dependent variables, varying according to what you wish to offer. For example, if I offer proposal-writing services only, I restrict my markets thereby to those individuals and organizations who pursue only contracts awarded through negotiated procurement. If I do proposal-writing seminars only, I restrict myself to a lesser degree, but still to only those firms pursuing contracts via negotiated procurement, and I exclude those who wish to have my help in writing proposals rather than, or in additon to, instructing their proposal writers. But if I expand my seminars or run additional ones covering government marketing generally rather than proposal writing, I broaden my marketing considerably to include those who pursue contracts resulting from bids as well as from proposals. Outside factors effect changes in markets, too, of course.

In consequence, you can define or identify your markets only with consideration of what you offer. The more diverse or flexible your offerings, the broader your market.

There is frequently an interrelationship among these alternative markets, so that publishing a newsletter or conducting a seminar often leads to a pure consulting assignment and vice versa; consulting clients may become your subscribers, and seminar registrants or clients for one kind of service may become clients for another service.

It is also true that the markets you can reach effectively may suggest what you should offer, so you must study the two problems, what to sell and to whom to sell it, together.

There is a third factor, how to reach the targets you perceive as your proper markets. It's of no avail to select a target you can't reach effectively. Here is an example:

In offering seminars in proposal writing, it was immediately apparent that my targets would not be individuals, for while the seminar would appeal to a few individuals, most of my proper prospects were companies, both small and large. I decided that my means of reaching them had to be direct mail. Producers of seminars directed at individuals, such as seminars in how to become a consultant or how to speed-read, are often sold via newspaper advertising because (1) experience proves that this is a good medium for reaching individuals and (2) it is not easy to put together a suitable mailing list of individuals for seminars on consulting, and it is more convenient to use print advertising.

Conversely, print advertising does not work too well when pursuing seminar registrations from companies. Experience demonstrates this, and evidently it has become conventional wisdom, for just about everyone who conducts such seminars uses direct mail.

GETTING NAMES FOR MAILING

Many people rent mailing lists for their direct-mail pieces and usually mail in great quantities, using bulk-mail rates (less than one half first-class postage), and many also arrange a tie-in with universities to get the very special rate offered nonprofit organizations (a fraction of the first-class rate). My own experience with rented lists has not been good, however; I have always fared far better with my own lists. Therefore, although it has been a great deal of work, I have laboriously compiled my own mailing lists over the years by a variety of methods, and these lists have worked rather well for me, A first-class mailing to only a few thousand names has produced for me as many registrations as bulk-mail pieces sent out to many thousands of names. Here are methods I have used to get the kinds of names I needed for my seminars and, later, for my newsletter and related mailings:

1. Help-wanted advertising. This has been one of my prime sources of company names and addresses. I have used the *Washington Post*, *The Wall Street Journal*, and the *New York Times* principally.

2. Membership directories of relevant organizations, such as professional engineers associations. Some of these are unavailable, but it is possible to get others.

3. Telephone Yellow Pages.

4. Companies mentioned in the many notices in the *Commerce Business Daily*, a federal government publication listing bid and proposal solicitations and contract awards, among other things.

5. Lists the government has supplied, such as a Navy directory of hundreds of Navy contractors and subcontractors and a New York City directory of minority contractors.

Using such sources and working hard at it, I have today nearly 25,000 names of organizations suitable for my own direct-mail needs. Moreover, they are a source of additional income if I wish to rent the names out to others. In fact, I can turn the list over to a list broker, someone who markets other people's mailing lists on a commission basis (usually about 20 percent). Many consultants earn substantial extra income by renting their mailing lists out to others. Good mailing lists rent from a low of about $35 to as much as $75 per 1000 names. They are rented, not sold; the renter has the right to use the list only once, and the list is salted with a few names that enable the list broker to detect unauthorized copying and additional use of the lists.

Another way to accumulate and compile names for mailing is by inquiry advertising. Inquiry advertising is used to generate sales leads and compile mailing lists, and there are several ways to go about using this:

One way is to offer free information in small advertisements. To generate enough inquiries to make the thing worthwhile, you have to offer something appealing. It could be the information itself, for example, "how to make $100,000 in your spare time", or a giveaway item such as a calendar, a brochure, or whatever is appropriate. Some of the names on my own mailing lists have come to me this way.

The idea here is to attract those who will make suitable prospects, so you have to select the medium in which you advertise and write the advertisement so that it draws the right names. For example, if you offer investment counseling or an investment newsletter, you'll want to advertise in the *Wall Street Journal* or another publication read by potential investors, such as perhaps *Money* magazine, rather than in one of those weekly newspapers sold in the supermarkets today, and, the advertisement itself must appeal to the kind of individual whose name you are seeking. If you are looking for those interested in an investment newsletter, you might want to offer a sample copy or perhaps a brochure explaining some little-known facts about investments today.

OTHER WAYS OF GENERATING LEADS: PUBLIC RELATIONS

One thing you must bear constantly in mind in marketing your consulting services is that what you are selling is, in the final analysis, a promise based on your own credentials and professional image. If you want clients to pay you for counseling them in their investments, whether on a direct consulting basis or by subscription to something you publish, you must have their confidence. You must therefore do those things which create, build, and enhance your professional image. While you need business cards and brochures, they are ancillary to your main marketing efforts; they alone cannot produce a significant amount of business. You must utilize some public relations tactics and strategy.

Manufacturers of new items like cigarettes, candy, cosmetics, household products, and other consumer items often introduce these items to the public and create a demand for them by a widespread distribution of samples. It's one way to persuade prospective customers to try the product, and it's all but certain that some people are going to like the sample well enough to buy the product. It's one of the oldest marketing devices known, and the fact that it is still in widespread use and the slower the economy, the more widespread the use of free samples demonstrates that it is effective.

The consultant can and should adopt the idea and adapt it to marketing consultant services. You can't stand out on a street corner and hand out samples of your consulting, and you can't mail samples to "Resident" either, but there are several ways in which you can offer free samples of your services and thereby generate some demand or at least some sales leads.

One way is by pursuing every available opportunity to speak to audiences of listeners who are likely to be good prospects for you. If, for example, you are that investment counselor I postulated a few paragraphs ago, find the audiences who would appreciate some free investment counseling. A meeting of a medical association might be such an occasion if it is as true as is generally alleged that medical people have too much uninvested capital and are actively seeking places to put it to work. There are many other meetings and conventions of people who would make good prospects. Volunteer to speak for an hour or whatever the program chairman will grant you. Be sure to bring along an ample supply of your cards and brochures, and samples of your newsletter or reports if you have either of those.

To get started in this, draft a letter describing what you wish to speak on and outlining generally what you will say, your personal credentials in the field, and whatever else you believe appropriate. Provide some references—names of people who will assure anyone who calls that you know what you are talking about and that it is worth taking the time to listen to what you have to say. Send that letter out, along with your card and a small brochure, to organizations in your area. If you want to improve your batting average in this, follow up the mailing by making telephone calls to each addressee.

Use any "contacts" you have, to promote such appearances, and when you do speak, make it clear to everyone who hears you that you are available to deliver such talks at other occasions. (Many of your listeners will also belong to other associations.)

In many cases, sponsors of national conventions invite people to speak, especially if the speaker will speak without compensation (except for expenses) or for a token sum. Many consultants take advantage of such occasions because they make new "contacts" thereby and often win business as a result.

Program chairmen and program committees of organizations are always on the spot to arrange things, and you'll find willing ears, in most cases, if you address your offer to these functionaries in associations.

It is useful to spend some time talking to people at your local Chamber of Commerce, Rotary, Lions Club, Elks, Businessmen's Association, and whatever else your community has in the way of business groups. These groups can be helpful in many ways.

Get in touch with talk-show producers of your local TV and radio stations and with the hosts of such shows as well. These people are often looking for new and interesting people to interview. A useful tip: Make it clear that you can be available on short notice, for emergencies. What often happens is that a scheduled guest or interviewee is unable to appear due to illness or some last-minute contingency, and the show has to try to find an instant replacement.

Be alert for seminars being held in your area. If you are willing to speak without fee, as in the case of conventions and meetings, seminar producers might be interested in having you appear. (Of course, the seminar must be relevant to your own field and needs.)

Very much the same things might be said about writing. You can write articles and columns about your specialty as free samples of your consulting services. Most associations have newsletters of some sort, and some of the larger ones even have slick monthly magazines. Offer them articles and columns as often as possible. Write letters to the editor as often as possible; you'll be surprised at how much (public relations value) you can get out of such letters.

Many companies or nonprofit organizations have their own newsletters and magazines, "house organs," as many call them. The editors of these are constantly looking for materials.

All these things are PR tools. "Public relations" means *publicity*, which in effect means free advertising. It is actually far more effective than advertising when skillfully handled, because it is editorial matter rather than paid-for advertising and so is far more credible; it "carries more weight" with the readers than does paid advertising.

One of the chief tools of the PR specialist is the *press release*, also called *news release* or simply *release*. It is sent out to "the media"—newspapers, newsletters, magazines, radio and TV newsrooms, commentators, and just about anyone else who might use some or all of it in their own publication or presentation. The objective is to get publicity, and the idea is that every editor, writer, announcer, commentator, and other individual involved in the media in any way is always hungry for material. Releases are therefore written and sent out by many public figures, by companies, nonprofit groups, associations, other organizations, and by just about everyone who has need of publicity. That adds up to a vast number of releases, and large newspaper and magazine offices are all but swamped with releases daily. It's a rare day that I don't get a few myself, since I edit a couple of newsletters.

The vast majority of these releases wind up in the wastebasket, principally because they are poorly conceived. They are not poorly written, but they have a common fault. There is no earthly reason, as far as most recipients of these releases are concerned, why they (the recipients) should use any part of the releases. They are not newsworthy. That does not necessarily mean that they are not news, for a press release does not have to be news to be used. But it does have to be worth inclusion in one's publication, broadcast, or presentation. It has to have information the editor (using that term to include commentators and others, from now on) believes will interest readers. That is the entire secret of success in getting your releases and other contributions accepted and published: You must sell the material (though "sell" does not mean get paid for, in this case) to whomever you have sent it to.

A responsibility of every editor faced with considering contributions is deciding whether readers will or will not be interested in seeing the material offered. There is more than one factor to be considered in most cases.

Is the subject generally germane to these readers and their interests? (Don't send news of a rise in precious-metals prices to a publication dedicated to race-track drivers.)

Is this aspect or treatment of interest to these readers? (Even *Wall Street Journal* readers are not likely to be interested in reading about precious-metals prices behind the Iron Curtain.)

Is this release in the right department? (The city editor of a newspaper is a busy person and may decide to trash a release that should have been addressed to the financial editor, rather than take the time to re-route it.)

Can I get the essence of this story from the first few lines, preferably from the headline? (If not, with so many other releases begging for at least a quick look, the editor is likely to waste no more time on it.)

Does the idea grab me right away, or do I have to ponder it a while? (Some linkage to the idea of the previous item, but not the same factor, as the following discussion will explain. However, busy editors generally don't lay releases aside for later consideration; usually, the release is either "in" or it's "out".)

The first three items require no extended discussion, but it is surprising how often people sending out releases do not consider them. I get many releases and even complimentary newsletters and tabloids that should not come to me because there is no earthly reason to believe that I would be interested in or have use for them. Getting your releases to the right people takes some time and requires some work, but it's futile to write and print the release if you are not going to get it into the right hands.

HOW TO WRITE A RELEASE

The physical format of a release is highly flexible, as figures 1, 2, and 3 reveal. Somewhere the thing must identify itself as a release and also identify the origin. For that reason, many organizations and individuals use their standard letterhead. Other items which should appear are these:

Contact—name, address, telephone number, and possibly title of an individual to call or write for more details. Sometimes an editor will want to expand on the release or do a more complete story of some sort, and information ought to be provided to help with that.

Dateline—while the letterhead may indicate the origin, it is customary to use a dateline for the editor's convenience in identifying city, state, and date of origin.

Release date—some organizations send out information they wish released on some coming date rather than immediately. This desire can be indicated by such notations as "For immediate release" or "Release on _____" with the date supplied. In some cases, the notation may use the term "embargo" until some date named, which means don't release this until the date named.

If the release is more than one page long, indicate at the bottom right corner that there is more to come by the word "more" and indicate that the story is ended at the bottom of the last page by any of the following: The symbol-30- (a telegrapher's sign-off), ###, or "The End."

Not every one respects the need for these things and follows the above practices. However, if you want to maximize the probability of your releases being used, it's helpful to make it as easy as possible for the recipient to use them. Bear in mind that, in a sense, you are asking the editor for free advertising space or offering a swap of what you purport to be useful editorial matter for advertising space. Therefore, it makes good sense to do all the above. That's the easy part of the answer to getting the space you want, because it is simply a matter of mechanical practice. More difficult and consequently more important is the matter of content. What content, organization, writing, and other such considerations make the difference

METRO

News Release

P.O. Box 61429, Houston, Texas 77208-1429, 713/225-1151

CONTACT: Janet Redeker

FOR IMMEDIATE RELEASE
January 27, 1982

The MTA Board of Directors voted today to authorize the Executive Director to establish a METRO Transit Security Department with expanded security enforcement. The Board took this action to enhance the safety and security of METRO's patrons, employees, and properties, and the general public.

Today's action gives Metro security personnel full peace officer status in a well defined jurisdiction which includes any land, easement, right of way, rolling stock(buses) or other property owned or controlled by the Authority. This is the first such program ever created in Texas, although 14 such departments exist in other transit systems such as New York, Washington, D.C., Los Angeles, and Atlanta. Other law enforcement agencies in the METRO service area such as Houston, Bellaire, Harris County, and Southside Place have expressed their positive support of the establishment of a Transit Security Department and mutual aid agreements with other agencies will be sought.

METRO's Security Department is currently staffed by 26 persons, including supervisory, operations, investigations and clerical personnel. Nine more patrol officers will be added by May 1, 1982, as part of the budgeted increase in 1982 security services. All of the current supervisors, patrol officers and investigators are certified peace officers and have an average of 7.4 years experience. Of the seventeen field personnel, eleven have college degrees and the other six have associate degrees or college credits.

-more-

FIGURE 1. First page of news release.

Coalition for Common Sense in Government Procurement

1990 M Street, N.W, Suite 570
Washington, D.C. 20036
(202) 331-0975

February 5, 1982

Contact: Gloria Gamble
(202) 331-0975

Coalition Supports OFPP Proposal for Advanced Notices to Industry of Agency Policies

Washington, D.C. -- The COALITION FOR COMMON SENSE IN GOVERNMENT PROCUREMENT has praised the recent attempts of the Office of Federal Procurement Policy (OFPP) to allow industry to comment on proposed policies and regulations being considered by federal agencies.

In his letter on its proposed "Public Participation in the Development of Federal Procurement Policies and Regulations" policy, Coalition President Paul J. Caggiano told OFPP that "we gladly welcome this proposed policy," saying that the Coalition has been recommending such a policy for years. "We have maintained that many internal agency procurement policies and regulations greatly impact federal government suppliers, but there has been no way for contractors to offer their viewpoints prior to the policy's implementation," Caggiano said.

OFPP's proposed policy would direct that "views of all interested parties, including government agencies, private organizations and associations, business firms, educational institutions and individuals be obtained and considered by any executive agency proposal to develop or amend a procurement policy, regulation, procedure or form."

The Coalition recommended only one addition to the proposal. It felt that OFPP's criteria for agencies to consider what proposed policies would be distributed for comment needed further clarification. Said the Coalition: "OFPP's draft policy letter says agencies' proposed issuances are considered to be significant if they have "any effect beyond the internal operating procedures of the issuing agency."

-more-

FIGURE 2. Another press release style.

"We would like to see something more definitive," says the Coalition, "something that recognizes the potential impact of the proposal on the business sector. For example, the following phrase could be added: ...and, if it changes, in any way, the procedure which contractors currently operate under to sell their goods and services to the federal government."

In explaining the reasons for Coalition support to its proposal, Caggiano told OFPP that currently, contractors are forced to accept new agency policies. "At times, a policy or regulatory change is learned about only when the solicitation for the new contract period is received by bidders. With closing dates as short as they are, offerors rarely have sufficient time to put together an offer much less register their complaints about an unfavorable policy. Besides, during this time government contracting officers have the upper hand and can threaten to disqualify the bidder or hold up his award indefinitely."

"Further," explained Caggiano, "OFPP's proposal makes government agencies more accountable for the policies and regulations they author. It provides industry a chance to get advance warning of potential changes; suppliers have an opportunity to point out any portions which will cause them unnecessary additional paperwork and costs; they can get clear and definitive interpretations of the planned issuances before they have to meet the requirement and agencies will have to use common sense and provide justifiable reasons for introducing new policies and regulations or amendments."

Caggiano also pointed out that the proposed policy could cut prices on what the government buys: "Suppliers know up front what is expected of them; less time is spent at the negotiating tables and contracts can be awarded more expeditiously," he explained.

The Coalition urges all associations and industry representatives to support OFPP's proposal.

The Coalition for Common Sense in Government Procurement is a nonprofit membership organization providing a multitude of services to large and small commercial product suppliers of the federal government.

\# \# \#

FIGURE 2. Continued.

between the release that finds itself being picked up and the one discarded immediately.

"NEWSWORTHINESS"

"Newsworthiness," as the term is used here, means simply having enough potential value to readers including listeners and viewers, (if the release goes to a radio or TV newsroom) to be worth using. The piece might fall into any of these categories:

Straight news.
Story behind a news story.
Novelty item.

News Release

GSA Chief to Close Seven Laboratories in Economy Move

Administrator Gerald P. Carmen said today he will close seven testing laboratories that have supported the General Services Administration's governmentwide supply system. He said the action will save $3.3 million annually.

Seventy-six employees will be affected by the closures. However, attempts will be made to reassign them into other elements of the Federal Supply Service in the same commuting area.

"Our Federal Supply Service is turning more and more toward procurement of off-the-shelf commercial items," Carmen said, "so there is less need for research and development to establish specifications for products or to develop government-unique testing methods. We will rely more on testing and quality assurance by reliable vendors and use of warranties and performance bonds to protect the government's interest. GSA will concentrate quality assurance efforts on warranty enforcement and audits of material."

Carmen said the change is in line with the Administration efforts to streamline and make government operations more efficient and to rely more heavily on the private sector.

The Research and Development Laboratory in Washington, D.C. will be closed December 31; Laboratories in New York, Chicago, Fort Worth and Auburn, Wash., will be closed by March, and those in Kansas City and San Francisco by August 1. This schedule will allow for an orderly transition to ensure that adequate contractual safeguards, such as extended warranties, are in place.

(MORE)

U.S. General Services Administration, Washington.DC 20405 (202) 566-1231

FIGURE 3. A federal agency news release.

106

Humor.

Noteworthy event that is not exactly a news happening.

Straight news can be many things which are broken to the press via releases—a merger of two companies or other financial/business event, action on some piece of legislation, a candidate announcing for office, introduction of a significant new product or process, or other such item which is truly news although not necessarily of general interest. Note that an item can be specialized news, such as financial, scientific, or otherwise of interest to some special group. For example, an item about the school system of a community is likely to be of general interest, but an item about some new idea in teaching is of interest usually only to those concerned with teaching. At the same time, it is often possible to convert an item from special interest to general interest or vice versa. That item about some special teaching technique can be rewritten from the viewpoint of the students, which is likely then to make it of general interest. And that is one of the techniques that the writer of releases can use—"slanting" an item to appeal to the group one wants to reach.

The story behind the story may also be of general or special interest. If you have some data on how a merger was brought about or how one company managed to acquire controlling interest in the other, you may have such a story. And if your release is highly technical—about tender offers, proxy fights, and financial manipulations—it is a special-interest story of how the merger was brought about. But if you choose to translate, interpret, and explain all that technical matter into lay terms, you may have a general-interest story showing the general reader how the movers and shakers in big business operate.

For most of us, true news items are hard to come by. Our own doings are rarely news of interest to anyone but ourselves. Releases offering novelties, however, are eagerly received, and they are not as difficult to generate as you might believe. For example, I used many releases to gain publicity for both my consulting services to help companies with their government marketing and for my government marketing newsletter. I had no difficulty coming up with several novelty items, some of which were also good for a chuckle, most helpful for these purposes. Here are a few of the release headlines I used, which pretty much explain the whole release:

I WAS PAID $6,000 TO ANSWER THE GOVERNMENT'S MAIL

U.S. GOVERNMENT AWARDS CONTRACTS FOR GO-GO DANCERS

GOVERNMENT RENTS MULES AND HANDLERS

GOVERNMENT CONTRACTS AWARDED TO BEST WRITERS

In each of these releases I made it clear that I was a government-marketing consultant, available to help write proposals, among other things, and that I was also the publisher of the *Government Marketing News*. I also listed in many of my releases the name and a brief description of some of my special reports, such as one called "Anyone Can do Business With the Government," along with prices.

The federal government is a natural for novelties and humor so it didn't take too much effort to find both in things connected with the government. However, it really doesn't take a great deal of effort to find novel and/or humorous items connected with any activity or field. It is a necessity for all PR purposes, speaking and writing as well as issuing releases.

In short, it amounts to this: Whether you are an experienced and "gifted" speaker or writer is far less important than whether what you have to say is interesting. The orator with the commanding, resonant voice is dull when the subject is dull. The writer with the magnificent style is also dull when the material is uninteresting. Don't worry about pear-shaped tones or polished phrases; worry about interesting material.

WHAT IS INTERESTING?

There is no scientific or procedural guidance anyone can give you for ensuring that the material you speak and write about will be interesting. It's far more an art and a sensitivity to what will interest others than it is a science or methodology. It is rarely that everyone is interested by the same materials and ideas. Still, there are some guidelines that will help you.

One thing that is guaranteed to stimulate another's interest is the other's *self*-interest—anything that affects the other's happiness, health, home, money, or other such personal factor is going to command interest. Studies conducted by *Reader's Digest* and others suggest strongly that some of the sure-fire topics are these: Lincoln, doctors, mothers, dogs. That led to the waggish idea that any story or article about Lincoln's mother's doctor's dog could not miss! Whatever the case, you may be assured that the other person is always interested in anything that is likely to affect him or her personally. Consider, for example, how many people now arise very early, put on exercise suits and torture themselves by running several miles in fair and foul weather because they have become convinced that this ensures good health.

Consider, too, how many people immersed themselves in books pledging to lead them to the Promised Land of financial security and even prosperity when the author's predicted economic collapse took place. Or how many people in the fifties spent many thousands of dollars to build elaborate backyard shelters against the day when the A-bomb or H-bomb would drop from the skies. Or how many thousands have been taken in by millenia of medical quacks, and how many people, even in this supposedly enlightened age, pop dozens of brightly colored but unnecessary vitamin tablets and capsules every day.

Talk about threats or benefits to health, home, money, career, job, family, future, children, or anything else that strikes as close to home, and you'll strike a nerve. Almost invariably, the other party will become interested if the linkage is close enough. You can't expect your listeners or readers to get greatly wrought up over millions dying in India or Madagascar, but they might become concerned over an epidemic across town. They have to *relate* to that potential threat or benefit and perceive it as a real possibility which affects them.

There are, however, other things that interest people. One is being "on the inside" or "getting the inside dope." That's why the "story behind the story" is so successful. Explain how the casino grows rich on a one-percent edge or how an investigative reporter digs up the dirt on public figures and contract scandals. Tell them the truth about how Howard Hughes lived and died, or how vitamins are made and where they come from. People have a great deal of natural curiosity as well as a desire to get the inside dope. The dullest technical data can become interesting, if you can make it easy for anyone to understand it and link it to your readers or listeners so that they relate to it.

Almost everyone likes to laugh, too, so humor finds ready acceptance. The problem here is that humor is extremely difficult to write, contrary to what a great many writing tyros think. Nothing is deadlier than attempted humor that does not succeed; it invariably becomes banality. So unless you happen to be one of those gifted with that rare ability to write or speak humorously, don't attempt it. Don't attempt to create humor, but if the material itself is humorous, use it. For example, I never tried to exploit the fact that the government awarded contracts for go-go dancers (for military service clubs), but the mere, unadorned fact that this had happened was enough itself to bring chuckles and grins if not belly laughter. Others always seem to find it amusing that the government sometimes hires contractors to answer mail and telephones, referee sports events, bag groceries, put on amateur theatricals, and perform sundry other services one is not likely to connect with running the United States Government.

LINKAGE WITH YOUR FIELD AND AIMS

It is necessary to speak and write in such manner and on such subjects as to further your own aims, which are one or more of these:

Provide samples of your work, skills, abilities.

Build your professional image to develop maximum credibility.

Improve your general visibility—make others aware of your existence and consultancy.

Generate leads for follow up.

To accomplish these objectives it is necessary that you not only be amusing, entertaining, and/or interesting, but that you also manage to make that interesting material exemplify your expert knowledge and abilities, and, as much as possible, provide a small sample of what you can do. That limits your topics somewhat, because they must be in your own general field. Therefore, you must find interesting material with direct application to your own services, somehow utilize material so that it can be linked to what you do professionally (or, as a final resort, used to "hook" your listeners or readers, after which you will get on to the less-interesting matters of what you do professionally). The latter should rarely be necessary if you work at it properly and if I am correct in my conviction that there are no dull subjects, but only dull presentations.

One thing that usually works is how-to success stories. If you can present the inside story of how people in closely related fields succeeded in doing what most of your audience would like to do or are ambitious to do, you have a sure winner in the glued-to-their-seats department. Tell an audience of investors or potential investors, for example, of how one investor succeeded in parlaying some relatively small sum of money into a large sum of money, a fortune, preferably. If you can make that almost a blow by blow description, providing the wealth of detail that truly shows how it was done, you'll surely hold the audience.

The same goes for almost every field. If you can relate this from your personal viewpoint if you were involved in some manner, preferably as a consultant, so much the better.

If you can, persuade the editor of a monthly newsletter or other publication to let you do a monthly column. A Q&A, Question and Answer column, is almost ideal for your purposes. Such a column demonstrates your ability to solve problems and help clients.

When you speak publicly, invite questions and comments. You want audience reaction for two reasons:

It enlivens the event by inducing listeners to get personally involved, to participate.

It helps you immeasurably in knowing what has the greatest appeal, thus helping you develop and design future efforts.

There really is a third consideration. Getting a lively exchange going with listeners is far more likely to produce good sales leads, I have found, possibly because it removes any barriers that might otherwise be perceived between the speaker and the audience. You'll find that if you are outgoing, friendly, and relaxed during your speech, many of the listeners will approach you after your talk and ask for your card or exchange cards with you.

FACE-TO-FACE SELLING SITUATIONS

The purpose of all these activities is primarily to develop sales leads. The more professional and capable an image you have managed to project, the more ready the prospects will be to agree to contracting with you. Still, contracts will rarely come your way without some final selling, what might be termed "face to face selling." It is the final showdown in the pursuit of the sale, that moment of truth when you will finally close that sale or lose it.

Don't be misled by the excessive zeal of sales trainers who insist that once you are face to face with the prospect, the ball is entirely in your court and, if you do not get the sale, you have somehow failed. It simply is not true for this reason: There are people who will deliberately waste your time. They've no intention and possibly no ability to buy what you are selling, but they have their own reasons for spending time talking to you. In some cases, they are callously and cynically trying to pick your brains for their own selfish purposes. Morally, this is no better than stealing, for they are trying to trick you into giving away what you ordinarily sell. There are also those junior people in organizations who have no authority to buy, and others who can't afford to buy but who are reluctant to admit this.

For this reason, it is perhaps even more important for the consultant to qualify prospects than it is for other people to do so. Qualifying prospects means determining whether the prospect has money and authority to buy or can get money and authority to buy. Those who fail to qualify prospects wind up wasting a great deal of time and sometimes money on sales efforts that could never succeed.

Qualifying a prospect is sometimes quite easy to do, sometimes difficult. If the prospect is someone in a large organization, it isn't too difficult because it can be done in the most impersonal of terms, such as saying to the prospect, before the conversation has taken too much of your time: "Is the budget available for this now, or would that have to win special approval?" Or: "Can you tell me how your company contracts for such things as this, that is, does your buyer issue a purchase order, or do you authorize a contract?" Such questions, dropped casually and with the obvious assumption that they are entirely impersonal, generally brings you the information you want and enables you to decide whether you are wasting your time and should cut your losses and run, have a serious possibility of doing business with this party, or need to investigate further and perhaps talk to someone a bit higher up in the organization.

On the other hand, if you are dealing with an individual consumer or the head of a very small organization, the situation is a bit more delicate. But it is still possible to phrase such questions as "Have you any money for this" tactfully and impersonally by using the right euphemisms. For example, you might ask the self-employed entrepreneur, "Have you budgeted this for the immediate future or are we talking about some distant time?" That kind of question is likely to bring you the information you need. But there are other ways, especially if you get an evasion rather than a straight answer and you begin to suspect that you are wasting your time. In those cases, it is often advisable to start talking about a retainer, meaning part of the payment up front. One way to do this is simply to explain that it is your standard practice or policy to require one third of the estimated total fee as an advance deposit. Another is to draw from your briefcase a standard agreement form and go over it with the prospect, pointing out the advance deposit. In either case, once you begin to talk money, the issue is forced, and you'll soon know whether you are well-advised to continue your sales effort or expend it elsewhere.

The time to do such things is when you have begun to doubt either the prospect's sincerity or the prospect's ability to afford you. There comes a time when you must decide that you have given away enough free information and it is time to close a sale or be on your way. As a last resort, you can always bring the meeting to a close and say some such thing as, "Why don't you sleep on it, since you seem to be undecided yet, and I'll give you a ring in the morning so you can give me your final decision."

That is not a good sales tactic when you think you have a good prospect and a good chance to close a sale. It is a last-resort tactic when you are all but convinced that you are wasting your time. (Still, you may be wrong, and someone who appears to be the worst possible prospect may turn out to be a worthwhile client, so even in this extreme, leave the door open a crack!)

Selling face to face, as in selling by any other medium, requires the use of the same good principles of sales. In the now-famous words of America's master salesman, the late Elmer Wheeler, "Sell the sizzle, not the steak." He meant, of course, sell the emotional appeal, the mouthwatering beauty of the sizzle, the benefit or much-to-be-desired result, as I prefer to explain it. Of course, the question of how you will do things and your ability to do them are likely to come up again and again, and will have to be fielded by you, but as far as possible, try to keep the presentation oriented to what your services will do for the client, what fantastic benefits they will provide. Whether the client realizes it or not, that is the ball you have to keep your eye on.

Make sure when talking to the prospect that you establish clearly in your own mind whether your prospect is troubled by a problem he needs help in solving or though not unhappy with how things are going, is interested in the possibility that you can provide enough improvement to be worth considering. Do not overlook the possibility that the prospect has a problem of which he or she is unaware, and which might be the best possible basis on which to anchor the sales presentation. However, be cautious, because even those prospects who have serious problems are not always ready to agree that they have those problems. Remember that it is the prospect's own perceptions that count, not yours. You must base your sales presentation and efforts on what the prospect perceives. Whatever you promise to do is not a benefit unless the prospect agrees that it is a benefit.

CLOSING THE SALE

The lay person thinks that *closing* a sale means getting the order, and in ordinary parlance that is true. However, in the special jargon of the sales profession, closing means *asking* for the order. And in the course of making a presentation and winning the order, a salesperson may close many times before actually getting the order.

Asking for the order is done indirectly, by *assuming* the order, thereby compelling the prospect to take some positive action to let you know that he or she has not yet agreed to give you the order. Therefore, to make it as difficult as possible for the prospect to stop you from writing the order up, closes are phrased so as to require only yes-yes answers, rather than yes-no answers. For example, you might say to your prospect, in closing: "Do you want me to start on this project Monday, or do you need my help sooner?" Or: "The retainer is $150. Do you want to have the agreement typed up on your letterhead, or would you rather issue me one of your purchase orders with your check?"

In one sense, this is a means for determining whether you have talked enough yet, whether the prospect is ready to buy. We all know about salesmen who have talked too long and killed the sale they would have had if they had shut up earlier and written up the order. But how do you know when it's time to shut up and write the order? The close is one way of finding out. If the prospect demurs, you must sell some more, then close again.

OBJECTIONS

When the prospect does demur after you close, you must assume that the prospect has some objection which must be overcome. One common problem in selling is that all too often a prospect will not agree to the sale because of some objection, but the prospect refuses to tell you what that objection is. That, of course, makes it more difficult to consummate the sale. Presumably, if you can learn what the objection is, you can overcome it and win the order. Therefore, if the prospect responds to your close with something such as, "Wait a minute, now. I really haven't decided yet," it's time for a next move by you. Typically, you are likely to respond with something such as, "Why, certainly. You must have a question or two. What point would you like me to go over again?"

It may take gentle probing and persistence, but until you discover what the true objection is, you are likely to be stymied. Why *true* objection? Because it is a common phenomenon for prospects to give you excuses instead of telling you their true objection. For example, a prospect may be ashamed to admit that he or she can't afford your services, or isn't convinced that you can do what you say you can do.

The only thing left to you is to start back through your entire sales presentation, in summary perhaps, but watching the prospect most carefully for some sign that you have struck a nerve somewhere, whereupon you are probably on the track of the true objection, and you can proceed to uncover it diplomatically and see whether you cannot make the sale now.

I have often run into prospects who felt that they could not afford my services at $500 a day when they would require several days of my time to help them in writing a proposal. Once I ascertained that as the problem, I could cope with it since I have long since worked out ways to deal with this problem of cost. (I do not believe that you should ever cut your rate, but there are some ways to reduce the cost to the client without cutting your standard rate, and I'll discuss these in a later chapter.)

BIDS AND PROPOSALS

In some consulting practices and situations, winning the sale requires that you submit a written bid or proposal. Because this is the main subject of a later chapter, I won't attempt to cover it here, except to note that it is a not-infrequent requirement in the consulting and professional-services field, so it is quite important that you master the art.

SALES MATERIALS

The principal sales materials used by most consultants, other than the bids and proposals required for specific sales efforts, are brochures, sales letters, and a special document generally referred to as a "capabilities brochure." There are also some special pieces, such as the "broadside," which refers not to a salvo from a battleship, but its advertising equivalent, a printed piece that unfolds to a large size such as 17 × 23 inches. Consultants also sometimes use advertising gifts and novelties such as desk calendars, rulers, key chains, and other such items which, it is hoped, help clients and prospective clients remember the consultant when help is needed. We'll discuss here three pieces, the regular brochure, the sales letter, and the capabilities brochure.

Your standard brochure—and you should have one, for a variety of uses—may be any size you wish to make it, from approximately 3 × 9 inches (equivalent to a standard sheet of 8½ × 11 inch paper, folded twice) to one 9 × 12 inches. My personal preference is for the small, approximately 3 × 9 inch size because it's convenient to carry a supply in pocket or purse, it's easy to hand out, and can usually be produced in quantity quite inexpensively and so dispensed freely, as brochures ought to be. Its obvious disadvantages are that it is easily lost, discarded, or overlooked and does not make that admittedly grander impression of the 9 × 12 inch brochure with stiff covers and elegant typographical style. The small brochure can present only a limited amount of information, but sometimes that's an advantage rather than a disadvantage.

Whatever the size and cost, what the brochure *says* is more important than how costly it is or appears to be. Even the most costly brochures are often dull, and no amount of expensive process color can compensate for the sin of having nothing to say. You are well advised to concentrate on the content, not the cosmetics, in practicing the art of brochuremanship.

INVISIBLE WORDS AND TERMS

The mark of the amateur copywriter, and the kiss of death on advertising copy, is over-writing, especially extravagant overuse of laudatory adjectives and adverbs, superlatives, and other hyperbolic excesses. The novice copywriter apparently reasons that readers will accept any claim that is outrageous enough and repeated often enough. Consequently, we find brochures peppered with such words and terms as these:

expert/expertise	adept	renowned	worldwide
highest standards	leading	tremendous	unique
remarkable	superb	worldwide	
outstanding authority	leader in the field	reputation	

Note that not one of the above terms is truly unemotional, objective, factual reporting or descriptive; all are emotional and all convey the bias of the writer's opinion. They are, in short, claims and self-appraisals, blatantly "Madison Avenue copy." Once, perhaps, these might have served well, but today our ears have been assaulted so often and at such length with such words and terms that we've come to dismiss them automatically and scarcely even hear them any more. Such words are, in fact, virtually invisible to readers as a result of overuse and overstraining of the reader's tolerance for hot air. Skilled readers instinctively speed-read their way past such language at speeds exceeding that of light, which, Einsteinian physics assures us, makes them vanish from view.

A brochure ought to follow the same basic rules laid down for any sales presentation or advertising copy, of which the first rule is to *get attention.* Unless you command the reader's attention, you can't get on with delivering your message. The second step, we are assured by the experts, is to *arouse interest.* You can't keep the reader reading unless you have commanded the reader's interest in some manner.

Many copywriters handle these two objectives separately. Note in TV commercials, for example, that some of them open with something only vaguely related to the main message, such as an automobile racing at breakneck speed and then abruptly coming to a shuddering halt inches before an obstacle. This is to get your attention, so that the movie star pitching the automobile can get you to watch the fine interior and exquisite styling of this fine, new automobile that enables you to drive like a maniac and still stop in time.

Advertisers do the same thing in print advertising, using attention-getting art, cartoon novelties, and other devices to catch the eye of the reader in the hope that the reader can then be induced to become interested in what the copy says.

This is a wasteful and inefficient way of doing it. There is no good reason I can see for not getting attention and arousing interest at the same time. That is, I advocate making the attention-getting device one that also arouses interest immediately. Since probably the most effective and certainly most useful way of arousing interest is to show the reader the benefit offered in terms of end-result, why not bring that into play at once? For example, a current print advertisement on my desk is by a company that offers instructional courses in writing, and the advertisement features a drawing of a lead pencil, with a small headline that claims the pencil is the greatest writing teacher in the world, and then goes on with text attempting to justify the mystic headline. Presumably, the reader is amused or is curious, and reads on. This advertiser evidently confuses being different or saying something cryptic with getting attention and arousing interest. It isn't until the middle of the body copy that the advertiser addresses the benefit promised, and not until nearly the end of the body copy that he provides specific reasons for the reader to buy. And the only evidence of capability offered is the claim of good results and experienced instructors. This is another case of too much cleverness and not enough salesmanship, an all too common ill of copywriters who are addicted to puns, double entendres, and other indulgences of their cuteness and literary pretensions or intellectual tours de force.

Sales copy is no place for subtleties. Quite the contrary, it is the place for the plainest communication possible. Little harm is done if each reader places a different interpretation on what the author of a poem or novel intended to convey, but ambiguities and other uncertainties about what the author of a piece of advertising or sales copy means to say is almost always fatal for the copy.

Open your brochure with a direct appeal to the reader's self-interest. One of my own small brochures announcing a seminar in proposal writing (see Figure 4) made an immediate "promise" (implication, that is) that attendees would learn how to win government contracts through strategy. It said other things, too, to capture readers' interest—that it would be an unusual and revealing session and that the truth about winning government contracts would be revealed. Note how much has been packed into a few lines of type, easily read in a few seconds:

1. The promise—learning how to win government contracts through strategy, using something called "proposalmanship."
2. A rationale to back up the promise of learning how to win contracts—the use of strategy.
3. The lure of getting "inside information" and learning "the truth" about the subject.

Note the absence of superlatives except for "most unusual and revealing" seminar/workshop, and even that was justified by the follow-up promise to reveal the truth.

FIGURE 4.   Cover of a small brochure.

The other panels of this 3 × 9 inch brochure pursued the promises made on the cover, elaborating on them and providing a program schedule and outline that furnished such specifics as these:

How to *appear* to be the low bidder and other basic strategies

Common proposal faults: how to avoid

How to turn liabilities into assets

How to combat competition

An education in costs and cost estimating

Other material in the brochure included a bio on myself as presenter (it is necessary to display your credentials), testimonials from attendees of previous seminars, names of prominent companies represented at previous seminars, and a form for submitting registrations for the sessions advertised. And all of this was so written as to minimize the use of adjectives and adverbs, and stick to the nouns and verbs. Note the items listed in the previous paragraph; they are verbs and nouns.

In a later chapter dealing with proposal writing, we'll delve more deeply into the art of writing persuasively, but bear in mind that to be persuasive writing must follow all the rules of salesmanship we have discussed. It must focus on the benefits promised and provide credible evidence that you can and will deliver. Using nouns and verbs which are specific and provide detail is a highly effective beginning at being credible. Unquestionably, "180,000" is more readily accepted than is "many thousands."

CAPABILITIES BROCHURE

In many situations, such as selling your services to government agencies and other large organizations whose needs are quite diverse, something generally referred to as a *capabilities brochure* is indispensable. A capabilities brochure is a basic marketing tool which professional-services organizations use freely, mailing them out to specific prospects and leaving them with prospects when making personal calls. They are often specifically requested by prospects, in fact.

Those organizations who contract for professional services frequently, and especially those organizations whose needs are so diverse that they are unable to predict what they will need in the future, either short or long-term, keep such brochures on file. The filed brochures are referred to when the organization wishes to solicit help, discuss needs with potential contractors, or make up a bidders list when seeking bids and proposals. Federal agencies often run notices in the *Commerce Business Daily*, a federal publication used to announce government requirements and solicit bids and proposals, inviting interested organizations to submit capabilities brochures.

Many consulting organizations have a single brochure, used for all purposes, including descriptions of their capabilities. In most cases, this does not work out well because the objective of the capabilities brochure is different from that of the small general brochure discussed earlier. In fact, the capabilities brochure may be exactly the wrong brochure to use when a general brochure is needed simply because it is too detailed and offers too much. In most cases the general brochure has as its objective a simple, preliminary introduction to your services while the capabilities brochure must, by its nature, be a fairly detailed and perhaps even laborious recital.

WHAT BELONGS IN A CAPABILITIES BROCHURE

The capabilities brochure goes counter to some things said earlier. Most sales and advertising copy must be focused sharply to be effective, and must not make you appear to be a jack of all trades, but rather a sharply focused specialist. The capabilities brochure, however, is not designed to sell anything except the probability that a client would be well advised to invite your proposal for any of the many services described in the brochure. Therefore, this brochure should have all the details that should not go into the small brochure. Here is what most prospects want to see:

The basic area(s) in which you function—civil engineering, psychology, urban studies, training, or other.

The specific services you provide—surveys, design, prototyping, field investigations, or other.

Your resources—facilities, staff (with detailed resumes of key staff members), and whatever else is relevant.

Other qualifications, especially summary descriptions of past projects, past clients, and past achievements.

The emphasis here ought properly to be on as many details as possible. The brochure need not be a flossy one, full of expensive color art, but may be quite simple. It should be professional looking and well indexed if it contains a great deal of material. However, I have found simple, typed presentations perfectly acceptable. The prospects are interested in content, not in cosmetics. By the same token, it is not necessary to have these reproduced in great quantity, for they have special application and are not designed to be distributed en masse.

SALES LETTER

A sales letter is quite a different proposition. It is normally sharply focused on a single objective or selling goal. It may be as broad as a general introduction of your services, with the intention of following up the letter with a telephone call or it may be a special offer of something.

Consulting Opportunities Journal

P.O. Box 17674, Washington, DC 20041

<u>$500 and more per day consulting, or grossing up to $10,000 and
more in a single day working a favorite profit center, today's
consultants are cashing in on growing demands for their knowledge.
The age of the consultant-entrepreneur is here</u>!

Dear Colleague,

You are sitting in a great position to turn your knowledge into "gold" in the months and years just ahead. And it doesn't matter if you're just starting out or an "old pro" in consulting, or whether you are part or full time in your practice.

The months and years ahead will bring unprecedented consulting opportunities to those men and women, in all fields, who are <u>prepared</u> for them.

<u>Consulting Opportunities Journal</u> (COJ) was founded to bring you information on those opportunities. We also report on trends, tips and techniques on how to <u>most</u> <u>efficiently</u> <u>market</u> <u>yourself</u> in today's potential-laden environment.

The response to COJ has been great. Being founded and written by consultants for consultants, the COJ has earned the reputation of a no-nonsense, straight-from-the-shoulder 'How-To' publication. No "ivory tower" stuff here.

Its writers earn their living from consulting in their various fields. So you can be assured that COJ's writers cannot afford (and neither can you) the luxury of writing about <u>theory</u> versus how it actually <u>is</u> "on the street." Each one of our consultant-writers, now and in the future, has faced and overcome the marketing problems, difficult client relationships, proposal-writing struggles and outright loneliness and more that we've all faced at one time or another.

Consulting is as much a <u>leadership</u> business as it is a <u>people</u> business. The COJ covers the people giving advice to the leaders of our society. The COJ is the <u>only</u> publication of its kind in the world. We are <u>dedicated</u> <u>to</u> <u>your</u> <u>success</u> <u>in</u> consulting, now, more than ever before.

It is to this end, to maintain our place of leadership in the consulting profession, that we are making you, what I believe, the <u>most</u> <u>generous</u> <u>offer</u> you have seen--from <u>any</u> national publisher in <u>any</u> field. First, let me tell you what subscribers are seeing in the COJ:

* How and Where to Get Consulting Leads (Self-Marketing
  Strategies that Can Be Used in Any Field)

* How to Set Fees (Also, What Others are Charging)

* How to Write Winning Proposals & Reports

* What Goes Into Launching a Successful Seminar or Newsletter
  (Information that can save you plenty!)

* IRS Proposals and Tax Considerations Affecting the
  Independent Consultant

* How and Where to Find Writing and Speaking Opportunities

(continued)

FIGURE 5.   Sample of a typical sales letter.

* Consultant Networks, Consultant Brokerages: What They Are,
  How They Work and How to Work with Them (Are They the
  Ultimate Income Source?)

* How to Discover, Develop and Market Information Products
  and Other Profit Centers of Your Own

* Data Banks, Research Centers, Make Them Work For You or
  Your Client, Telephone Marketing and much, much more!

Along with covering scores of publications to bring you the happenings in the
booming consulting industry, we have just acquired Consultant's Digest and merged
it into COJ--at no extra cost to subscribers. There's even a Q & A column where
you can get specific answers from specific questions from COJ's own consultant to
consultant editor, Herman Holtz.

When you come right down to it, the COJ could be broken up into several
newsletters--each with the same or higher subscription rates. There could be one
on Self-Marketing Strategies, Consulting Contracts/Fee Negotiation, Direct Mail
Marketing/Advertising Strategies for Consultants, Developing and Marketing Seminar
and Newsletter Properties and others. But these are all included in your COJ
subscription.

A year's subscription to COJ is only $24 for six full issues. And it's
totally tax-deductible along with a money-back guarantee. Plus, there's no extra
charge if we increase our publishing schedule during your subscription term.
(Saves $6.00 over single copy)

Those watching the mushrooming consulting industry tell us that, within two
short years, a weekly publishing schedule will be needed to touch all the bases.
We don't know about weekly, but from the looks of things now, a monthly publishing
schedule is not far off!

A 2-year subscription is just $39 (a savings of $21.00 off the single-copy
price), and a 3-year term is only $57, a big $33.00 savings over single-copy!

Now, let's get back to my "most generous" offer I mentioned earlier. We've
just made a special purchase of 7 top-selling titles of consulting guidebooks from
The Consultant's Library, the nation's leading consulting book publisher (See the
attached list).

As if all the foregoing benefits of a COJ subscription weren't enough, now you
can get up to 3 (THREE) books FREE--up to an $80 value with your paid subscription!
You simply select one book FREE for each year of your chosen subscription term.

This is a limited-time offer and may be withdrawn soon. To ensure your
selections, order today on the special order form enclosed. Use the handy postage-
paid envelope for additional speed and savings.

Isn't it time you discovered all the benefits to you and your family from your
own consulting practice?

                              Yours for a successful consultancy,

                              J. Stephen Lanning
                              Publisher

FIGURE 5. Continued.

The sales letter is ordinarily a form letter. Although typed and reproduced by offset printing so that it is not readily apparent that it is printed
rather than individually typed, most recipients are well aware that it is a
form letter. It is not necessary to follow the traditional letter format and
address "Dear friend" or some similar banality. Some people are very

"turned off" by such obvious insincerity, and modern practice in sales letters is to avoid the pretense that it is truly a personal letter. Instead, it is now perfectly acceptable to use a headline or two and launch abruptly into the body of the letter without a salutation, as in Figure 5. The letter need not be one page, either, as in the figure; it can be more than one page, and it can be signed as you might sign any letter.

All the standard practices and principles of writing advertising and sales copy apply here. The only difference is that the sales letter is typewritten rather than typeset.

Use simple, straightforward language in a sales letter, and get right to the point. People who get your sales letters don't want to read flowery language or spend time deciphering your meaning. Be brief, make your points one by one, summarize quickly, and close.

5

Marketing to the Public Sector: Federal, State, and Local Government

Out of nearly 13 million businesses in the United States, only about 2 percent do business with government agencies. Ignorance of government markets and the opportunities there is the principal reason.

A GLIMPSE OF THE PUBLIC-SECTOR MARKETS

In the past two generations, and particularly in the past one, government agencies have become important markets for virtually the entire spectrum of man's goods and services. Where once the governments represented markets for only office supplies, street paving, and other construction-related public works, today the governments buy almost every service, product, and material offered in the marketplace generally. Moreover, governments are the only customer for many things: Who else would issue a contract to have groceries bagged and carried to waiting cars, rather than hiring boys? Who else would issue contracts to sell contraceptives on the streets in Pakistani cities or pay contractors to run travel bureaus and rent cabins in National Parks?

The federal government employs approximately 2.8 million civilians, nearly three-quarter million in the Postal Service alone. (Sometimes federal civilian employment is erroneously reported as 2.1 or 2.2 million, because of the mistaken belief that since the Postal Service is now a government corporation, the employees are no longer civil service people.) Approximately 130,000 of these are in positions directly related to federal purchasing and procurement—contracting officers, contract negotiators and administrators, accountants, clerks, and sundry other people assigned to procurement offices. At the moment, the annual procurement budget is over $125 billion for all federal offices and agencies and rising every year despite Administration efforts to reduce it. The various bureaus and administrations (referred to generally as "agencies" here and in most publications dealing with the subject) number nearly 2,000 and together make over 15 million separate purchases every year. Nearly 98 percent of these purchases are small purchases, not more than $10,000 each, although over 85 percent of the procurement dollars are spent on the larger purchases, many of which run to millions of dollars each, and occasional ones even to billions of dollars.

It should come as no surprise that roughly three quarters of all this procurement and purchasing is done by the Department of Defense (DOD), which includes the armed services and a number of other DOD agencies, such as their own supply service (the Defense Logistics Agency or DLA). However, all the other Departments and agencies do some purchasing, and several do a great deal. (See *Directory of Federal Purchasing Offices*, by Herman Holtz, John Wiley & Sons, Inc., New York, 1981 for complete details on agencies and lists of goods and services commonly purchased by each agency.)

SOME SERVICES PURCHASED BY FEDERAL AGENCIES

The following is a partial listing of the types of services federal agencies buy. In some cases, such as data processing and other computer-related services, virtually any agency might be a customer; in other cases, only certain agencies would be good prospects. R&D (research and development) services related to agriculture, for example, would be useful to only a few of the agencies. The following have been taken from official reports for the fiscal year 1981 (October 1, 1980 to September 30, 1981, inclusive.) These are general categories which usually do not describe precisely what the services are but, rather, what areas of interest they cover.

R & D (Research and Development)

Insect and disease control

Agriculture production

Crime prevention and control

Fire prevention and control

Community services, rural

Community services, urban

Aircraft, missiles, space

Ships, tanks, weapons, automotive

Electronics, communications

Textiles, clothing, equipage

Fuels and lubrication

Construction

Economic growth, employment

Manufacturing technology, productivity

Education

Coal, gas, geothermal, other energy

Pollution control, air, water

General science

Housing

Income security

Medical, biomedical

Health services, mental health

Natural resources

Social services

Aeronautics, other space

Transportation, modal and general

Mining, hazardous materials

Metallurgical

Natural Resource Management

Aerial fertilization, spraying

Aerial seeding

Forest range fire suppression

Forest tree planting

Tree breeding

Wild horse-burro management

Social Services

Care of remains, mortuary services   Chaplain services
Recreational, rehabilitation   Geriatrics
Government health insurance   Other social services programs

Quality Control, Testing, and Inspection

Weapons, fire control equipment   Vehicles
Railway equipment   Safety equipment
Communication equipment   Marine equipment
Electrical equipment   Construction material
Aircraft components   Plumbing, heating, ventilation, and air
Chemical products   conditioning, HVAC equipment, systems
Tires and tubes   Industrial machinery
Pumps and compressors   Valves
Ships, small boats   Rope, cable, chain
Containers, packaging   Fuels, lubricants, oils
Guided missiles

Technical Representative Services

Covers generally the same areas and items as "Quality Control, Testing, and Inspection" categories.

Medical Services

General health care   Laboratory testing
Nursing services   Nursing home care

The list goes on to include most medical specialties, such as anesthesiology, cardiovascular, dentistry, geriatrics, neurology, and others.

Professional, Technical, and Management Services

Architect-Engineer services, all   Automatic data processing
Other ADP services, general   ADP systems development and
                                    management

Program evaluation

Operations research

Advertising

Public relations

Studies and surveys, all

Data collection

Technology transfer

Program design, development

Photography

Publications services

Training development, services

CONTRACTING ARRANGEMENTS

Some agencies have permanent or semi-permanent requirements and authorization for consultants, usually as some specific number of "slots." For example, one office in OSHA (Occupational Safety and Health Administration, Department of Labor) with which I happened to do some business had three consultant slots and had consultants on an annual contract to give this office three days a week of their time. I was retained to do one specific task that would require a number of weeks and access to government facilities and resources. I was therefore furnished a desk, typewriter, and other resources in the office for the duration of the project.

Government agencies may have a need for consultants for literally any function, even those they normally carry out in-house with federal employees. Here are a few examples of work I have known to be done by consultants which is ordinarily done in-house:

Public information services, including development and sending out of press releases, handling telephone requests and written requests for information from press and public in general, and preparing monthly magazine for printing by Government Printing Office every month.

Developing work statement and other information necessary to issue Request for Proposals (RFP) or bid solicitation.

Reviewing, evaluating, and scoring proposals received and selecting winner of competition.

Answering government's mail and telephones.

PURCHASING AND PROCUREMENT SYSTEMS

There are several levels of government in our system, and each level has some purchasing or procurement functions. These are the levels:

Federal

State, territory (Puerto Rico, Virgin Islands, Guam)

County

City

Town, township

In addition to the 50 state governments and the territorial governments, there are in the United States approximately 18,000 cities and towns of size and about 3,000 counties. The size and variety of procurement carried out by each of these jurisdictions vary according to the size of the jurisdiction. Not surprisingly, California and New York state governments have larger procurement budgets and more formally structured and organized procurement systems than do such small states as Delaware and Rhode Island.

Each government has its own system, since each is an independent entity and free, within reasonable bounds, to set up any system it sees fit. However, almost all tend to certain policies and practices, usually patterned roughly after the federal model. There are necessary differences, too. For example, the federal government has its own publication, the *Commerce Business Daily*, in which to announce its needs and bidding opportunities, whereas most other governments must rely on newspaper advertising. Both maintain bidders lists and provide roughly the same methodology for getting your name listed on bidders lists. The following will describe the procurement systems in general, but will go into detail only when what is being discussed bears some direct relationship to marketing consulting or similar professional services to government agencies.

THE FEDERAL PROCUREMENT SYSTEM

Federal procurement is accomplished under the control of and procedures dictated by the Defense Acquisitions Regulations (DAR), formerly the Armed Services Procurement Regulations (ASPR); the Federal Procurement Regulations (FPR); the NASA Procurement Regulations (NASPR); and literally thousands of bulletins, memoranda, and other miscellaneous documentation. There is today an Office of Federal Procurement Policy (OFPP), which is part of the Office of Management and Budget (OMB), an agency with very close ties to the President, as his own budget and management staff. Under legislation authorizing it, OFPP has carried out a project in which the aforementioned potpourri of procurement regulations and documentation has been assembled and integrated into the Federal

Acquisition Regulations (FAR). This is not yet law, FAR has not yet replaced all the other procurement regulations, but it is expected to do so ultimately. Even so, the practical changes in the procurement system will not be great, but redundancies, anomalies, confusion, and disputes should be reduced significantly when FAR makes its predecessor regulations obsolete.

The general philosophy of the federal procurement system is one of competition. Originally, the idea was to give everyone a fair chance to compete for government contracts but with competitive bidding to "keep the game honest" and give the government the lowest possible prices. The procurement methodologies grew up around this idea and were designed to produce open and honest competition for all federal purchases.

It soon became apparent that finding the lowest bidder was neither appropriate nor practical for all procurement. There were many cases where it was absolutely necessary for the government executives to decide which bidder was truly capable of producing what the government required, which was most dependable, and which truly understood the government's requirement and would produce what the government wanted and would find acceptable. Sad experience demonstrated that in many cases what the low bidder produced was simply unacceptable.

One answer to that is specifications—provide the bidders a detailed description of what must be supplied and caution them to bid realistically because government inspectors will examine the product and will reject it if it does not meet the specifications completely. Under those circumstances, the contractor offering the lowest bid to produce what has been clearly specified is the awardee.

It soon developed that it was not always possible to furnish specifications, particularly when the contractor was to carry out an R&D project. Who could foresee exactly what was going to prove possible in developing a faster airplane or more sophisticated radar set? It is the R&D contractor who develops the specifications, based on what he has been able to develop and prototype.

If an agency wants a survey made or some kind of social study undertaken, providing specifications is, again, an impractical idea. There are many other kinds of procurement in which specifications can not be furnished except perhaps in the most general sense, and then the description of what is required is not a specification at all. It is an item description in rather general terms or, as it is called when it is a service rather than a product that is being procured, a *statement of work.*

Therefore, when the government is able to specify exactly what is wanted in such terms that it is possible to reject a result that does not meet the requirement, a bid is requested, and the competition is strictly one of price. The document the federal government issues is an Invitation for Bid and Award (IFB), Standard Form 33. This type of procurement is referred to as "advertised" or "formally advertised" procurement. All that is requested of bidders is a price quotation or set of quotations and filling in the various blanks on the forms provided. (See Figure 6.)

The form lists a time and place of bid opening. The various bids are sealed until then. At the exact time and place announced, the bids are opened publicly. Anyone who wishes to may attend the opening and listen to the bids read aloud. Usually, those bidding attend the opening and record the bids.

The low bidder is ordinarily awarded the contract. (Not at the opening, however, for the contracting official must check all the arithmetic and verify a few other items.) I say ordinarily because there may be an irregularity, such as the low bidder having forgotten to sign the bid, which disqualifies the bid irretrievably. Other than some such irregularity or any other factor which might disqualify the low bid (such as false statements made in the bid documents), the award is controlled by the low bid; the contracting officer is compelled to award the contract to the low bidder. The strategy for winning an IFB-announced contract is simple enough: Be the low bidder, and have everything in good order. It is rarely quite that simple. It is not always easy to determine who is the low bidder, and there are certain cost strategies possible in many cases. (We'll discuss these later in another chapter.) By understanding how the system works and how to devise certain cost strategies, it is sometimes possible to *appear* to be the low bidder although you may not be.

If you will refer to Figure 6, you'll see that there are two boxes at the top: ADVERTISED (IFB) and NEGOTIATED (RFP). The same form is used for both types of solicitation. Whereas an "advertised" procurement consists of submitting sealed bids and selecting the low bidder, a "negotiated" procurement consists of soliciting proposals and evaluating them to select that one which appears to be "in the best interests of the government, price and other factors considered," and opening negotiations with the proposer. The government is not required to award the contract to the low bidder under the regulations governing negotiated procurement, but is permitted to decide which proposal represents the best offer. (The subject of proposals and proposal writing is taken up in detail in a later chapter.)

The government has assigned a set of descriptors to the various categories of services and goods bought. In general, goods are purchased under numbered categories—for example, 69: Training Aids and Devices. Services are described by letters. Those most pertinent to consulting and professional services are described as follows:

| STANDARD FORM 33, NOV. 1969
GENERAL SERVICES ADMINISTRATION
FED. PROC. REG. (41 CFR) 1-16.101 | SOLICITATION, OFFER,
AND AWARD | 3. CERTIFIED FOR NATIONAL DEFENSE UNDER
BDSA REG. 2 AND/OR DMS REG. 1.
RATING: | 4. PAGE
1 | OF |

| 1. CONTRACT (Proc. Inst. Ident.) NO. | 2. SOLICITATION NO.
RFP-SBA-7(i)-MA-78-1
☐ ADVERTISED (IFB) ☒ NEGOTIATED (RFP) | 5. DATE ISSUED
11/14/77 | 6. REQUISITION/PURCHASE REQUEST NO. |

| 7. ISSUED BY   CODE
Small Business Administration
1441 L Street, N. W.
Washington, D. C. 20416 | 8. ADDRESS OFFER TO (If other than Block 7)
Contracting Officer, c/o Program Manager
Small Business Administration, Room 610
1441 L Street, N. W.
Washington, D. C. 20416 |

SOLICITATION

9. Sealed offers in original and __6__ copies for furnishing the supplies or services described in the Schedule will be received at the place specified in block 8, OR IF HAND-CARRIED, IN THE DEPOSITORY LOCATED IN Rm. 610, 1441 L St., N.W., Wash., D.C. until 5:00pm EST (local time), FRI, DEC 16, 1977. If this is an advertised solicitation, offers will be publicly opened at that *(Time, Zone, and Date)* time. CAUTION—LATE OFFERS. See par. 8 of Solicitation Instructions and Conditions.

All offers are subject to the following:
1. The attached Solicitation Instructions and Conditions, SF 33-A.
2. The General Provisions, SF 32 _____ edition, which is attached or incorporated herein by reference.
3. The Schedule included below and/or attached hereto.
4. Such other provisions, representations, certifications, and specifications as are attached or incorporated herein by reference. (Attachments are listed in the Schedule.)

FOR INFORMATION CALL (Name and Telephone No.) (No collect calls.):
Lillian Harris, Program Assistant, AC 202/653-6894

SCHEDULE

10. ITEM NO.	11. SUPPLIES/SERVICES	12. QUANTITY	13. UNIT	14. UNIT PRICE	15. AMOUNT
	Provide technical and management assistance as specified in Parts I thru IV of the Schedule to individuals or enterprises eligible for assistance under Sections 7(i) and 7(j) of the Small Business Act, as amended. This solicitation is a 100% small business set-aside.				

OFFER (NOTE: Reverse Must Also Be Fully Completed By Offeror)

In compliance with the above, the undersigned offers and agrees, if this offer is accepted within _____ calendar days (60 calendar days unless a different period is inserted by the offeror) from the date for receipt of offers specified above, to furnish any or all items upon which prices are offered, at the price set opposite each item, delivered at the designated point(s), within the time specified in the Schedule.

16. DISCOUNT FOR PROMPT PAYMENT (See Par. 9 on SF 33-A)
_N/A_ % 10 CALENDAR DAYS; _N/A_ % 20 CALENDAR DAYS; _N/A_ % 30 CALENDAR DAYS; _N/A_ % _N/A_ CALENDAR DAYS.

| 17. OFFEROR   CODE   FACILITY CODE
NAME & ADDRESS

(Street, city,
county, state,
& ZIP Code)

Area Code and Telephone No.
☐ Check If Remittance Address Is Different From Above - Enter Such Address In Schedule. | 18. NAME AND TITLE OF PERSON AUTHORIZED
TO SIGN OFFER (Type or print) |
| | 19. SIGNATURE   20. OFFER DATE |

AWARD (To Be Completed By Government)

| 21. ACCEPTED AS TO ITEMS NUMBERED | 22. AMOUNT | 23. ACCOUNTING AND APPROPRIATION DATA |

| 24. SUBMIT INVOICES (4 copies unless otherwise specified) TO ADDRESS SHOWN IN BLOCK | 25. NEGOTIATED ☐ 10 U.S.C. 2304(a)( )
PURSUANT TO ☐ 41 U.S.C. 252(c)( ) |

| 26. ADMINISTERED BY   CODE
(If other than block 7)
Small Business Administration
Office of Management Assistance
1441 L Street, N.W.
Washington, D. C. 20416 | 27. PAYMENT WILL BE MADE BY   CODE
Small Business Administration
Budget and Finance Office, Room 405
1441 L Street, N.W.
Washington, D. C. 20416 |

| 28. NAME OF CONTRACTING OFFICER (Type or Print) | 29. UNITED STATES OF AMERICA
BY: _____
(Signature of Contracting Officer) | 30. AWARD DATE |

33-128   Award will be made on this form, or on Standard Form 26, or by other official written notice.

FIGURE 6. Standard Form 33, for solicitations.

A   Experimental, developmental, test, and research work

H   Expert and consultant services

L   Technical representative services

M   Operation and maintenance of government owned facility

Q   Medical services

R   Architect-engineer services

T   Photographic, mapping, printing, and publication services

U   Training services

X   Miscellaneous

HOW TO FIND OUT ABOUT OPPORTUNITIES TO BID AND PROPOSE

The *Commerce Business Daily*, is a newsletter-sized 5-days-a-week publication of the Commerce Department, printed and mailed by the Government Printing Office. In it the various agencies announce their needs, in synopses, with information on where/how to request the entire solicitation package. Other information carried there includes notices of awards, and these are often excellent sales leads, for many of those winning substantial contracts are in need of support services.

Procurement offices of agencies that buy more or less regularly also maintain bidders lists and furnish a form, Standard Form 129 (see Figure 7), for suppliers to fill out and file.

Government procurement offices also keep a file of all current solicitations available for anyone interested. The large procurement offices which do a great deal of purchasing often have a "bid room," with a bulletin board on which are posted copies of all current solicitations. You are free to visit these rooms and see if there is anything there of interest. Where the procurement office does not have a separate bid room, the outstanding solicitations are generally kept in a binder, also available for your inspection upon request.

It is advisable, if you are seriously interested in pursuing marketing opportunities with federal agencies, to utilize all these methods. This will result in maximum coverage, for no single method is foolproof. Even with Form 129 filed in every office of interest to you, you won't see every solicitation that interests you, nor will you find everything in the CBD (*Commerce Business Daily*), for there are the inevitable slip-ups there, too.

BIDDER'S MAILING LIST APPLICATION	INITIAL APPLICATION	FORM APPROVED OMB NO.
	REVISION	29–R0069

Fill in all spaces. Insert "NA" in blocks not applicable. Type or print all entries. See reverse for instructions.

TO (*Enter name and address of Federal agency to which form is submitted. Include ZIP Code*)	DATE

1. APPLICANT'S NAME AND ADDRESS (*Include county and ZIP Code*)	2. ADDRESS (*Include county and ZIP Code*) TO WHICH SOLICITATIONS ARE TO BE MAILED (*If different from item 1*)

3. TYPE OF ORGANIZATION (*Check one*)	4. HOW LONG IN PRESENT BUSINESS

INDIVIDUAL	PARTNERSHIP	NON-PROFIT ORGANIZATION
CORPORATION, INCORPORATED UNDER THE LAWS OF THE STATE OF		

5. NAMES OF OFFICERS, OWNERS, OR PARTNERS

PRESIDENT	VICE PRESIDENT	SECRETARY
TREASURER	OWNERS OR PARTNERS	

6. AFFILIATES OF APPLICANT (*Names, locations and nature of affiliation. See definition on reverse*)

7. PERSONS AUTHORIZED TO SIGN BIDS, OFFERS, AND CONTRACTS IN YOUR NAME (*Indicate if agent*)

NAME	OFFICIAL CAPACITY	TEL. NO. (*Incl. area code*)

8. IDENTIFY EQUIPMENT, SUPPLIES, MATERIALS, AND/OR SERVICES ON WHICH YOU DESIRE TO BID (*See attached Federal agency's supplemental listing and instructions, if any*)

9. TYPE OF OWNERSHIP (*See definitions on reverse*)	
MINORITY BUSINESS ENTERPRISE	OTHER THAN MINORITY BUSINESS ENTERPRISE

10. TYPE OF BUSINESS (*See definitions on reverse*)		
MANUFACTURER OR PRODUCER	REGULAR DEALER (*Type 1*)	REGULAR DEALER (*Type 2*)
SERVICE ESTABLISHMENT	CONSTRUCTION CONCERN	RESEARCH AND DEVELOPMENT FIRM
☐ SURPLUS DEALER (*Check this box if you are also a dealer in surplus goods*)		

11. SIZE OF BUSINESS (*See definitions on reverse*)		
SMALL BUSINESS CONCERN*	OTHER THAN SMALL BUSINESS CONCERN	
*If you are a small business concern, fill in (a) and (b):	(a) AVERAGE NUMBER OF EMPLOYEES (*Including affiliates*) FOR FOUR PRECEDING CALENDAR QUARTERS	(b) AVERAGE ANNUAL SALES OR RECEIPTS FOR PRECEDING THREE FISCAL YEARS

12. FLOOR SPACE (*Square feet*)		13.	NET WORTH
MANUFACTURING	WAREHOUSE	DATE	AMOUNT

14. SECURITY CLEARANCE (*If applicable, check highest clearance authorized*)

	FOR	TOP SECRET	SECRET	CONFIDENTIAL	NAMES OF AGENCIES WHICH GRANTED SECURITY CLEARANCES (*Include dates*)
KEY PERSONNEL					
PLANT ONLY					

THIS SPACE FOR USE BY THE GOVERNMENT	CERTIFICATION
	I certify that information supplied herein (*Including all pages attached*) is correct and that neither the applicant nor any person (Or concern) in any connection with the applicant as a principal or officer, so far as is known, is now debarred or otherwise declared ineligible by any agency of the Federal Government from bidding for furnishing materials, supplies, or services to the Government or any agency thereof.
	SIGNATURE
	NAME AND TITLE OF PERSON AUTHORIZED TO SIGN (*Type or print*)

129–105

STANDARD FORM 129 (REV. 2–77)
Prescribed by GSA, FPR (41 CFR) 1–16.802

FIGURE 7. Standard Form 129, Bidders List Application.

135

INFORMATION AND INSTRUCTIONS

Persons or concerns wishing to be added to a particular agency's bidder's mailing list for supplies or services shall file this properly completed and certified Bidder's Mailing List Application, together with such other lists as may be attached to this application form, with each procurement office of the Federal agency with which they desire to do business. If a Federal agency has attached a Supplemental Commodity List with instructions, complete the application as instructed. Otherwise, identify in item 8 the equipment, supplies and/or services on which you desire to bid. The application shall be submitted and signed by the principal as distinguished from an agent, however constituted.

After placement on the bidder's mailing list of an agency, a supplier's failure to respond (submission of bid, or notice in writing, that you are unable to bid on that particular transaction but wish to remain on the active bidder's mailing list for that particular item) to Invitations for Bids will be understood by the agency to indicate lack of interest and concurrence in the removal of the supplier's name from the purchasing activity's bidder's mailing list for the items concerned.

DEFINITION RELATING TO TYPE OF OWNERSHIP
(See item 9)

Minority business enterprise. A minority business enterprise is defined as a "business, at least 50 percent of which is owned by minority group members or, in case of publicly owned businesses, at least 51 percent of the stock of which is owned by minority group members." For the purpose of this definition, minority group members are Negroes, Spanish-speaking American persons, American-Orientals, American-Indians, American-Eskimos, and American-Aleuts.

TYPE OF BUSINESS DEFINITIONS
(See item 10)

a. Manufacturer or producer—means a person (or concern) owning, operating, or maintaining a store, warehouse, or other establishment that produces, on the premises, the materials, supplies, articles, or equipment of the general character of those listed in item 8, or in the Federal Agency's Supplemental Commodity List, if attached.

b. Regular dealer (Type 1)—means a person (or concern) who owns, operates, or maintains a store, warehouse, or other establishment in which the materials, supplies, articles, or equipment of the general character listed in item 8 or in the Federal Agency's Supplemental Commodity List, if attached, are bought, kept in stock, and sold to the public in the usual course of business.

c. Regular dealer (Type 2)—in the case of supplies of particular kinds (at present, petroleum, lumber and timber products, machine tools, raw cotton, green coffee, hay, grain, feed, or straw, agricultural liming materials, tea, raw or unmanufactured cotton linters). Regular dealer—means a person (or concern) satisfying the requirements of the regulations (Code of Federal Regulations, Title 41, 50–201.101(b)) as amended from time to time, prescribed by the Secretary of Labor under the Walsh-Healey Public Contracts Act (Title 41 U.S. Code 35–45). For coal dealers see Code of Federal Regulations, Title 41, 50–201.604(a).

d. Service establishment—means a concern (or person) which owns, operates, or maintains any type of business which is principally engaged in the furnishing of nonpersonal services, such as (but not limited to) repairing, cleaning, redecorating, or rental of personal property, including the furnishing of necessary repair parts or other supplies as part of the services performed.

e. Construction concern—means a concern (or person) engaged in construction, alteration or repair (including dredging, excavating, and painting) of buildings, structures and other real property.

DEFINITIONS RELATING TO SIZE OF BUSINESS
(See item 11)

a. Small business concern—A small business concern for the purpose of Government procurement is a concern, including its affiliates, which is independently owned and operated, is not dominant in the field of operation in which it is bidding on Government contracts and can further qualify under the criteria concerning number of employees, average annual receipts, or other criteria, as prescribed by the Small Business Administration. (See Code of Federal Regulations, Title 13, Part 121, as amended, which contains detailed industry definitions and related procedures.)

b. Affiliates—Business concerns are affiliates of each other when either directly or indirectly (i) one concern controls or has the power to control the other, or (ii) a third party controls or has the power to control both. In determining whether concerns are independently owned and operated and whether or not affiliation exists, consideration is given to all appropriate factors including common ownership, common management, and contractual relationship. (See items 6 and 11.)

c. Number of employees—In connection with the determination of small business status, "number of employees" means the average employment of any concern, including the employees of its domestic and foreign affiliates, based on the number of persons employed on a full-time, part-time, temporary, or other basis during each of the pay periods of the preceding 12 months. If a concern has not been in existence for 12 months, "number of employees" means the average employment of such concern and its affiliates during the period that such concern has been in existence based on the number of persons employed during each of the pay periods of the period that such concern has been in business. (See item 11.)

● **COMMERCE BUSINESS DAILY**—The Commerce Business Daily, published by the Department of Commerce, contains information concerning proposed procurements, sales, and contract awards. For further information concerning this publication, contact your local Commerce Field Office.

129–105

STANDARD FORM 129 BACK (REV. 2–77)
☆U.S. Government Printing Office: 1977—261-047/3836

FIGURE 7. Continued.

TYPES OF CONTRACTS

The federal government awards several kinds of contracts, but all are either cost-reimbursement or fixed price, although some may be hybrids, with elements of both cost-reimbursement and fixed-price contracting. Contracting officials would usually much prefer fixed-price contracts, just as they would prefer that all solicitations be sealed bids, with award to low bidders. However, it is not always possible to do things this way, because in many kinds of contracting, such as R&D, for example, it is not always possible for the contractor to do more than guess at the probable costs. For this reason, the government often finds it necessary to award a cost-reimbursement contract, in which the contractor will agree to some set of maximum unit rates (the units being labor hours, units of product, or other identifiable entities) and maximum overhead rates, with a fee generally fixed as some agreed-upon percentage of the total cost estimated. Under this arrangement, the contractor will earn the exact fee agreed upon, but will be compensated for all reimbursable units he can document to the government's satisfaction. (A matter of recordkeeping.)

The simplest type of contract, then, is the contract to carry out some single task or project—write a training manual, for example—for a fixed price, often identified on the solicitation form as "FOR THE JOB: $_____" where you are requested to enter your quotation. This is generally used for small jobs, although not necessarily *small purchases*, which are defined under current law as not more than $10,000 each. However, an agency may ask you to quote only a bottom-line final price on, perhaps, a $25,000 project. On the other hand, for larger projects—$100,000, perhaps—it is likely that you will be required to furnish more details about the price. That may still be a fixed-price job. Whether you are required to furnish cost analyses has nothing to do with whether the job is fixed-price or cost-reimbursable. (Although you may be sure that you will be required to furnish backup cost analyses for cost-reimbursement contracting, for it is not possible to negotiate such a contract otherwise.)

There are several types of cost-reimbursement contracts, of which the well-publicized cost-plus-fixed-fee (CPFF) is best known and least often used, at least not in its original form, under which the contractor took virtually no risk and "got away with murder" again and again. Following are the basic types of contract you are most likely to encounter, other than the firm fixed price that contracting officers prefer. You'll find some elements of both cost-reimbursement and fixed price contracting in these.

Basic Ordering Agreement, or BOA

This is generally an annual contract under which the contractor lists prices for hours of labor for each labor category and other work units such as pages of typing. The government issues "task orders" against such a contract, which the contractor must execute at the rates stipulated and agreed to in the master contract. Usually the agency issues the task statement with a request for estimate. The contractor estimates the job using the rates scheduled, and begins work when the agency approves the estimate.

Time and Material, or T&M

Similar to the BOA, except that it is generally issued for a project of indeterminate size rather than for a year's services.

Purchase Order

A government purchase order may be issued instead of a formal contract, for any small purchase (not more than $10,000). By its nature, this is normally a fixed-price contract. Exceptions: Purchase orders may be used to contract for tasks under master contracts, such as BOAs or Federal Supply Schedules (which are really BOAs), in which case the Purchase Orders may be for more than $10,000 if the master contract so authorizes.

Among these basic types of contracts there are other variable factors. The original bid or proposal submitted to win the contract may have called for fixed unit prices which included all overhead and profit—billing rates—or they may have required a full cost analysis to show how the various rates were derived and arrived at. The contract may permit the contractor to bill at the precise rates scheduled in the contract, or it may require billing of "actuals", listing individual names of those employed in the work, with their hours and their actual rates of pay. In the latter case the contractor will have to bill the actual total of hours and other costs, even if the estimate was for a higher figure and was accepted. In many of these contracts, however, once the agency has accepted the estimate of the task, the estimate becomes a fixed price regardless of the contractor's actual costs.

There are also contracts that call for small fixed fees, with provision for award fees. These are fees set by a committee which judges how well the contractor has performed and stipulates a fee accordingly.

One major point: It is usually best to avoid using the term consultant in bidding, proposing, and/or negotiating a contract with a federal agency. Try to keep the term completely out of the picture, for two reasons:

1.   Many agencies have fixed daily rates for consultants, and by policy are unable to pay more. These rates are generally most unrealistic, and you will have a problem with them.

2.   There is a distinct prejudice against consulting in the OMB and a few other federal agencies, where they tend to believe that "consulting" describes work that should be done by federal executives.

It is almost always advantageous, from both viewpoints, to have the work described as a project of some sort, preferably in terms of the nature of the work, such as survey, design, study, research, development, analysis, or other such functional term, and specify the product, too—manual, report, program, specification, design, drawings, or whatever will result. (There is almost always some physical product, such as a report or manual.) Then price the project as a whole rather than specifying some daily or hourly consulting rate.

One prejudice many government executives have, inspired perhaps by Congressmen and Senators who investigate what they believe to be abuses of the procurement process, is that a consultant ought not to earn more per hour or day than the government employee who does similar work. Superficially, this may appear to make some sense, but it neglects to consider these factors:

Government employees are the recipients of one of the most generous fringe-benefit packages to be found anywhere in the world. This includes up to over 10 weeks paid time off annually (this represents a full 20 percent higher actual hourly rate than their nominal hourly rate), hospitalization payments, a superb retirement plan, and excellent prospects for promotion.

Although it is possible to be laid off a government job, the relative security of the job is far greater than in most commercial organizations.

The consultant has been called in, in many cases, because the federal employees are not capable of handling the problems or satisfying the need.

For these reasons, at least, you are entitled to a considerably higher rate of pay than is your opposite number (if there truly is one) in the government agency. Have no hesitancy about charging your full fee or rate, no matter how aggressive you must be or what ploys you must resort to.

SELLING TO THE GOVERNMENT

There are several government agencies who will help you pursue government contracts: The Business Service Centers of the General Services Administration, the various District Offices of the Small Business Administration, and the Small Business Representatives who are to be found in a great many government offices. (See "The Reference File," last chapter, for more details.) From such federal offices you can get brochures of various kinds and some direct counseling. However, what you get is information and guidance in how the federal government buys, and that is not exactly the same thing as selling to the federal government. Basically, selling to the federal government is not that much different from selling to commercial accounts, with the following principal exceptions:

1. The federal government is more bureaucratic than are most for-profit companies, and there is more paper work and formality to the procedures.

2. A private company can do business with anyone they wish to, without explanation to anyone (although most tend to follow the same basic principles that government does). However, the government is ruled by statutes which control them to some extent, and you must understand what the law requires if you are to market effectively to government agencies.

3. Federal agencies often give you a great deal of trouble as a consequence of normal bureaucratic characteristics; they have trouble reaching decisions, they change their minds frequently, they ask for more than the contract entitles them to, and they otherwise extract from you a pound of flesh on every job if you permit them to. Even when you have learned to protect yourself in every way possible, you still often wind up wishing you hadn't taken the job unless you have anticipated the probability of trouble and gauged your prices accordingly. The upside of government contracting is that you can usually get a far better price from a federal agency than you can from a private firm, so you are paid for your aggravation. Expect it, plan for it, and price for it. (Sometimes, private-sector firms are even more bureaucratic and troublesome than federal agencies are, and you aren't even getting your price with the private firm, as you are with the federal agency.)

You can sell a federal agency across the counter in much the same manner that you do a private-sector firm, especially if the project is for not more than $10,000, a small purchase as defined by law. (Legislation is in the hopper to raise this figure to $25,000 in view of inflation. It has been $10,000 since August 1974, when it was raised from its previous $2,500 level.) A federal executive who wishes to contract with you can issue a purchase order for that amount which requires only superficial competitive bidding, so for all practical purposes, any federal official who has the budget available and the authority to spend it can issue purchase orders for up to $10,000 spontaneously. It is therefore entirely feasible to make calls on federal agencies as you would on privately-held companies, and to use just about any other marketing tactic you might use elsewhere.

There are various strategies, technical and cost, that you can employ when selling to government agencies which are not usually as helpful when selling in the private sector. You can protest to the Government Accounting Office or the agency's Contracting Officer if you think you have been unfairly treated or have not been given a fair and equal opportunity to compete for the contract. This is purely an administrative procedure, so you do not need a lawyer, but need only write a letter of complaint and follow up when the agency responds, as they definitely will.

One other advantage is this: You can, under the authority of the Freedom of Information Act, demand to see other proposals and contracts and get relevant information, such as what the government agency paid for similar work in previous contracts and who is currently doing the work or who did it last year. Such information is exceedingly helpful in your marketing and especially in making up your bids and proposals. In many ways, you have a much greater freedom in pursuing government business than in pursuing private-sector leads if you take the trouble to learn about them and exploit them.

STATE- AND LOCAL-GOVERNMENT PURCHASING

The federal procurement system is something of a model for the purchasing administrations of most states and local jurisdictions. In some cases (notably, California) the state has even patterned its designators of supply categories closely on the federal system. However, there are a few significant differences:

1. Most state governments tend to centralize their purchasing in a single supply agency in the state, from which the various state agencies requisition what they need. This is almost universally true

for commodities such as office supplies, construction supplies, and other common-use items. It is true in some states for certain services, too, such as printing.

2. Most states also tend to delegate purchasing authority to the various state agencies when the agencies have need of specialized services, such as consultants are likely to offer. There is usually some paper work involved. The agency has to get an approval from the supply or procurement official, but it is pretty much a routine procedure.

3. *Small purchases* in state procurement systems tend to be quite small, compared with federal standards, usually on the order of a few hundred dollars.

4. States and local governments do not have anything like the federal government's CBD. Therefore, it is common practice for state and local governments to announce their procurements and bid/proposal opportunities in the major local newspapers printed in English. The announcements are generally found among the classified advertisements under the heading "Bids and Proposals."

There are also similarities between the state and federal systems.

1. The advertisements are synopses of the requirements, and each notice advises the reader where and how to get the entire solicitation package or "bid set."

2. Bidders lists are maintained, and in most cases the state or local government has forms of some sort to fill out to get your name listed on the appropriate bidders lists.

3. Many states maintain offices which are the equivalent of the General Services Administration (GSA) Business Service Centers and/or the Small Business Administration (SBA) District offices, to help entrepreneurs in various ways, through small business programs and minority-entrepreneur programs they operate. (See The Reference File, last chapter, for more information on this.)

WHAT STATE AND LOCAL GOVERNMENTS BUY

A list of goods and services purchased by state and local governments resembles that of the federal government except that it is not nearly as diverse. Taken in the aggregate, the purchasing by state and local governments totals considerably more than the procurement budgets of the federal government. Therefore, regarding all state and local governments, rather than any single one, the total procurement is as diverse as is that of the federal government. In terms of consulting and related technical/professional services, purchasing by state and local governments appears destined to grow, since the Administration in Washington has declared its intention of turning over as many programs to states as possible.

CAN YOU DO BUSINESS WITH ANY STATE/LOCAL GOVERNMENT?

Obviously, a state or local government is compelled to go outside its own jurisdiction frequently to buy what it needs, and each jurisdiction's procurement regulations and legislation acknowledge this. In fact, many states have specific small-business programs and set aside certain procurements or otherwise give small business preferential treatment. However, such preference is usually given only to businesses within the state. A business can qualify, ordinarily, only by being incorporated in or having its principal offices within the state, as well as by meeting other criteria.

SMALL BUSINESS CRITERIA

A small business is generally defined as one that is not dominant in its industry and meets whatever size standard has been established for businesses in that industry. The Small Business Administration has long had the federal responsibility for determining size standards for small businesses, and has established different standards for different industries, such as the maximum number of barrels a day capacity for a refinery.

For consulting and other technical/professional service industries, federal standards tend to be in terms of either average annual sales (for three years prior to time of determination) or number of employees. At the moment, the maximum average annual gross sales a business may have to qualify as a small business is $3 million, $5 million, or $8 million, and when number of employees is used as the yardstick, the number is 500 employees, maximum. So "small" is very much a relative term, even within the federal SBA definitions. When the various states and local jurisdictions define a small business, they are somewhat more conservative, although some use the federal SBA size standards.

TYPES OF AGENCIES AND THEIR NEEDS

The federal establishment has been growing steadily from the day of its initial establishment. Growing and spending money appear to be two primary functions of any government upon which you can always depend. In the past few decades and especially since the early sixties, the growth rate accelerated sharply, creating new departments—Transportation, Health and Human Services, Housing and Urban Development, Energy, and Education are all relatively new departments—and there have also been independent agencies, such as the Environmental Protection Agency and ACTION, the volunteer agency that took over the old Peace Corps.

Some other agencies are of less recent vintage. The Department of Commerce and Labor, created in 1903, was split into two separate departments in 1913. The military services were assembled into a single, cabinet-level department (DOD) in 1947. The Coast Guard, established in 1915, became part of Transportation in 1966. While some new departments have been created from the ground up and others have been created by assembling various bureaus and independent agencies—both Energy and Transportation are largely aggregated elements that had been long in existence—some are created by splitting of a subdivision, as Education was split off Health, Education and Welfare (HEW), where it had been an Office. And many new agencies are created by setting up new bureaus in existing organizations, so that existing departments and independent agencies grow on their own.

All of this makes it increasingly difficult for the entrepreneur to find his or her way around the establishment, even with a road map. Those who know the federal establishment reasonably well are in general agreement that selling to the federal agencies is not nearly so difficult as finding them. In fact, often the sales are all but automatic once you find the right doors.

In my own experience, I found this to be entirely true. Calling on a bureau of the Labor Department on one occasion, I spent several hours visiting different offices to which helpful employees directed me in response to my questions. My question, in each case, was to whom would the individual I was speaking to recommend me. (I had explained, in each case, what sort of services I provided.) Eventually, after talking to several individuals, I stumbled into the right office, one in which I was all but welcomed with open arms, and where I did considerable business soon after. Moreover, as a result of this contact, I was recommended to other government executives. Each time I met anyone in government, whether we did business together or not, I solicited his or her recommendations as to other likely prospects for my services.

The needs of each agency vary with the nature of the agency, its mission or charter, its problems, its staffing. Some agencies are heavily staffed and have less need for consulting services than do others which are less well staffed. However, there are some generalities that can be made:

If the work is of a nature that is labor-intensive—computer programming, for example—it is highly likely that the agency will have to "contract out" for at least some of its work, since only rarely is a federal agency heavily staffed with relation to its needs. That is, in this example, if the agency does more than occasional computer programming. (Example: the NASA Goddard Space Flight Center, which has over 200 computers on-site and therefore uses a great many contract programmers and analysts.)

If the work is highly technological, particularly if it is "state-of-the-art" (advanced technology), it is unlikely that the agencies will have all the technological specialists they need, and they are likely to have substantial consulting needs. (NASA, Environmental Protection Agency or EPA, Bureau of Standards, OSHA.)

If the agencies are highly visible (prominent, frequently the subject of newspaper stories, recognized widely by the general public) and especially is under severe pressure because they are working on pressing problems (such as pollution, transportation, safety, and unemployment), it is likely that they have frequent need of consultants. (EPA, Transportation, Labor.)

If an old-time agency (Treasury, for example) has no special problems but is engaged in strictly routine work, there is less pressure on the agency to get things done, and they have probably built up an able in-house capability over the years so that they are not especially good prospects. However, if they are handed special problems—such as complying with a new law, like the one on equal employment opportunity—they are likely to need help.

HORIZONTAL AND VERTICAL MARKETS

In marketing to the government establishments, I have conceived of the markets as being "horizontal" and "vertical." That is, computers and computer services represent a horizontal market to me because any agency may be a good prospect, and most agencies have at least some use for services related to computers. On the other hand, I can't think of any agency other than the U.S. Army who would have need of 155mm howitzers, or anyone other than the U.S. Navy who would be likely prospects for peri-scope gear. Therefore, those items represent vertical markets.

These are extreme cases, and most cases fall between these extremes. There are more than a few agencies who might buy hand guns—the mili-tary agencies and all the law-enforcement agencies: FBI, Secret Service, CIA, and even a few others, such as the building guards where an agency runs its own security instead of contracting out for it.

In terms of services the same considerations apply. Almost any agency may contract for training services, but if you specialize in some training area, you may or may not be constricted to only a few government mar-kets. Most agencies are at least prospects for general management train-ing, office skills training, and several other kinds of training. Some are highly specialized: the Postal Service, for example, sometimes found it necessary to contract out only to former Postal Service employees because they were the only ones who knew the system well enough for some kinds of training. Even if you specialize in a fairly popular subject, electronics maintenance, for example, you must pick your targets, for only a few fed-eral agencies have use for electronics training. (Postal Service and the mili-tary agencies, primarily.)

You should study the various government markets and what they have use for and try to broaden your services as much as you can in order to broaden your market and sales possibilities.

State and local governments operate bureaus which in some cases are similar to federal agencies, but in other cases are quite different. For exam-ple, all governments have some law-enforcement responsibilities, so they must buy equipment and services relevant to carrying out that responsi-bility. But local and state governments also operate bureaus or agencies that are quite different from those found in the federal establishment, such as these:

Public libraries	Public school systems
Fire departments	Institutions—mental, old age, for example
Universities	Sanitation departments
Public roads bureaus	Examination boards and licensing

STUDYING, SURVEYING PUBLIC-SECTOR MARKETS

Reading the "Bids and Proposals" notices in the newspapers and reading the synopses published in the *Commerce Business Daily* (subscription information found in last chapter, with information on where to see cop-ies) for a few weeks will give you a clear idea of what is being purchased and by whom. However, that is a "snapshot," a view of the markets at that time. Government markets change, as do all markets, and it is necessary to keep up, if you wish to do business with government agencies. You must be aware of new programs, new interests, and new trends.

For example, a few years ago the federal government established the Pension Benefit Guaranty Corporation as an independent agency, a government corporation. The agency started by borrowing temporary staff from other federal agencies until it could hire and train its own employees and then began to contract out for a variety of services it found it could not depend on its own staff for, particularly training in such things as actuarial work and pension programs. That's been the history of many new agencies—Transportation, Office of Economic Opportunity and Job Corps (OEO now defunct, Job Corps now in Labor Department CETA program), and other new agencies. The Office of Economic Opportunity was a particularly rich source of consulting business in its early days, and many new businesses were launched entirely on the strength of OEO contracts.

Don't be misled by budgets. Sometimes an agency has an exceptionally large budget—the Department of Transportation (DOT) was an example—and finds itself besieged by people seeking contracts when the agency has few contracts to give. A large budget does not necessarily mean a large procurement budget; it is necessary to see how the agency's budget is to be allocated. In the case of DOT, much of its large budget went to subsidize operations at state- and local-government levels, so that relatively few contracts were let directly by DOT.

Times change, too. Not too long after the new Postal Service was established as a government corporation, after having been the Post Office Department for many years, the corporation established a training organization, as an institute for training employees in management and in technical subjects. For years this institute was a mother lode of contracts for projects connected with both development and delivery of training. Then, almost overnight, the stream of contracts dried up. The institute continued to operate, but with sharp restrictions on its freedom to contract out for services. More than one small company (some one-person enterprises) went out of business rapidly thereafter, a small-scale repeat of the aftermath of OEO's dissolution. It is essential, in contracting with government agencies, to be aware that your source of business can dry up suddenly, so see to it that you are not entirely dependent or excessively dependent on any single source.

HERE/HOW TO GET DETAILS

In the last chapter of this book are directions to sources of information on states that offer programs for small business and supply useful information on their procurement activities. Useful addresses, for example, the Chamber of Commerce, are provided also for a number of major cities. Writing or calling these sources will generally bring you the detailed information you need to pursue business opportunities there. In the case of state governments, there is usually a specific purchasing office and, in many cases, one or more special program offices, since over one half of the states operate special programs for small business and minority entrepreneurs.

In some cases SBA district offices and GSA Business Service Centers have compiled useful lists of local government agencies. It is advisable to request these, too, from any such office or center in an area where you wish to do business.

6

The Initial Meeting
With the New Client
or New Prospect

*To solve a problem, you have to understand it and define it first.
Especially in consulting, that usually means listening, which is something
that many of us have never learned to do. A successful working
relationship requires that both parties listen to each other and reach
complete agreement on the project.*

RULE NUMBER 1.   Have a Clear Understanding from the Beginning.

There are many circumstances under which you might have an initial meeting with a new client or prospect. By "meeting" I do not mean a casual introduction or handshake at some professional function. I refer to a contact in which you have a serious discussion with the new client or prospective client, in which you size the other party up as a business prospect (possible sale), and the other party sizes you up as a possible source of help (support service or advisor). The following discussion refers to any occasion on which you and that other party talk business seriously for the first time.

This could be under a wide variety of circumstances, from a casual but extended conversation at some professional or business function such as a conference or convention to a formal, pre-arranged meeting in either one's office. In most cases this first meeting is going to be with a prospective new client because you will not often have made a sale to a new client without a preliminary discussion, usually on a face-to-face basis. It is possible, however, because of the nature of consulting and what you charge for (your time), that some confusion may arise at this first meeting over whether the other person is actually a client or only a prospective client, especially if the meeting is formal, pre-arranged and in the other's office. To put it another way, there may be confusion as to whether you may bill for the time you spend discussing the other's needs and/or diagnosing the possible problem(s). Failure to clarify this and establish the exact nature of your relationship at this early time may cost you money and may even cost you a sale. If, for example, you believe that you have already been retained and are talking to a client on billable time, as distinct from exploring a sales possibility with a prospective client, you may very well waste your time, give away what you normally sell (time and information), and create a dispute that will cost you the sale you might otherwise have had. It is therefore essential that you and the other person have a clear mutual understanding at this first meeting, of the relationship between you.

For example, in a recent case one of the attendees of a seminar I presented invited me to have lunch with him a few days later. At the outset of our lunch he stated quite clearly that he was not trying to get something for nothing, and if I thought that what I said to him over lunch constituted billable consulting, I was to send him a bill, which he would pay. (I chose not to bill him, but if I had, it would not have created any problems between us because of our clear initial understanding.)

There are, however, many people who will "pick your brains"—use your consulting services free of charge—if you permit them to do so. Sometimes the larceny is deliberate, but not always. In many cases, the other party honestly believes that you are willing to give away what appears to be merely conversation. In either case the result is the same; you are "giving the store away."

It is a difficult situation in many ways, especially for the individual who is new to the consulting profession and happens to be an open and outgoing individual. It takes self-discipline and extended self-training to keep in mind always that time and knowledge are the consultant's inventory, and if you give them away, what will you have left to sell? There is an anomaly here, too. In making a presentation, you must generally demonstrate your knowledge and ability, so you must frequently give a little away while being careful not to give too much away. We'll be returning to this problem again later in this discussion and in discussions of proposal writing and of consulting processes, where the problem inevitably resurfaces and must be handled with skill and care if it is to be solved.

RULE NUMBER 2.   Be a Dignified Professional—Always.
What you are selling is essentially your own stature or image as a learned and skilled expert in some specialty. Your success lies largely in how much confidence you can inspire in others, how much respect you command as the professional specialist. The client's confidence in you is as important to your success as the patient's confidence is to the medical practitioner. Therefore, you must manage to strike the proper balance between maintaining a suitable professional dignity and being a stuffed shirt, for appearing to be a pompous ass is as deadly to your image as is being totally without dignity or "unprofessional," as some would put it.

One of my own clients is an executive with a government agency which deals largely in technical work and contracts with many consultants for services, usually with a requirement for a proposal. My client has told me quite plainly that if a proposal appears unprofessional to him in any way, he is immediately prejudiced by this, and is unlikely to do business with that individual. Even if he likes a given proposal, but the proposer conducts himself or herself in some manner my client deems unprofessional during a contract negotiation or related discussion, that negative factor may result in the consultant losing the contract.

Professional dignity, image, decorum, stature—whatever term is applied—is difficult to define precisely, let alone prescribe a formula for. The individual can be jovial, congenial, amiable, even mildly humorous, without losing dignity. It is not necessary to be somber to achieve the proper image. The consultant should be easy for others to talk to and to relax with; a tense prospect is more likely to be mildly hostile than receptive to your sales appeal. Although no one can teach you how to present exactly the right image, here are some general guidelines to help you at least avoid some of the pitfalls.

Dress conservatively. That does not mean that you may not be stylish and well-dressed, or that you must wear "banker's gray" or undertaker's black. But do avoid the extremes of ultra-loud sports clothes and other informal wear. Wear a businesslike outfit, "sensible" shoes, and compatible accessories.

Don't try to be Bob Hope. Above all, do not tell ethnic jokes or racy jokes, if you must tell jokes at all. It is not necessary to be a comedian or a clown, and it is always risky to do so, especially at a first meeting. Be amiable, smile easily and frequently, and if you risk a witticism, be sure it's at your own expense. Do not be dogmatic; do your best to appear knowledgeable, yet open-minded and flexible.

Keep your voice soft and warm. Avoid being loud or appearing to be trying too hard. Try, instead, to radiate quiet self-confidence, without going to the extreme of "coming on strong." Don't brag unnecessarily about how good you are, on the one hand, but don't be too modest, either, for you can't be excessively modest when you are trying to sell something. There is a "trick" to selling the quality of what you do without appearing to be a braggart. Later, in discussing proposal writing, we'll discuss the art of persuasive writing, and there we'll deal with this subject again. But the following covers this topic briefly.

SELLING WITHOUT BRAGGING

Here are three simple "don'ts" which will immediately assist you in mastering the art of telling others how good you are without appearing to brag:

Don't use hyperbole—"millions" of projects, when you really mean a few dozen and expect the listener to understand that you are exaggerating for effect, not for literal reporting.

Don't use superlatives—*most, best, greatest, largest, fastest,* and so forth. They have the same effect as hyperbole; they're rarely believed.

Don't use adjectives and adverbs at all (with permissible exceptions as indicated by following discussion).

The significance of these admonitions will become clearer in a moment as you review the following "do's" and the discussion that follows those:

Do confine yourself principally to nouns and verbs.

Do present reports rather than claims.

Do quantify as much as possible when quantification has impact.

Bragging, at least as far as the prospect's impression is concerned, is what you are doing when you say such things as "You can't find anybody in the whole country who can do as much for you as I can," or "Mine is easily the most effective service available." It's bragging because you are making claims and because you are offering absolutely no evidence. Your claims are totally unsupported, and you are demanding that the prospect just accept your assurances. Consider the difference in impact between the following two statements made to a prospective client:

1. "When I design your system and write your programs, Mr. Murray, you can be sure that they will be more efficient than what you have now."
2. "Mr. Murray, Excelsior Supply said that the system I designed for them reduced their computer time by twelve percent and saved them over thirty-three thousand dollars last year."

Note that the second statement does not furnish absolute proof—Mr. Murray would have to call Excelsior to verify the claim—but neither is it bragging; it's reporting, and it's quantified, not in sweeping, grandiose hyperbole, but in what appears to be precise numbers. That quantification is so persuasive that Mr. Murray is almost sure to accept the report without calling Excelsior (although he may decide to do that, so you must not make claims you can't back up).

Go to meetings and presentations armed with as many *facts* as possible that speak in your favor. It is never bragging, nor is it ever in bad taste, to report facts. Make it your business to learn the facts and compile those that will help you make credible presentations, whenever you must speak face-to-face with clients or prospective clients.

THE MOST IMPORTANT THING YOU CAN DO

It is well accepted that everyone performing a sales function is most effective when also performing a consulting function, that is, every salesperson is or ought to be a consultant, no matter what he or she is actually trying to sell. If you are selling cosmetics, you will sell them far more effectively by taking a sincere interest in the prospect's needs and suggesting cosmetics that will truly help solve a problem.

To be a consultant, in this sense, you must do three things:

1. Learn the prospect's situation, symptoms, desires.
2. Analyze the situation, symptoms, desires, and define the base problem(s).

3. Formulate an approach to a solution by explaining to the prospect how what you offer can meet the need, solve the problem, improve the situation, or otherwise prove helpful.

To put this another way, which may make it easier to grasp the basic idea of being a consultant while selling, you have to provide a useful service by showing the prospect how whatever you are offering can help. For this to be effective, it must be specific rather than general. This is very much along the lines of what we have just discussed—how to put your best foot forward without bragging. One key requirement for being credible is specificity. Don't make vague and generalized statements (such as "I always try to write my programs to use the least amount of computer time") and do make specific, detailed statements (such as "Every program I write is subjected to several screening analyses, one of which is a comparison of alternatives to see which will require the smallest amount of computer time"). This is akin to the difference between using adjectives and using nouns only; there is an almost instinctive skepticism aroused by adjectives, superlatives, hyperbole, and generalities, just as credibility is inspired almost automatically by quantifications, specificity, strong nouns, and strong verbs.

You cannot perform a complete analysis or provide a set of consulting services free of charge in the sales effort. So we come to the problem of how much you can give away when you are actually giving a sample of what you ordinarily sell. The simple answer is, *Just enough to close the sale*, but the real question is, *How much is that?* An answer to that question is, *Just enough to demonstrate that you can provide the necessary help, but not enough to enable the prospect to do it without your help.*

FIRST STEP IN ANALYSIS

Some prospects' needs require nothing more than expert advice, your know-how. That is, armed with your know-how, the prospect can handle the problem without further help from you. In other cases, the theoretical knowledge alone is of little help without the specific services you would provide.

The hazard of giving too much away in demonstrating your capability is far greater in the first case than in the second one. You must therefore probe cautiously if there is a possibility that you are dealing with a situation of the first kind, and be guarded in how much information you part with at no charge. An anecdote will illustrate this:

In my work as a marketing consultant, I am called on frequently to assist a client in writing a proposal or, in some cases, to write it entirely my-self. There are also cases where I am called on by a client simply for help in analyzing the requirement and deciding on a basic proposal strategy.

In such a case, when I am sitting in the offices of a prospective new client reviewing the proposal solicitation, the client expects me to make some observations that will demonstrate that I am capable of suggesting a useful proposal strategy. At the same time, if I say too much before the client has agreed to retain me, I will have suggested the strategy and my services will no longer be of any particular value. I am therefore in that all-too-typical dilemma of how much can I afford to give away?

I will usually suggest only the kind of strategy I believe will be decisive—that is, technical or program strategy, presentation strategy, or cost strategy—without further detail. I might say, for example, something like this:

"It appears to me that the customer here is greatly concerned with costs, yet fearful that the contractor might sacrifice quality for costs. I believe that we can work out a strategy to keep costs low while ensuring that quality will not suffer. I believe I would need [some estimate of hours or days, as appropriate] to develop this for you."

This is one case where, if the prospect tries to push me to go beyond this, I would be deliberately vague and general, pleading, by way of justification, that I need time to work out the answers. I thus make it clear to the prospect that I will offer nothing more unless I am retained, while I turn my attention to pressing for the sale (probably a close here).

If you are facing the alternative situation—one in which it is the specialized services you can perform that are of the essence—you can usually afford to be a bit less guarded in how much theoretical information you give away. In that situation, the information is of correspondingly less importance in making the sale except as it helps convince the customer that the services you provide are the ones he needs. Bear this in mind as you offer information, so that the information you offer is designed to persuade the prospect of the need for your help, as well as of your technical/professional abilities.

PRICING

At some point a prospect invariably asks, "How much?" Conventional wisdom in the field of selling says that a smart salesperson never volunteers a price, but always waits for the prospect to ask the price, since that, in itself, can be useful information. Here are three general truths about prospects asking the price:

The prospect who asks the price almost immediately,before learning anything of what you offer and what it can do for him or her, is generally price-shopping. That means that this prospect already has a pretty good idea of what you are offering and what its potential value is, and has already talked to one or more competitors. Or it may mean that the prospect simply can't afford the service, but is still probing, almost desperately, for that remote possibility of finding someone who will work much more cheaply than the others.

The prospect who asks the price only after listening to your presentation, asking interested questions, and discussing different related matters with you, is probably a serious prospect who can be sold.

The prospect who listens to your presentation with obvious boredom or disinterest and asks no questions or makes no comments, is merely being polite, even in asking the price. You are probably wasting your time if you pursue the sales effort further. (The prospect who fits this description is, however, unlikely even to ask the price. He or she just isn't that interested.)

When a client asks the price after exhibiting sincere interest, it's a good signal for an effort to consummate the sale if you have by that time covered all the points you believe necessary to the close. There is a simple test for that—your ability to answer the inquiry as to price, that is, if you have gathered enough information and done enough discussing to have arrived at an estimate of the amount of time and other expense to do the job. If you have not, however, the question is premature and needs to be responded to differently. Conventional wisdom is that a salesperson should never quote a price, not even in response to a specific inquiry as to price, until ready to close. A premature price quotation, according to this principle, is likely to destroy the possibility of making the sale. This reasoning hypothesizes that the prospect's attention is diverted to price rather than to potential benefits and this may be fatal to the sales effort.

In the case of quoting consulting services, there is first the matter of the consultant's *rate*—hourly, daily, or other—and second, the total price, which must take into account the amount of time the consultant estimates as required as well as any other expenses. One way to defer quoting a price, if the question comes up prematurely, is to observe that you'll be quite pleased to quote as soon as you have gathered enough information, but that you need just a few more minutes. Even if the prospect asks specifically for your rate, you can postpone answering the question in the same manner by observing that a flat quotation of your rate is really not at all helpful in determining what the total cost will be, because once you have gathered all the data, you'll be able to work out the most efficient way to organize the project. It is usually not difficult then to persuade the prospect to wait a few minutes for a quotation.

HOW TO QUOTE PRICES

Even in today's grossly inflated economy, many prospects find a quotation of several hundred dollars a day or even of $75 an hour somewhat shocking. Inflation has ballooned prices so rapidly in the past several years that most of us are still having trouble adjusting our thinking to the new scales. Therefore, when a prospect asks, "What's your daily rate?" a casual answer of, "Five hundred" sometimes sends the prospect into near-shock. So it is wise to anticipate this and ease the shock. There are several ways consultants do this:

Some believe that quoting $75 an hour is less shocking than quoting $600 a day.

Some quote a figure and follow up immediately with an explanation that there is never a premium charge for overtime or holidays, or that the daily rate means for a day which may well run over 8 hours without penalty to the client.

Some prefer to quote a relatively low rate, but charge overtime premiums for hours over 8 in a day or 40 in a week, for holidays, for weekends, and for anything other than the normal business day. The question is therefore answered by quoting the relatively low hourly rate without elaborating as to the other matters.

Some think it best to quote for the entire effort if they have been able to work out an estimate of time required and can guarantee this as a firm fixed price.

Some offer to submit a written estimate and try to defer all pricing information until they have time to study the thing and reach a conclusion as to best pricing strategy.

A few consultants have sliding scales and offer different rates for different clients and different situations. For example, some will offer a lower rate per day or per hour for extended assignments, such as several weeks rather than a few days. I once offered a special, lower rate to minority-owned firms, on the theory that most of them were struggling to get established. (I found it impractical and eventually abandoned the practice, although I continued to be generous in calculating the time I charged to minority entrepreneurs, with probably the same net effect. However, it did away with the problem of having more than one basic rate.)

WHERE TO CONDUCT INITIAL INTERVIEWS

Your first contact with a prospect is frequently at some event, such as a meeting or convention; a telephone call from the prospect as a result of a recommendation; or a telephone call to the prospect as a result of a lead that came along in one manner or another. Often the question of "your office or mine?" comes up. If the prospect is coming to your city from some other place, you will have to either receive the prospect at your office or arrange a meeting somewhere else—possibly a hotel lobby, a cocktail lounge, or someone else's office. Barring that, however, it is usually a better practice to call on the prospect at his/her offices. This is usually most convenient and comfortable for the prospect. (In any meeting or exchange the person behind his/her own desk has a psychological advantage, feeling more secure and more dominant when you are on his/her own grounds. That is likely to work out to your advantage in terms of closing a sale.)

The prospect may suggest lunch, or you may have suggested it. Don't fight the prospect over the check. Whoever suggested or invited the other to lunch would normally expect to pick up the check. If the prospect is putting up a real fight to pick up the check, however, don't contest it. For some people, losing such a contest is a put-down and is resented, whereas it is a distinct feeling of success to win such a contest.

The question of whether to have a drink at lunch troubles some people in business. I have never known it to harm a business relationship but I have heard others report different experiences. I therefore recommend only that you use your own best judgment, and if you do drink at lunch, confine yourself to only one or, at most, two. If you drink enough to loosen your tongue too much, you will almost surely lose the sale.

THINGS THAT SHOULD BE SETTLED AT FIRST MEETING

One of the things that causes the greatest amount of trouble, and in extreme cases may easily lead to business failure, is failure to reach a complete understanding with your prospect and soon-to-be new client. Amazing though it may seem, again and again consultants undertake assignments without having established precisely what they have pledged themselves to do and/or exactly how much they are to get for their services.

Clients are guilty also of agreeing to projects without clear understanding of the agreement and then, of course, there are problems between consultant and client. Nor is the contract per se an answer to this problem, for a contract is merely a documentation of the agreement. If the agreement is not clear, the fact of a written document will not clarify it.

The problem arises all too often because the consultant, eager to make the sale, operates on assumptions or wishful thinking rather than pinning the client down on specific points before agreeing to start work. This matter comes up again when dealing with proposals, but often a consultant is hired to provide services without the formality of a proposal. This matter will be covered once again in connection with contracts. When consultant and client reach the point where they have agreed to do business together, it is essential that the business relationship be crystal clear in both qualitative and quantitative terms. The best way to settle disputes is to prevent them by being absolutely specific about what the consultant is to do and what the client is to pay.

Here are some of the points about which there should be no confusion; definitions are usually necessary, depending on the nature of the work and the contracting arrangement:

Precise number (maximum and/or minimum) of hours, days, or other units of time allowable

Precise costs, either in fixed price or unit rates

Allowable other costs, such as per diem, travel, printing, postage, or whatever is relevant

Precise end-product required and agreed to, quantitatively as well as qualitatively

Scheduling commitments

What each party, consultant and client, must do (In some cases, client must agree to use of certain facilities, reviews, other such cooperation.)

Contingencies—what alternatives are, if some of foregoing run into difficulties

Liquidation, if signatories are to have options to terminate

It is rare that all of the above are relevant and need to be spelled out, but these are some of the kinds of matters about which conflicts can arise. These should be considered when getting down to specific agreement in meeting with the new prospect, not necessarily so that each can be made an item in a formal, written contract, but so that the two parties may be sure that they understand each other and are in basic agreement on who is to do what. While you are yet consultant and prospective new client, everything is still open for discussion and agreement, but once you have reached agreement and you are consultant and new client, it is too late to discuss these matters. They were agreed to, and discussion of them now may lead to amendment of the contract (verbal or written), but it may also lead to dispute, something that neither party really wants. So it is important to settle all these matters now, in the consultant-prospect stage. The success of the project, the business relationship between you and your client, and any future business relationships probably depend heavily on how well this first project goes, and that is likely to depend heavily on the quality of the understanding.

INITIAL MEETING WITH NEW CLIENT

Most of what we have discussed has been on the assumption that you are meeting for the first time with a prospective new client, so that much of what you do and do not do is directed to advancing the probability of making a sale. But there will be cases of closing a sale or getting an assignment without ever having actually met the new client or, at least, without having had a chance to do much more than be introduced to each other and shake hands. Even so, at least some of what has been presented in the past few pages is appropriate to the first meeting, but not all of it since the basic purpose of a first meeting with a new client is quite different from that of a first meeting with a new prospective client. Where it is your purpose to sell your services to a prospect, in a first meeting with a new client you have already made the sale and are trying to get the project off the ground. Where you have tried to analyze the prospect's situation and customize your services to the prospect's needs, you are trying to analyze the client's situation so that you can devise and conduct the most efficient consulting service possible.

It is possible that you are already familiar with the client's problem as a result of the earlier analyses and sales effort, although that will not always be the case. However, it is rare that you do not need a kickoff meeting with a new client, for the objective of the analysis is entirely different now. When the other party was still a prospect, you were analyzing the situation to find ammunition for your sales effort; now you are trying to decide on the most effective approach to satisfying the client's needs.

THE KICKOFF MEETING

No matter how much preliminary discussion there was, and despite the written explanations of need issued by the client and the proposal submitted by the consultant, both parties generally feel the need for a kickoff meeting once they have agreed to do business together and the client has contracted for the consultant's services. Details that seemed relatively unimportant before a contract existed must now be settled. Minor objections the client had to certain things the consultant proposed must now be surfaced and resolved. Now the client must pass on to the consultant everything he or she knows and can suggest, and the consultant must sound out the client on many matters of procedure. Sometimes the client wants the consultant to provide a revised schedule and description of certain functions; sometimes the consultant simply wants the client to affirm the originally agreed-upon schedules and procedures. In any case, the initial meeting after reaching agreement on doing business together clears the air and provides the launching pad for the project.

7

Proposal Writing: A Vital Art

It is abundantly clear that when proposals are required of those competing for contracts, it is the best proposal writers, but not necessarily the best performers or most qualified proposers, who win the contracts.

SOME USEFUL BACKGROUND ORIENTATION

A few years ago, a sales proposal was little more than a price quotation. A proposal simply listed or described what was to be done or delivered (usually citing or reproducing customer-supplied specifications, if the proposal was to provide some set of services or construct something to custom requirements), presented the costs, and stipulated some basic contract requirements. (In many cases, the latter was a "boilerplate," or standard, form.) Even today, a customer sometimes calls for proposals but actually requires little more than that described here when the contract is for some standard construction work or sale and installation of equipment. More and more, however, the concept of what is termed a proposal is patterned on the model of what federal government agencies require when they request proposals. When a prospective client, whether a government agency at any level, a nonprofit institution of some sort, or a profit-centered corporation, asks for a proposal from a consultant, the request is invariably for something more comprehensive than a price quotation and set of contract terms. Therefore, the guidelines, models, and recommendations made in this chapter are generally appropriate to all proposal requests the consultant is likely to receive from any prospective client, and even from foreign governments, which often issue what they refer to as "tenders," rather than "requests for proposals" (RFPs), as we are more likely to do in the United States. (Foreign governments and foreign organizations are often far less demanding in what they wish to see in a proposal than are American government agencies and companies. Experience has demonstrated that responding to foreign tenders as though they were American RFPs is quite effective in winning new business.)

WHY PROPOSALS ARE REQUESTED

The organization issuing an RFP is sending out some implicit messages by the mere action of issuing an RFP, aside from what the words of the work statement and other documentation say:

> We need help of some kind. (See contents for details.)
>
> We are seeking the most qualified proposers and/or best plans, programs, prices, and/or other considerations.
>
> We want you to study our needs as we describe them here and give us your best opinion as to what we ought to do and what you propose to do for us, along with your qualifications for doing the job and the evidence that yours is the best plan for us.

That sums up what the prospective client is trying to achieve in issuing an RFP. Price is only one of many factors, and a low price is no inducement if there is no persuasive evidence that the program will achieve all its objectives satisfactorily. Price will be a factor, but it is of lesser importance than a number of other factors such as quality, reliability, timeliness, and effectiveness of the program.

The mere act of RFP issuance tells you that the prospective client (hereafter called the "customer" for ease of reference) needs help to decide who is the best contractor for the customer's purposes. Procurement regulations, even in a privately-owned corporation, may mandate that an RFP be issued and proposals evaluated in this situation. That does not, however, change the fact that the purpose of the request is to solicit from prospective contractors their proposed plans or programs and their own credentials or qualifications. Since the customer's judgment as to which proposer appears to be the best-suited for the project is based on what the proposal says, it is clear that proposal-writing skill is one of the most important marketing skills. (In a great many cases, it is far and away the single most important marketing skill, the principal factor in the success of many technical/professional services organizations.)

BASIC ELEMENTS OR INGREDIENTS OF AN RFP

A request for proposals generally has four elements, usually along these lines:

A letter explaining who is the issuer, when proposals are due and where they are to be delivered or sent, whom to call if questions arise, and what contractual arrangement is envisioned

Information about what should be in the proposal, how it will be evaluated, any special admonitions or advice deemed necessary, and sometimes one or more forms to be filled out and signed, including quite frequently (especially if the request is from a government agency or some large corporation) special forms on which to record cost estimates or prices.

Some standard (boilerplate) information relating to the issuer's regulations, contract terms, method for invoicing, and other data regarding how the issuer proposes to do business under the impending contract.

A statement of work, describing the customer's problem(s) and/or requirement(s) which are the reason for issuing the request for proposals. This statement is supposedly a complete description in enough detail to enable the proposer to analyze the customer's stated problem(s)/need(s) and devise a proposed program that reacts suitably to the solicitation.

KINDS OF INFORMATION AN RFP CALLS FOR

To fulfill its mission of discovering which contractor has the best program and best qualifications and ought therefore to be awarded the contract, the customer organization wants these specific kinds of information in most proposals:

> An analysis and/or discussion of the stated requirement to demonstrate that the proposer does, indeed, fully understand the customer's need or problem, knows how to go about developing a fully detailed program that will solve the problem(s)/satisfy the requirement(s).
>
> A preliminary program design or approach, with sufficient explanation to demonstrate the suitability of this design or approach.
>
> A specific proposed program, with adequate details of staffing, organization, schedules, end-products, interim products, procedures, management, quality control, and whatever the proposer deems important enough to merit specific discussion in the proposal. (These vary with different requirements.) Cost estimates must often be in great detail.
>
> The proposer's qualifications to carry out the proposed program successfully. This includes knowledge, skill, facilities, and any other resources necessary for success in the proposed project.

Depending on the size of the RFP—which, in turn, depends on the size of the project—the above factors may be spelled out in multi-page detail or they may be summarized briefly. A small project, perhaps a $2,000 or $5,000 project, may be described in a one- or two-page statement of work and call for a single for-the-job price rather than a detailed cost analysis, and require a simple proposal consisting of only two or three pages. (This is often referred to as "letter proposal" because it is informal and actually contained in a letter.) A project running into many millions may well call for an RFP which is actually a cartonful of manuals and reports, perhaps 5,000 pages of material, requiring a multi-volume proposal, often with an entire volume devoted to costs alone. Projects of this size are beyond the scope of this book and are mentioned for information only. The proposals you are expected to become involved in producing are likely to range from letter proposals of a few pages each to, at most, proposals of 25 to 50 pages, and even then a large portion of those pages essentially duplicates other materials you use.

WHAT IS A PROPOSAL?

It may seem unnecessary, after all this discussion, to pose the question of what a proposal is; have we not already answered that question? In fact, we have and we haven't. We have answered it partially and generally from only the customer's viewpoint, as a source of information to help the customer make a determination. But we have not truly answered the question from the proposer's viewpoint, your viewpoint as a consultant writing a proposal in the hope of making a sale. From your viewpoint you must regard the proposal as a sales presentation. Bear these factors in mind as we explore the development of proposals in greater depth:

> With only an occasional exception, there is only one winner in a contract competition. All the others are losers, and coming in second is no better than coming in last.

> It is not enough to demonstrate that you can do a good job. So can all other proposers, presumably, so that isn't a basis for awarding you the contract. You must be better than good.

> It is unrealistic to expect the customer to perceive that the plan you propose and the qualifications you describe are superior. You have to explain why your proposed program designs and approaches are superior, and why your own qualifications are superior. In short, you must do more than present your program and qualifications; you must sell them. That is truly what a proposal is all about, and a proposal is successful only if and when it does sell.

PROPOSAL SITUATIONS

The most common situation that leads to proposal writing is that of an organization reacting to a felt need by inviting all interested parties to submit proposals. The basic situation here is one of competition with other consultants. Presumably, one of you is going to win the contract. (I say "presumably" because there have been occasions when the customer was not pleased with any of the proposals submitted and therefore simply cancelled the procurement.) Ordinarily, you know nothing about the procurement until the organization announces it, either by sending you a bid set (if you are on their bidders list) or by advertising the requirement in some medium you read. At that point, you review the requirement and decide whether you will submit a proposal. This, however, is not the only situation that leads to proposal writing; there are at least two others.

One comes about when you know something about the customer and decide you have an answer for one of the customer's problems. Or when you believe that you have something of value to offer the customer and choose to do it via a proposal rather than some other means of presentation. This is often referred to as an "unsolicited" proposal because the customer did not initiate the action; the proposer did.

Another situation can easily come about as a result of your having made some sort of oral presentation to a prospective client. You may have met the other party at some event, and during the course of conversation discovered the existence of a problem for which you have the solution. Or it may result simply from a routine sales call you made. In either case, it is not uncommon to the consulting industry to have an interested prospect say something along the lines of, "That's an interesting idea. Why don't you send me a proposal, and I'll consider it seriously."

Even in the course of doing small consulting jobs, it is quite common for prospects to ask for something on paper, usually meaning a rather informal letter proposal.

WHOM MUST YOU SELL?

Interestingly enough, you are often asked to submit a proposal even when you have thoroughly convinced your prospect that what you offer is worth buying. The prospect may not call it a proposal, but may say some such thing as, "Write this up in a letter to me, won't you?" It is often not despite but because of convincing your prospect that you are asked for that informal proposal. The reason is simply that the prospect may need to get approval internally or the organization may require "a piece of paper" to back up a requisition and generate an order for anything.

This has happened to me in federal agencies as well as in privately-held companies. Having essentially made the sale in discussion with the executive, I have followed up with a letter proposal describing what I am going to do and what it will cost. The executive abstracts from my letter proposal a brief description of the requirement, and that is entered into his requisition and into the purchase order which is ultimately issued. Without my letter proposal, the executive has a most difficult time doing his own paperwork and getting the purchase order or contract issued.

There have been numerous cases in which the prospect has needed my proposal to explain the project to whoever must give approval in the organization and to get the approval. Therefore, I have often found it necessary to do the entire selling job in my proposal despite the fact that my prospect is already sold. In short, I am arming him to sell it "upstairs" in his company.

There are, therefore, truly no situations in which a proposal ought to be anything other than a sales presentation. It is futile to design a fine program and then fail to sell it. And the principles of selling are not different in proposals than they are in any other kind of sales presentation. It is always necessary to give the customer reasons for buying from you rather than from someone else and for buying your proposed program rather than someone else's. The basic appeal is the promise of certain beneficial results. Ordinarily a proposal is an effort to sell competitively. That is, typically in proposal situations, and invariably when the customer has asked for proposals, there is a customer who wants to buy, and you are not trying to persuade the customer to buy the service per se but rather to buy the service from you rather than from one of your competitors. It's important to make that distinction in your mind so that you focus your sales arguments appropriately and address the right objective in your proposal. When the opposite situation prevails and you are volunteering a proposal in the hope of selling what you offer on a sole-source basis, keep that distinction clearly in mind, too. As in all selling, you must try to view the situation from the customer's perspective. In one case the customer is being asked to decide between buying and not buying; in the other case, it is a question of buying one offered plan versus buying another offered plan.

Again and again proposal writers make the mistake of failing to understand or remember that difference. They waste time persuading the customer of a need the customer has already become convinced of instead of focusing on the special virtues and advantages of their own proposed program or services versus those of anyone else.

PUBLIC- VERSUS PRIVATE-SECTOR PROPOSALS

What must be in a proposal in terms of customer-dictated requirements is not always the same as what must be in a proposal in terms of necessary sales arguments. There are certain distinctions, particularly between the proposals requested by private industry and those requested by government. One reason for this—and one of the chief distinctions in general between procurement by private industry and procurement by government organizations—is that various statutes apply to and exercise some control over governmental procurement. The best models for proposal requests and responses are those of the federal government agencies, and they will be used as examples here. As far as possible, those features and characteristics which are to be found primarily in the government models will be pointed out as such. So do not assume that when a private-sector organization requests a proposal the request will include all the typical requirements explained here.

However, those elements that must be in a proposal to persuade the customer to buy from you are as important in one case as in the other. The public and private sector organizations and their special requirements differ, but each employs humans motivated and influenced by the same appeals. The sales arguments that are effective in one sector are effective in the other.

One of the basic differences between the two sectors in proposal requirements is this: In the private sector, when a customer requests a proposal, the request is made on the assumption that anyone offering their goods or services is properly qualified and equipped to do so. The government proposal demands that the proposer prove his or her own competence, facilities, experience, resources, and whatever else will demonstrate that he or she can handle the requirement capably.

What this means is that the customer is evaluating not only the merits of the program you propose versus the merits of competitive programs, but also your credentials versus the credentials of your competitors. You find invariably in the RFPs issued by federal government agencies a requirement to present your qualifications as individual practitioners (professional resumes of staff) and as an organizational entity (even if you are a single person).

Today, even private-sector organizations tend to request such information, but whether they do or not, it is excellent sales strategy to include this information. If you fail to do so, and your competitors do include such information, they are certain to enjoy an immediate advantage over you.

One reason government agencies ask for such information is that they are required by procurement regulation, which has the force of law, to make an objective evaluation of each proposal, and each proposer's qualifications is one area of specific evaluation.

THE EVALUATION SYSTEM

The procurement regulations do not suggest precisely how a federal agency must evaluate proposals, except in general terms. For one thing, technical proposals must be entirely free of price information so that they may be evaluated on the basis of their adjudged technical merit. Those evaluating technical proposals are not permitted to see or learn the contents of the cost proposals, which are separate documents, secured by the contracting official of the agency until the technical evaluation is completed. Only then, when all technical proposals have been awarded specific point scores (usually on the basis of 100 points maximum) does price become a factor in the evaluation.

Because the regulations are rather general, evaluation systems vary enormously from agency to agency. The proposer is entitled to know generally how the proposals will be evaluated in any given competition, but the variance is so great as to provide a basis for proposal strategies in some cases, whereas the evaluative criteria listed in another case may bring little but confusion to the proposer's search for strategies. Here are examples of typical evaluation criteria which you can encounter, and which illustrate the wide range of specificity:

1. The following are the criteria on which proposals will be evaluated. Item (a) has twice the value of Item (b), which has one half the value of Item (c)

    Item (a): Understanding and approach.

    Item (b): Qualifications of proposed staff.

    Item (c): Qualifications of organization as an organization.

    Award will be made to that proposer whose proposal is deemed to be in the best interests of the government, costs and other factors considered.

2. Evaluation criteria are as follows:

(a) Understanding of the problem:	0 to 5 points
(b) Practicality of approach:	0 to 10 points
(c) Evidence of realistic anticipation of problems and planning for contingencies:	0 to 10 points
(d) Proposed management and organization:	0 to 10 points
(e) Qualifications of proposed staff:	0 to 25 points
(f) Qualifications of organization:	0 to 25 points
(g) Resources offered:	0 to 15 points
Maximum possible points:	100 points

In some cases, evaluation criteria are even more greatly detailed than in Example (2) above, with blocks of text explaining each factor and even showing subordinate elements making up the various evaluation factors and range of weights possible for each. In some cases, costs are assigned specific weights as well instead of being part of a general, final consideration. Aside from that general "costs and other factors considered," so often found in government RFPs to explain how costs are evaluated, there are two basic systems for weighting costs on a more objective scale:

In some cases, costs are simply assigned a weight, such as 0 to 25 points. That means that the proposer with the highest cost is assigned zero for costs, while the proposer with the lowest cost earns 25 points. All other proposed costs are prorated between the extremes, those extremes thereby establishing the reference standard or scale.

A somewhat more sophisticated method consists of dividing the costs proposed by the technical score awarded the technical proposal, to ascertain a cost per technical point, with the objective of awarding the contract to the proposer achieving the lowest cost per technical point. To make this workable, however, it is necessary to confine this competition to those proposers whose technical proposals are in the competitive range, which means those whose proposals are technically acceptable to the agency. Both systems make it possible for someone scoring below the top technically to wind up with the best overall score, where low price compensates for lower rating technically. In both cases the evaluation is comparative rather than absolute. This is a point that many proposal writers miss.

The presentation of an allegedly objective evaluation leads many to the mistaken belief that the evaluation points are awarded against an absolute scale. They are not because they cannot be. Take, for example, the qualifications of a proposed staff as a factor. If the maximum is 15 points, that suggests that the proposal offering the perfect staff would earn 15 points. But how can that be? Who is to make that judgment and how can it be made? Inevitably, the evaluators will award 15 points for that proposed staff they consider to be the best of those offered, and all others will be rated in comparison. In short, proposals are necessarily evaluated by comparison with each other, and that means that it is always important to consider whom the competition is and how you compare with your competitors in all areas.

Even when proposal requests do not specify evaluation criteria, these factors are influential, and it is often helpful to write your proposal as though you were indeed subject to an objective evaluation.

One other major difference between public- and private-sector proposals is that a private-sector requestor may be as just or unjust as suits his or her desires, whereas public-sector organizations do not have that freedom because they are spending public money and are subject to statutes.

In most cases, and certainly in the case of federal agencies, you have the right of appeal when you believe you are treated unjustly. The first step is an administrative procedure and is called a "protest." You may protest against any irregularity or "defective" procedure. Here are some specific examples:

> Most people think of a protest as something you file after you have lost out in the proposal competition and the contract has been awarded elsewhere. The bulk of protests are, in fact, protests against the award of a contract, made by the losers, who think they were entitled to more consideration. Protests here are frequently based on the protester's claim to have offered the lowest price or an allegation that the party who won was not properly qualified. In most cases these protests are based far more on emotion and disappointment than on fact and logic.
>
> A client who found a procurement announced only a few days before the proposals were due asked for an extension on what appeared to be reasonable grounds of simple fairness and equal opportunity to submit a proposal. Refused by the contracting official, the client protested formally and the extension was granted, as it inevitably had to be under any fair interpretation of the law.
>
> Many announcements of procurement are made with the stipulation that the announcement is for information only because the procurement is to be on a sole-source basis, deemed to be justified. If you believe that this denies you a fair opportunity to bid or propose and you believe that the justification is unwarranted, you are free to challenge it with a protest. (Many sole-source procurements are unjustified but go unchallenged.)
>
> You may challenge by protest just about anything you believe inequitable—evaluative standards and criteria, provisions or requirements in RFPs, and all other details.

There are two ways to file a protest: You can write a letter of protest to the contracting official of the agency whose action or solicitation you are protesting, being sure that you make it plain that yours is a formal protest calling for action and not merely an expression of opinion, or you can address that letter to the Comptroller General of the United States in his capacity as the head of the General Accounting Office (GAO), an agency of the Legislative Branch of the government. It costs you nothing but your time, and you do not need legal counsel. GAO will respond, advising you of the next steps. Even if the decision goes against you, you are still free to sue in federal courts if you choose to. This administrative procedure does not compromise your legal rights and options in any way.

These are the major differences between proposal requirements and options in the public and private sectors, although there are likely to be many minor differences. If you have doubts, the requirements made by federal government agencies for proposals are the most comprehensive, hence the ones least likely to lead you astray. By following those practices and procedures, you may be providing far more information than is required, but that is certainly preferable to not providing enough. I offer the following ideas, suggestions, guidance, and recommendations as appropriate to all proposal requirements where you do not have specific reason to believe that they are inappropriate.

FORMAT AND GENERAL RATIONALE

In some cases, an RFP mandates a specific format for your proposal when you are responding to a specific request for proposals. It is wise to comply completely with the instructions furnished. In practice, this is the exception, and RFPs call for certain information but rarely dictate how the proposal is to be organized and presented. Where you are submitting a proposal of your own volition, the choice of format and organization of contents is entirely yours, although it is often helpful to ask whomever you are dealing with in the customer organization if there is any preference or suggested format. Unless you have a preprinted, boiler-plate proposal that you send out generally, you should not undertake the writing and submittal of any unsolicited proposal without advance preparation and arrangement with someone in the customer organization.

The following is an outline I have found to be appropriate for almost all cases, and proposals written in this format have produced many contracts. The titles are generic, to indicate the content of the section or chapter generally. Later, we'll take up the matter of specific titles for the sections or chapters.

Section I. Introduction

Divided into two subsections, one introducing you and offering your qualifications in summary, with the notation that details of your qualifications will be presented later; the second subsection summarizing the customer's problem or requirement as you understand or interpret it, in your own words, and serving as scene-setting for the next section.

Section II: Discussion

The conclusion of Section I was the cue for this section, which begins to explore the customer's problem or requirement in depth and scope. The objectives in this section are these: To demonstrate conclusively that you do understand the customer's problem/requirement, possibly better even than he does; to show that you have the necessary technical knowledge, familiarity with the field, experience, and creative imagination to handle the problem/requirement satisfactorily; to show that you have analyzed and reasoned matters out and arrived at the best possible approach; to present that approach with the rationale that proves it best (that, in fact, *sells* it by explaining exactly why it is better than anything others can offer); to introduce whatever major factor(s) you believe will make the critical difference in making this sale; and to introduce the specific proposed program which will follow this section.

Section III: Proposed Program

Everything that has gone before has been preparation for this section, where you are going to be specific and detailed, quantitatively as well as qualitatively. The program you describe here must be that which you promised and "proved" most appropriate in the previous section. There you included a prescription; here you fill the prescription. As appropriate to the situation, this section should include some or all of the following specifications: How the project is to be organized, how staffed, by whom staffed, how managed, procedures to be employed, quality control, cost control, schedules, descriptions of interim- and/or end-products, resumes of proposed staff. It may include a project organization chart if the project requires the services of a multi-member staff, a milestone chart, and other details. The overall objective is to be as detailed and specific as possible. The previous section was heavily sales-oriented, but a large part of the sales burden rests on this section, too.

Section IV: Experience and Qualifications

This section is devoted to demonstrating that the organizational entity is highly qualified, experienced, has the necessary resources and track record to do the job dependably, and is a thoroughly responsible contractor. Names of references help here, too.

These are the basic sections of a standard proposal format, but they are not all the elements of the proposal. In addition to these, most proposals have at least some of the following (with the exception of letter proposals, which offer similar information, but in much abbreviated, informal presentation):

Front Matter:
Copy of letter of transmittal
Title page
Foreword, abstract, or executive summary
Table of contents
Appendices or "Exhibits":
Complete text of reports or articles referred to in main text
Samples from prior projects
Detailed explanations, not appropriate to main text
Other information of interest only to some anticipated proposal readers

GENERAL IMPACT A PROPOSAL MUST HAVE

Bear in mind that vague generalizations are never convincing or persuasive. Whether the prospect reasons it out consciously or not, every prospect is at least subconsciously aware that anyone can make vague observations and general promises, but you have to truly know what you are doing and what you are talking about to be absolutely specific. It is not surprising then, that specifics are far more believable than generalities.

The overall concept in the proposal format just presented is based precisely on that truism. Throughout the proposal, an effort is made to be as specific and objective as possible. Minimize the use of adjectives and adverbs and stick with the nouns and verbs. Never use approximations when you can offer exact figures and exact quotations. Never use guesses when you can make estimates. Never round off numbers; use the most exact number you can, even if you have arrived at it by estimate. That is, if you have used some formula to estimate and the formula produces a result of 186,793, don't round it off to 190,000, or even to 187,000; report 186,793 as your best estimate. Otherwise, the customer may assume that you are guessing rather than actually estimating, and will be sure that you are stacking your guess in a way most favorable to your own purposes.

Always appear scientific and objective. Always be as positive as possible. Never use such phrases as "may tend to indicate . . . " Say "indicates." It says the same thing, but is far less redolent of hesitancy and uncertainty.

If you appear uncertain, your reader is certainly not going to feel very confident in what you say.

The proposal format recommended here is designed to build to a climax of detail and specificity. It begins with a general understanding of the customer's problem or requirement, with even that made as specific as it can be made in an introductory presentation, and a similarly general introduction to the proposer, with a brief glimpse of the proposer's qualifications. It then goes on to discussions which grow steadily more detailed and more specific as they approach the presentation of the specific, detailed program. That, Section III in the format recommended here, is the climax of the proposal, what the proposer (you) specifically proposes to do for the price (which may be contained in another document). That is your promise of what you will do, what results you will achieve, how you will go about it, when you will deliver, and why you are qualified to do the job.

A major worry every contracting officer and purchasing agent shares (and this includes every manager who is buying something, whether formally a contracting or procurement official or not) is this: Will this contractor or supplier deliver satisfactory products or services on schedule? Costs cannot be the first consideration in many kinds of procurement; absolute assurance of performance is often more important than lowest cost.

This means that the customer must have faith in you. You must manage to persuade that prospective client that you are not only technically and professionally competent to do the job, but are a reliable contractor as well. In effect, every proposal tries to offer evidence of

1. An attractive, practical program that appears well suited to do the job
2. Complete technical competence and all necessary resources to execute the program properly
3. Absolute reliability and responsibility, virtual guarantees of carrying out the program conscientiously and unfailingly

Customers will inevitably evaluate you on all these grounds, and weakness in any may cost you the contract. But note this carefully: The weakness that costs you the contract may be apparent but not real. We are talking again about the customer's perception. If you appear to be weak in one of these areas because you have failed to make your strength plainly apparent, the effect is just as deadly as though you were, in fact, weak in that area. Here is an example of that:

An organization in Phoenix, Arizona, had been one of the contractors to the Department of Commerce's Minority Business Development Agency (MBDA) for several years. Each year this organization responded to MBDA's RFP and won another year's contract. After about four years they found themselves beaten by another firm, and they protested. The agency explained to them that a major weakness in their proposal was their failure to fully explain their experience and track record in the work.

"But you know us and what we do," the organization complained to MBDA. "After all, we've been your contractor for years."

They were shocked to learn that under the law, MBDA proposal evaluators could not credit them for anything that was not specifically stated in their proposal. The 10 points they lost in their technical score was fatal, even though they were well qualified.

STRATEGY

Over 20 years of experience with proposals has convinced me that successful proposals are most often those based on specific, well-thought-out strategies. Again and again, I have seen the "dark horse proposer," the one the customer and the competitors had never even heard of before, upset the cart for those who thought they would win easily, because the dark horse candidate tried harder and worked at developing a winning strategy and implemented it well in proposals. All sales and marketing effort ought to be based on specific strategies, but proposals even more so because each is an individual, custom requirement, and the customer is often all but pleading in the proposal request for help in choosing a winner. If you read RFPs carefully and between the lines, you will hear customers begging you, "Don't stop at describing and explaining your program to me; *sell* it to me. Make me understand why I need it, why it is better than any possible other program. Give me what I need to choose you as the winner."

Sometimes I have heard neophytes, working at possibly the first proposal they have ever attempted, mumble as they pore over the RFP, "I wonder what they really want." Such proposal writers have the feeling that the issuer of the RFP is playing some kind of game in which the proposal writer must guess at what the customer really wants, with the contract-prize going to the proposal writer who guesses correctly.

If that is sometimes the case, it is by chance and not by conscious design on the part of the customer. It may well be a "Eureka!" situation, in which the customer reads a proposal and exclaims, "That's it! That's it exactly!" as the proposal explains what the customer really did not understand when the RFP was issued. If you are fortunate enough and clever enough to offer a proposal to a customer that results in such a reaction, you are likely to win the contract. Many RFPs and their work statements are most unclear and vague, leaving the reader somewhat confused as to just what the customer wants or needs. When that is the case, it is almost always because the customer doesn't really know any more than the RFP and "SOW" (statement of work) impart. That is often why a consultant is invited to submit a proposal—because the customer is well aware of the need for help, perhaps even help in diagnosing the symptoms and identifying the problem. Perhaps the customer believes that the RFP/SOW do describe the problem, when in fact they are describing symptoms.

If you are to devise an effective strategy and stand a reasonable chance of winning the contract, it is critically important that you analyze and understand the basic situation. Decide first of all whether the customer understands and has identified the problem or requirement accurately, or is being misled and confused by symptoms and distractions. Having done that, work next at deciding what the customer's real need is. In some cases you may be able to make a good estimate of what the true problem is from what the SOW says. In other cases you may decide that it is not possible to identify the problem without doing some actual consulting first.

A first step in development of a proposal strategy is painstaking analysis of the requirement, as described by the customer, to arrive at an opinion as to which of the following best describes the basic situation:

1. The customer has a good and probably accurate understanding of the actual problem or requirement.

2. The customer all but admits that what are described are probably symptoms and that the contractor will have to discover what the problem or requirement is and what to do about it.

3. The customer claims or professes to know what the problem or requirement is, but is probably mistaken; it is necessary to discriminate between what the customer thinks the problem is and what the real problem is. ("Problem" also meaning need or requirement.)

Not every RFP calls for services to solve a problem. In many cases the customer simply needs to enhance the in-house capability temporarily with more hands and feet, or to carry out some specialized, one-time project such as doing the initial programming for a new computer just purchased. In such cases as these the RFP generally makes it clear that the customer knows specifically what is needed, and is looking for a proposal making the best offer. Best in this case may mean price, technical competence, schedule, or other things; it is necessary to study the RFP carefully to decide what "best" means to the customer, and that becomes the basic strategy.

On the other hand, the customer may have a problem but not the faintest idea of what the real problem is. Perhaps the symptoms are late and inaccurate reports from the computer, with the customer admitting that work is needed to find out where the trouble is, as well as how to solve it best.

The customer with the woes of late and inaccurate reports may advise readers of his RFP that he has computer program problems and wants a specialist to straighten them out. Reading the RFP, you may decide that the customer has drawn an entirely unwarranted conclusion, and the reason for the faulty reports may well lie in any of several other possible places. Or the details in the RFP may even convince you that the problem is definitely not related to the computer program, but is related to data forms and data-gathering procedures.

Each of these situations calls for a different strategy. In all cases, it is important to view the program needs from both the customer's viewpoint and the contractor's viewpoint, to try to establish several points:

1. What appears to be the best (fastest, most efficient, least expensive) way to do the job?
2. What prejudices does the customer appear to have about the need?
3. What appears to be most important to the customer? (Cost, schedule, technical approach, staff qualifications, contractor qualifications, working relationship, other?)
4. How do these factors relate to each other? (What incompatibilities exist? How can they be resolved best?)

For example, it may well be that the method you believe to be best for serving the customer's need is directly contrary to what the customer has clearly indicated is of great importance. The RFP may insist on some requirement that adds needless expense to the project, while also insisting that cost is an important consideration. You must have a strategy for coping with this, and there are strategies possible. Each case is an individual problem, to be solved individually, and no solution is possible until you have established clearly where and what the problem is. One strategy is to admit frankly that you perceive a possible anomaly in the customer's stated position, and then offer the customer an option, leaving it to the customer to decide whether you are right but not nullifying the customer's right to proceed according to his desires, regardless of your ideas. Many proposal writers would choose to simply ignore this, if they had indeed conducted an analysis in this depth, and cater to the customer's stated desires and prejudices. The strategy suggested here, however, is likely to disqualify such a proposer as being too superficial or not honest enough. There is a serious risk in neglecting to do this analysis and/or in being less than completely honest in revealing your analysis and professional opinions to the customer.

This is a program or technical strategy, based on whatever you believe is most important to the customer or can be shown to be most important. But it also entails elements of what may be called "presentation strategy" because it includes an effort to capture the customer's interest and favor through making an honest appraisal and recommendation and offering the customer options.

Where cost appears to be a major consideration, perhaps even the most important consideration once capability is established, a cost strategy may be used. There are two possible approaches to cost strategy:

1. Program-design considerations which are aimed specifically at reducing the costs of the program, so that these are program/technical and cost strategy elements.
2. Several methods for *appearing* to be the low-cost proposer or bidder.

Some RFPs call for what contractors refer to as a "laundry list" of services to be performed and/or labor to be supplied. For example, contracts calling for professional engineering services may list several grades of engineers (graded according to years of experience and academic degrees, for example), draftsmen, and designers, and may call for original design, redesign, reverse engineering, and value engineering. The bidder or proposer is asked to list standard rates for each of these on some unit basis such as hours. Frequently, a bit of investigation will reveal that the customer rarely if ever calls for one or more of those services or classes of labor. In responding to this RFP, then, it is possible to "low-ball" those services and labor classes, taking the relatively slight risk that you may have to supply them occasionally at the quoted low prices, but also all but guaranteeing that you will emerge the apparent low bidder.

In some situations, an experienced contractor can determine that there is a certainty of changes in the work later, after the contract has been awarded and work has begun. Each of these changes requires a negotiation with the contracting official on amendment of prices. Experienced contractors have long since learned that it is worthwhile to "buy in"—win the contract by bidding a breakeven or even a below-cost price—because they can recover everything and turn a profit in negotiating the changes later. (Construction and many other kinds of engineering work, for example, inevitably involve changes during the life of the program.)

There are often proposals which are so deficient in specific information that it becomes almost impossible to estimate the cost. A request to perform a study which will result in a computer program or lengthy report may not furnish the proposal writer enough detail to judge how big that end-product will be, hence what it is likely to cost. Here is an opportunity to devise and employ a cost strategy. The approach is to make a best judgment as to what the simplest and lowest-cost method of performance likely to satisfy the customer's need is, and to so propose. You may also offer the customer options, should he wish to spend more and achieve a more elaborate or larger result. You can offer what appears to be a low price, without taking away the customer's freedom to opt for something greater, more elaborate, and more costly. In fact, you are all but compelled to do this when the RFP is such that pricing becomes most difficult.

There is, finally, the matter of what may be called "capture strategy," that strategy which is expected to be the decisive factor in winning the contract. It is usually coincident with one of the other strategies, and it may even be the sum of all other strategies if you have been unable to reach a conclusion as to what will be most important to the customer and most decisive in directing the customer's decision.

When you are responding to an RFP which spells out the evaluation criteria to be employed, these criteria give you suggestions for strategy evolution by defining what the customer believes to be most important. But don't be misled; often, in government agencies, a group borrows some other agency's RFP format and uses it, with no intention of being ruled precisely by it. That is, the actual evaluation may or may not coincide with what the RFP states. Gather information by every means available to you. Don't depend on the RFP alone, but do study it closely and read it over and over. Most RFPs contain far more information than you can glean in a first reading. You get a bit more information at each reading, some of it quite important.

Don't neglect to read it all, either. In one case the sheaf of "boilerplate," which is usually laid aside and neglected, contained the single clue that enabled the winning proposer to find the winning strategy. It was the customer's own specification of a typed page of manuscript, but it had a great effect on cost.

Don't neglect the presentation strategy, either, for this often determines the success of your other strategies. If you have devised a marvelous technical or program strategy, it can be effective only if it is presented properly, if the customer understands and appreciates it and its overall impact on the whole program. Your presentation—the writing and the physical proposal itself—must get the point across effectively if it is to help.

DO'S AND DON'TS OF PROPOSAL WRITING

A few paragraphs ago you were shown how to handle the impossible-to-price RFP by devising and offering the customer a base program and one or more options to elaborate on that program. The procedure recommended was intended to provide insight into one of several possible cost strategies. However, another reason for handling the problem in the manner indicated has even greater implications.

The reason for being impossible-to-price is usually the failure of the customer to provide detailed specifications. If a customer wants you to propose the development of a training program but fails to specify the medium, the number of hours of material, the number of illustrations, or anything else you need to know to prepare a cost estimate, what should you do?

People who do not know better react by either discarding the RFP (especially if they have other opportunities to respond to) or by calling the customer and asking for more information. In my opinion, both of these are directly counter to your interests, for these reasons:

1. If you discard the RFP, you are quite likely discarding a good opportunity to win a contract. I have always favored the vague RFP over the crystal clear one because I have almost always been more successful in responding to the former type. The reason? Others are discouraged by such RFPs so you almost always have far less competition. You have much more flexibility in your response, as you will soon see, and far greater opportunity to devise effective strategies.

2. If you call the customer and ask questions, two things can happen: The customer may cancel the requirement (I have known this to happen) and may or may not reissue it later; the customer may provide the specification details requested, but they will be sent to all your competitors as well as to you. You may very well give your competitors more help than you got yourself out of those answers. You have certainly thrown away an advantage you could have had.

The most advantageous thing to do is to propose your own specifications with or without options. Sometimes the options are helpful, but the important principle is never to submit a proposal that commits you to anything not quantified. You cannot possibly agree to deliver something of an undefined size for a defined price unless you are truly reckless or quite careless, yet many contractors make this mistake. It leads to disputes later as the customer demands more than you expected to supply, and you've no basis whatsoever to dispute the legitimacy of the demand.

You can combine this kind of situation with the "changes" strategy mentioned earlier. Without mentioning options, you "low-ball" the specification of end-product, hours, or whatever units form the basis for specifications and costs. That is, you offer whatever you believe are the smallest quantities that appear credible for the requirement. If and when it becomes apparent that more is needed, the customer's demand for more becomes a change to be negotiated, and you are legally protected.

Simply make this your rule: No proposal will be submitted in which whatever constitutes units costing money are not clearly specified and quantified. If the customer fails to provide the specifications, the proposer must provide them, but they must be there in the proposal (because the proposal is usually the basis of the contract).

One other common mistake many proposal writers make is to be deliberately vague about the program because the RFP and SOW were vague. The rationale is that if the customer had not been very specific about what is to be done, it is risky for the proposal writer to be specific. The reasoning goes on to assume that if the proposer is specific, there is serious risk that the customer will not like or will not agree with the courses of action proposed, and will therefore reject the proposal. According to this line of reasoning, there is consequently far less risk in being somewhat vague and general.

The reasoning is specious, however. While there is the possibility that the customer will neither like nor agree with the proposer's program, there is the certainty that the customer will not award a contract for a vague and undefined program. The risk of rejection for being vague and indefinite is even greater than the risk of rejection for marching to a different drummer than the customer does. It is my firm conviction that it is far better to develop and clearly spell out your program design. However, you can still "lay off your bet," to reduce the risk that the customer will reject your proposed plan because of disagreement as to what is needed or how the need is best met. It is always possible to stipulate in your proposal that the proposed design is preliminary, is based on information supplied in the RFP and SOW which is probably not enough to base final design decisions on, and is therefore offered as a tentative design, to be made final, possibly with revisions and refinements, after award.

Bear in mind that the customer does not have to make a final decision based solely on what the proposals offer, but is free to call in any or all proposers for formal presentations, discussions, proposal supplements, and negotiations. Anything you can provide in your proposal to stimulate or provoke the customer into inviting you in for discussions is a definite plus. Offering a highly specific approach and design, with the proviso that you are open to changes as a result of further details becoming available to you, often does cause a customer to invite a proposer in for discussion. I have found, too, that offering the options gambit frequently results in the customer inviting the proposer in to discuss the very questions the proposer has raised. It has been an unusually successful stratagem in my own experience.

One of the most common mistakes of tyros in proposal writing is the rush to paper and pencil; they begin to write far too soon, before they have fully analyzed the problem or requirement and, therefore, before they have fully understood it. And, of course, before they have devised a strategy or even an approach.

A second common mistake, related to the first, is that those not truly familiar with writing tend to the assumption that writing consists solely of words and sentences. They neglect to consider other, often far more effective, ways of conveying information and ideas—graphic methods, charts, photos, graphs, diagrams, and drawings of various kinds. Many proposals fail to make their points with the maximum impact possible simply because the writer has failed to employ graphic aids.

One can truly kill two birds with one stone here. The following method is synergistic and produces results far beyond the simple sum of the two functions accomplished with one act. It is a method I call "graphic analysis," and it produces at least these results:

It greatly facilitates the analysis and understanding of the REP and the problem or requirement described there.

It speeds up and materially assists the development of an approach to and design of a program.

It provides a virtual road map for writing the proposal, while it also lessens the burden placed on words alone to present the main messages.

It furnishes, ready-made, an effective drawing to help the customer follow your proposal.

Even these are largely understatements in situations where the benefits and overall impact of the method are overwhelmingly great and have made possible proposal efforts which would have been far more difficult if not impossible otherwise.

FUNCTIONAL FLOWCHARTS

The basis for the method is the functional flowchart, which is in fairly common usage in engineering and data-processing fields, although the latter use such charts in a highly specialized genre, not really suitable for the purposes to be described here. For our purposes, we wish to use functional flowcharts in the simplest form possible because, for some reason, people who have not been exposed to them before appear to have some difficulty in using and understanding them. Therefore, it seems advisable to offer some rather general introductory material about them first:

A functional flowchart is a simple representation of the steps in any process, simple or complex. Preparing a plain omelet, for example, might be represented so:

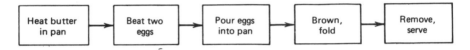

The flow is from left to right, as in reading (some people use vertically oriented charts, but I think they are easier to read when they are left to right, as in reading). The chart can contain as many or as few steps as you think necessary for your purposes. You might prefer this:

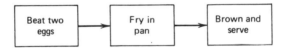

You may find it desirable to show phase relationships—how different events are related in time. The first two flowcharts were entirely sequential, one event following another. But suppose we want to show that we can have the butter heating in the pan while we beat the eggs? We'd do that this way:

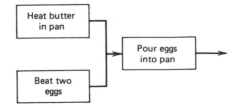

Such drawings show not only the specific steps in as much detail as we think necessary, but they also show how the steps relate to each other. If you were to write a recipe based on this chart, you'd probably start this way, under the direction of the chart:

> Heat butter in small frying pan. While butter is heating, beat two eggs in bowl. When butter begins to brown, pour beaten eggs into pan.

It's easy to write according to the chart, simply elaborating on each step in the chart, using the chart as a guide. Anyone could write up the recipe with such a chart as a guide, explaining each step in somewhat more detail than the chart does. It's not the function of a flowchart to present all the minutiae, but only to show all important steps and their relationship to each other.

It really isn't necessary to repeat all the words that are already in the chart, is it? All that is really necessary is to cover those points not covered in the chart, such as how to know when the pan is at the right temperature, how to judge when to turn the eggs, and other such amplifying detail. The chart takes over much of the burden of presentation, and, if well designed, displaces its own weight of words.

A reverse process is possible; a functional flowchart can be derived and constructed from written description. That is, text can be converted into a graphic representation. One very useful application of this is to translate the work statement of an RFP into a functional flowchart. There are several salutary results:

> It is far easier to perceive the discrete steps and their relationships to each other when presented graphically.
>
> Anomalies and redundancies stand out plainly.
>
> Inefficient processes stand out, pointing the way to improvement.
>
> It is relatively easy to experiment with approach and design alternatives until the optimal design is found.

If this is done first, before making serious efforts to begin writing, the writing is enormously simplified because the program is designed. Moreover, the final chart is now available for inclusion in the proposal, while the original chart is a guideline to explaining to the customer the pros and cons of the proposed program and how the design was reached.

The process consists of doing what is represented succinctly in the following functional flowchart:

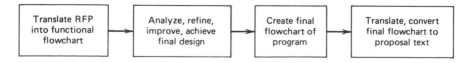

This is an abbreviated and simplified explanation of the process, assuming a sequential, straight-line process, whereas in actuality few processes are ever purely sequential. Most processes are generally sequential in macroscopic overview, but have numerous concurrent or parallel events (or functions) and iterative steps (feedback loops). In practice you would be studying the RFP/SOW and first drawing a rough-draft flowchart of what is described there. Rereading the RFP/SOW, you would begin to refine the first draft of your flowchart, going back to the first block and modifying it. You would probably do this several times as you gleaned more and more information from your study of the solicitation, until you finally felt reasonably sure that your chart was a fair representation of the project as the customer saw it or, at least, as the RFP/SOW described it or suggested it.

By this time you would probably have expanded and detailed that chart, and you would probably be in some disagreement with it. Remember that at this point you have charted what the customer has defined, described, or implied in the solicitation and work statement, which is not necessarily what you believe is the best approach to satisfying the requirement. Now it is time to begin revising that flowchart according to whatever approaches and design strategies you have evolved to achieve whatever benefits you believe possible in terms of dependability, cost, efficiency, schedule, or other parameters. That, in fact, is the main objective of this exercise—to aid you in finding and evaluating all possible alternatives.

In a sense, this is a brainstorming session. (I like to refer to it as "idea storming," for what I hope are obvious reasons.) It enables you to carry on a brainstorming function on a solo basis although the method was developed for use by a group. But it is also most useful in a group session if you are working with others to develop a proposal. Here are two ways this can be used in a group effort:

1. One individual can study the solicitation and draft a functional flowchart from it, make copies of the rough-draft flowchart and distribute the copies to the members of the group. Using this as a starting point and working under a leader at a blackboard, the group brainstorms the design and revises the draft flowchart.

2. In some cases, it is more practicable or more desirable to develop every version of the flowchart, including the first rough draft, in a group session. This can be done best on a blackboard, a leader translating the decisions of the group into the diagram.

Sometimes the SOW does not provide even a clue as to just what the customer envisions or what principal functions are contemplated for the project. The proposal writer(s) must work from the ground up. That may be somewhat more difficult, but there are a few basic principles which help the proposal writer or team in getting started. A first step is to identify or define precisely what the end-product is to be, for there is almost invariably an end-product. Even a survey or study, conducted to resolve one or more questions or to provide some specific data, must be documented, so that the final report, manual, tape, or whatever medium of documentation is used is the end-product. Even if there is no physical item which might be identified as the end-product, there is a service to be so identified. If, for example, you were proposing to be one of the MBDA-funded organizations, one end-product and, in fact, the main objective of the contract, would be the set of services to be MBDA clients.

Once you have defined the main objective of the effort to be proposed, you can make that the right-hand box of the rough-draft flowchart:

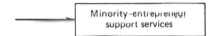

From this point you can develop the chart in reverse. First you must decide what is immediately necessary to provide that end-product, the various support services. One need not be a Phi Beta Kappa to begin to list the prerequisites:

Office facilities

Staff of specialists

Literature

Liaison with banks, investment companies

Liaison with industry

Training, lecture facilities

These must be organized into some logical arrangement to precede the end-product box on the chart. Note that these are not sequential functions, but are functions, factors, and conditions which must be performed or be in place on a concurrent or parallel basis.

Each of these is the result of earlier functions. Literature of clients must be developed. Liaison with lending institutions, investors, and credit companies must be established. Liaison with industry for contracts, subcontracts, and sales must be developed. Consulting and training materials and facilities must be created. The organization's own staff must be oriented and trained.

Another way to begin the development of a functional flowchart when the RFP/SOW furnishes virtually no clues as to any ideas the customer has of how the process should work is to begin with the simplest of functional diagrams, such as this:

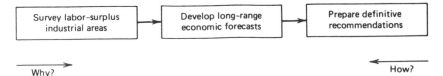

It is always possible to sketch in at least three or four basic functions including a starting point, an end-product, and a basic process to get from the beginning to the end if the functions are described in such general terms as these. The next step is to take each of the boxes in this completely vague and generalized beginning and develop it into a reasonably well detailed series of functions or processes. Ultimately, a detailed flowchart emerges, as you ask yourself, "How?" for each box on the chart, until you are satisfied that "how" is self-evident.

One test of your chart, incidentally, is to ask "why?" of each box, going from left to right (starting point to finishing point, if you choose to use other than left-to-right sequence). The next box should furnish the answer. Going the opposite way, from end-point back to origin, the question is "how?" and each prior box should furnish the answer. Example:

Why survey labor-surplus industrial areas? To develop long-range economic forecasts.

Why develop long-range economic forecasts? To prepare definitive recommendations.

How to prepare definitive recommendations? By developing long-range economic forecasts.

How to develop long-range economic forecasts? By surveying labor-surplus industrial areas.

The questions and answers make sense in a most general way, but they are entirely unsatisfactory as precise explanations, descriptions, or justifications. That's because the chart is far too rough a draft yet. That is what makes the how-why check useful; the answers are an excellent indication of the rationality of the chart as well as its adequacy. The answers reveal the need, if any, for additional information by exposing any missing steps or functions in the chain.

SOME WRITING AND PRESENTATION CONSIDERATIONS

One basic rule of selling and advertising is to get attention first. Notice how many TV shows, especially movies, begin with sharp action to capture your interest so that you will endure the endless roll of titles and credits and a few dozen screamingly boring commercials. That is a rule for all writing, although many writers appear to be totally unaware of it. The concept is adaptable to proposal writing, and its use is part of what is referred to here as "presentation strategy."

The idea is to open with something that will arouse the reader's interest or curiosity or appear to promise something humorous or beneficial, or otherwise provide some inducement to read on.

One example of how this works was in a proposal to the Job Corps. The Job Corps wanted proposals to train illiterates in electrical-appliance repair, a field that makes it necessary to be able to read at least the manufacturers' service literature, and one in which it is rather difficult to teach theory (Ohm's Law, for instance) to students who cannot master at least simple math and basic algebra. The winning proposal pointed all this out on page 1 of the proposal, but pledged, before going on to page 2, that the proposal would reveal a number of innovative methods which would surely cope successfully with these problems. It was a spectacularly successful effort, as the proposal reviewers at the Job Corps freely admitted.

The general rule that may be employed in adapting the principle to proposal writing is this: Select the most interesting, startling, or striking idea in your proposal and introduce it on page 1, as close to the opening sentence as possible. Only introduce it; do not explain it, but indicate clearly that details will appear later in the proposal. As they say in show business, leave something for the encore. The success of the device depends on arousing the reader's eagerness to know more about it.

One problem that troubles many consultants in writing proposals is the problem of giving too much information away, particularly if the proposal goes into some detail on how to solve some problem. Many proposal writers fear that the customer may appropriate information, some of which may be proprietary, without compensation, or may even utilize it to direct a competitor's services. It's a real enough problem, and one without any completely satisfactory answers. There is this to be said, however: The problem exists primarily with regard to the private sector. It is rare that a government agency will misuse information contained in proposals, especially if the proposer advises the agency that certain data is proprietary and not to be released. RFPs from the government today carry instructions on precisely how to notify the agency which data is proprietary and must be kept confidential. It is a good idea to use such notices when submitting proposals to private-sector organizations or individuals. The cautionary note alone is usually enough to give the reader pause, if he or she were contemplating using the information improperly.

When submitting proposals in the private sector, it is also a good idea to copyright the proposal, a simple process. On the title page of your proposal make the notation: "Copyright 19__ by _____. All rights reserved." This won't protect the information because you copyright specific arrangements of words, not ideas, but it may remind the reader that he is reading proprietary information of value to its originator.

Making the notation described affords you common-law copyright. It is not necessary to register this copyright with the Copyright Office of the Library of Congress unless you get into litigation. You can register it at that time, so it is unnecessary to do so in advance. But do use the notice, or you may be unwittingly making a gift of your material to anyone who wants it.

A common problem with far too many proposals is that they are not only extremely dull and unimaginative, but they also fail to take advantage of all possible opportunities to sell. One of the areas in which a proposal can and should exercise more salesmanship is in the use of headlines, captions, and titles.

In suggesting a format for proposals a few pages ago, I noted that the titles used there were all generic and not the titles I would actually use. For example, I used *Introduction* as a title for Section 1, which is just about as unimaginative as one can get. I do not suggest that there is any other title that should be used as a standard title. Rather, an appropriate title ought to be selected for each proposal, and that title ought to do some selling. It should at least give the reader a reason for *wanting* to read what follows the title. Suppose, for example, that you are submitting a proposal to develop a training program for someone, and you have some new idea you believe is most appropriate and will bring great benefits. You might open your proposal somewhat along these lines:

Section I
A Giant Step in Training Technology

Here, for the first time, is a simple, inexpensive method for designing training that will not overtrain, but will be totally specific to the need.

Even this is somewhat general, and I would try to make the section title not only attention-getting and interest-arousing, but as closely related to the specific project as possible. And I would use a blurb following the headline, as shown above. It's most appropriate to a sales presentation, giving you an unequaled opportunity to stress, dramatize, and draw special attention to your major selling points.

This principle ought to be followed for all headlines, figure titles and captions, and other such matter. An organization chart should not be labeled *Project Organization*, but something such as *Organization for Results*.

Most of these headlines and captions must be devised after the copy has been written and the drawings and charts developed. Until then, temporary headlines may be used. "General Background" is pretty bad as a headline, but it will serve the purpose if it is to be replaced after you have had time to study what the text says and determine what the main emphasis or selling point of that text passage is.

Creating the selling headline after the text is written has another advantage. If you find it difficult to decide what the main selling point of that text passage is, it is possible that the text does not have a selling point, in which case it ought to be rewritten. The purpose of a proposal is to sell, and it ought to sell on every page, in every line, and by every means possible. If you do not win the contract, it ought not to be because you failed to put forth that last extra ounce of selling effort.

FRONT MATTER

You may recall that in earlier pages the subject of front matter—pages preceding the main text of the proposal—was raised, with the notation that included in front matter was a foreword, or executive summary. Let's consider what such material does for your proposal and how to use it properly.

Theoretically, if you have something called "Executive Summary" included in your front matter, that would be a type of abstract, summing up the main points of your proposal for managers who have no need to read all the technical details of your proposal but want a summary of it. In practice, an executive summary is used most effectively to summarize the main selling points of your proposal, those sales arguments you believe to be most persuasive.

An executive summary or foreword ought to be as short as it is possible to make it without sacrificing important information. "Short" is, of course, relative to the size of the overall proposal, so a 150-page proposal might have an executive summary of 2–4 pages, whereas a 50-page proposal might be able to summarize everything important in a single page. Bear in mind that an executive summary is designed for top-level managers who want to digest the meat of your proposal in a very few minutes, but in practice everyone will read the executive summary, even if he or she is going to read the entire proposal. Write an executive summary with that expectation, write it with this mental set: "This is what I have to offer you, and these are the reasons that you should award this contract to me, the reasons you will find it to your greatest benefit to do business with me rather than with anyone else." Do not be wordy in your executive summary; be as terse as possible, even to the point of using telegraphic style for effect, this being a means of recognizing that the purpose of the executive summary is to provide the essence of the proposal only. For example:

Executive Summary

PDQ Associates offers XYZ Corporation the following benefits in the program proposed in these pages:

Cost-minimization through Phase-1 analysis inclusion of cost-alternatives determinations

100 percent sampling for quality control

Completion dates 60 days earlier than RFP calls for

100 percent backup planning for contingencies

Innovative technical approach

This kind of format makes it possible to present 10 to 20 items in a single page. A good plan is to list after each item the page(s) on which the reader can find details or full explanations of how the promised benefit will be produced. This adds greatly to the impact in two ways: 1) it draws attention to the item, and 2) it adds heavily to the credibility of the claim by advising the reader just where the proof of the claim is to be found—exactly what the cost alternative determinations are to be, for example.

COST/BUSINESS PROPOSAL

Government RFPs call for submitting the costs in a separate proposal, which may be in the same package as the technical proposals but must be bound separately. The purpose is to make the technical evaluation as objective as possible by withholding from the evaluators all knowledge of costs, at least until they have completed their technical scoring of all the proposals.

In many cases this is quite a slim volume and sometimes is merely a set of cost sheets (usually a government standard form) folded and sealed in a separate envelope. When the RFP calls for a separate "business proposal," this generally includes items of various kinds such as these:

Estimated costs for the program proposed

The organization's financial status—annual report if a public corporation, annual sales, other such information

Description of the parent organization, particularly with regard to its business practices

Method of subcontracting and purchasing

Personnel policies and procedures

Backup data on costs such as expense pools for overhead and General and Administrative costs (G&A) and fringe benefits if separate from overhead accounts

Name of contract administrator, qualifications for such responsibility

The commercial or private-sector client does not usually ask for this volume of data, especially not the financial data. (In the private sector, many would consider such information none of the customer's business!) Nor do private-sector clients usually request that costs be documented separately, although they may. However, it is probably a good plan to do so, even if the client has not requested it.

8

Negotiations, Fees, and Contracts

Consulting is a business as well as a profession, and you must never lose sight of that. If being businesslike ever costs you a client or a sale, it is almost certain that the client or sale would not have been worth having.

FEE STRUCTURES

On a federal government standard cost form (DD 633 for the Defense Department, Form 60 for most other federal agencies), the next to last line says "fee or profit," using the terms as interchangeable synonyms. These forms consider that the contractor's fee is what he is paid over and above costs, an idea undoubtedly stemming from the prevalence of cost-reimbursement contracting some years ago. When the typical consultant uses the terms *fee*, the term refers to a billing rate—what the client is to pay the consultant, whether by the hour, day, week, or month. If, for example, a given consultant charges $500 a day, that is the daily fee, and it includes the consultant's normal business expense for automobile, parking, telephone, office, postage, and other such costs.

Not every consultant charges in this manner, although flat rates per unit time (hour, day, week, month) is probably the most popular basis consultants use for charging their private-sector clients.

In the public sector it is not always possible to charge such flat rates, for at least two reasons:

Many government agencies have standard consulting rates, varying from agency to agency, and will therefore insist that you charge neither more nor less than those standard rates.

In most agencies, if the total cost exceeds some given amount, the agency will not agree to unit-rate billing at all for custom projects, but will require contractors to submit a full cost analysis to demonstrate how they have arrived at their final cost estimates or prices. This varies, too, from agency to agency and even from job to job within the same agency sometimes.

STANDARD RATES

In general, the government agencies are unrealistically conservative about what they consider to be fair and equitable standard consulting rates. Even today, with galloping inflation and exceedingly high costs of doing business, there are government agencies who think that $200 is a most generous daily fee for a consultant. The bureaucratic mind never ceases to amaze, and an understanding of bureaucratic thinking can be exceedingly helpful, as witness the following episode:

A few years ago, the Region III office of what was then OMBE (Office of Minority Business Enterprise) asked me to conduct a seminar of about one-half day duration for the staffs of OMBE-funded support contractors (consulting organizations) at an annual Region III meeting of representatives of these organizations. I prepared a simple letter proposal describing the proposed program, and priced it at $300 plus travel. The meeting was to be held in Wilmington, Delaware, to which I proposed to drive from my offices in Washington, DC.

The agency agreed, I carried out the seminar, everyone was satisfied, and the agency paid my invoice without difficulty.

Shortly after, the headquarters office of OMBE, in Washington, DC, asked me to propose to them a similar half-day seminar for OMBE staff to be held in Washington. I prepared a similar letter proposal, and priced the half day at $300. No travel expense was involved this time.

A few days later the agency called me to explain that their maximum consulting fee was $150, and there was no way that they could pay me $300 for the day. I explained that their own regional office had had no trouble with it, but they insisted that that had nothing to do with it. The regional office could do as they liked, but the central office could not pay more than the maximum of $150.

I agreed to submit an amended proposal, and I rewrote the proposal, making it identical in all respects except for the cost notations which I changed to read thus:

Preparation for seminar presentation:	$150
Presentation of seminar:	150
Total fee:	$300

The central office of OMBE had no difficulty whatsoever with this, and I was issued a purchase order and subsequently paid $300 without a murmur!

What was important here to the agency staff was not the cost itself, but justification of costs. Justification is magic in dealing with bureaucracy; proper justification can get you virtually anything and everything. In the case presented here, I made the mistake of assuming that the bureaucrats realized that it always requires some preparation to present a seminar, and that the preparation was included in my costing. Obviously, they did not realize that and had to have it explained to them.

COST ANALYSES

In projects of any size—typically, anything that goes above $25,000, although in many cases even for projects much smaller than that—government agencies demand that the proposer do more than present a total cost bottom line; the proposer is required to show how he has reached that bottom line. The reason for this is quite simple. In most cases, procurement officials really have no way of judging how fair your prices are unless they can see the entire cost picture. So if you are permitted simply to quote a flat price—let us say, $97,000—for a custom project, the agency has no way of satisfying itself that your price is fair and reasonable for such a job. The procurement regulations therefore require that the procurement officials examine your entire cost basis, and the extent of detail required depends to some extent on the type of contract and on its size. Let us consider first a relatively small, fixed-price proposal for $100,000. Here is what the standard cost forms would require you to explain:

1. Direct-labor costs
2. Labor overhead
3. Other direct costs
4. Various other items which are really "other direct costs," such as other consultant specialists brought in, materials, travel and per diem, and subcontracts

On the basis of seeing these, a contracting officer is in a far better position to evaluate the propriety and fairness of your bottom line. Let's take a look at these items, to see just what they are and what the terms really mean.

DIRECT LABOR

Direct labor is that labor which is applied specifically and directly to the project or contract, as distinct from indirect labor. For example, if the contract is for the development of a computer program, the systems analyst and the computer programmer(s) actually doing the work are direct labor. A secretary who types up the reports and other material for the job is also direct labor if you keep an accurate accounting of the hours she spends at this, for it is only that portion of her time that is direct labor.

It is not too difficult for a contracting officer to determine whether the direct-labor rates you charge are reasonable. It's rather easy to check on what the industry pays for a programmer, analyst, secretary, and others. Moreover, for a really large contract, the contracting officer may come to the contractor's office and ask to see some payroll records to verify the data in the proposal.

LABOR OVERHEAD

For most service or labor-intensive businesses—and consulting is almost without exception a labor-intensive enterprise—the chief basis for establishing an overhead rate is direct labor because it is direct labor that is the chief item of cost. Overhead will include those items suggested in Chapter 3, and the rate will be derived as explained there. The contracting officer has a fair idea of what overhead rates are reasonable for a service business, from lows of 40-60 percent to highs of 100-150 percent as a rule.

OTHER DIRECT COSTS

Other direct costs may include such items as postage, long-distance telephone calls, printing, computer time, travel expense, per diem costs (lodging and meals for travelers), and other costs incurred especially for the contract if accounts are kept so that these costs can be identified as incurred solely for the contract to which they are charged. Any costs which cannot be linked directly to a specific contract or project must be charged as indirect costs—overhead or G&A (General & Administrative) costs. If you wish to keep your overhead rates as low as possible—and there are usually benefits in doing so—keep the most detailed records possible of all costs and charge as much to direct costs as you can, thereby minimizing what you charge to overhead expense pools.

FEE OR PROFIT

The "fee or profit," as government cost forms list the item, typically represents a percentage of all other costs. If you examine a federal Standard Form 60, Contract Pricing Proposal (Research and Development) (see Figure 8), you will see that it is line 14, of 15 lines, that is labeled "fee or profit." The line above it is "total estimated cost," and the line below it—that famed *bottom line*—is "total estimated cost and fee or profit." Typically, contractors request a fee or profit which is a percentage of the figure on line 13.

How much you may ask as a fee varies with the nature of the contract. You may ask more for a fixed-price contract because the risk is somewhat greater than in the case of a cost-reimbursement contract. Even in the latter case contracts vary greatly, and the risks vary greatly accordingly, so

CONTRACT PRICING PROPOSAL
(RESEARCH AND DEVELOPMENT)

Office of Management and Budget Approval No. 29-RO184

This form is for use when *(i)* submission of cost or pricing data (see FPR 1-3.807-3) is required and *(ii)* substitution for the Optional Form 59 is authorized by the contracting officer.

	PAGE NO.	NO. OF PAGES

NAME OF OFFEROR

SUPPLIES AND/OR SERVICES TO BE FURNISHED

HOME OFFICE ADDRESS

DIVISION(S) AND LOCATION(S) WHERE WORK IS TO BE PERFORMED

TOTAL AMOUNT OF PROPOSAL

$

GOV'T SOLICITATION NO.

DETAIL DESCRIPTION OF COST ELEMENTS

	EST COST ($)	TOTAL EST COST[1]	REFER-ENCE[2]
1. DIRECT MATERIAL *(Itemize on Exhibit A)*			
a. PURCHASED PARTS			
b. SUBCONTRACTED ITEMS			
c. OTHER—(1) RAW MATERIAL			
(2) YOUR STANDARD COMMERCIAL ITEMS			
(3) INTERDIVISIONAL TRANSFERS *(At other than cost)*			
TOTAL DIRECT MATERIAL			
2. MATERIAL OVERHEAD[3] *(Rate* %X$ *base=)*			

3. DIRECT LABOR *(Specify)*	ESTIMATED HOURS	RATE/ HOUR	EST COST ($)		
TOTAL DIRECT LABOR					

4. LABOR OVERHEAD *(Specify Department or Cost Center)[3]*	O.H. RATE	X BASE=	EST COST ($)		
TOTAL LABOR OVERHEAD					

5. SPECIAL TESTING *(Including field work at Government installations)*	EST COST ($)		
TOTAL SPECIAL TESTING			
6. SPECIAL EQUIPMENT *(If direct charge) (Itemize on Exhibit A)*			
7. TRAVEL *(If direct charge) (Give details on attached Schedule)*	EST COST ($)		
a. TRANSPORTATION			
b. PER DIEM OR SUBSISTENCE			
TOTAL TRAVEL			
8. CONSULTANTS *(Identify—purpose—rate)*	EST COST ($)		
TOTAL CONSULTANTS			
9. OTHER DIRECT COSTS *(Itemize on Exhibit A)*			
10. TOTAL DIRECT COST AND OVERHEAD			
11. GENERAL AND ADMINISTRATIVE EXPENSE *(Rate* % *of cost element Nos.*)[3]			
12. ROYALTIES [4]			
13. TOTAL ESTIMATED COST			
14. FEE OR PROFIT			
15. TOTAL ESTIMATED COST AND FEE OR PROFIT			

OPTIONAL FORM 60
October 1971
General Services Administration
FPR 1-16.806
5060-101

FIGURE 8. Standard Form 60, government cost form.

This proposal is submitted for use in connection with and in response to *(Describe RFP, etc.)*

and reflects our best estimates as of this date, in accordance with the Instructions to Offerors and the Footnotes which follow.

TYPED NAME AND TITLE	SIGNATURE	
NAME OF FIRM		DATE OF SUBMISSION

EXHIBIT A—SUPPORTING SCHEDULE *(Specify. If more space is needed, use reverse)*

COST EL NO.	ITEM DESCRIPTION *(See footnote 5)*	EST COST *($)*

I. HAS ANY EXECUTIVE AGENCY OF THE UNITED STATES GOVERNMENT PERFORMED ANY REVIEW OF YOUR ACCOUNTS OR RECORDS IN CONNECTION WITH ANY OTHER GOVERNMENT PRIME CONTRACT OR SUBCONTRACT WITHIN THE PAST TWELVE MONTHS?

☐ YES ☐ NO *(If yes, identify below.)*

NAME AND ADDRESS OF REVIEWING OFFICE AND INDIVIDUAL	TELEPHONE NUMBER/EXTENSION

II. WILL YOU REQUIRE THE USE OF ANY GOVERNMENT PROPERTY IN THE PERFORMANCE OF THIS PROPOSED CONTRACT?

☐ YES ☐ NO *(If yes, identify on reverse or separate page)*

III. DO YOU REQUIRE GOVERNMENT CONTRACT FINANCING TO PERFORM THIS PROPOSED CONTRACT?

☐ YES ☐ NO *(If yes, identify,)*: ☐ ADVANCE PAYMENTS ☐ PROGRESS PAYMENTS OR ☐ GUARANTEED LOANS

IV. DO YOU NOW HOLD ANY CONTRACT *(Or, do you have any independently financed (IR&D) projects)* FOR THE SAME OR SIMILAR WORK CALLED FOR BY THIS PROPOSED CONTRACT?

☐ YES ☐ NO *(If yes, identify.)*:

V. DOES THIS COST SUMMARY CONFORM WITH THE COST PRINCIPLES SET FORTH IN AGENCY REGULATIONS?

☐ YES ☐ NO *(If no, explain on reverse or separate page)*

See Reverse for Instructions and Footnotes   OPTIONAL FORM 60 (10-71)

2

that while some cost-reimbursement contracts are almost totally risk-free, others entail a substantial risk. Therefore, fees may and do vary from 5 or 6 percent of the line 13 figure to 15 to 20 percent of that line.

Note, especially, the nature of the items you must break out to show how you arrive at your final price. These are items that must bear up under scrutiny—under audit, in fact, if the contract is large enough. That's not to say that every large contract will be audited, but every large contract of $100,000 or more is subject to possible audit to verify that the charges are all allowable under the terms of the contract and the general provisions of the procurement regulations.

There are other ways of costing out bids and proposals, and not all of them require revelation of all elements entering into making up the bottom-line figure. In some types of contracts, particularly Basic Ordering Agreements, Time and Material contracts, and similar arrangements where usually there is a laundry list of labor classes and/or kinds of service functions on an indefinite quantity basis, it is fairly typical to have such contracts bid/proposed and drawn up on the basis of billing rates for each labor class and/or service function. Such a quotation might look like the following:

Labor Category/ Service Function	Billing Rate	
	Per Hour	Per Page
Engineer I	$15.50	
Engineer II	15.50	
Illustrator	9.40	
Technical Writer	12.65	
Editor	10.90	
Typing		$3.68
Proofing		4.95

The rates listed are to include direct labor, overhead, all other costs, and profit. If the contract is a large one, and especially if it has any kind of cost-reimbursement provisions or a provisional overhead rate, there may be a requirement to provide a full-scale cost analysis and presentation, but quite often such quotation as the above is entirely acceptable.

PROVISIONAL OVERHEAD

Government cost forms have a line on which the bidder/proposer is asked to state whether he has had a government audit of the books during the previous 12 months. This is supposed to satisfy the need to verify the contractor's claimed burden (overhead, G&A, and other indirect costs, if any) rates because the results of audit are on record. However, if no such audit has been performed the bidder is proposing a *provisional* overhead, even a provisional G&A. That is, a rate that will be acceptable (subject to audit) upon which final adjustments will be made according to whatever the contract provides in that respect. So it is entirely possible to employ estimated burden rates. These can be employed at any time. If you have had an audit but you believe that your overhead is higher now than it was when audited, you can offer a provisional rate subject to later verification.

There are a few cases where the government wishes to make a pre-award audit. There are no hard and fast rules for this, but the contracting officer of the agency is always at liberty to require this if it appears that the best interests of the government so dictate. More often, however, a contracting officer will make a "facility inspection," which means a visit to your offices to verify that you are equipped and have the resources to perform properly. This may include a look at your financial reports, too, if the contracting official believes it necessary to verify your financial responsibility.

This does not mean that you must have offices in some commercial space, such as a high-rise office building. I have had such inspections of my office at home and "home" at that time was an apartment with one room in full-time use as an office. It may be that a local zoning commission will object to your conducting a commercial enterprise from or in your home, but the state and federal government are totally unconcerned with this. What they wish to verify is simply that you are capable of and equipped to carry out the terms of the contract properly, and without violation of state or federal laws.

PRIVATE-SECTOR PARALLELS

Over the past few decades the federal and state governments have become major markets, together not less than 10 percent of the GNP (Gross National Product), which means that they purchase well over $200 billion annually in goods and services, with the figure growing constantly. This has had a pronounced effect on much of the private-sector marketplace. One thing that has happened is that the size of government contracts has grown. Some 20-odd years ago, the U.S. Government let a contract for slightly more than $1 billion for the first time in history. This was the BMEWS (Ballistic Missile Early Warning System) contract let to RCA to build the basic installations at Thule, Greenland and in Fylingdale Moors, England, and later expanded to include installations at Clear, Alaska. A huge undertaking at the time, the work entailed over 300 subcontracts. In fact, the 300 subcontractors earned approximately two thirds of the $1 billion total cost of the contract, with RCA handling the remaining one third of the work in their own facilities. This is typical of large contracts; the prime contractor almost invariably must subcontract much of the work, for nobody—not even America's supercorporations—does everything, and many major contracts call for virtually everything. They often call for basic research, development, prototype construction, testing, demonstration, production, training, and documentation. Even when a prime contractor has all the facilities and resources to do everything, schedules and other commitments usually make it impossible or at least impractical, so the prime contractor lets many subcontracts.

The government agency customer is well aware of this, and while it may not impose many restrictions on a prime contractor when a small contract is involved, a large contract is an entirely different consideration. In the case of large contracts, where it is all but certain that the prime contractor will be compelled to award a number of smaller subcontracts, the basic contract imposes certain conditions and requirements on the prime contractor.

For one thing, the government has conducted a competition to decide where the prime contract will be awarded, and the government has no intention of permitting the spirit and intent of competitive procurement to be frustrated by using non-competitive methods for awarding substantial portions of the work as subcontracts. So the contract usually requires that the prime contractor use procurement methods which are similar, in principle, to those under which the prime contract was awarded. To minimize the risk of legal difficulties, prime contractors tend to emulate government procurement methods as much as possible. Therefore, even when bidding in the private sector, and especially when bidding for a subcontract on a government prime contract, you may find yourself operating under the principles we have discussed here.

Even when there is no government contract involved, or when the government contract does not specifically require compliance with the principles of competitive bidding and the federal procurement regulations, you may run into similar requirements simply because the prevalence and scope of government procurement has established models, and many private-sector organizations find it expedient to emulate those models.

This should be of particular interest to the independent consultant, for while there are opportunities to win small prime contracts with government agencies, there are even more opportunities to win subcontracts with larger organizations.

GOVERNMENT CONTRACT "PAPER"

In most cases the federal government's Standard Form 33 (Figure 6) is the actual contract between the government and the prime contractor. When the contractor submits the bid or proposal, the contractor's official signature—that of whoever is authorized to commit and bind the contractor—is inscribed in box 19 of Form 33. When and if the government agrees to accept the offer and award the contract to that bidder, the government's authorized contracting official fills out the bottom section labeled "AWARD" and signs it. A contract now exists. In short, when you sign in box 19, you have already signed a contract. All that is needed to complete the transaction now is for the government to sign.

In the case of advertised procurement you are generally cautioned to check your figures and other elements of your bid most carefully because all the government must do is sign the contract you have already signed and you are committed. The government can legally insist that you perform as bid, even if you have made some gross error. (In practice, the government rarely does this because it is not in their interest to force you to perform on a contract which is not to your advantage, but it is possible for the government to do so, and there have been cases where they did.) The total contract includes by reference the relevant portions of your bid or proposal and the relevant procurement regulations.

In the case of negotiated procurement, it is rare for the government to sign Form 33 without some actions justifying the term "negotiation," although those actions may not be true negotiation. What they are depends primarily on how large the contract is and other factors. It is fairly obvious that it is not in the government's interest to generate many thousands of dollars' worth of expense to conduct negotiations on a small contract of perhaps $25,000. It is more likely that the proposer would get a letter or telephone call from the contracting official asking for verification of the price, or perhaps asking for a best and final offer.

BEST AND FINAL OFFERS IN GOVERNMENT PROCUREMENT

It is customary for government agencies to request best and final offers from one or more proposers whose technical proposals have been found to be satisfactory. This does not mean that the proposer's cost quotations are necessarily deemed excessive, but it is standard practice in many agencies as part of the negotiation process. For small contracts, the usual procedure is a simple request by letter or telephone, with the proposer responding by letter or addendum to the original cost proposal. For larger proposals, the usual procedure is somewhat more elaborate.

In a typical case—and practices do vary widely, so that not all agencies conduct negotiations in this precise manner—the contracting officer will invite several of the top proposers to come in one by one to discuss their proposals, answer questions, and if they wish, make formal or semi-formal presentations to the agency staff. As a result of this conference, the proposers are usually asked to document the answers they have provided in an addendum to their technical proposals, and are almost always also invited to review their cost proposals and make their best and final offer.

According to other factors, such as the size and importance of the contract, actual negotiations across the table may ensue. It is the contracting official's duty to get the best deal he can for the government, and there are some official guidelines circulated in the government to instruct contracting officials in proper negotiation methods and procedures.

NEGOTIATION OF GOVERNMENT CONTRACTS

It is my personal conviction that it is much easier to negotiate with the government than it is to negotiate in the private sector, although not everyone will agree with this. One reason I believe this is that I have learned the magic of justification. Government contracting officials are trying to get the best deals they can for the government, and that means the lowest prices for what the government requires. But because price is not the sole consideration, and because the environment is a bureaucratic one, the "best interests of the government" are not always to us what they are to the government officials.

One cost item that I have found most contracting officials almost invariably concerned with is overhead. Regardless of what the bottom line turns out to be, most contracting officials are upset by any overhead figure they deem to be excessive. If, for example, a typical overhead in your field happens to be 65 to 75 percent of direct labor and you offer a cost proposal that is based on a 110-percent overhead rate, you are likely to be asked why your overhead rate is so high, with the intimation plain that you are a high-cost producer, hence probably inefficient or self-indulgent.

You must also bear in mind that you are never dealing with a proprietor or a profit-motivated individual in doing business with government agencies, so your appeal can never be to such motives as profit or they will miss the mark completely. You must be aware of what motivates government procurement officials, both in general and in particular. There are some generalities that can be pointed to, but in many cases there are special situations that will be of great help to you in carrying out negotiations successfully if you are aware of them.

In the middle sixties, when Lyndon B. Johnson's Administration was dedicated to warring on poverty, the contracting official of Johnson's new Office of Economic Opportunity made a pledge to a Congressional committee that no contractor would get more than 4.7 percent fee or profit on an OEO contract because all OEO contractors should feel it their duty to forgo at least some of their profits to help in this holy crusade to wipe out poverty in America. Any contractor who attempted to win more than 4.7 percent profit was simply wasting time, and those who understood in advance that that was the figure for line 13 could negotiate contracts at OEO with relatively little difficulty.

However, the Chairman of the Board of one rather large corporation thought that it would help him win one of the sought-after Job Corps Centers if he offered to undertake the contract for a fee of $1. The corporation won a contract, but not on that basis. In fact, he was advised that his offer was an embarrassment to OEO, and that they desired that no one get more or less than 4.7 percent profit.

In another case, the bidder proposed an overhead rate of 47 percent when negotiating a fairly large contract with a federal agency. The government officials were incredulous at what appeared to be an unrealistically low overhead rate, and that alone nearly soured the negotiations by making the government negotiators suspicious. Perhaps a private-sector negotiator would have quickly seized the opportunity to get such an apparent advantage, but the government procurement officials operate on the reasonable premise that the government loses, not gains, if the contractor goes broke on the job and can't perform as promised and contracted for. It is rare for a government agency to seize and press an unfair advantage despite some popular mythology to the contrary.

PRIVATE-SECTOR CONTRACT "PAPER"

It was once my task to prepare a proposal for the development of a training program for the American Red Cross. After I had written the proposal and priced it at approximately $26,000, I submitted it, and in due time the ARC invited our marketing executive to come in for discussion. During that discussion, ARC's training specialist called me to discuss technical points in the proposal which he either disagreed with or which were not clear to him. I managed to satisfy him and agreed to send him an official addendum, modifying our original proposal as we had agreed via telephone. Price was not affected, nor did ARC even discuss price; they accepted the price as reasonable.

A few days later, after ARC had our addendum in hand and was satisfied, they called and asked us to send someone to their offices to finalize and execute an agreement for the project. Our marketing director elected to go personally, but he decided that he ought to have legal counsel, and he asked our staff lawyer to participate with him.

The discussions never took place. As soon as our marketing director introduced our lawyer to the ARC representatives, they demanded to know why we thought it necessary to have lawyers present for a simple matter of a small contract. Our marketing director managed to say the wrong things, which only increased the ARC suspicions of our intent and our apparent mistrust of them. The ARC decided not to do business with us, and that was the end of it.

This is not an unusual case, but it illustrates something about contracts and legal overtones in small projects. My own experience, and this appears to be paralleled by that of Hubert Bermont, a Washington, DC, consultant, is that demanding that clients sign formal contracts for small consulting projects is often risky simply because it usually alarms clients. Today, almost everyone has been made conscious that it is unwise to sign anything without reading it carefully, and concomitant with that is the general suspicion of fine print and legal phraseology. Lawyers are trained to use Latin terms and legal jargon—*torts, habeas corpus, flagrante delicto*, and other terms—which most of us who are untrained in formal law are totally confounded by and therefore highly suspicious of. (So even if we do read the contract with the greatest of care, we are not at all sure what it said!)

The best thing that can be said for formal contracts, with all the *whereases* and *parties of the second part*, is leave them in your lawyer's office. Even the U.S. Government today writes contracts in English and keeps them relatively simple. Those formal, multi-page contracts, on legal-size sheets, bound in blue binders and bearing many seals and witnessed signatures, have no place in the lives and practices of independent consultants. They are useful and appropriate only in major business undertakings, where each party is represented by legal counsel and there is enough money involved in the whole thing to make such elaborate proceedings necessary. Spring such a document on a prospective client as a condition of doing business with you and you will probably lose the sale in every case.

This is not to say that there should be no "paper" between you and your client. In most of my consulting projects nothing more exists between me and my client than a handshake and a verbal agreement arrived at in discussion. Perhaps that is because I deliberately keep my conditions and terms as simple as possible so that we really do not have a great deal of need for even a letter of agreement, although I do recommend that others execute such informal agreements. Let's consider what a contract is and why it is executed on paper as a document.

First of all, a contract is an agreement. It is not the document that we so often refer to as "the contract." That is merely the documentation of the agreement, so that the contracting parties do not have to rely on memory. In many contracting arrangements the agreement is fairly complicated and it would be unreasonable to expect the parties to recall precisely what agreements were reached, especially if they were reached during and after the course of drawn-out negotiations.

There is also the question of simple honesty. A motivation for signing a formal document is often the fear that the other party will not live up to the verbal agreement. Verbal contracts are binding, but there is the problem of proving that the verbal contract exists if it gets into litigation. I believe that one should not do business with anyone who appears to be less than honest. I firmly believe that no contract, no matter how many *whereases* and *wherefors* it has in its paragraphs, is worth more than the sincerity of the parties' intent.

In any case, I generally use a simple, one-page Letter of Agreement when I feel a need for a written agreement. I have a suggested form, on my own letterhead, with blanks to be filled in and space for two signatures and dates. I find that many clients prefer that the agreement be drawn on their own letterhead, simply copying my form with the blanks filled in per our verbal agreement.

There have been a few cases where I had to resort to special measures to collect fees due, and it is because of this that I have such a form and sometimes ask the client to sign it with me. Those are the cases where I entertain some doubts about the client's ability or willingness to pay, and yet have nothing substantial enough to justify refusing to do business with the client. I have found it a wise precaution in those cases.

FEES AND COLLECTIONS

We have discussed generally the matter of fees earlier but we have not yet discussed the matter of collecting your fees, not an unimportant matter nor one to be taken for granted. Let's consider first the matter of collecting what is due you when you enter into contract with the federal government.

A common complaint by government contractors, especially the smaller ones for whom cash flow seems to be an eternal and universal problem, is that the government takes too long to pay its bills. The complaint is so widespread that there are currently two separate bills in Congress to try to compel the agencies to pay their contractors more promptly.

I do not believe that legislation will help. The contractors complaining about the problem are asking Congress to do for them what they ought to do for themselves—handle their own collection problems.

I have found it easier to collect from government agencies, in many cases, than from commercial corporations. Perhaps this is because often the private-sector company is deliberately aging its payables to minimize its own cash-flow problems, and deliberately stalling when you call, and giving you "the check is in the mail" excuses. When federal agencies are slow in paying, and they tend to be slow if you permit them to be, the problem is bureaucratic fumbling and sloth. This is much easier to cope with and overcome, and only once did I have any real difficulty in overcoming it.

In most cases, especially for small contracts and small payments due, the government can process your invoice and have a check in your hands in about 21 days and in only rare cases does the normal processing routine require more than 30 days. I have sometimes been paid in as little as 15 days, which is quite fast for a government agency. Here are some of the problems that delay payments:

You sent your invoice in duplicate, but the process in the agency requires three copies of the invoice. Someone may make a copy, but sometimes no one does, and the invoice lies in the in-basket indefinitely.

The agency lost your invoice, and they are waiting for you to do something about it, despite the fact that there is no way you can know that your invoice has been lost.

Somewhere in the process, someone has failed to sign the necessary piece of paper or has put your invoice at the bottom, in a bureaucratic last-in, first-out procedure.

It's a principle of bureaucracy that a bureaucrat rarely if ever exercises initiative of any sort at any time in any situation. The bureaucrat is unlikely to ever call or write you to ask for a duplicate of your invoice or anything else which would straighten out the situation. I once waited eight months for a $13,000 payment because I was managing a fairly large organization at the time, and my accountant never thought to advise me that the payment had never arrived. Investigation proved that our invoice was still resting in the first in-basket it had been consigned to on its arrival eight months earlier! An angry telephone call to a contracting officer who was at first incredulous, then furious (with his own people), and then thoroughly apologetic produced payment with unusual speed.

The way to avoid the problem or solve it quickly when it arises is to take the following steps:

When you sign the contract, ask specifically what the invoice processing procedure is—exactly who must sign, what are the various specific steps, how long should each take? Record this for future reference.

Allow the agency whatever their normal processing cycle is (I generally wait for 30 days, maximum). If you have not gotten your check by then take the following action(s).

Call and begin tracing by telephone. Ask exactly where your invoice is, physically, at the moment—that is, in whose hands. Don't permit yourself to be put off with promises to "check into it" and "get back to you." Those are stalling tactics and only delay resolution of the problems.

Once you find out exactly where your invoice is and what the problem is, find out to whom you send duplicate invoices or whatever you must do to straighten the thing out.

In only one case did this procedure fail to get me paid with reasonable promptness after my follow-up. In that case I had great difficulty in getting any answers or finding anything out from people in the Commerce Department, for whom I had done the work. I wrote a rather sharp letter to the Secretary of Commerce, who was annoyed with me for doing so, though she should have been annoyed with her own staff for their bumbling. But I did get paid promptly after that.

This is a good practice to follow when you are dealing with a large corporation, too, for large corporations can become as bureaucratic as government agencies. Do not be fearful that demanding your money will cost you the good will of the client. If insisting on being paid with reasonable promptness costs you a client, it is a client not worth having.

Under federal law a small business is entitled to get progress payments when working on a government contract that will run to more than a few weeks. Most contracting officials are entirely willing to work out a plan for progress payments, based on units of work completed or elapsed time. Many large cost-reimbursement contracts, for example, authorize the contractor to bill each month for expended labor and other costs. You should ask for similar arrangements with private-sector clients if the project will run to a period longer than you believe you can work without ongoing compensation. There is absolutely nothing unbusinesslike about such a request, and you should have no hesitancy about asking for progress payments.

RETAINERS

Federal procurement law makes provision for advance payments, but such payments are the exception rather than the rule, and it is not too likely that you will find contracting officers receptive to such requests from you, especially when you have no real justification for such a request. The private sector is an entirely different matter, and the subject of retainers is a most legitimate one in the consulting profession as it is in the legal profession. However, the term is subject to at least two interpretations:

If you perform services of a nature and for clients such that you are likely to be called upon frequently by any given client, the client may be amenable to an annual retainer arrangement. This usually takes the form of monthly payments, with the consultant's guarantee that he or she will be available whenever needed. The monthly payment guarantees the client some given number of hours or days, additional ones to be billed as they are ordered. Sometimes payment for time not used each month is forfeit, and each month starts anew. In other cases the consultant permits the client to accumulate unused time throughout the year as a credit. Almost invariably the slate is wiped clean at the end of the year, and everything starts new again.

I often ask for retainers at the outset of specific projects. When I am dealing with a substantial company or with someone already well-known to me, I agree to bill at the end of the job. On the other hand, when I am dealing with very small organizations, particularly those not known to me, it is my usual practice to ask for a retainer before starting work, usually approximately one third of whatever I estimate the whole project will cost. There have been cases where the wisdom of this was proved later, including more than one case where I discovered it had been wise to refuse to begin work, because the client could not or would not furnish a retainer.

In general, it's a good practice to get a retainer as "earnest money" as often as possible, but especially if the client is totally unknown, not rated, or otherwise something of a risk to extend credit to. For that is what you are doing when you begin work without a retainer; you are extending credit and trusting that the client can and will pay you later. A retainer up front reduces the risk, and by the time you have provided services equivalent to the amount of the retainer, you should have been able to gather some impressions about the client. It has been my experience that where I have gotten a suitable retainer I have collected my final bill, usually without undue difficulty. The only exception was a case where it was obvious to me that the client was having some difficulties in scraping the retainer together, and I undertook the project with some misgivings. I finally paid an attorney a substantial fee to collect about 75 percent of the remaining fees due me.

A bad debt is often a double loss because you not only lose the money for which you have worked but you lose the client as well. It can be argued that such a client is not worth having, but that is based on the assumption that the client was a deadbeat who deliberately defrauded you, and that is not always the case. I have often nursed a potential client along for many months (two years, in one case), giving bits of information and advice by telephone when I perceived that the prospect could not afford to retain me yet but was likely to do so at some future, more prosperous time. I have found this to be a sound policy, and my willingness to do this has earned me many fees I might not have earned otherwise. However, had I insisted on charging the client for the time and extended credit therefor, I would almost certainly have wound up with a bill which the client would not have been able to pay within any reasonable period. Asking for a retainer, then, is one way of qualifying the prospect—determining whether the prospect has the funds to retain you. Once you know the answer to that, you can use your own best judgment as to whether working on credit is a good risk or whether it is better to stick politely but firmly to a policy of retainers, where the client is not rated or shows no persuasive evidence of being solvent enough to afford what is needed.

NEGOTIATING TIPS, TACTICS, AND GAMBITS

In any negotiation, whether it is with a government agency or a commercial client, each party is trying to "psych out" the other—read the other's intent and strategies. The buyer is trying to get the lowest price possible, while the seller is trying to get the highest price possible. The buyer has built-in advantages—he knows what your competitors have bid, whether you are or are not in a number one position, and what his own intentions are. You are trying to work out the best deal you can for yourself without overreaching so that you lose the contract you now believe is close to realization.

The thing you need most here is information. It's easy to be a brilliant negotiator if you know that you are already the low bidder or that the client is not seriously considering anyone other than you as suitable for the project. So you are asking questions primarily in the hope that the other party will let some useful gems slip out which will help you judge how close you really are to the goal and how you compare, both in costs and quality, with competitors. You want to know how hard you can press or how stubbornly you can hold out for what you want without losing the contract.

I am constantly surprised at how many people resort to all sorts of devious means for getting information when there are straightforward ways that are worth trying first, such as simply asking direct questions. In trying to find out how the customer really feels about my price or how important it might be to find some means for reducing the price, I have had success by simply asking along these lines:

"Mr. Granitejaw, I have put together here a fairly elaborate plan on the basis of what I know at this point. Are there provisions in my plan for things you feel you do not need, where we could cut the cost or beef up some other area?"

The answer to this type of question may be evasive or it may be revelatory; I have often found it to be the answer to my mental question about the price I quoted versus what the client wanted to spend or had been quoted by others.

In the case where you have priced by offering a basic model and several options (as in the automobile business), a leading question concerns what Mr. or Mrs. Prospect thinks of the options.

Another way to get at this is to suggest that you'd like to go through the entire plan, step by step, with the client and discuss each step. Before this joint review has gone very far, you'll begin to size up the client's ideas from the remarks made.

There are cases where the client will tell you directly that your price is high and may even state on what basis—by comparison with what the client has budgeted or estimated in advance or by comparison with other bids. This may or may not be on the level; some negotiators will say this even if you are the low bidder, trying to drive your price lower still. It's fair, in such a case, to ask:

"Ms Clientprospect, may I ask on what basis you find my price high? Are you comparing my price to someone else's price on a dollar-for-dollar basis without analyzing the value of what I offer versus what others offer?"

Regardless of the answer you get to this, the idea is to get into discussion of the value you are offering, and if the client even suggests that you are offering a limousine when the need is for a tin lizzie, turn to the gambit suggested earlier. Discuss what you have proposed, step by step, and explore ways of reducing or simplifying the plan.

I believe that you should do this even if you know that you can afford to cut the price without running serious risks. To simply reduce the price for the client is to admit that you have overpriced the project. For the sake of your own image—to keep yourself looking respectable and to counter any notion that you are desperate for the contract—always make the client pay some price, however small, for a price reduction. That is, cut something out. It may be so insignificant as to lead the client to chuckle inwardly at how shrewdly he has gotten you to yield substantially on price while he gave up virtually nothing. Nevertheless, it's a good tactic: do you really care that the client believes that he or she is a far better negotiator than you are, as long as you win the contract? Actually, this is a plus and helps persuade the client that it is in his or her interest to award you the contract.

In one case where I was negotiating a small contract for services to a small company, the prospect made what I could almost call "the usual proposition," because it has been made to me so often. My payment would be some percentage or portion of the contract, given me in the form of a lucrative subcontract. I politely but firmly made it clear that I do not work on speculation or on contingency. He apparently was prepared for that because he immediately proposed that I take part of my fee in cash and part as a portion of the project. Since the cash figure we referred to was enough to cover my costs and fees, I took time to appear to be in deep thought and then with apparent reluctance agreed. The fact was that I did not expect this client to make good on the agreed-upon subcontract any more than had numerous others who, early in my consulting career, had defrauded me with similar promises. He did not disappoint me, either; he did win the contract, and I heard no further from him. The point is, however, that I was quite satisfied to settle for the cash figure we agreed on, and my client was sure that he had outfoxed me, so he hastened to agree to any minor refinements I asked for, which had no bearing on price but were of some importance to me.

The fact that I have come to a firm policy of refusing to work on speculation or contingency need not influence you. It has proved to be an unwise option for me because of human cupidity. The cases in which the client made good on his promise to me regarding some subcontracted portion of the project turned out to be the exceptions. In every case, I believe, the client meant well enough, but after winning the contract with my assistance managed to convince himself or herself that I had not really done much, and left it to me to sue them. I chose not to, and after a half-dozen such experiences I simply refused to work that way again. Your case may be different, depending on the nature of what you do and the specific situations. At least one prominent independent consultant of my acquaintance undertakes contingency assignments on occasion, but his are situations which afford him some almost automatic protection against being cheated. It is a good bargaining chip if you need one in your negotiations and if it is a practical alternative for you.

Probably your worst enemy is your own greed. Individuals go to the bargaining table determined not to settle for less than the other party will yield and thus lose everything. In one case, while still employed as a local manager by a multi-division firm, we were invited by NASA to discuss our proposal, submitted in pursuit of a contract for about $500,000. We knew that NASA had budgeted that amount, so our program was designed to the price.

The "discussion" was a form of negotiation which ended with the invitation extended to us (with studied casualness, as though it were a last-minute thought) to review our cost figures and submit a best-and-final price. It was now obvious that we had to decide whether to reduce our price. Since we had designed to a cost, we had a good bit of flexibility and could have cut a good bit. Opinion among those of us who had participated in the discussion was divided, but the conclusion we reached was that we were so far ahead of our competitors technically that we could afford to hold out for our price. We lost to a competitor who was about $35,000 lower than we were.

If you worry that you may accept less than the amount you could have gotten, you will make this mistake, and you will lose some projects you could have and should have won. The proper approach, I believe, is to remember that you have lean and hungry competitors in virtually every case, and there is almost invariably at least one who is lean enough and hungry enough to accept the lowest price that he can live with. Negotiating a final figure that is somewhat less than you know or believe is the figure a client has budgeted is not necessarily leaving money on the table at all. The figure you have to meet or beat, usually, is the lowest competing bid.

There are undoubtedly cases where there are no direct competitors, especially when the project is a small one. But where the amount of money involved is substantial, there are directly competing bids and proposals, and it is *these* against which you are bidding.

This does not mean that you must always underbid to win contracts. There are cases where yours is a superior position, perhaps because your technical proposal was superior, perhaps because you have an outstanding reputation in your field, or perhaps because the prospect has been exceptionally well impressed by you. In such cases, usually, you need merely be in the competitive range or not excessively higher in cost than your competitors. But you must not overestimate the superiority of your position, either; overconfidence is as deadly as greed, and some consultants find it easy to convince themselves that they are so superior that they can command any price they ask for.

Listen and watch for the signals. In one major contract negotiation at which I happened to be an observer rather than a participant, the contracting officer tried several times over nearly a half hour to signal the contractor that his proposed prices were too high. Since the contracting officer asked pointed questions about various centers of cost and appeared interested in discussing these more than anything else, he ought to have gotten the signal. But he remained obtuse until the contracting officer became so frustrated that he violated usual practice by almost shouting, "Damn it, we like your technical proposal and we *want* to do business with you, but not at these prices!"

Usually the other party is not trying to signal you; the signals are unconscious and unintentional. Still, they are sharp and distinct enough to alert negotiators.

Some may be body language. Some opinions on the subject are that when the other fellow steeples his or her fingers, it signifies confidence, perhaps pontification of views. Folding one's arms across the chest indicates stubborn opposition to being persuaded or swayed from a conviction. Unbuttoning one's jacket is claimed to be a signal of acceptance—readiness to agree on the current position. But these are *maybes.* Maybe the other fellow is just more comfortable with his jacket unbuttoned!

More dependable as a signal is careful analysis of what appears to concern the other party most, and the primary indication of that is where or about what are you being most closely queried. That should give you an excellent clue as to whether the prospect is concerned primarily with costs or primarily with project technicalities.

The point of this is to psych out the client's "worry items," matters of greatest concern. Listening carefully can also give you clues to competitors' approaches: The client may inquire into other technological approaches or design ideas which are so specialized technically that he or she would ordinarily be unlikely to know about them. The probability is that these were inspired by a competitor's proposal or presentation. The questions are therefore often excellent clues as to what you are competing with technically. The same thing may apply to cost items if the client appears to have some already-fixed notions about what various elements of the program ought to cost.

Some consultants, especially those pursuing fairly large and complex projects, deliberately plant "throwaway" items in proposals and cost estimates to serve later as bargaining chips at the table. They include costs which are either inflated or not truly necessary with the expectation that they can use these as things to yield on during negotiations, while not giving up anything of real value. The problem with this is that it assumes that you are bargaining only against the client's own budget and notion of what things ought to cost, whereas you are probably bargaining against what competitors have proposed and estimated. This is a popular device, the use of which deceives no one, but it helps each party to accomplish his or her mission. If you choose to use it, this is the best way to go about it:

First, do not use useless or meaningless costs as gambits to be thrown away. This is senseless. It assumes that the other negotiator is naive and does not perceive that these items were designed to be pawns.

When you design the program you propose or present, design a full-scale program, the way you would prefer to carry it out. Then go through it and identify for yourself those items that you would cut out of the design if you were compelled to carry out an austerity program while still achieving the original main objective of the program.

Determine the costs of those items and how much you can reduce costs by eliminating them.

Those are your proper bargaining chips. They are entirely useful to the design, but they can be dispensed with and not endanger achievement of the end-purpose of the program. Make it clear to the client that the objective can be achieved despite cutting costs, but at some inconvenience or at some sacrifice to speed of execution or whatever must be compromised to realize the cost reduction.

Any time you feel that you are fighting a battle of who is the low bidder, this is an approach to consider. Don't wait for the client to ask you about cost reduction; volunteer the idea. You are likely to be surprised at how often a client concerned with price does not want to save money if it requires even a slight inconvenience. But be sure that the client understands clearly the three conditions you can pledge:

1. A specific reduction in costs.
2. Achievement of the main objective.
3. Sacrifice of some sort.

9

Consulting Processes and Procedures

Here are three rules which will help you succeed as a consultant both in the stages of making the presentation and winning the sale, and in conducting the analyses and carrying out a satisfactory and rewarding project.

We have already established that the term *consulting* is so broad that it all but defies definition with any great precision. Consequently, it is all but impossible to prescribe any except the most general set of consulting processes and procedures that will even approach universality. In this chapter, and to a large extent in most of the remaining portions of this book, will be offered guidelines that are both as general as recommended ethical standards and as specialized as descriptions of certain useful analytical methods.

THE ART OF LISTENING

Much more attention has been devoted to the need for and the art of listening in the past two decades than in the centuries preceding it. Possibly this is because most of us now hear less and less of what others say. We have become accustomed to living in an environmental cacophony, trying to listen to TV, spouses and children, and other distracting noises which all compete for our attention. Or we are trying to ignore all the environmental noise while absorbed in some task or in reading. In any case, most of us have learned how to tune out those sounds which are not of focal interest at the moment and somehow manage not to be distracted by them or—and perhaps this is a more apt analysis—we have learned how to select from the hubbub those signals we wish to hear, "straining" the unwanted out, as Isaac Asimov has put it.

In many of us today this has become an ingrained action, perhaps a necessary defense against a constant aural assault, but nevertheless an almost involuntary and certainly unconscious screen we erect and maintain. Unfortunately, it has led to a recognized and acknowledged problem, the subject of much corrective effort—failing consistently to really hear what others are saying.

There are other factors in this failing; we are under much pressure and we begin to unconsciously speed things up, even listening. We tend sometimes to "speed listen" as others speed read, grasping the main message in general, perhaps, but missing the important details, a defect that results in failed communication. Some of us are even guilty of preemptive judgment in listening, deciding prematurely what is significant and what is trivial in the information being passed to us, what data will be accepted as valid and which rejected as invalid.

Some of us may go to the opposite extreme, accepting everything without question, without weighing anything for its validity, importance, or general significance. This is just as deadly to communication and just as hazardous to a successful initiation of a consulting project.

In consulting, listening is not entirely a passive act for it is rarely 100-percent listening in the literal sense; in virtually all cases it is necessary to guide the client in initial sessions by asking a few judicious questions. It is true that your main activity is listening in the beginning, but it is also true that few clients are able to judge precisely what you need to know, and few provide all the information you need without the careful prodding of your own questions.

But if it is often necessary to guide the client by asking an occasional question, it is also necessary to have an objective, to know what you want to know. And your objective when you are listening to a prospective client describing the need is quite different from your objective when you are listening to a client in your first meeting after contracting for your services. In the first situation, your overall objective is (or should be) to gain enough information to enable you to formulate a strategy for winning the contract, whereas in the second case you are trying to start organizing the project.

LISTENING AS A SALESPERSON

Let us not be coy about the need to be salesmen and saleswomen in the consulting profession. To pretend that it is beneath the professional dignity of a consultant to engage in anything so crass as direct selling is nonsense. As an earlier chapter pointed out, the key to selling most things, and especially custom-designed professional services, is consulting itself. Who is better qualified to sell than the consultant? So make it a rule when you are listening to a prospect explain his or her needs, to gather what will assist you in devising a successful sales presentation.

This is not quite as cynical as it may sound to you. It does not advocate deceiving a prospect into believing that you are sincerely interested in helping him or her solve problems and meet needs while you are truly interested only in making a sale. This is one case where you can have it both ways—you can and should be sincerely interested in what the prospect has to say, but you are not going to be able to apply your own talents to solving the problem unless you can make of that prospect a client. Therefore, you must do first things first, and the first thing is to gather information for sales purposes (although most of it will also be useful later, after contract award when you undertake the project). Here are the things you want to know:

The essential problem or need

The prospect's own notions, if any, about how to approach the problem/need

Whether, in fact, the project does entail a need to solve a true problem (as distinct from providing some specialized services, for more or less routine work)

Any specific constraints or related requirements, such as cost and time limitations

The prospect's intent—whether firmly intent on retaining someone to help, simply considering the possibility/desirability of doing so, or merely making conversation and, possibly, trying to pick your brains

Let's consider some of these in greater detail.

The Essential Problem or Need

We've all experienced situations wherein individuals offer solutions for which there are no problems, trying to force-fit their prejudices into every situation. For example, I know some computer programming specialists who can see problems only in terms of writing or rewriting programs. They are apparently convinced that any program written by anyone other than themselves is poorly done and needs to be tightened up, at least, and possibly even scrapped and replaced with a really good program.

There are prospective clients who are no less prejudiced and short-sighted in describing their own needs. Some go so far as to do their own diagnosis and seem intent on hiring a specialist primarily to verify their own diagnosis. They really want to handle their own problems or appear to be doing so, and are most reluctant to ever appear to need someone else's expert knowledge. They will hasten to assure the consultant that they can handle the problem themselves but simply don't have the time, and that that is why they are considering hiring a consultant for the job.

From a sales viewpoint, the smart thing is to appear to go along with the prospect's play acting; to embarrass the prospect is surely to lose the sale. But you still need to know what the real need or problem is if you are to make an intelligent presentation. For example, when an executive in the General Services Administration asked for my help in producing a brochure and manual explaining new methods for awarding A&E (Architect-Engineer) contracts, he advised me that he had written the two publications and wanted me to edit and ready them for printing by the Government Printing Office. I agreed tentatively, but asked for a few moments to look at the manuscripts. As I had feared, they were truly dreadful, and no amount of editing would correct their problems; they needed extensive rewriting, including reorganization. Instead of saying so to my prospective client, I remarked that they would need a rather heavy edit if he wanted really first-class products. He readily agreed that he wanted the products to reflect credit on his office and gave me carte blanche to do what I thought had to be done. I priced the work for rewriting, although I suffered the purchase order to describe it as editing.

A client often has a problem which can be stated in a few words, but he has surrounded the basic problem with so many observations and re-counting of incidents that it takes a bit of sifting and straining all the language to determine what the essence of the problem is. For example, the U.S. Army Corps of Engineers at Fort Belvoir, Virginia, issued a request to propose a set of engineering-support services in connection with certain night-vision (infrared) equipment development in their laboratory. The RFP made it appear that the major need was for value engineering, a discipline that determines whether an item can be designed and manufactured more efficiently. Consequently, the proposers were required to present their credentials as value engineers, which is a highly specialized field. Despite the focus on value-engineering capability in each proposal submitted, the bulk of the work proved to be something generally referred to as "reverse engineering," wherein engineering drawings are made up to match the equipment, because engineers often develop their products without taking the time to prepare accurate drawings. So in this case it was necessary to focus on value engineering to win a contract which would require extremely little value engineering. Had the proposers known this in advance they would still have found it necessary to concentrate writing effort on value-engineering coverage, because that's what the client thought was needed.

So it is necessary to identify the essential need without casting out the prospect's own notions, right or wrong, about the need.

The Prospect's Own Notions

Quite often, despite recognizing the need to retain the services of a technical expert, a client is prejudiced about how to go about organizing and running the project necessary to satisfy the need. In some cases the client may even furnish a functional flowchart of sorts, reflecting his own prejudices about how such work ought to be done.

Here again you must proceed with caution. Certainly the last thing you want to do is have an eyeball-to-eyeball confrontation with the prospect. You can't do anything but lose that kind of contest. On the other hand, you can't afford to agree to a plan that is clearly unsuitable and will not produce the needed results, or at least not produce them on any acceptable level of efficiency. You must manage somehow to reconcile the problem without damaging your own position.

One way is to probe and find out whether the prospect is truly committed to the ideas he or she has put forth or is merely trying to be helpful. In the latter case a proper approach is to simply suggest that you will certainly consider the ideas and appreciate the contribution. But if the prospect is firmly committed—has taken such a firm stand that it would probably be humiliating to be forced to retreat—diplomacy is definitely in order. A face-saving remark such as the following may solve the problem:

"Well, that seems to me to be an excellent way to go at this, but since we are in an advanced talking stage and I haven't had time yet to become really familiar with the project why don't we discuss the specific approach later?"

That alerts the prospect diplomatically, without actually challenging his or her ideas, to the fact that you have some reservations or, at least, are not prepared to accept the ideas without discussion. One reason it is helpful to do this during early discussions rather than to appear to go along and bring it up only after a contract is signed is that experience shows clearly that both parties lose in a confrontation. When you are trying to win someone over to your view, it is a definite mistake to force your arguments and "prove" the other party wrong. This only solidifies the other's position and all but compels him or her to find additional arguments to back up the position already taken. On the other hand, you may offer a few arguments, casually and without anything resembling table-pounding, and then deliberately leave the subject for a few days. Go on to other things. Permit the other party to mull over what you have said without being forced into a firmly established position. The other person can begin to come over to your viewpoint gracefully and without loss of face. This is far more effective and often accomplishes what could never be accomplished in a shouting match or even in a lengthy, good-humored technical argument where the two positions are solidified and polarized.

Whether the Need Is a True Problem

Much as we like to believe that the primary function of consultants is to solve problems, the majority of consulting assignments do not involve any but minor problems. For the most part, the services are the provision of certain special skills and knowledge to conduct a survey, design a system, perform a study, write a report, plan a project, evaluate a set of results, determine a training need, or otherwise perform services which are more or less routine for the consultant.

That is not to say that a specific problem to be solved is never the main objective of retaining a consultant. When the Postal Service (then the Post Office Department) computerized its payroll system at Paramus, New Jersey, it found the payroll program taking nearly 24 hours to run on its computer, whereas it should have required only a fraction of that time. Tightening up the program required more or less routine services, but it was still a problem, especially as the contractor was compelled to estimate whether the original program could be saved and utilized to any extent or whether it would be more efficient to write a completely new program. (In this case there were unforeseen problems in that the computer, a new model, had faults in its own compiler.)

A prospective client always wants to gain some insight into your technical capabilities and needs to have some confidence in them. When the work involves finding a solution to a true problem, when it entails troubleshooting, the prospect also wants some assurance that you have a capability for solving the problem. Therefore, you need to draw out of the prospect enough information to discover whether you will be doing some preliminary troubleshooting as a first order of business in the project.

Specific Constraints or Related Requirements

It is important for you to find out if there are any special constraints or requirements such as a not-to-exceed cost figure established in advance or a schedule date that must be met. Here are a few other constraints you may run into and should be alert for:

Requirement that contract and work be approved by a higher-up individual or a review committee of some sort. (The latter can be trouble; committees are almost always trouble unless they are under the firm control of a decisive individual.)

Progress reports. These can slow you down, cost you money. Be sure you know all reporting requirements when pricing the job.

Government-type cost analysis and cost revelations in your formal bid or proposal. Some people object to making such disclosures and won't do business with government because they object to such requirements. If you are one who feels this way, now is the time to find out about it.

Turnkey requirement—requires that you install system you design and train client's staff to run it. Sometimes clients forget to mention such things. Be sure that you know what you are to deliver.

The Prospect's Intent

It has been observed that there are many individuals in organizations who have little to occupy their time. This is especially the case in large, bureaucratic organizations such as governments and large corporations. People in such positions get bored and lonely, and they are entirely willing to listen to what you wish to offer for as long as you wish to talk. They appear sympathetic and receptive, and you soon begin to feel that you are very close to a good sale. Unfortunately, you are deceiving yourself, for the individual has absolutely no budget and no authority to command funds for your services.

This is why all good sales training calls for qualifying a prospect before spending too much time with the prospect, to determine whether the prospect *can* buy from you.

This is not to say that you must immediately abandon a prospect who, it turns out, can not buy from you. That prospect may easily be the key to meeting or making a presentation to someone who *can* buy from you. That is part of the qualification process, determining whether the prospect who for one reason or another can't buy from you can help you make a sale to someone else.

It is essential that you ask the question correctly to find this out. First you must inquire whether funds are currently available for the project being discussed. If not, when will they be? Will the individual you are talking to be able to commit them now, in advance, so work can begin as soon as the funds are released?

If these questions do not produce the information you want to hear, a second set of questions will revolve around what it takes to get the project authorized and funded, as a preliminary to follow-up sales effort, introduction to someone else, or whatever may be a suitable next step. (That suitable next step may be to simply close your brief case, say goodbye pleasantly, and go on to a more fruitful call.)

LISTENING AS A HIRED CONSULTANT

We have been talking about the listening for information which will help you close the sale. Now that you have closed it and won the contract, you are on chargeable time. The client is now paying for your time, perhaps on an hourly or daily basis, perhaps in a fixed-price arrangement. But you are not through listening yet; now you want information to meet a different objective. You want to gather as much information as possible about the need or problem so that you can function as effectively and as efficiently as possible. As the client describes things to you, you need to decide whether you are learning of symptoms or problems; many people who are not trained problem-solvers tend to confuse the two. One of my clients, for example, told me that his problem was that he was not winning enough government contracts. I agreed that that was a serious problem for him since he was in the contracting business and virtually all his business was with the government. However, his lack of success at winning contracts was not his problem but was a symptom of—what? His problem could have been any of the following or some combination of several:

Poor proposal writing

Addressing the wrong government market segments

Failing to keep in touch with all relevant requirements

Overreaching—trying to win contracts in areas for which he was not well qualified

Poor past performance

Poor past contract administration (Even good technical performance can be offset by careless administration.)

Overpricing or poor estimating

In any case, for the purpose of conducting troubleshooting analyses the identification of the problem must be such that it points directly to the *cause* of the main symptom(s). Even that is only a first step, and the process must often be repeated. For if the real reason my client was not winning a satisfactory number of contracts was any or a combination of the causes listed, then those causes must be treated as symptoms also and analyzed in the same manner. For example, let us suppose that my client was not winning contracts because of poor proposals. Let's regard poor proposal writing as a symptom and consider what some of the possible causes could be:

Poor program design

Weak staff resumes

Weak organization credentials

Unpersuasive and unconvincing writing

Unimaginative presentation

Complete lack of strategy in planning

Once again, each of these may be analyzed in the same manner. Poorly designed projects may be caused by any of many factors, such as these:

Proposal efforts totally unorganized

Inexperienced people used on proposals

Staff has weak technical capabilities for program design

No true analysis of customer wants

At this point the analysis is reaching rock bottom, that point at which it is possible to do final troubleshooting and pinpoint the true problem(s). Let us suppose that all four items listed above prove to be true. Each suggests in itself the possible remedies, and taken together they point clearly to a need for more highly qualified staff and a much more highly organized and disciplined proposal-writing system.

Note that in each listing prior to this last one, the possible causes were stated in somewhat vague and general terms which may have pointed to possible problems but were not yet truly *diagnostic*. That is the main objective of a troubleshooting analysis—to be diagnostic so that possible problem solutions are clearly indicated. Most of the time the final solution must be selected from among options. Consider, for example, that my client is totally unorganized in his proposal efforts. What are the possible solutions? I can think of at least the following:

Hire an experienced proposal manager to organize a proposal department

Use consultants to help develop proposals and especially to direct the efforts

Bring in a consultant to train someone on staff as a proposal manager

What a client elects to do depends on other factors—whether he has enough proposal activity to justify a full-time proposal manager, for example, or even whether he can find such an individual. He may be compelled to bring in a consultant to help with proposals and also help to organize a proposal department and train a proposal manager.

Most problems do have more than one possible solution, although in some cases one solution is clearly far better than any others. In other cases it is not that cut and dried, but must be determined by further study. A project that involves the solving of a true problem must proceed along lines that include these major steps:

Initial data gathering: Listening to the client, examining any documentation the client can offer or direct you to, studying other relevant documentation you know about or discover through your own efforts, and whatever other activities enable you to assemble or learn all facts you believe relevant.

Troubleshooting: This includes the type of analyses already reviewed, in which symptoms are examined to determine their possible causes, and each cause is checked out to verify it. The process is repeated until you are down to first causes, where the statement itself identifies, or at least strongly suggests, the remedial actions possible.

Resolution of alternatives: With the first causes identified, the possible alternative solutions are investigated and possibly discussed with the client to evaluate the practicality of each and the pros and cons of each, so that a specific recommendation can be made or the solution implemented as the project requires.

A BASIC APPROACH TO ALL ANALYSIS: FUNCTION

Analysis means separating something into its constituent parts to determine what it is made up of and how it all functions together (qualitative analysis) and the proportions of the various components (quantitative analysis). We are primarily concerned here with qualitative analysis, although occasions arise where quantitative analysis is required, too. We are concerned not only with analysis, but also with *synthesis*, the assembly or combination of elements to make up an end-product. In most cases analysis is not an end in itself but a means to an end, a necessary preliminary to the synthesis which is the true objective of the whole project. It is fair to say that the chief objective of analysis as far as we are concerned here is to find causes, while the chief objective of synthesis is to develop and apply remedies.

The key to analysis of most things, whether we are analyzing a physical device, an organization, a management system, or virtually anything else, is *function*. While the item being analyzed is subjected to an identification of all its component parts, each of these parts is identified also as a function. This functional analysis separates all the component functions of the item, whatever it is, and then sorts them out into their various classes, describing the contribution of each to the main function, which must also be identified as a first order of business in the analysis. This is the basis for that discipline known as *value management* (also known as value analysis and value engineering), and describes generally that which has come to be called *systems analysis*.

The basis for it all is that we are rarely really concerned with what something *is;* we are usually concerned with what it *does.* A wrist watch indicates or keeps time, and the chief reason for owning and wearing one is so that you can determine what time it is any at moment. Most wrist watches are also decorative jewelry, and some are extraordinarily expensive. Being decorative is another function, but one that has nothing to do with the main or basic function of keeping time. That is not to say that it is unimportant or that it is without value, but it is a secondary function that makes no contribution whatever to keeping time accurately.

If we begin to break the watch down into its component parts and examine their functions, we must identify the function of the hour and minute hands as that of *indicating time,* which is in direct support of the main function. Without those two hands, the watch could not keep time and function usefully.

Everything has some main or primary function, and most things have a number of secondary functions, some of which contribute to the main function and some of which do not. A simple paper clip has only one part and usually only one function, keeping papers together. But if you are holding one of those paper clips that has serrations or little cuts along its surface, you have one with a secondary function of adding gripping power. It supports the main function by making it a bit more effective despite the fact that the paper clip would still work without those serrations.

Identifying main functions is not as easy as it may appear to be. In many cases it is easy to guess wrong. Let's take that device used to enter the figures on a check with perforations and colored inks. Generally referred to as a "checkwriter," its function would be mistakenly assumed to be writing checks. Not so. If we spent money to buy such a device simply to write checks, we would be going at it rather inefficiently. For one thing, it doesn't really write checks because it writes only the figures, and a typewriter, which already exists in every office, is a far more efficient tool with which to write a check.

The true function of a checkwriter machine becomes apparent when you ask yourself *why* one uses such a device. In this case, the purpose of the device is to perforate the check when writing the figures in so as to make it all but impossible to "kite" the check—to raise the face value, as some skilled forgers are quite accomplished at doing with ordinary typed or handwritten checks. That is, the true function of the device is to protect you by "kite-proofing checks."

There are several basic rules or procedures which are of great importance in functional analysis and consulting generally. Here is the first one:

RULE NUMBER 1.   Functions are always described as a verb and a noun—two words—although an additional word is permissible if necessary to compound the verb or noun for clarity of meaning. But no adjectives or adverbs. In the check-writing example I used a compound verb, kite-proofing, to describe the function.

The main function generally reflects or states the purpose of the item. If it does not, it should be studied carefully to see if the true main function has been identified. In a workshop session on functional analysis, a group decided that the main function of an overhead projector was to project images. It took extended discussion to demonstrate that this was incorrect. While it is true enough that an overhead projector projects images, the purpose of the device, the reason anyone uses it in presentation, is to present a large image. Projection in this case is a means, not an end. As far as the presenter is concerned, a slide projector or a film-frame projector would be entirely satisfactory to do the job, but so would a set of large flip charts, posters, or TV monitors and videotapes. The presenter simply wants images that all can look at together, and it is in examining that purpose that the key to main function lies.

Another way to pursue this is to consider the need: What need does the item satisfy? The answer to that will either define the main function or put you on its track. Let's put this to the test in terms of a job rather than of a mechanical device.

Consider the proper functioning of a secretary, since few executives make proper use of a secretary. What is the true reason an executive needs a secretary?

If you think in terms of how most executives actually employ secretaries, you'll have visions of typing, filing, answering the telephone, fetching coffee, making plane and hotel reservations, keeping an appointment book, and reminding the boss when it's his wife's birthday or anniversary time. Small wonder, then, that Robert Townsend and other executives decided that it was wasteful for them to have private secretaries and found other means for getting their typing and filing done, while they kept their own appointment books and made their own reservations and hotel arrangements. Small wonder that fewer and fewer women are willing to accept positions as secretaries, given the array of menial tasks the position usually includes. But let's analyze it: What is the true purpose, the justification, of having a busy executive supported by a secretary? Is it for convenience or to glorify the exalted position the executive occupies? Is it to find an inefficient means for getting typing and filing accomplished? Or is it, in its original concept before the original purpose of a secretary was lost to view, to save the executive's time? Time is that precious commodity which is apportioned equally to all of us, regardless of rank, position, ancestry, personal wealth, and other endowments or handicaps. The busy executive who is paid an annual salary in six figures because he has special talents, wisdom, and judgments to offer never has enough time, and his or her time is quite expensive, often running to several hundred dollars per hour. At that cost, imagine the waste of an executive calling an airline for reservations, going to the pot to get coffee, poring over routine correspondence, and otherwise spending that hundreds-of-dollars-an-hour time on trivial tasks.

Unfortunately, while it is apparent that a busy executive should not be employing his or her expensive time making Xerox copies or assembling the pages of a report, it is not evident to most that neither should that executive be answering routine correspondence, shooing uninvited salesmen and other time wasters from the office, and otherwise spending much of the day in tasks a secretary could and should do. The simple fact is that secretaries are almost invariably underutilized, and that is at least in part because neither the secretary nor the boss has ever thought the matter out and taken the appropriate steps to assign to the secretary *all* the tasks a secretary can and should handle.

Once I had the good fortune to have such a secretary assigned to me. She had once been secretary to Harold L. Ickes, Franklin D. Roosevelt's Secretary of the Interior, understood what a secretary ought to be able to do and she did it. If I were on the telephone and it became apparent that I was agreeing to travel somewhere, by the time I had hung up Peggy was already calling the airlines. When she brought me the morning's correspondence, she had already pulled the pertinent files and brought them in with the letters I needed to answer, and sometimes she had already drafted an answer and brought it to me for approval! She understood the concept of secretarial help, and she implemented it well.

Here again, the answer becomes apparent when the question of need is raised. If the executive's need was simply for typing and filing, and perhaps for fetching coffee and other minor chores, he could hire a typist for far less than one usually pays a secretary. That's why Robert Townsend insisted on not having a secretary assigned to him, but called for someone from the typing pool when he needed a letter typed.

The same reasoning can be applied to an office procedure, a printed form, an organization, or an entire system. First identify the need which it is the purpose of the item to satisfy. Purpose, need, and main function are most closely related, if not identical with each other. It must also be borne in mind that the same item may be viewed somewhat differently by different parties. Take, for example, that government form, Standard Form 129, Application for Bidders List. It serves a purpose and fulfills a need for both the contractor and the contracting officer. The contractor has a need to be on bidders lists and to receive bids to which he can respond. The contracting officer has a need for bidders to whom he can send solicitations for bidding. Both needs are satisfied by this form when it is properly filled out and filed, fulfilling its function of describing interests or wants.

In making these functional analyses, you often find secondary functions which not only do not contribute or are not necessary to the main function, but also do not appear to be of any particular value. Such secondary functions add to cost and sometimes are sources of malfunctions or other problems. Incredibly, they often exist merely because the designer had a whim or a bias which impelled an illogical act. On the other hand, often a needed secondary function is lacking because the designer failed to anticipate or perceive the need for it. One company, for example, employed several thousand people scattered through over 40 offices throughout the United States, but generated the payroll every week on its own computer in the home offices in New York City. The people who designed the system failed to consider several other needs which could have been easily served automatically by the same system, such as keeping track of each employee's annual leave and sick leave allowances, and there was an endless chain of problems revolving around disputes between employees and managers about earned time off. But at the same time, the computer spewed out report after report every week, most of which were of no perceptible value to the managers to whom they were sent in a steady stream of fat brown envelopes. The cause? Designers decided what managers' needs were; they chose not to ask the managers what their needs were.

In one case an engineer employed by the Navy started his own engineering-services company and began to win contracts from the Navy. His little firm prospered and grew until he occupied a fair-sized building of his own and employed several dozen people.

One day he decided to quit listening to what the client wanted. He decided that he knew what the client needed far better than the client did, and he began to give the client what he deemed suitable. His company is no more. After many efforts to make him understand that he had to satisfy the needs they perceived, whether he perceived them the same way or not, the Navy just took its business elsewhere. Need is what the client perceives. If you do not agree with the client, you are always at liberty to try to change the client's view. But you can never decide for the client—unless specifically authorized to—what the client's need is.

RULE NUMBER 2. Be sure that you and the client are in agreement on what the need is. If you think the client is wrong you can either try to change the client's mind or you can withdraw from the project, but you can't function directly counter to the client's wishes. In most cases it is possible to persuade the client to change his view after you have done enough analysis to demonstrate that you are right and if you use a bit of tact or diplomacy. Example: "Mr. Client, I had the same idea you did when we started, but I have learned that I was wrong. Here is what I found out by research and analysis." This kind of opening is disarming and permits Mr. Client a face-saving, graceful way out because even you, The Expert, were led down the garden path by early appearances, and you are not ashamed to admit that you were forced to change your views.

In the formal value-engineering discipline, the practitioner asks a series of questions about the item under study: *What is it?* (Descriptive, functional name.) *What does it do?* (Main function.) *What else does it do?* (Secondary functions.) *What does it cost? What else would do it?* (The same main function, with no less reliability.) *What would that cost?*

These questions are asked in value engineering because the usual purpose of value engineering is to find ways to reduce costs—usually of manufactured items—without compromise of quality, dependability, or other important features. Using the basic method for trubleshooting problems or designing projects does not entail all these questions, usually, although it may entail alternate versions. If you are considering alternatives, you might wish to ask yourself, "What else will do it?" and bring up all possible alternatives. It is necessary to have defined "it"—main function—first. If you are engaged in analysis for troubleshooting purposes, you may wish to go through the analysis first, identifying the main function and all the secondary functions. Once you have identified all the component parts and functions, and mated each component part with its intended function and relation to the main function, you can begin to examine and study each component part to determine whether it is functioning properly, with the objective of finding malfunctioning components so they can be replaced or redesigned.

In recent times value analysis has been applied to other objectives than reducing costs, for the concepts work equally well for other parameters—conserving energy, saving time, reducing the use of scarce resources, and other such needs. For example, the EPA (Environmental Protection Agency) found itself in some difficulties a few years ago in spending the money budgeted by Congress for grants to communities whose water-treatment facilities need renovation. The problem was that it was taking approximately two years to process the application of a community for one of the grants, and time limits on the authority to award the grants were in danger of expiring before all the grants were approved. Meanwhile, EPA contracted with an engineering firm to provide certain skills in inspecting and evaluating the needs of water-treatment plants and arranged for that contractor to subcontract with a team of value engineers. It would be the responsibility of the latter team to uncover the cause of the delays and demonstrate a method for speeding up the process. The objective of the value analysis was, in this case, to save time rather than money.

In doing this, the questions concerning money are modified to address the question of time. *What does it cost?* becomes *How long does it take?* and *What would that cost?* becomes *How long would that take?*

The step-by-step analysis first uncovered all the main functions required to go from application through a variety of engineering tests and evaluations, through reports, and to final approval and award. Time required for each function was identified and charted, and the problem surfaced almost immediately. The final engineering report was taking many, many months to write, although no one could find any logical reason or justification for this. Troubleshooting that specific problem—foot dragging on writing a final engineering report—brought relief, and EPA managed to achieve their grant-award objectives.

Value engineers—most are certified by their national organization, the Society of American Value Engineers (SAVE) as Certified Value Specialists (CVS)—use a charting or diagramming method which is quite similar to the functional flowcharts discussed earlier. (See Figure 9.) The left block describes the need, and the blocks to the right of the broken line list, in order, the main function and the secondary or support functions in their

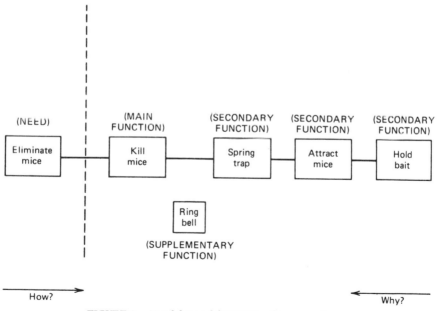

FIGURE 9. Need for and functions of a mouse trap.

logical cause-effect order. Reading from left to right you get HOW and from right to left you get WHY. Eliminate mice by killing mice, kill mice by springing trap, spring trap by attracting mice, attract mice by holding bait, and so forth. In the opposite direction, hold bait to attract mice, attract mice to spring trap, spring trap to kill mice, kill mice to eliminate mice.

By checking this logical sequence you can determine 1) whether the sequence is complete or something has been left out, and 2) whether the secondary function is a true support function, actually contributing a necessary support of the main function, or is a supplementary function that may have value but is not necessary to carrying out the main function. The expressed need should fit logically into these chains of reasoning.

In many cases there are secondary functions which are supplementary to and not in support of the main function. In this case we have a special mouse trap that rings a bell when a mouse has been caught. This is a useful function, announcing a successful action, but is not related to the main function of eliminating mice by trapping and killing them. Therefore, it does not belong in the direct functional flow. (However, it is positioned to show its relationship to the other functions; the positioning reveals that it is when the trap is sprung that the bell is activated and rings.) If you try to insert this functional block anywhere in the functional mainstream, the WHY-HOW question sequence will soon reveal that it does not belong there.

This is entirely functional as a diagram in that it does not describe or identify components. It is easily possible to do that by dividing the boxes in two parts, one of which describes the function and the other describing or naming the component which performs the function. It is also possible to note the actual cost of each function or the time required to perform it or whatever other quantifying parameter you wish to address.

What many value specialists do is to write out all the functions on cards, along with any other information deemed useful, and then arrange the cards in the sequence shown in Figure 9. The advantage of doing this rather than sketching it immediately is that the cards may be manipulated freely while studying the problem and especially when the WHY-HOW check reveals something amiss in the functional flow.

BRAINSTORMING

The method referred to as *brainstorming*, invented by Alex Osborne, an advertising executive, has become well-known, and good results have been claimed for it by many. The method was devised for use by a group of people rather than by individuals, and has been consistently advocated as a method for evoking creative contributions from a group.

Basically, the method calls for three major phases of activity:

1. The group is assembled, with a leader. The leader asks a question or calls for ideas along some specific avenue, such as slogans for a new soap product. Everyone is invited to make suggestions, with all suggestions accepted and strict injunctions against evaluative comments—derision, applause, laughter, or other. All ideas are recorded, preferably on a blackboard, where everyone can see what has been suggested and perhaps be inspired to "piggyback" ideas on some already recorded.

2. When the group runs out of steam, the ideas are evaluated. Some are thrown out, some modified, some perhaps combined, but this phase results in a collection of ideas acceptable at least on a tentative basis.

3. Final evaluations are made to either make a final selection or choose a few of the leading candidates (perhaps to offer a client for final decision).

It is possible for an individual to do something of this sort on a solo basis. Although we now have a good idea of how the creative process works, few recognize that it is brainstorming (I prefer to call it *idea-storming*) carried out on an individual basis. The creative process consists, in essence, of having your own subconscious mind record all the ideas you can come up with, do the evaluations, and make the final choice. Here are the three steps described almost universally by inventors and others who come up with important new ideas frequently:

1. Concentration: Intensive thought, with deliberate effort to develop ideas, analyze matters, try different notions "for size," and otherwise cogitate as long as it appears to be at all fruitful.

2. Incubation: Go on to other things. Deliberately put the matter out of mind and concern yourself with totally unrelated matters. Let the material incubate.

3. Illumination (often called inspiration): The solution pops into your head, most often when you are relaxing, playing golf, swimming, sunbathing, reading a book, or otherwise free of tension. Inspiration is often the first thought in the morning or may wake you up in the middle of the night.

Consider the example of Archimedes, who was asked by his king to determine whether the king's crown was all gold as it was supposed to be, or whether it had been adulterated with base metals. Archimedes pondered long on the problem without success. Then one day, while relaxing in his bath, he was inspired with the answer—he could learn the volume of the crown by measuring how much water it displaced. From there it was a simple matter to weigh the crown and make the determination the king wanted.

When you try as hard as you can to recall a name and cannot, but it pops into your head unbidden at some later time while you are thinking about something entirely unrelated, you have a similar manifestation of the unconscious mind at work.

This is not to say that you may not come up with good answers as a direct result of and during conscious deliberation and effort. With enough practice you will train your own mind to seek out problem solutions and new ideas. You will, in fact, probably be surprised at how many ideas you can generate when you have made conscious efforts to do so over some period of time. Eventually, even the effort is almost unconscious. That is, your mind begins to seek out answers and new ideas almost by reflex if you condition it to do so.

SPELLING OUT THE AGREEMENT

The need to specify what you are to do and what you are to deliver has been stressed several times. It has also been stressed that the matter of formal, written contracts be handled judiciously and diplomatically for fear of upsetting the apple cart. But that is not to say that you should not have some form of written agreement, which is likely to be an informal or semiformal letter. Nor is it to suggest that because the agreement is written as an informal document it should not be entirely specific and clear.

For some reason, many people appear to have trouble specifying and quantifying when the project is a custom-designed one. The client apparently thinks that the consultant is best qualified to suggest specifications, and the consultant tends to think that the client ought to know exactly what he or she wants and also how much of whatever that is. All too often, the result is that an agreement is entered into without proper specifications, and the later dispute becomes almost inevitable.

RULE NUMBER 3.   Never sign an agreement that does not specify exactly what you must do and/or deliver (both qualitative and quantitative) and how much or on precisely what basis you will be paid ("how much" if it is fixed-price, "on what basis" if it is a time-based fee).

It is rare that a project, even one calling for specialized technical or professional services, does not involve at least one specific deliverable item, such as a definitive final report. In many cases there are several reports required during the course of the project. Often the final document, whether it is a report, manual, design plan, or something else on paper and bound between covers, is truly all the client has to show for the money spent with you. If your project was to conduct a study or design a system, the end-of-project documentation represents the entire cost of the project.

Let's suppose that you were retained to conduct a study of some sort and you were required to submit a final report but the client hasn't the foggiest idea of how to quantify or specify that in advance. (You may be sure that if it never gets specified in the agreement, whatever you deliver later will be unsatisfactory!) Perhaps you do not have too clear an idea either of what a final report will entail for this project. How to proceed? Should you press the client to give you a specification? Or gamble on your own guesstimate?

It is almost never wise to press the client for specifications in such cases as these. You may ask diplomatically what preconceived notions the client has about the size and content of the final report, but you will probably not get an answer. It's up to you to make an estimate that you can live with. Consider that a 100-page report, typed double space (as many business people like typed reports), is about 25,000 words, a fairly extensive report for a small project. But consider also the probability that you will have to include some illustrations, charts and graphs, for example. If you propose to have these done by a professional illustrator, they can cost you a good bit of money. However, with graphic aids available today in any well-stocked artists supply house, almost anyone can do a decent job of creating charts, graphs, schematic diagrams, and other simple line drawings that are, if not fully professional in appearance, at least not too amateurish.

Make your best guess. The client will almost certainly accept your estimate. Base your price on that estimate and make sure that it becomes part of the agreement specifications.

WHAT THINGS MUST BE SPECIFIED

There is no hard and fast rule on what things must be specified, either qualitatively or quantitatively, except this: Specify anything and everything that represents items of cost, items for which you make specific charges, and/or items which represent to the client what he or she is buying. You must interpret this injunction sensibly. If you anticipate several hundred dollars' worth of printing or travel expense, you must include your estimate of this in the agreement or, if it is to be a fixed-price agreement rather than some fee-plus-expenses arrangement, be sure that you have included these items in your flat-price quotation. (In small consulting projects the arrangements are usually for fee plus expenses.) On the other hand, it is not necessary to include a few dollars' worth of postage or duplicating costs, which are properly absorbed as part of your overhead. It is important, however, that you have studied these areas and estimated realistically. For example, it can easily happen that you have estimated $10 worth of miscellaneous postage and copying costs only to find later that the client insists on having 200 copies of the final report. Such a thing actually happened to me in connection with the development of a special training program for a large manufacturer of cans and other containers. The program included a fairly substantial student manual to supplement the 35mm film reels which presented the main training materials. The contract called for delivering 50 copies of these manuals to the client.

One day, the marketing executive of my company called me to request that I send the client an additional 150 copies, gratis. I objected to this, pointing out that we had already met the terms of our contract, which had not been a particularly profitable one in any event. Our marketer insisted on making this expensive gift to the client, and I insisted that my own department was not going to stand the loss. (How easy for the marketing executive to give away something for which his department would not pay!)

Instead, I called the client and carefully explained that we had satisfied our contractual obligation and would gladly supply 150 additional copies of the manual at our cost (which would, of course, include our overhead and G&A burdens).

I had no difficulty whatsoever in getting the client's cheerful agreement to my entirely reasonable position. (I have never found it disadvantageous in any way to be entirely businesslike—agreeable, even amiable, but businesslike.)

This was made possible by the fact that in this contract we had been wise enough to specify, and to make specifications quantitative where appropriate. But let's look at other situations where such quantifying is less clear-cut. Consider the case of a project in which you are not at all sure just how many days or hours of your time are going to be required. This is a situation I face frequently and not always under the same conditions.

In one kind of case, especially when I am doing work for an established client, I offer a rough estimate of the time required and specify what I am to produce as nearly as I can estimate it. I do my level best to live with that estimate. If the project takes a bit longer, I absorb the difference and bill the client on the original estimate. If the project threatens to run over the original estimate by a considerable amount—especially if it is the result of changes or additions by the client, as it almost always is—I discuss this with the client and get approval to amend the original estimate.

There are some cases, especially when I am working for a new client for the first time and the client wants some assurance that he is not giving me a blank check, where I agree to a fixed price or a not-to-exceed maximum figure. This may sometimes entail risk on my part; it is not always possible to foresee everything that can go wrong and take up your time, but neither can you estimate for every possible contingency and expect the client to accept a gross overestimate. You simply must accept some risk in consulting, as does everyone engaged in any enterprise. The idea here is not to eliminate risk but to minimize it.

With the unit of cost to the client being some hourly or daily fee, it is that unit which must be specified. There are situations, however, in which it is totally impossible for you to make even a rough estimate. These are situations in which the client hires you on an indefinite basis with the option of terminating your services abruptly and without notice. (That is part of the risk and justifies, to a large extent, the relatively high hourly or daily rate most consultants command.) All that you can specify, in such cases, is the rate per unit time, the type of work you are to do or service you are to provide, where you will work (your office, the client's premises, or both), and how you are to be paid (billing periods).

In doing work with large companies, such arrangements often start out on the premise of being for a few days or even a few weeks, and wind up running for a number of months. One of my consultant acquaintances is working at this moment in the offices of a Connecticut firm on a project that was originally to have lasted for two months, is now in its sixth month, and appears likely to continue for an untold number of additional months. Some projects of this type have run for years. The Xerox training-development facility at Leesburg, Virginia, for example, hired a number of consultants, planning to use their services for a few months, and kept them all busy for over five years!

That possibility raises a question about the rates. To a large degree, your rates are a reflection of how many chargeable (paid) hours or days a year you manage to work. All other hours you consider to be part of your normal working hours are overhead. For example, if you want to pay yourself $25 an hour but manage to average only 20 hours per week of paid time, you have to charge clients $50 an hour, plus whatever your other costs are, to do so. Your overhead is automatically going to be over 100 percent since overhead is generally calculated as a percentage of direct labor.

But suppose you get a long-term assignment running into many weeks or even months. Should you still charge the same basic rate?

Feelings are divided on this, and the decision is not one of honesty, either. There are many consultants who would not vary their rate; they charge as much per hour for six-month assignments as they do for two-hour assignments. Some say it's a matter of principle, on the premise that having different rates for different clients or different projects is somehow dishonest or, at least, unscrupulously "sharp." There are others who object on the grounds that it is undignified and unprofessional, especially since they see it as a kind of Middle East bazaar bargaining.

Some of the arguments can be turned around and rationalized to prove the opposite point. For example, since a long-term assignment drastically lowers that portion of your overhead which must pay for your idle time or marketing time, is it honest to charge the long-term client the same rate, which includes that overhead, as you do the short-term client?

The fact is that neither practice is dishonest, unethical, or undignified unless you indulge in unethical tactics. A client offering you months or even weeks of full-time consulting is in the same position as a customer buying an extraordinary quantity of something; it seems reasonable to him that he is in a position which justifies negotiating a special rate.

The decision is your own personal one, but you can make it with a clear conscience, guided only by what you believe is your own best interests. If you ordinarily command $500 a day, but a client offers to pay you $300 a day for a guaranteed minimum of 60 days, you decide whether it is in your best interests to accept it, reject it, or try to compromise on some figure between $500 and $300. (The probability is that the client expects to negotiate in that range, and may very well settle with you at considerably more than $300 per day.) If you flatly reject the idea of negotiating your rate, however, you run the risk of not getting the contract. If the client believes that what he offers is important enough to justify negotiations, the risk is great indeed that the client, having his offer to negotiate the rate rejected out of hand, may feel that he has lost face and is therefore obligated to break off the talks and seek help elsewhere. On the other hand, if you indicate a willingness to discuss the rate, you are signaling clearly that you will accept less than your stated rate of $500, and any failure to negotiate in good faith is certain to cost you further consideration for the work. Once you agree in principle to negotiate, you must accept the fact that you are going to work for less than your usual rate and negotiate then in good faith.

It is here that the question of how to specify and quantify arises. It is easy enough to specify the hourly or daily rate in your agreement, but since such agreements are almost always subject to cancellation by the client, sometimes at the option of either party, how do you protect yourself against being negotiated into a reduction in your rate and then given only a few days' work at that special, reduced rate?

The necessary guarantee can be written into the agreement in either of two ways:

1. Specify a minimum number of hours/days at the rate agreed on—a not-less-than number of days or dollars.
2. Specify that the rate is contingent on being paid for some minimum number of hours/days, and that in the event of the project running for less than that number, you are to be paid at your standard rate.

The second alternative is usually somewhat more palatable to clients while still protecting your position. But the first alternative is probably more favorable to you if you can make the guarantee sufficiently high. So from the negotiating viewpoint, it is a good tactic to begin with the first alternative and get that if you can, using the second alternative as a fall back position if you are unable to reach agreement on the first one.

If you are writing an agreement to do work which is to produce an end-product that is the objective of the work—a manual, training program, computer program, or organization design, for example, you must consider everything that is involved in costs to you when you specify the deliverable items. A publication of any kind, for example, usually consists of both text and illustrations, and while contractors may remember to specify the number of pages the publication will include, they often overlook the need to estimate the number and kind of illustrations and, in some cases, the source. Sometimes the client can furnish some or all of the illustrations, while in other cases the contractor must furnish them. Bear in mind, too, that there are differences in cost among various types of illustrations—photographs, line drawings, engineering drawings, renderings, and others. Moroever, it must be specified what form the end-item(s) will be delivered in. If, for example, the end-product is to be prepared for printing in color, the art work is somewhat more complicated and expensive than it is for black and white reproduction.

When preparing an audiovisual training program on American Indians for the U.S. Forest Service, I was neatly mousetrapped by a supplier who pledged to supply me with all the 35mm colored slides I would need at reasonable prices. Unfortunately, I never got the commitment in writing. Instead, the supplier kept promising that the shipment was on the way. In the end, I had considerable expense that I had not anticipated, as well as a great deal of trouble and extra work, before I managed to satisfy the needs of the project for slides.

Training programs entail the direct program material, which may be in the form of lesson plans, lecture guides, student manuals, slides, transparencies, filmstrips, tapes, posters, flip charts, or other learning aids. To fail to specify and agree on these in advance is foolhardy and likely to create a disaster for you. Many training programs, however, also require other ancillary materials, such as instructors' guides, administrative manuals, and standard tests. These are just as important and just as costly.

Computer programs usually require some sort of documentation—reports and/or manuals explaining the program, how it's designed, what it does, how to install it, how to operate it. These manuals ordinarily require a number of flowcharts of the type that programmers and systems analysts favor.

Engineering projects often require finished engineering drawings (as distinct from rough drawings), and these can be quite costly. Most engineering projects require reports, too, and what has been said generally about reports and publications applies here. If the project is aimed at developing a design of some sort, it probably also requires the delivery of a prototype. For example, as an employee of a small electronics company I prototyped the first solid-state (transistorized) model of an RCA electronic voltmeter. (Formerly it was called a "VTVM," for vacuum tube volt meter, but once there were no longer vacuum tubes in the device, it was no longer a VTVM!) That sort of thing usually calls for two prototypes: 1) an engineering prototype to demonstrate a functionally feasible design, and 2) a manufacturing or production prototype to serve as a model for manufacturing the device efficiently. Engineering consultants who are emotionally more scientists than engineers sometimes forget that a second, production prototype is necessary.

In general, if the project requires that anything at all be produced and delivered by you as a result of your work, study that most carefully and make a realistic, worst-case estimate. If the client objects to your estimates, simply offer to make all items in dispute cost-reimbursable, but be sure that you don't straitjacket yourself with unrealistic not-to-exceed limitations.

10

Final Reports, Presentations, Other Products

Reports and other products are sometimes the most important aspect of the consulting project. In any case, they are always a reflection of you, the consultant—how well you perform and how effective your services are. But they tend also to become permanent records and leave permanent impressions.

WRITTEN REPORTS

Most consulting projects entail some physical product, written reports not the least common. If the project is of relatively long-term duration, and especially if the client is a fairly large organization with several levels of management, you will be required to submit progress reports, probably on a monthly basis, as well as a final report at the conclusion of the project. Written progress reports, submitted in multiple copies (frequently as many as 10) every month, enable several levels of management to maintain oversight of your work to satisfy themselves it is making progress toward the goal and not wasting time and money. It also aids that executive who authorized the project and contract to report "upstairs" in his company, both via the formality of whatever memoranda and reports he or she is required to generate, and by arming him or her for the inevitable boardroom meetings and inquisitions.

From this it should be clear that reports you prepare and submit are more than window dressing or trivial routine. They should report accomplishment that represents progress toward whatever the ultimate goal(s) of the project are, and they certainly should be well-written—lucid, accurate, informative, complete, and completely upbeat. At the same time, they must be dignified and objective in tone as well as credible. As in the case of proposals and similar documents (see Chapter 7), reports must not make unsupported claims, but must report only facts and data based on demonstrable fact, carefully avoiding hyperbole and superlatives. It is information, not rhetoric, that is the raison d'etre of the project report.

Progress reports are generally written in a narrative, chronological format. That is, they report events in the order of their occurrence, describing each event or action that has taken place during the reporting period, what resulted, what it led to, or whatever the significance was. When you prepare a progress report, bear in mind that the principal objective of the report is to record and report on progress. Therefore, it is in terms of progress, distinct movement toward the goal of the project, that everything reported assumes importance or the lack of it. Whatever has happened that moves the project toward the goal is progress and is therefore important. Whatever has little or no effect on progress is unimportant.

Some report writers allow themselves to confuse effort with importance. An event or function which entailed great effort automatically appears to be important, although it is actually of little or no importance. Suppose, for example, that certain data you were seeking proved difficult to get, and that it was only by great effort and ingenuity that you finally got it, only to find that it did not affect your results at all. There is an all-too-human tendency to gild the lily and make a great thing of how hard you worked and how clever you were in unearthing this data. Yet you can't show that this represented progress or contributed in any way to progress. Heroic and brilliant although you may have been, you must be truthful about the importance of this data and mention it only in passing if at all. (However, it may be worthwhile to note, for future projects, that this data is not worth collecting.)

Perhaps it's cruel, but it's nonetheless true in most situations, including report writing, that no one cares about the storms you met at sea; they ask only if you brought the ship home. Only results count.

ORGANIZATION AND FORMATS

Information can be organized in a variety of ways, and there are different kinds of reports for different kinds of needs. Among the several ways information can be organized are these:

Chronological or order of occurrence

Historical—similar to chronological, but not necessarily in strict order of occurrence

Reverse chronological—tracing events back to origin or first causes

Order of importance—least to most important or vice versa (most often vice versa)

The general to the particular or vice versa

Syllogistic—beginning with premises and developing arguments

Deductive—stating principle(s) and analyzing facts to relate logically to stated principles

Inductive—examining facts and organizing them for logical inference of governing principles

A chronological narrative is probably the most often used organization for progress reports. However, because most reports have several sections, the data is generally organized differently in each section according to the purpose and utility of the section. Some clients, especially those who authorize projects more or less regularly, may have their own standard report format. In such case, you will of course use the client's preferred format. Often, the client either has no preferred format or has only the most general of guidelines governing the preparation of written reports. Then the format is left to you, but that does not relieve you of the obligation to furnish the kinds of information the client wants and should logically have if the report is to be useful.

In most cases the opening introduction of a report is a narrative, along the following general lines:

1. Background information. If a final report or the only report, this is likely to be a recapitulation of the overall objective of the project, the general strategy and principal functions, and other data which would bring the reader "up to speed" about the project. If this is one of a series of progress reports, the introduction need merely furnish a brief transition from the prior progress report and introduce the general objective of this just-expired reporting period's effort.

2. A narrative recounting of all events of the reporting period or total project, usually in chronological order. If necessary, linkages to or transitions from the prior report may be included in introducing the various elements of the reporting period's efforts.

3. Problems encountered. This should include complete accounts of the problems encountered and how they were overcome or solved. Probable linkages to projections made in prior report.

4. Examination of results. In some types of projects, such as studies and surveys, the data collected needs to be presented in full detail, discussed, and analyzed. This is generally syllogistic, may involve mathematical presentations, must usually show methodology of analysis, present results such as logical conclusions to be drawn or premises established for future investigation (next reporting period, perhaps).

5. Plans for next month (if progress report). Links from this report logically, projects problems anticipated and how they will be handled, and also attempts to project next month's achievements. Must usually project goals for next month.

6. As an alternative to (5), if this is a final report this section will probably be one of extending examination of results on a total-project basis and extending conclusions drawn in (4) to final recommendations.

Obviously, some of these sections require different formats and organization from others. Raw data, for example, may be presented as a straight, chronological narrative, but when the data are to be examined and analyzed, they must be arrayed, grouped, and processed to reach conclusions through correlations and other manipulations. Here the data must dictate, by their very nature, how they will be organized. In fact, it may very well be necessary to organize the data several times, in several different patterns, to get a complete picture of what the data mean.

Syllogistic presentations are inescapable; the client wishes to know how you reached conclusions and on what basis you offer your recommendations. Where you must explain a premise or a principle upon which you base some of your work, it may be necessary to make an explanatory excursion, which will probably require a from-the-general-to-the-particular presentation, or even a reverse-chronology of effect-cause to trace something back to its source or origin.

Project reports, then, tend to be both reportorial and, to at least some extent, speculative. Most have sections which ought properly to be confined strictly to factual reporting, while other sections may speculate—albeit with syllogistic logic—on the meaning of the facts presented earlier. Even here it is necessary to be entirely objective in tone and method, and to offer no conclusions, recommendations, or even general opinions for which you cannot or do not demonstrate a logical chain of reasoning supported by demonstrated facts. That is absolutely vital to the overall credibility of your report, and it is essential that you preserve that credibility with scrupulous care. Once lost, such as through anything clearly and indisputably demonstrated to be error, credibility is difficult to regain. This does not refer to trivial errors such as minor spelling or typographical errors, but to errors of fact or method. These put into question your professional consulting skills and your professional reputation, which you must guard jealously.

One common error often made by consultants is the assumption, perhaps unconscious, that his or her professional reputation and image are such that clients will accept anything he or she says on "authority" alone. It may even be true that some clients will accept what you say as absolute truth and even wisdom simply because you say so. But it is hazardous to depend on this presumed authority. Even when a client calls me on the telephone in distress over something and wanting immediate counsel, I always explain why I am advocating whatever course of action I advocate. Make it an ingrained habit that whenever you write or speak professionally you think syllogistically, and you always report objectively, even in recommendations where you are reporting conclusions drawn from logical analysis. For example, suppose a client asks me whether the General Accounting Office will always compel a contracting official to allow bidders enough time to respond. I must honestly answer that I cannot guarantee it, but they should do so, and they have done so in previous cases, which I then cite. The logical conclusion is that the GAO ought to be expected to do again what they did previously in similar circumstances, and that protesting to the GAO is a proper thing to recommend to my client in such cases. I have not only given my client good advice, but I have shown the client clearly the basis on which I offer my recommendation.

This may run counter to the business philosophy of some consultants,

who believe that their methods and knowledge ought to be held as closely
as possible, to make clients dependent on them. They fear that if the client
learns too much, the client will not require the consultant's services in the
future. This is at least partly why many professionals develop a mystique
about their professions, often with a cabalistic jargon to aid and abet the
mystique.

This is clearly evident in the use of Latin in medicine and law, for example, and in the distortion of word meanings to make jargon of them. For
example, in a dispute with my insurance company many years ago, I was
dismayed to find that the word *premium* on my policy meant *payment*. It
had never occurred to me that the insurance company would mask the
idea of payment with this unlikely euphemism. But accountants offset
items in their work, and when they say *sales* they don't mean what you
and I mean when we use that word. Neither does *cost of sales* refer to the
cost of the selling effort, nor does keeping books on a *cash basis* mean that
literally. To a psychologist, *behavior* means something other than deport-
ment, and *reflex conditioning* proved to be too nearly self-explanatory so
most psychologists today appear to favor the newer term *operant conditioning*, which is more satisfactorily obscure and vague.

To some degree, we all fall prey to habits of jargon that we use as a kind
of shorthand. I confused someone with whom I corresponded by using
what is to me a most common term, *sign off*, to mean approving by signature. My correspondent was not familiar with the usage, but thought the
term referred to saying good night, as when radio announcers used to
"sign off." That made my letter nonsensical as a result. A scientist may refer to an environmentally-caused mutation, but that is a shorthand other
scientists will recognize as a kind of code for the perpetuation of muta-
tions that, because of environmental circumstances, made the species
better suited for survival as a result of the mutation.

Such jargon and codes are all very well when professionals of a given
kind communicate among themselves, but I believe them to be out of
place in communicating with others, and especially so when they are
used to deliberately surround one's profession with an impenetrable mystique for the purpose of self-preservation.

I freely admit that I am probably very much in the minority in this position. Many other consultants believe that their knowledge and skills are
their stock in trade, and to educate their clients too much in the consulting methods and skills is "giving the store away." Aware as I am that other
consultants believe as they do and can make a rational argument for their
position, I cannot take the position that it is morally wrong or dishonest to
play your cards close. Like sliding fee scales, good arguments can be made
on both sides of the question. My position has always been that when a

client has paid me the fee I ask for, the client has bought all of me—all the technical/professional help I can provide, including orientation, indoctrination, and training. (One of my services, in fact, is to conduct training seminars for client companies.) I believe—and I think this is a matter of policy rather than of ethics—that the client is morally entitled to understand exactly what I am doing in his or her behalf and why I am doing it. But there are at least two other considerations here.

1. Lectures, seminars, training, and other information about that in which I specialize are of themselves profit centers, as you'll see in a later chapter.

2. The basic fear is largely ungrounded. It is far more the exception than the rule that a client studies what you do and does it for himself or herself the next time. If you have performed well, and the client needs such services again, it is almost certain that you will be favored with the client's patronage once again. (Such has been my experience.)

For the above reasons I believe it essential that your reports be as lucid as you can make them, and that they should not withhold anything. Surrounding your work with a mystique has its downside as well as its upside. What you may gain in making the client dependent on you may be more than nullified in a corresponding failure to be entirely credible and so to inspire the client's total and complete confidence in you.

LEVEL OF DETAIL

Aside from the question of revealing precisely what your methods are, there is the question of how detailed reports should be.

Unless the client has mandated some specific, detailed specification of reporting format, this is largely a matter for your own judgment. Here are the factors to consider:

Objective of the Project. If the project is designed strictly to reach some end-goal, such as the development of a computer program, it is generally not necessary to go into painstaking detail in the reports but merely to report on progress, problems, and whatever else will demonstrate progress, account for time and money spent, and assure client that the project is moving along. On the other hand, if the project is designed to devise a system or methodology, or to design something, it is likely that the client will want considerable detail. If much of your work consists of making decisions and acting on them on some regular basis, the client is likely to want full details.

Client's Technical Level.   The client who is a technical or professional in your own field generally requires far less detail to understand precisely what you are reporting than does one whose field is entirely different from your own. For example, if you are designing a computer system for a client who is also highly knowledgeable about computer technology, you can probably use the jargon of your profession and obviate the need for detail that explains the obvious to the professional in your field. But if you are writing a report for a client who hasn't the foggiest idea what *multiprocessing* means and has no idea what "generation" his own computer belongs to, it is absolutely necessary to translate your professional jargon into everyday English or, at least, explain the terms when you use them. That means going into painstaking detail in most cases.

Objective of the Report Itself.   Some reports are more or less routine and of relatively little importance once they are read for their immediate message. But some reports are, themselves, either the objective of the project or the end-product that represents the objective of the project. It was once my obligation to do a survey and prepare a report for a government executive who needed the report per se to submit with his budget request as justification for the funds requested. Sometimes a client wants certain information which is best presented in a report. In another case, my final report presented a model for training evaluation as its concluding section, and it was that model that the client wanted; the rest of the report was relatively unimportant except as it explained the model.

There is at least one other consideration, one that justifies a special discussion, the potential of the report for generating additional business. A report represents such a potential or can be made to. Some excursive discussions are needed to sketch in the background and explain this fully. An anecdote will illustrate one relevant situation:

Some years ago, while I was the general manager of a technical-services organization, a government executive with whom I was acquainted approached me about an idea he had. He was sure that one of the operations of his agency could be done far less expensively by contracting the work to a private firm such as the one I was employed by. His idea was to have me write an unsolicited proposal, which he believed he could get approved.

I found the notion appealing, and we spent a day together, visiting nearby installations of his agency and discussing what was to be done, after which I returned to my own office to ponder the matter.

It was soon evident, as I explored the proposition, that the proposal would be extremely expensive to write and would require a massive effort. I would have to do a great deal of research into several areas and do most exhaustive cost analyses. All of this with no guarantee that we would ultimately get the contract.

I found the prospect an unacceptable one, and I was reasonably sure that my company would agree with my own appraisal. I therefore visited the government client and so advised him. But, I added, I could suggest what I thought to be a reasonable alternative: If he could award us a suitable study contract, the resulting report would provide him with information worth the cost—I was prepared to demonstrate that most clearly—and enable us to write the proposal at an acceptable cost. Doing such a study would undoubtedly disqualify us from winning the contract on a sole-source basis, but it would enable the agency to "go out on the street" with the solicitation (invite proposals from everyone interested), because the information could be made available to everyone. I found that a better gamble because I had little doubt that I could write the winning proposal. At any rate, I was prepared for that gamble.

There is nothing improper about this. The government cannot solicit proposals without preparing an internal estimate of cost, nor can a government agency expect contractors to submit proposals if the cost of the proposals is prohibitively high. It is not likely that anyone would have been willing to prepare a proposal without more information than existed at that time under the circumstances. The only thing unusual about this was the way in which the entire thing came up. Usually, when an agency wants to investigate the possibility of using outside contractors for projects, some sort of study is undertaken first so that the statement of work can be written. If the study required is too extensive for an in-house effort by the agency, it is customary to contract the study out. In short, there is nothing truly unusual about using contract services to gather the necessary background data for a procurement.

This is usually a direct result of a government agency's initiative, but it sometimes happens that a contractor doing work for a government agency—especially research and development work—perceives needs and/or opportunities for the government to benefit by further work based on the project being conducted currently. For example, a contractor developing a better fighter aircraft may uncover some entirely new and radically different approach to a related area, perhaps a better rocket fuel. This possibility may take the shape of an unsolicited proposal, resulting in a new contract to develop that possibility into a reality.

It is not uncommon, therefore, for contractors to make active searches for and carefully consider all possibilities for follow-on contracts. The alert contractor finds or makes opportunities to use project reports as preliminaries to proposals for new contracts. In fact, the *recommendations* section of a report may be, in effect, a preliminary proposal itself.

When considering what level of detail to go to in a project report, consider this possibility and be guided accordingly, especially if your client is a private-sector organization where the client makes whatever rules suit him at the moment. (As distinct from government bureaus and others who are bound by statute to follow certain procedures in procurement.)

ORAL REPORTS AND PRESENTATIONS

Frequently a client requires an oral report or presentation, usually in addition to rather than in place of a written report. Generally, this is because the client wishes to ask questions and explore areas of special interest, and if the client is a fairly large organization, it is likely that you will be asked to make this presentation to a group. The larger the group the more questions and comments will be voiced.

Sometimes these questions are not sincere quests for information. Participants at such an event are frequently relatively low-level people in the organization who want to be noticed and recognized as being alert and intelligent, so they formulate questions intended to demonstrate those qualities. Sometimes there are people present who are merely combative and feed their egos by attacking the speaker, whom they hope to disgrace or at least to embarrass. Some are employees who simply resent you as an outside consultant earning more money than they do, and possibly being a threat to them and their jobs. Sometimes these latter individuals even feel that they have been put down by the act of bringing in an outside consultant expert to do whatever it is that the boss could not or would not entrust to in-house staff. You, of course, are made the object of any resentment at any fancied put-down.

Don't expect a completely receptive audience at such a presentation, then, especially if the group you must speak to is fairly large. Be prepared to keep your sense of humor, pretend you don't recognize the hostile nature of some of the questions and comments, and don't engage in a battle of barbs. Disarm the opponent by a simple device of appearing to agree. Example:

I once undertook to develop a model evaluation system which would make a direct measure of training transfer—make qualitative and quantitative comparisons of actual job performance improvements resulting from training. This was a pioneering effort; such a model had never been attempted before, and I was cautioned by those expert in that field that the job was an impossible one. Still, I persisted and produced what I thought to be an acceptable first model, with a thoroughly detailed final report. The client asked me to make a formal presentation before a group.

I found the group to number over 20 education-and-training specialists, and after I had introduced and explained the model, I was bombarded with questions. For the most part, the questions expressed skepticism regarding the model, its validity, practicality, accuracy, conformance with accepted training-evaluation technology, and numerous other fine points.

I found it relatively easy to answer all questions and disarm all hostility by the simple device of saying, "Yes, but—." I answered a number of questioners in a single answer in somewhat this manner: "Yes, I agree that this is a somewhat crude model and needs much more development, but I remind you that this is a Model T evaluation method, and we can only develop the advanced, V-8 model by developing and using this and then going on."

Several times I had to point that philosophy out, using different analogies and metaphors so that I did not repeat myself despite the fact that the question was being repeated. I kept my good humor throughout the session and gave no hint of my real annoyance at the petty sniping, which in this case was due in part to resentment that I had done what some of these experts said couldn't be done. I tried to minimize the embarrassment of anyone who thought he had been humiliated by being proved wrong through candid confession that my model was a crude first effort. (I didn't and do not now really believe that. It was a first model and I hope has been considerably improved since then, but it was not at all crude.) I even admitted that it was almost entirely theoretical, and we wouldn't know whether it really worked until after extensive tryouts.

The head of the client organization was quite satisfied with the model and the presentation. In fact, I strongly suspected that the chief reason for the presentation was to respond to criticisms being voiced in the organization that the task was a total waste of time and money, and nothing worthwhile could come of it. Perhaps he began to have some doubts, too, and wanted to see how I would field complaints and criticisms, and whether I could win over any of the doubters. I probably did not actually win any of them over, but at least I opened their minds a bit on the subject and quieted the criticism. (I could not have achieved this result if I had been combative and given critics a concrete reason to be hostile.)

Not all presentations fit into that category. Most are sincerely inspired as a perceived necessity, even if some of the attendees may not feel exactly warm towards the consultant interloper. Unless you definitely know something to the contrary, you must approach and plan a presentation as a sincere effort to present results and answer questions. You must be prepared for a complete exposition, even if you have furnished a detailed written report beforehand.

The key to a successful presentation is thorough planning and preparation. Unless you are able to speak well spontaneously, you would be well advised to write out your entire text on cards or in an actual script which contains notations of any visual aids—posters, slides, transparencies, or other—that you have had prepared.

THE IMPORTANCE OF VISUAL AIDS

Visual aids serve a number of most useful functions in a presentation:

> They aid the attendees to grasp what you are presenting.
> They aid you in speaking by taking much of the pressure off.
> They add interest and help hold the listeners' attention.

The question of which to use—posters, flip charts, slides, or transparencies—is often debated. There are a number of considerations that ought to be taken into account when making the decision. The whole matter of visual aids and public speaking will be discussed in more depth in Chapter 12. For now, let us just make the point that it is to your advantage in at least those ways listed here to use as many visual aids as possible. These do entail some expense, so it is wise to discuss any anticipated need for such formal presentations when negotiating the original contract.

HANDOUTS

Another useful aid in making presentations is the handout—items you distribute to everyone in attendance. You use handouts in various ways and for various reasons, according to your situation. Here are some of the ways and purposes of handing out material to attendees:

> Handouts may be visual aids, used simply because it is much less expensive to type and duplicate information than it is make up original artwork and have it made into posters, slides, or some other form for

presentation. Handouts may be a way out when you have been given an unexpected requirement for a formal presentation and have not budgeted money for visual aids.

Handouts are sometimes used because the information is too extensive to put on any kind of visual aid, and you believe that it is unnecessary to recite it all, or you have statistical data and other material you believe the listener must be able to scan several times to grasp it all and understand the significance of what you are presenting.

Handouts are used often to give attendees something to carry away from the session as a permanent reference.

For some types of presentation, handouts are given to listeners as samples—if, for example, you are presenting some new and improved product.

Handouts, then, offer much the same advantages that visual aids do, although they are less effective in some respects. They also can do some things that visual aids can't do, as the foregoing list reveals.

For some presentations, if your budget can endure it, you may wish to make up a handout package of all the visual aids, reduced to 8-½×11 inch size. This is not an uncommon practice, and we'll talk some more about it later.

OTHER PRODUCTS

Many consulting projects require the delivery of other products than reports. These include, but are not restricted to, manuals of various kinds, instructional materials (which may or may not include manuals); audiovisual materials; drawings; computer programs in the form of manuals, tapes, or other; designs; and perhaps even other end-products. The most common problem concerning such requirements is defining them properly in advance to avoid disputes and even possible litigation later. The danger—and this has been mentioned before, but is serious enough to warrant repetition—is that you and the client may think you understand each other and are in agreement as to what the end-products are to be, and find only when the project has ended that you were not in agreement at all. This can result from a mutual lack of knowledge of what such end-products ordinarily are or from such dangerous and misleading euphemisms used in business contracts sometimes as guarantees of "best commercial practice." (Imagine trying to agree in a court of law on just what that means?) Here are a couple of examples of how such problems can arise:

In a contract to produce a multi-media training program, we stipulated each item to be delivered and specified that the copy would be "camera ready," a common enough phrase that I believed to be well enough understood among all in our field.

To my utter frustration, the client kicked up a terrible fuss when he saw the camera-ready copy. He objected violently to the spliced-in corrections and the paste-ups, threatening to refuse final payment. He insisted that the copy was not camera-ready, despite my careful explanations that we were using a universally accepted practice and that none of what appeared to be flaws to him would show up in the printed copy. I had a most difficult time resolving the matter, but finally had him go and check with several printers, who assured him that what he had in hand was indeed thoroughly acceptable camera-ready copy.

This is an unusual case. Not all clients are that ignorant nor that obtuse and stubborn, and it is almost impossible to guard against that kind of ignorance. However, it is not always the client who is obtuse.

In a contract covering an extensive program to be conducted on the client's facilities, there was a clause authorizing the contractor to sell his own project up to $75,000 worth of his own books, "at prices not to exceed those charged the most favored customer." In pursuit of the $75,000 so authorized, the contractor set about developing $75,000 worth of books which could be used on the project. Finishing the books, the contractor had them printed and bound, delivered them to the project for use, and billed the client $75,000.

The client refused to pay the bill on the grounds that it was for unauthorized activity, a "not allowable" expense. Months of haggling and arguing followed without resolution.

It finally occurred to someone to bring in special help to resolve the problem. The specialist brought in began by studying the wording of the clause. He decided almost immediately that he had the answer.

"Your problem is," he told the unhappy contractor, "that you are billing the client $75,000 for R&D for developing these books, and that is not what the contract authorizes. What it authorizes is the sale to your own project of up to $75,000 worth of your own, proprietary books, books off the shelf. That's what is meant by 'at prices not to exceed those charged the most favored customer.' No other interpretation is possible."

He resolved the matter by establishing list prices and discounts for the books and billing the client for $75,000 worth of those books at maximum discounts. Thereupon the client paid the bill without a murmur.

The meaning and intent of the contract was clear enough, but the contractor, who had no proprietary books, misinterpreted the description in the only terms that fit his own normal situation. This illustrates once again the importance of being able to view situations from the client's viewpoint.

(It also illustrates that an accurate definition of the problem points directly to and often even specifically identifies the proper solution.)

There are cases, also, of winning Pyrrhic victories. One such case, which is distressingly typical, occurred when a federal agency awarded a contract to a fairly large behavioral-sciences consulting firm to develop a training program. The firm proposed to develop a program consisting of two end-items, a student's manual an an instructor's manual, and they proceeded to do just that in a project costing approximately $50,000. Eventually they delivered those two end-products.

The client ran into trouble immediately when he attempted to use the two manuals to develop classes. For one thing, he was unable to find a functional relationship between the two manuals. Each appeared to be extensive in its coverage, but the instructor's manual gave no hint of how to organize the program and use the two manuals. An effort to compare the two side by side left the client baffled.

He went back to the contractor, who simply pointed to the contract, the terms of which they had fulfilled. Whether the products were useful to the client apparently was of no concern to the contractor.

The client called in another consultant, who managed to straighten the problem out by developing an administrative guide and curriculum plan which prescribed methods for using the existing manuals. This was information that should properly have been part of the instructor's guide, but both client and proposer neglected to determine that when writing the contract. The contractor was therefore on good legal grounds, but his indifference to the client's interests earned him only the client's enmity and resolve that never again would that client agree to an award to that contractor.

Such things happen with a fair degree of frequency. When the client is a private firm, such cases often wind up in litigation because clients refuse to pay the consultant. When the client is a government agency or a large corporation, and when the contract is for a relatively small sum of money, the client often chooses to pay and then turns to other sources for relief.

This is a short-sighted policy on the part of the consultant, for it ordinarily costs far more to acquire a new client than it would have cost to adjust whatever was wrong and keep the good will of the existing client. But some consultants are unthinking of the long-term results and proceed on the premise that it is the client's fault if he (the client) failed to foresee whether the end-product specified would satisfy the need.

In another case in my experience, the client was dissatisfied with the quality of the product delivered and rejected it. The consultant patched the work up, but it was still unsatisfactory. The client finally came to the conclusion that the consultant could not do better and paid, but made it known throughout the agency that this consultant had done poor work and could not do better. This was a case where the consultant would have been well advised to seek out someone to help make the client happy, as some consultants wisely do when they encounter such problems.

What is at question here is not whether you have delivered what the contract specified, but whether what you delivered or are about to deliver is 1) a proper product, useful to the client in satisfying the original need which was the reason for engaging your services, and 2) of adequate quality to satisfy the client's needs.

This is not to say that you must necessarily make good any deficiencies out of your own pocket. More often than not, if you and your client have discovered that what you originally agreed upon as a product is really not exactly what is needed, the client will agree to amend your contract and pay you whatever is necessary to produce the needed end-item. The importance of specifying it precisely in the contract now appears; it provides both the moral and legal basis for renegotiation.

It is a mistake to assume automatically that whatever you specified in the contract to be done and/or produced is correctly conceived. It may well be, but it may not be. When undertaking custom projects, especially when there are elements of research and development involved, it is often not possible to be sure what the end-product ought to be exactly; the design needs often surface only during the earlier phases of the project. It is wise, therefore, to be prepared to amend the original project design and the contract if the design changes affect costs. This means periodic evaluations as the project progresses to compare the needs of the client as they now appear with the end-item(s) conceived earlier.

It is very much to your interests to operate on this basis, inasmuch as this often results in a great deal more business developing even before the current project is completed. This was particularly true during the great weapons and space programs of the fifties and sixties, when many large electronics, aerospace, and other high-technology firms ballooned relatively modest initial contracts into much greater undertakings. Whereas additional business sometimes results from what has been learned in a project and the final report can be virtually a proposal for another contract, there are also cases where original contracts can be amended and grow to much larger sizes simply by discovering a need or opportunity for different outcomes than those originally contemplated.

COMMON MISTAKES IN REPORTING

One of the most common mistakes made in progress reporting is in estimating that percentage of the project completed and that remaining to be done. The common mistake that so many make is to measure not the portion of work actually accomplished, but the proportion of time or budget (in effect, the same thing) expended. If the project is estimated to require 100 professional days of effort and 25 days have been expended, the consultant tends to report the project 25 percent accomplished, with 75 percent yet to go. If the project is based on, let us say, a 6-month effort, with each month approximately equal in days or hours to be devoted to the project, here is a typical month-by-month projection of percentage completion:

Month Number	Percentage Completed	Remaining Effort
1	16	84
2	33	67
3	50	50
4	60	40
5	65	35

The trend is obvious. As the time grows short, the consultant begins to realize that percentage completion—nearness to the end-goal(s) of the project—is not keeping pace with percentage of budget expended. Now, with only 15-20 percent of the time left, he realizes there is probably not more than one half the work finished.

The problem is that you can't measure anything by itself. You must find some external measure, something totally objective and unrelated to the budget of time or dollars. (The chief purpose in such measurement is to compare the two and determine whether the project will be completed on schedule and within budget.)

Management specialists freely admit that one of the more difficult things to do in management is find the means for measuring progress and achievement in a number of fields. This is particularly difficult in activities where there are a large number of diverse functions, and it is difficult to estimate the time required for each. Many custom projects, especially R&D efforts, fit this category. Nevertheless, it is necessary to try, and there is a method which has proved to be reasonably successful even in these extreme cases. It is based on making certain arbitrary assumptions which take advantage of the laws of probability. Briefly, these are the steps:

1. Break the project down into as many distinct steps, phases or functions as possible, trying to make each of approximately the same time/budget requirement and trying to specify at least 50 such steps or functions.

2. Arbitrarily assign each such step a value of 2 percent of the project overall.

3. Monitor each step each month. (Some will be concurrent while others are sequential, so each must be monitored separately.)

4. Use the following scoring method:
    A step not begun is zero percentage.
    A step in progress but not complete is one half done.
    A step completed represents whatever percentage was assigned it.

If you had 50 such items, any step in progress, whether just begun or nearly complete is one percent. Add up the one- and two-percent steps each month, and report the total, *regardless of how that total correlates with the percentage of your time or dollar budget expended.*

According to how they correlate, you can judge whether you are behind, on, or ahead of schedule and budget, and that tells you what you must do.

This system works reasonably well if it is followed faithfully. The normal error in estimating each step tends to cancel itself out if there are 50 or more steps and the rules are followed. (The greater the number of elements or steps, the more effectively probability law operates to minimize total error.)

Another common error in report writing is the tendency to attempt to use text for all presentations except numerical data. For some obscure reason, report writers operate on the assumption that only numbers lend themselves to tabular presentation. Later, in discussing consultant skills (Chapter 12), we'll discuss this matter in greater depth and demonstrate the conception and construction of tabular presentations.

11

Fees and Collections

We all pay for our education, in one way of another. There are ways to minimize that cost and avoid being tricked or trapped into working for nothing. Here are a few things you ought to know.

THINGS ARE RARELY WHAT THEY SEEM

The practice of requiring one third of your total fee upon contract signing, one third at some identified mid-point, and one third upon delivery and acceptance of the final product or service is a fairly common one in commercial trade. One reason for operating on this basis is that the first one third serves as "earnest money," demonstrating the client's ability and intention of paying your fees. But another excellent reason is your own cash-flow need; as a small, independent consultant, you simply cannot afford to "carry paper," nor can you discount it at the banks very easily. (Banks are notoriously reluctant to finance service businesses, largely because there are few tangible assets to seize in case of default.) I have had reason (40,000 reasons, in fact!) to regret my frequent failures to insist upon this arrangement. Here is how many consultants learn bitter lessons:

In a typical case the consultant is invited to visit the client, who is comfortably situated in a well-furnished office in a modern office building located in a good business district. There are several offices in the suite, a reception area, and several secretaries and other people busily engaged in a variety of functions—typical busy office of a presumably successful business.

The client is well dressed, smilingly affable, obviously at ease in the environment, may even get on first-name terms with you immediately. He says something along the lines, "George—may I call you 'George'?—we have a lot of work here, and we can keep you pretty busy. Now here is what we need." And he goes off into a discourse of their needs which holds the promise of much profitable work for you.

You raise the question of a retainer. "Sure," you're assured, "No problem. Take a few days, of course, for the paper work, but we'd like you to get started in the meanwhile."

Because the operation appears to be substantial and successful, you go along. (You may even be reluctant to bring up the subject of a retainer.) Surely this successful company will have no problem with the few hundred or few thousand dollars your service will cost.

Some time later, when all your diplomatic inquiries into getting paid run into a wall of excuses and evasions, it begins to dawn on you that you've been taken in by appearances. It may well be that the client owns absolutely nothing in the office except perhaps his own brief case. It's not too difficult to rent or lease-buy all furniture and office equipment, and it is commonly done today. Even if you were to sue successfully, you might not be able to satisfy a judgment. If you are surprised that your client was far less successful than he appeared to be and that he was unable to pay your bill, you may be even more surprised at how easily you can win in court and still lose in the end.

WARNING FLAGS

One reason you should have a signed agreement with your client is in the event that you must undertake some legal action to collect your bill. Of course, you would not have undertaken the project if you had had any reason at all to suspect that you would have such difficulty. Because you found the client to be so eminently and obviously successful and open, you may have hesitated to insist on a signed agreement between you. Your client may even have suggested that his word was like money in the bank, and that he was a great believer in doing business on a handshake and gentleman's agreement.

Those are danger signs, red flags that should alarm you immediately. In today's environment, most businesspeople expect to do business via written agreements, even if they are simple letters of agreement, and it is rare indeed that any businessperson will object to your being businesslike and expecting the client to be businesslike also. Any client who appears reluctant to sign an agreement with you—provided that the agreement is a reasonable one—is probably telegraphing something that should be interpreted as a danger sign.

Whether you insist on an advance payment or retainer is up to you, although you should probably insist if there is the slightest reason to suspect any danger of having difficulty in collecting your fees. Granted that you may run into difficulties in collecting advance fees from some of the large corporations, due to ponderous corporate procedures or policies preventing such payment in advance, but in that situation there is no doubt as to the client's *ability* to pay, and you should have no difficulty arranging for progress payments if the project is long-term. It may also be, in dealing with such a large corporation, that the corporation has its own standard agreement forms or wishes to issue you a purchase order, which has the force of a contract. But it is rare that you will have difficulty arranging for some written commitment from a large corporation. If you are dealing with such a large firm, their purchase order may have a preprinted standard clause explaining that payment will be made upon completion, when you will use one of the copies of the purchase order as an invoice.

There is a danger in this, if you are given a purchase order for a long-term project, and you agree to begin work without reading the fine print that specifies payment only upon completion, you may have great difficulty in getting progress payments. The time to settle the matter of payments is when you are making your initial agreement. If a purchase order results, read it carefully, and if you object to any of its terms, raise the matter immediately and get it settled. Arrangements can usually be made at the beginning. But even though the company may be flexible, the individual with whom you have made the agreement may be reluctant to go to the trouble later of modifying the terms of the purchase order or making special arrangements for you. You may be assured that it is not unreasonable, in a long-term project, to ask for progress payments at not more than 30-day intervals, and it is generally acceptable to request that your invoices be paid at two-week intervals.

The importance of settling all this in advance is illustrated by my experience in negotiating several contracts with the Bureau of Naval Personnel. The Bureau Counsel was also the Bureau's contracting officer when the Bureau contracted for special services independently of the centralized Naval supply service. Although he was a most jovial individual, he was also one who hewed to the line exactly. He negotiated shrewdly, as might be expected, going over the proposal and contract terms point by point. But only after we had agreed on all points and he was about to approve the contract did I think to bring up the matter of progress payments. At this point the gentleman frowned and said that while he had no objection to making progress payments, to negotiate those now meant that the entire negotiation was nullified, and we would have to go back to square one if I wished to negotiate a different payment schedule than one of billing upon completion. After that experience, I was careful to stipulate the mode of payment in my proposal and make sure that it was mentioned early in the negotiation. Not all contracting officials are quite that exacting, but occasionally you will run into such situations.

Clients who agree too readily to my terms, who appear willing to forego all discussion of rates and total estimates, for example, alarm me. It comes across to me as a signal that perhaps the client does not intend to pay me, anyway, so why worry about what I charge?

A variant of this is the client who indicates a willingness to engage you without even inquiring as to your rates and estimate of the total project cost. That is truly alarming. What responsible businessperson agrees to a blank-check assignment?

There are also situations where it is by no means clear whether the client has indeed agreed to your services or not. There have been situations in which the client asked all the right questions—how much I charged, what my estimate of the job was, and when I could start—and appeared to be agreeing to my starting, but did not actually say so. In one way this is somewhat upsetting because it is just too easy; I can't help but be uneasy when a sale comes without even a slight struggle, especially when the money involved is a considerable sum.

All of these situations ought to be regarded as mandating a retainer or advance payment and a carefully drawn Letter of Agreement. I would personally be most reluctant to begin working on a project under these circumstances without those two items. It's entirely possible—I have actually encountered this problem—that the individual to whom you are speaking is satisfied with everything you have said and proposed and wishes to proceed but is not empowered to proceed on his or her own authority. Asking for a signed agreement and a retainer will straighten this question out soon enough.

DECIDING WHAT THE MID-POINT IS

If you proceed on an agreement to get one third of your fee on signing and the next one third at mid-point, you have the problem of reaching agreement on what that mid-point is. For some kinds of contracts, that is fairly easy; for others, it may prove difficult.

In the case of developing training programs, manuals, and other such written products, I found it expedient to utilize the fact that normally such projects entail a rough draft and a revision process. For such projects I usually designated acceptance of the rough draft by the client as representing midpoint, calling for the payment of the second one third of the fee.

Not all projects lend themselves so conveniently to a natural mid-point. (Of course, the client must agree to your mid-point designation.) It should be a point at which the client can express satisfaction with what you have done so far, but is still firmly committed to you and needs your services to get the job done. Perhaps this is a cynical observation, but the cynicism is based on regrettable experiences. Bear in mind that in most agreements for consulting services, clients wish to have a clause that permits them to discontinue the arrangement upon suitable notice. (You may hear this referred to technically as a clause providing for liquidated damages or liquidating the contract, because it's a common enough provision in contracts for services.) It is therefore not unheard of for a client to opt for termination of the contract at whatever point the client believes he can take over and finish the project without your help. So while this may appear to be in conflict with what I have said earlier about being totally open and frank in giving the client complete access to your knowledge, that is for his or her potential *future* needs; I do not assist the client in cutting short the project we have contracted for. I do not advocate being unduly suspicious of a client who has given you no reason for suspicion, but neither do I advocate being completely ingenuous or naive.

COLLECTIONS

If you have the good fortune to contract exclusively with AAA (that is, triple-A credit rating) clients you may never have a collection problem. However, the nature of consulting is such that most of us have an occasional problem collecting a receivable or, at least, collecting with reasonable promptness.

As in all other problems, prevention is far better than correction, and the details of payment should already have been agreed upon and understood. Even then you may run into payment problems. I have found that large corporations tend to get as bureaucratic as do government agencies, and what has been said about doing business with government agencies is often apropos here, too. With large corporations it is usually helpful to know exactly how the invoice-processing and check-issuance system works so that you can troubleshoot delays effectively. In large corporations as in governments unreasonable delays are rarely due to poor systems; they are almost always the result of bureaucratic ills, chiefly indolence, indifference, and bungling by bureaucratic personnel.

You may have the occasional problem of trying to collect from a client who can't or won't pay without some collection pressure. The typical collection procedure pursued by most businesses is one of increasing insistence and pressure, each step predicated on the hope that the client will pay and not compel the collector to undertake the next step. Here are the typical steps:

1. Normal billing—submittal of your regular invoice.
2. Statement of money due at some regular interval, usually once a month, at either mid-month or end/beginning of month.
3. Courteous letter, reminding client of debt and asking plainly for payment, albeit in diplomatic language.
4. More insistent and less diplomatic letter.
5. Telephone inquiry, reasonably courteous, but still insistent.
6. Severe letter, threatening legal action or formal collection action, such as turning over to collection agency, turning over to lawyer, otherwise increasing pressure.
7. Turning matter over to collection agency, lawyer, or bringing suit.

If you are forced to resort to any of these latter steps, it is not likely that you wish to do business with this client again, so you probably decide to take the gloves off at this point and be as rough as you must be to collect. Anything you do in steps (7) or thereafter is going to cost you something. A collection agency keeps something on the order of one third to one half of everything it collects, a lawyer will charge you for what he does (possibly also a contingency fee as in the case of a collection agency), and going to court will cost you something since you need a lawyer here, too, unless the amount is small enough to take your case to small-claims court. That costs you a relatively small fee, and if you have an open and shut case you usually do not need a lawyer. Here is an example:

A client retained me to help him by developing a sales brochure for his product. We agreed on $600 for my work, and he paid me $300 retainer. I prepared several roughs and we went over them together, after which he selected one to be put into final draft. While I was doing so, he suddenly called me to report that he was selling out and did not need the brochure after all. I agreed, thereupon, to let the matter drop where it stood and to liquidate the contract for the retainer of $300 already paid. The client demanded that I return the $300, but I refused, pointing out that I could sue him for the entire remaining amount, but was willing to accept one half the fee, already paid, for having done about three quarters of the work. At that point, the client sued me in small claims court.

I wasted more than one half day waiting for the case to be called. When the judge heard the details from me and from my erstwhile client, the case ended abruptly with the judge advising my former client that he was way off base in demanding a refund of his money, since it was he, not I, who had breached the contract, and I had done most of the work. The hearing itself took only a few minutes, but the case cost me most of a full working day.

That's one of the problems with suing, it's time-consuming, and the time you lose may be worth more to you than the fee it will cost you to retain a lawyer or turn the account over to a collection agency for action.

Serving your client with a legal notice that you are bringing suit may itself be enough to bring about settlement. In those cases where I found myself forced to this extreme, I found that the client was in financial straits and finding it difficult to pay rather than being unwilling to pay. In every case, therefore, I found it necessary to compromise rather than press the suit and win judgment.

JUDGMENT

A great many people appear to misunderstand just what a judgment is and what it is not. In a civil action such as a lawsuit to collect money due you, you ask the court to enter judgment against the defendant in the amount due you. If you win your suit the court does so, ordering the defendant to pay you whatever that amount is, which frequently includes your legal costs. You are given legal documentation attesting to that judgment. You are now legally entitled to collect that amount of money from the defendant.

If the defendant is an insurance firm or any organization with obvious assets, you will usually be paid as a matter of course. However, if the defendant should simply refuse or fail to pay you, the court cannot take further action. The court will not collect your judgment for you; that's your job. If the defendant chooses to defy you and your judgment, you have the task of seizing some assets of the defendant—bank account, furniture, or other asset—to realize payment. But the defendant who defies you to collect may either have no assets you can seize or have them well hidden. For example, if the defendant has office furniture and equipment he has rented or is lease-purchasing and has little equity in the property, you can't seize it because the owners of the property have a prior claim. If the defendant has bank accounts, you have to find them; the court will not attempt to do so for you.

It is not at all uncommon for individuals to take steps to make themselves "judgment-proof"—arrange their affairs so that it is all but impossible to collect a judgment entered against them. Obviously, there is little point in suing and winning judgment against someone from whom you cannot collect. Therefore, that must be a sober consideration before you sue a client.

CREDIT

In a very real sense, you are extending credit to a client when you agree to be paid for work after the work is done. You may have already noted that many firms extend credit only to "rated" firms, which means firms having a Dun & Bradstreet credit rating. Unrated firms must pay in advance or upon delivery if the purchase is of goods rather than service. If you do a major part of your work with small business firms, it may be worth your while to enjoy the Dun & Bradstreet service or to pay for another credit-reporting service in your area.

If you get an advance retainer and progress payments, you have already reduced the risk and established the client's credit through your own experience, which is often far more reliable than any credit rating awarded by an outside agency of any sort.

MECHANIC'S LIEN

In general, the law holds that a mechanic may hold your property, which he has repaired and has in his possession, for payment of his justly due bill if you fail to pay. If your failure to pay continues, the mechanic may take measures to entitle him to sell your property for his bill.

It may well be, in some situations, that you are in the position of the mechanic, with some property of your client in your physical possession and a client who has failed to pay or indicates an unwillingness to pay. You should consult an attorney for specific counsel and guidance, but presumably the mechanic's lien will justify your holding the client's property, pending payment.

THE COSTS OF COLLECTION

The costs you experience in collecting your bills are part of your overhead expenses, and should normally be charged there, as should any business losses. If you are unfortunate enough to have some such losses regularly, you will soon learn what the percentage is and consider this part of your cost of doing business. For example, some entrepreneurs who are paid principally by checks and whose sales tend to be small ones almost inevitably have some small percentage of checks that bounce and are too small to go to great expense to collect. Most businesspeople find it more practical to simply write off these small losses as part of their overhead expenses.

It has been my experience that there is ample work available for anyone who is willing to work for nothing, and accepting all assignments without sober consideration, written agreements, and proper payment guarantees inevitably leads to doing some of your work for nothing.

12

Consultant Skills
You Need, How
To Develop Them

As a consultant, you must present to your prospective clients the face of a specialist. Actually, you must be a generalist, possessed of many diverse skills, especially if you are an independent consultant and must rely on yourself for all functions.

CONSULTING: BUSINESS OR PROFESSION?

Consulting is both a business and a profession. It is a profession in that as a consultant you must be the master of some set of special technical/professional skills, which you can employ in either your own independent practice or in the employ of a larger organization. But it is also a business, in that it is a service you sell to clients, and your success as an independent consultant depends on many skills other than your technical/professional ones.

There are two distinct sets of skills you must master. One is the set of business skills—marketing, administering, and managing your enterprise. The other is a set of technical/professional skills which support, enhance, and/or supplement your basic consulting specialty. Some of these skills are necessary as direct support of the basic skills you sell as a consultant, while others are necessary to broaden your base of income-producting activities. Some of these supplementary skills serve both ends.

The most common failing of beginning consultants, you will recall from an earlier chapter, is the failure to establish and build a broad enough business base. In the next chapter we will be discussing this specifically and offering guidance. To take advantage of this it is necessary to recognize the various skills you need and learn how to develop them fully. These skills are not only necessary to your success generally, but are the key to building your practice and possibly developing it into a much larger business. (We'll look at how some other consultants have done just that, in the next chapter.)

The two basic skills this refers to are those of writing and speaking but especially writing, because while your normal consulting practice demands that you be able to write reasonably well, no matter your technical/professional specialty, writing skills also offer you many opportunities to expand your business base. Let's look first at speaking, however.

PUBLIC SPEAKING

Most people are reluctant to speak publicly, especially if they have never done so before, and if the audience is made up of complete strangers. The neophyte speaker is sure that he or she is going to appear a fool. But it isn't only neophyte speakers who are petrified at the thought of standing up before a crowd of strangers and speaking at length; a number of experienced professional speakers never get over being nervous and must drive themselves to the dais every time they speak. They just never feel truly comfortable on the platform. It is therefore futile and would be dishonest to assure you that "you'll get used to it" and speak easily and comfortably after you've gained some experience. You probably will, for most people do, but there are some who never do feel really at ease on the platform. That, however, does not prevent them from appearing there and doing an excellent job every time they speak.

Perhaps you are under the delusion that some people are born speakers while others are not and can never be good speakers. That is sheer nonsense. What is true is that some people are fortunate enough to have good speaking voices, resonant, pleasant voices, while others have raspy or squeaky voices and perhaps even impediments, such as a slight lisp.

Strangely enough in light of this misconception, some of the most successful speakers belong to the latter class; their voices offer more handicap than aid to their speaking careers. (Take Barbara Walters, for example, an exceptionally highly paid interviewer, who has a rather irritating, squeaky voice and a pronounced lisp as well as being rather lacking in what some would call a "platform manner" or "stage presence." Despite these handicaps, she is considered an outstanding interviewer and appears to be not the least conscious of these vocal faults.)

The key to successful public speaking is quite simple. If the fear that paralyzes the inexperienced speaker is the fear of appearing foolish, then the solution is to take measures which will avoid this possibility. If the fear of appearing foolish is, in essence, the fear that you will either appear not to know what you are talking about or present your material poorly, then what you must do is simply be sure that you do know what you are talking about and are completely prepared to make your presentation.

The key to speaking successfully is to have something to say. Again and again we are put to sleep by speakers who drone on, saying so little of note that we are not sure that they have anything to say, much less have prepared themselves to say it well. They appear never to get to the point, which suggests that they really have no point to make but are simply rambling aimlessly. Whether this is truly the case or not, the appearance that it is destroys listener interest.

You may be blessed with an ability to speak well extemporaneously or with a minimum of time needed for preparation. Few people are, although there are some gifted individuals who can do this. There are also some gifted individuals who are entertaining even when they have no special point to make, simply because they either have a ready store of entertaining stories or because they happen to have that rare charismatic quality that enables some speakers to be interesting if they stand on a platform reading the dictionary aloud! Most of us do not have the good fortune to be so magnetic a presence, and we must therefore rely on certain sound principles which will give us the confidence we need to make an interesting, if not entertaining, presentation:

Address a specific purpose or objective in your presentation.

Organize your material so that it has a beginning, middle, and ending.

Identify those specific main points you must make to achieve the overall objective of your presentation, and make those points.

Be prepared. (This is an absolute essential to having confidence.)

PLANNING THE PRESENTATION

It is a wise individual who operates on the general assumption that nothing desirable ever happens all by itself; only disasters happen that way. Those things we want will happen only when we make them happen, and that means planning and preparation. This applies to making a presentation of any kind as much as it does to anything else. Many speakers write out their presentations in full text and even memorize them; others prepare outlines, notes, guidance cards, or other aids less than a full text, and speak from those. You should use whichever method works best for you, but that may not be the same method in every case. There are circumstances where I speak from only the sketchiest of notes or even spontaneously because I have spoken on the subject many times and need only those notes which will remind me of major points or topics so that I don't forget to cover them. But when I speak on subjects I know a great deal less about, I spend much time in preparation of well-detailed notes —sometimes even a full-blown lecture guide.

If you are not accustomed to speaking before a group or are apprehensive about doing so, it is probably a good idea for you to prepare a full text of your remarks even if you know the subject thoroughly. Then, if you get stage fright or mike fright and everything you ever knew flies out of your head, you can at least read your presentation. If you are a good reader, that may be an excellent way for you to make the presentation. For one thing, having a full, well-prepared text before you helps greatly to lend you confidence. Many fine speakers—such as the late Franklin D. Roosevelt—frequently read from texts when making public speeches. The quality of your presentation, as far as content is concerned, depends entirely on the quality of your preparation. Good preparation assures you an acceptable presentation, and good preparation begins with planning.

GOALS AND OBJECTIVES

A first step in planning any presentation, written or otherwise, is setting a goal—defining what the presentation is to accomplish. Here are a few examples of types of goals a presentation might address or pursue:

How to solve a problem of some sort

How something works

How something came about (its history, causes, origins, etc)

New developments in a given field

How to do something

Arguments for or against something

Presenting a report of some kind

There are a few other general categories which are not really germane to this discussion, such as introducing another speaker, making an award, and entertainment (telling funny stories). But even those have their goals, and the presentation must be structured accordingly, keeping in mind always that the listeners must be made aware of the goal or final objective of the presentation.

This means that the presentation must make its goal clear by some means other than a bald statement that such and such is the goal. The idea was expressed once by a writer who allegedly heard a rural speaker advise others that the way to make a presentation was to "Tell them what you're going to tell them, tell them, then tell them what you told them." That is a pungent way of explaining the need to telegraph your goal to your listeners—let them know where the presentation is headed, present the body of information, and then sum it all up in concluding remarks. That is simply another way of pointing out not only the need to have a beginning (introduction), middle, and end (summary), but identifying what each of those parts should do or be.

It is well established that an effective presentation covers only one major point or goal rather than a multiplicity of points. This is open to some interpretation, however, as we tend to use synonyms interchangeably so that we do not always communicate effectively. That is one reason I prefer to use the word *goal* to refer to the main purpose or objective of a presentation, and *objective* to refer to some milepost on the way to reaching or achieving the overall goal. Suppose, for example, that I wish to explain to an audience how to market to government agencies, and my main point is that learning *where* the government buyers are is at least as important as learning *how* they buy. If this is the only major point I wish to make in helping my listeners begin to address the government agencies as market targets, I might organize my presentation along the following general lines:

> *Main Goal.*   Demonstrate the need to learn where the government buyers are.
>
> *Objectives.*   Explain number of government purchasing offices and procurement specialists.
>
> Describe number, scope of geographic distribution of agencies.
>
> Describe scope, diversity of government organization, both superstructure and infrastructure.
>
> Explain how agencies buy both nationally and locally.

How detailed I get in developing all this will depend primarily on how much time I have and on what my listener's needs/interests appear to be. If, for example, I am addressing a meeting of milk suppliers, I would focus on those government markets which are good targets for milk and milk products, which would mean primarily military bases, VA hospitals, and a few select other government organizations. Of course you must address your listeners' interest if you expect to get and hold their attention. My presentation would then be structured along these lines:

> Because milk is perishable, government installations that use milk buy it locally instead of through centralized purchasing. One major class of customer is the military base; each base has procurement offices because it must do some buying locally. But there are a few other government facilities that are good prospects for milk and fresh milk products, including VA hospitals, which exist throughout the United States, Coast Guard stations, and a few government residential schools, such as the Postal Service schools at Norman, Oklahoma, and Bethesda, Maryland. Each of these has its own procurement office. Here is how you can find out what government installations of such types are in your own area.

In terms of a beginning, middle, and end, my beginning would present the main idea, along these lines:

> There are several things to learn about selling to the federal government, but the most important thing is where the federal procurement offices are. Once you locate those, the procurement officials at those offices will help you file the proper forms to get on bidders lists and submit your bids.

As an end, after presenting the information on where and how to find those government purchasing offices, my summary would be along the lines of the following:

> Now that is the real secret of selling to the government—finding the buyers. For most people finding the buyers is the hard part; selling them is the easy part. The contracting officers want to help you. Hunt them up, the way you've just heard, and ask them for help. That's really all there is to it.

Now this is the easiest kind of presentation to make successfully because it is aimed directly at the listeners' interests—it tells them how to do something they want to do. It contains elements of three of the types of goals presented a few paragraphs ago:

How to solve a problem (sell to the government)

How something works (local buying of some government agencies)

How to do something (find the proper government purchasing offices)

The content alone is all but guaranteed to hold the interest of your listeners because it serves one of their needs. Any time you can make a presentation that strikes a nerve in this manner, you are pretty sure to be a hit. But that does not mean that you cannot be equally successful when addressing other goals, such as explaining how something works or what new developments have been occurring in some field of interest, or even in presenting arguments for or against something. There are certain ways you can pique your listeners' interest, no matter the subject matter or the overall goal of your presentation. Here are a few things that motivate most people:

Inside Information. Most people are titillated by the idea of being made privy to information known to only a select few.

Newest Information. Most of us are eager to learn what's new, very much along the same line of reasoning as that which impels us to be interested in inside information. It makes us especially privileged.

Curiosity Arousing. Often it is possible to use the novelist's device of arousing curiosity by creating something of a mystery. Example: *Every competent engineer knew that the automobile self-starter was an impractical idea. Even Charles Kettering knew it, when Ransome Olds asked him to invent a self-starter. But Kettering was sure that he could do the impossible.* This could go on, to explain exactly what made the self-starter an impossible idea. Once the listeners' curiosity is so aroused, it's important to make them wait a while for the answer.

Eye Opening.   Sometimes it is possible to make the audience sit up and pay attention by throwing out an attention-getting opener, such as what I like to refer to as "startling statistics." For example: *The U.S. Government spends over 700 billion dollars a year now—that's a seven followed by eleven zeros. It also comes to about one and one-third million dollars spent every minute of the day, every day of the year.* For even greater dramatic effect, you could write this on a blackboard to show what all those zeros look like. Most of us have trouble visualizing even one billion dollars, much less 700 of them.

Amusing.   Many speakers open with a funny story of some sort. This is a wonderful device if you can do it. It is also highly dangerous if telling stories well is not one of your natural talents. Beware of this unless you are sure you can handle it well.

Gimmick.   This is also a dangerous device, although effective when handled well. For example, suppose a speaker carries a wrapped package or a glass globe to the dais and deposits it carefully on a table in plain sight. Perhaps he even spends several minutes fussing with it, grins knowingly at the audience, and then begins his address with no further attention to package or globe. He is almost certain to have everyone's attention, at least in the beginning, because everyone wonders what the thing is, what its significance or part in the presentation is, and when the speaker will reveal the secret. The danger is that the device will so distract the audience that they will not give the speaker their full attention. If the speaker finally reveals that his gimmick had nothing whatsoever to do with his presentation, the listeners may feel betrayed and unhappy at being tricked. If you use a device of this sort—and it can be quite effective if handled well—be sure that it does have something to do with your presentation, and that you finally let your audience in on your secret.

For the most part, these devices are means for getting attention. They will not of themselves hold the audience unless you follow with a worthy presentation—useful or interesting information, properly presented.

SOME PRINCIPLES OF PRESENTATION

One essential in making a presentation is that of using terms and words that your listeners will understand. This is not to say that you must talk down, or that you must low-rate your listeners' intelligence and education, but you must be aware that there are many regional differences. When I was first in Chicago many years ago, having morning coffee at a lunch counter, I asked for a "coffee cake," which was what I had learned to call in Philadelphia what I soon learned Chicagoans called a "sweet roll," and many others call a "danish." And what Philadelphians called a "soda" Chicagoans called a "phosphate" and New Yorkers called a "pop."

Because of television and the fact that most of us travel freely around the country today, there are probably fewer such regional differences in expressions, but they have not been completely eliminated, and they still present some barriers to complete communication. Even more to the point is the matter of general vocabulary.

The English language is an extremely rich one, perhaps because English includes so many words that are not English at all, but have come to us from many other languages—Latin, French, German, Spanish and Italian, to name only a few. There are possibly as many as 500,000 general words and as many more technical terms in the language we refer to as English. A quick skim of any unabridged dictionary provides a rough idea of just how rich the language is.

The average person's vocabulary ranges between 12,000 and 15,000 words, rarely much more than 20,000, sometimes well below 10,000. Those scholars and writers among us with larger vocabularies—and some range to 40,000 words—are in the minority, and often fail to communicate when they use their full vocabularies.

If you happen to be one of those whose vocabulary ranges to 20,000 or more words readily at your command, a good piece of advice is to forget about one half your vocabulary in writing and speaking, except perhaps in some unusual circumstance which justifies or requires your special vocabulary.

This is not to say that having a large vocabulary is a disadvantage or is in any way a handicap—unless you permit it to become one. Many people believe that the possession of a large vocabulary is a great aid to clear thinking, since we do at least some of our thinking in words, rather than images, and a large store of words aids us in reasoning and analyzing ideas. It has been claimed that a large vocabulary is often characteristic of those with high intelligence quotients. Just bear in mind that communication is not a unilateral process but is bilateral: When you speak, you send messages, and if your messages are either not received or are received but not understood, communication has not taken place.

UNDERSTANDING VERSUS BELIEF

It is commonly supposed that understanding precedes belief or, conversely, that belief is the result of understanding. For example, we believe that the Earth is round because we now understand global geography. Or is that a fact? Do we believe that the Earth is round because we understand the geography of earth, or do we understand that geography because we believe that the Earth is round? Relatively few of us have ever seen the physical evidence, such as a ship at sea coming over the horizon, or a view of Earth from space, as our astronauts have seen Earth. We are taking most of the evidence for a round Earth on acceptance of what we have been taught.

Or take the atomic structure of matter. Our most powerful electron microscopes, even those that can photograph the larger molecules of matter, are not powerful enough to verify our theory of atomic structure. Yet, we "understand" it purely because we believe it.

There is no doubt that we tend strongly to believe that which we want to believe. Religious beliefs bear ample witness to that; adherents of each of the many religions in the world tend to believe strongly, and many even insist most vigorously, that theirs is the only true belief, and they can "prove" it by the "logic" of their faiths. We find the same kind of logic in our political views, where people of varying political faiths argue their proofs.

In all things, although an understanding of anything may rest on a thoroughly acceptable syllogistic chain of logical reasoning, somewhere at its roots it has to rest on one or more basic premises which are accepted on faith. In the end, it becomes most difficult to separate *understanding* from *belief* in terms of cause and effect. It is evident, in any case, that people always tend to believe what they want to believe, even those who fancy themselves to be skeptics who believe only what they have good evidence for. An atheist, for example, may maintain quite stoutly that he will not believe in God when he has been offered no evidence that God exists. But he is quite oblivious to the argument that neither has he been offered any evidence that God does not exist. He has decided which of the two alternatives he prefers to believe and understand.

"COMMUNICATION" IS REALLY PERSUASION

The translation of all of this into practical, working terms is this: To "communicate" with others you must be persuasive. If you want others to "understand" what you say (or write), you must *persuade* them to *believe*. To persuade them, you must not go directly counter to their established prejudices. No amount of logic will change hardened opinions; only persuasive techniques have even a chance of doing so, and even then it is far from easy to accomplish. The true hazard, however, is this: When you are presenting information about which people have no bias—about which they are still open minded—carelessness can antagonize them into rejecting what you wish to offer. That is, if you once take a position your listeners find highly offensive, they are likely to reject everything you say, no matter how open-minded they may have been earlier about other matters. What has happened is that you have lost credibility with this audience because you have said something to arouse their hostility.

I recently listened to a speaker explain to a room full of people how they might go about becoming published authors. Unfortunately, he used the pronoun "I" unwisely, failing to make the point that he was using his own experiences as examples, and coming across to many listeners as a braggart. He so aroused the hostility of several listeners that in the lecture-evaluation sheets they were asked to fill out, many of the listeners excoriated this speaker although he had actually made an excellent presentation, had good stage presence, and a fine, resonant speaking voice.

If you are very experienced and find your own experience the richest lode of illustrative examples, be as sparing as possible in using that first person singular pronoun. At the least, if you find it necessary or helpful to point out that the anecdote is from your personal experience, don't make yourself the hero of the story. Tell the story as an observer rather than as an active participant, or as a minor character rather than the protagonist. On the other hand, if you are describing a horrible example of what not to do, it may be helpful and even advisable to make yourself the leading character in the story. It's perfectly acceptable to explain how you did something stupid or embarrassed yourself, whereas some listeners will find it objectionable to hear you tell how some other person made a stupid mistake. Such confessions of your own foibles and failings are usually good for laughs if you appear sheepish enough and are willing to laugh at yourself. For example, when the question of "wiring" a request for proposal comes up ("wiring" means arranging things so that one bidder is given advantages which make it almost certain he will get the contract), I usually get a laugh by telling a story from my own experience which I generally introduce along these lines:

> "When it comes to wiring proposal requests, you're listening to an expert. I am about to tell you how I very cleverly managed to lose a contract which had been wired expressly for me."

How can you hate a guy who admits his own stupidity and invites you to join in laughing at him? Listeners are all but compelled to warm up to such a speaker. That points out one mistake some speakers make: Don't appear to be pompous, a poseur, or overly impressed with your own importance. Such images almost always arouse audience hostility. The trick is to be entirely at ease, relaxed and self-confident, and yet have the utmost respect for your audience. Somehow, how you *feel* about your audience manages to come across to them. If you feel contempt for them, they will sense it just as they will sense it if you respect and like them. An audience tends to mirror your own feelings, returning the emotions you radiate. If you are to be persuasive at all, you must be liked and respected by your audience.

SOME DO'S AND DON'TS

Here are a few items to keep in mind when speaking to a group:

Don't display nervous habits, such as fidgeting, pulling your ear lobe, knotting the microphone cord, and other such things. These things distract your listeners from what you are saying, may lend the impression that you are amateurish or a bit weird.

Don't try to explain everything with words alone when clearly you need a blackboard, a model, a poster, a handout, or some kind of aid. Better not to make the presentation at all than to make a poor one.

If you are new at speaking, overly nervous, or have trouble standing in plain view, you can put yourself at greater ease by standing behind a podium or sitting at a table. Don't make it harder on yourself than necessary.

Don't make it harder on your audience than necessary, either. Often you have the choice of having the room arranged classroom style or theater style, at tables or with rows of chairs. Classroom style is far more relaxing and comfortable, puts your listeners at greater ease and makes them more receptive and patient.

Don't try to be Bob Hope. You can use humor without being a comedian or an accomplished teller of funny stories. However, it is not necessary to be Will Rogers, a humorist, either. Use humor only if it comes naturally and comfortably from you, preferably with anecdotes that relate directly to your subject and which you and the audience can enjoy together.

Learn how to stop. If you have been given one hour, prepare a one-hour presentation. Make your points, respond to comments and questions, if appropriate, thank your audience for their attention, and STOP. (The applause may be gratitude because you have stopped, but it's still applause.)

Don't follow the oft-given advice to select one person in the audience as the target for your remarks. For one thing, it's discourteous to appear to ignore everyone else. But it's also somewhat disquieting to listen to a speaker who never glances your way and makes some people feel as though they were eavesdropping on a private conversation between two strangers. Let your eyes roam the room, addressing every section, if not every individual. Make it clear to everyone that you are talking *to* them, not *at* them.

In a remarkably short time you'll find yourself performing like a professional on the platform and probably even being entirely at ease and actually enjoying your speaking chores. Most people do enjoy speaking publicly once they have mastered the art of appearing to be worth listening to and have gotten a few rounds of appreciative applause. But the road to becoming an accomplished speaker requires actual experience, just as learning to swim requires finally taking the plunge. Perhaps the greatest satisfaction is in learning that it is not as difficult as it once appeared. In fact, it's really quite easy, requiring only that you do these things:

Know what you are talking about—be prepared.

Relax on the platform and be your usual, likable self.

Like and respect your listeners.

Focus all your attention on giving your listeners what they came to get—some information and/or ideas—not on how you look and sound.

Do these things and you will find that your listeners will help you to be a complete success on the platform.

WRITING SKILLS FOR THE CONSULTANT

A great deal of what has been said about public speaking applies equally to writing, so some redundancy is inevitable. Much of what a consultant must write is simply written presentation—reports, technical articles, papers for professional journals, and even books.

Hardly anyone in the business or professional world today can escape the necessity for writing. More and more, we have become a society of paper, the inevitable requirement of our exploding technologies and the increasing complexity of our society. It is estimated, for example, that some 95 percent of all the scientists who ever lived on this planet are alive today. This is a way of dramatizing our age's explosions of science and education which are linked to the technological explosion. (It's not clear which is cause and which is effect.)

This is not the case in engineering and hard sciences only. Modern times have seen the same order-of-magnitude expansions in such fields as psychology, sociology, information sciences, economics, and all other technical/professional fields. The expansion is at exponential rates, feeding on itself to a large degree, with paper necessary to document, record, report, and teach new knowledge to students and practicing professionals, while the rapidly growing ranks of newly graduated professionals are at work, making still further advances and generating still more paper to perpetuate change and advancement. It is not only the growing volume of practitioners and knowledge in all these fields, but also the growing complexity of new developments that mandates still more paper to make the new knowledge available to others. It has reached the stage where the practicing professional's work is almost useless, or at least not worth its cost, if it is not properly documented for reference and dissemination.

This dramatizes one major difference between written and oral presentations: An oral presentation can reach only that limited number of listeners in hearing range, and even then it is transitory, its usefulness limited to even the hearers by the constraints of their memories and the completeness and accuracy of the notes they take. But written presentations—products of the pen—are permanent records, always available for study and available to anyone and everyone with access.

The same considerations apply to the quality of the information. Mistakes or incomplete accounts delivered orally can be tolerated and are to be expected; few oral presentations are designed or expected to include all the painstaking detail. In written accounts, however, because of their permanency a much greater effort must be made to achieve painstaking accuracy and provide all necessary detail. (There are exceptions, principally in those circumstances where the account is obviously not a permanent record, such as a newspaper account, or is necessarily lacking in minute detail, such as in a news release or newsletter.) It is because of that that a handout is in order when it is necessary to provide listeners with details for future reference.

We have covered a few of the relevant areas such as news releases and reports as far as their purpose, use, content, and general approach are concerned. We have not yet gone into depth on writing per se, nor on other products of your pen such as newsletters, books, and papers. In the next few pages we'll explore such matters as usage and style, and in the next chapter we'll take the subject up again from another viewpoint, that of speaking and writing activities as independent profit centers for your enterprise rather than as supporting activities for your consulting services.

CONCEPTION AND INITIAL PLANNING

A written product requires the same beginning as the development of an oral presentation. Both stem from some overall goal or purpose, some response to a need. Written presentations are designed to report, advise on how to solve a problem or class of problems, explain how something works, instruct in how to do something, argue for or against something, or otherwise satisfy some perceived want. As in the case of marketing and selling your services (or anything else, for that matter) you may be addressing a felt need (one that potential readers already are aware of) or attempting to create a need (make potential readers recognize the need for what you are offering).

This is inherent in conceiving the idea initially. If you are preparing a report which your consulting contract calls for, you and/or your client conceived the need early when you were drawing up your agreement. You agreed then that the client would get progress reports or a final report, and you probably agreed, at least in general, what would be in that report. (For example, if you contracted to develop a computer program of some sort, you almost surely agreed to provide the typical documentation that clients ordinarily require when they have computer software designed.) The first step in preparing something in writing is conceiving the basic idea, and this ought to start with the recognition of a need that should be satisfied.

There are several ways in which that recognition can come about. You may become aware of some problem or of the fact that the problem is a common one, that you have an answer or solution for that problem, and that relatively few people appear to be aware of it. For example, before I began to write extensively about marketing to the U.S. Government, I simply had not been aware of how little written information was available on the subject. (Most of what was available was government-furnished literature which explained how the government buys, which is not the same subject as how to sell to the government.) As I became aware of this problem, I began to write on the subject.

Usually the concept is not as broad as that. In some ways it is easier and even more effective to address a more narrowly oriented problem and need, such as how to sell motorcycles to the government, if you believe that there are enough vendors of motorcycles who would be interested in your information.

In a way, this is a how-to-do-something idea, but how-to information is quite often problem-solving information, too. How to sell motorcycles to the government helps those for whom selling motorcycles to the government has been a problem. A how-to is not necessarily addressed to a specific problem; it may be how to do something to make one's life more pleasant or how to save money on your income taxes.

These are not the only topics that impel people to read. Some of us have a need for escape or entertainment, or a need to satisfy our curiosity about some things. We therefore read things that offer us no practical or tangible benefits, but do answer at least some of our needs for reading matter of one kind or another. So your conceptual idea might be in any of the following general categories:

Problem-solving and/or how to

Believe it or not—intriguing and unusual information

General interest—how a computer works, the body's immune mechanisms, and so forth

New developments—the latest in antibiotics, new home appliances, and so forth

Useful reference information—home remedies, household hints, and so forth

Scholarly reports—the minute, technical detail, profound analysis, learned opinions, and so forth

Note that in developing your basic idea you are already suggesting the specific goal or objective of whatever you propose to write, whether it will teach a method for solving a problem, instruct in something or other, amuse and satisfy curiosity, add to the reader's store of technical/professional knowledge, or other. You should have a clear understanding of what your proposed writing is to do for the reader if you are to plan and execute it successfully.

A next step is to proceed from initial concept to general plan. Even the most gifted and accomplished professional writers must do some planning for even the briefest article or paper. Let's try charting the process of developing the idea. (See Figure 10.)

You begin with a concept and you formulate a logical goal or main objective. If you were to plot the development of the concept into a piece of writing, you might use this approach since you now have the two ends of the chart, the starting concept and the final goal. Even this is still a rather

FIGURE 10.   Flowcharting the development.

vague beginning. It would be more helpful to start charting the concrete functions and products as in Figure 11:

FIGURE 11.   Flowcharting the first function and end product.

Virtually every piece of writing requires initial research and data gathering, unless you happen to have all the information already at hand for one reason or another (the exceptional case). Even before you begin research, you will have made at least a tentative decision as to just what form your writing is to take. In this hypothetical case we have decided it is to be a magazine article. It is necessary to make this decision and even to estimate about how long the article is to be before you can undertake your research and data gathering. (Most magazines measure articles in number of words.) Obviously the research and data gathering for a 5,000-word magazine article is of an entirely different scope than it would be for a 600 page book. (That would be on the order of a quarter-million words.)

You could draw up a preliminary plan before completing or even starting your research, but you would have difficulty in finalizing your plan (which some people call a "book plan," even though it is not for a book) before you have looked over the available data. The rest of your plan is a plot or itinerary for getting from the research stage to the finished-article stage. The typical steps are these:

1.   Concept and goal
2.   Identification of specific end-product (article, paper, book, etc)
3.   Research, data gathering
4.   Plan—content outline, spelling out each main topic, progression, subordinate objectives, main points, illustrations

5. Writing—first (rough) draft

6. Editing, corrections, revisions, rewriting

7. Writing—second draft (May be final or there may be one or more additional cycles of revision and rewriting before a final draft is produced.)

By far the most difficult and complex function is planning and outlining the proposed content. Writing can be easy or it can be quite difficult. It depends primarily on how thorough, detailed, and effective the planning and outlining have been. Good plans and highly detailed outlines simplify the writing task enormously, and the reverse is equally true. Probably every hour spent in planning and outlining saves at least one hour of writing time and reduces the number of drafts needed to get to the final draft.

There is little doubt that by far the most common fault of those who write poorly is the failure to carry out these first few steps. Study of poor writing almost always reveals that the writer was not at all sure what he or she was trying to say, had really not decided what the main objective or main point was, and consequently had resorted to a tidal wave of rambling, pompous, overblown and totally obscure prose to mask that simple truth. This is not necessarily a conscious action, either; many writers unconsciously create rambling prose which they hope will obscure the fact that they have nothing to say, or that what they have to say is hardly worth saying. For example, you will find some reports and journal papers reporting on test series and their analysis saying such things as, "This tends to indicate the possibility of . . . ." In short, says the writer of such language, I don't really have any idea what conclusions we can draw here; I'm not even sure what the maybes are.

It is commonly assumed, when one uses polysyllabic "jaw breaker" words and rare words often found only in the unabridged dictionary, that the perpetrator is bent on displaying his or her great erudition. I'm not at all sure that that is the case, for in most such cases which I investigate by analyzing what the writer has actually said, I discover that the writer has said nothing worth saying or has somehow missed the point entirely. I believe many writers start out with only a rather vague or most generally defined objective and point to make, and somehow they lose sight of that point somewhere along the way. For example, one writer of a text on solar energy apparently wished to make the point that all energy on Earth has its origin in the sun, but due to grossly convoluted sentence structure, he managed to appear to be making the point that the sun is a reservoir of an unimaginable quantity of energy. That latter is true enough, but it's also a *non sequitur*, a totally irrelevant observation in the context in which it was used.

In another energy-related paragraph, found in a government publication, the writer furnished what he apparently thought was a profound or sage observation about how to compare government activity in energy conservation with private-sector activity in energy conservation. When the awkward sentences were deciphered, unscrambled, and translated into everyday English, it became apparent that what the writer had said is that to compare government activity with private-sector activity, one needs only to compare what the government spends on energy conservation with what the private sector spends on it. This is so painfully obvious and such a trivial observation that the writer evidently felt a great need to be less obvious and chose clouding his language as a means for doing so.

We manage to deceive ourselves about how well we understand what we are trying to explain, analyze, or comment on. We deceive ourselves in more than one way, use more than one rationale in persuading ourselves that we know precisely what we are doing. For example, many people firmly believe that having memorized something is equal to understanding it. For them explanation consists of repeating someone else's account. ("Someone else" may have had a less than perfect understanding, too.) There are also a great many people who have learned the jargon and how the jargon is used, and they mistake the ability to use the jargon knowingly as proof of knowledge and understanding. There are also those who make a quantum leap to conclusions by learning the rudiments of a subject and deciding that they now know what they need to know, or that the matter is almost exactly the same as some other matter they had learned about previously.

I found this to be the case in several situations. In technical writing organizations, for example, I found that most of the poor writing being done by technical writers was due to hasty analysis of the equipment and systems they wrote about. In almost every case the writer knew and understood far less about the equipment or system than he thought he did. The convincing evidence for this was the remarkable improvement in the writing which came about when the writer was compelled to return to his research for a few days. More than one writer admitted sheepishly that additional research forced him to conclude that he knew far less of the equipment than he originally thought he did.

In the training-development activities I found much the same situation, with many of those who wrote confusing knowledge of technical terms with understanding of the concepts they represented. Many writers of training materials, for example, used the terms *behavior* and *behavioral objective* without truly understanding what they mean as used by behavioral psychologists. One supervisor was quite upset to find that a section of a proposal failed to specify that the proposer would develop behavioral

objectives. He had failed completely to recognize the meaning of a paragraph that explained carefully the plan to determine what things a learner
ought to be able to do as a result of the training, and to structure the training accordingly. He failed, in short, to recognize the description of a behavioral objective because the jargon term *behavioral objective* had not
been used!

There is a simple way to determine whether one has a true understanding of any given matter: Anyone with a true understanding can *translate*
the jargon into simple language which any lay person, even a child, can
readily understand. Even the concepts of Einstein's Special and General
Theories of Relativity can be put into simple language for everyone, and
more than one writer has done so successfully. To say that "The earth is
an oblate spheroid" is not really explaining anything to anyone who does
not know what "oblate" and "spheroid" mean. But if you really grasp the
meaning and are not merely repeating memorized jargon, you can explain
quickly and simply that the earth is shaped somewhat like an orange,
round, but flattened slightly at each end. Anyone who has ever seen an
orange can easily grasp that. Perhaps more important, you can demonstrate your own understanding to yourself. Whenever you are having
trouble translating your material into simpler terms in trying to explain
something, you should begin to suspect that perhaps your understanding
of the matter is less perfect than you think it is. I have always regarded
with great suspicion the professed knowledge of anyone who says, "I understand it, but I can't explain it." To the contrary, it has been my experience that the problem of the writer who really understands the material is
not in finding a way to say it, but in deciding which of many possible ways
to say it is the best way.

THE INTENDED READER

One key factor in deciding how to say it is the reader—for whom is the
writing intended? If for a scientist, *oblate spheroid* may be the right term.
(But as the writer, you should have been able to visualize an oblate spheroid, even if it appeared to you as an orange!) It is possible for writing to fail
its purpose because it is wrong for the reader, not because it is inaccurate
or badly written. It is necessary to take into account, when planning whatever you propose to write, for whom you have intended the information. I
refer to this as a *reader profile*, and I specify my typical (intended) reader
in terms of interests, education, age, and reading level. I have written some
of my books for beginning, small entrepreneurs, while others have been
intended for executives of well-established businesses of considerable

size. Some have been aimed at those having general management responsibilities, while others have been directed to marketing executives or project leaders.

All my writing to date has been directed at adults with professional or
business interests, although some of my material might be of interest to
retired individuals wishing to establish additional retirement incomes.
(But that makes them people with business interests, after all!)

Reading level is another matter, which justifies its own discussion.

READING LEVEL

It usually comes as a surprise to those who learn it for the first time that by
far the majority of people—even college graduates—do not read well any
writing rated above eighth-grade level. That is about the level of the material in the extraordinarily successful and popular *Reader's Digest*, which is
quite often used as a standard. Perhaps there are cases where it is necessary to write at much higher levels and to be difficult to read, such as in
writing a highly technical paper for a professional journal. These are the
exceptions, not the rule. In almost every other case, it is acceptable, desirable, and even necessary to write at about *Reader's Digest* level.

Even so, the professional consultant cannot escape the necessity for
using technical terms and other jargon peculiar to his or her professional
field. If you are an electronics engineer writing to other electronics engineers, you are compelled to use such terms as *positive feedback* or *regen-
eration*, and you would not explain or translate them since their meaning
is common knowledge to anyone schooled in electronics. On the other
hand, if you must use such terms in writing to an audience not so
schooled, it is necessary to make the meanings of those terms clear when
you use them. Even in writing to other electronic engineers, if you are
presenting new technical terms concerning new concepts or new research, you probably must explain these.

It is not solely the reader's obligation or responsibility to understand
what you write; it is your obligation and responsibility to use the right
terms and concepts for your intended reader. That means you must have
decided who that reader is to be.

Reading level or level of difficulty in reading any given piece of writing is
a grossly misunderstood matter. There are those who advise that if you
keep your sentences and words short, you will be far easier to read. This is
a partial truth of limited usefulness. The length of words and sentences
are not necessarily in direct proportion to their reading level or level of difficulty. That sentence presented a few paragraphs ago, *The earth is an ob-*

late spheroid, is shorter and the words have fewer syllables than *The earth is shaped like an orange, round but flattened slightly at each end.* The longer version is easier to understand because it uses *familiar* words and a familiar *referent,* the orange. Vocabulary and referents are also principal players in determining the reading level of any writing, and the Dale-Schall method is based on lengthy vocabulary lists of words deemed suitable for each grade level for which they are designated.

The problem is, principally, that despite all methods for making the structuring of writing to a given reading level a matter of science, it is still primarily a matter of art. Using such methods as "fog index" and the Dale-Schall measures undoubtedly help greatly, but they are ponderous and not entirely practical approaches. The writer must simply strive to develop some intuition for the right reading level and be always sensitive to the reader profile so that he or she can almost automatically sense the right words, the need for an explanatory digression, the desirability of some kind of aid to understanding such as a diagram, and otherwise be entirely in empathy with the reader. (Several methods will be discussed presently.)

OUTLINING

There are only two kinds of outlines, despite various people assigning various adjectives to the word *outline.* They are these:

1. An outline of what you plan to write about
2. An outline of what you plan to write

An illustration will probably make this clearer if it is not already clear enough what the distinction is. Here is an outline of what a writer might plan to write about:

Symptom Diagnosis of Malfunctioning TV Receiver

1. Visual/aural inspection, picture and sound

    (a) Video
    (b) Audio
    (c) Raster
    (d) White noise

   2. Functional checks

      (a) Front-panel controls
      (b) Rear-panel controls

Here, for comparison, is how the same outline might be written in the second manner categorized—what you plan to write:

Symptom Diagnosis of Malfunctioning TV Receiver

   1. Visual/aural inspection, picture and sound

      (a) Is raster present? If so, is there video information?
      (b) Is audio present? If not, is there white noise?
      (c) Conclusion as to principal trouble symptom—for example, high voltage, no raster, loss of video, loss of sync.

   2. Functional checks

      (a) Rotate brightness control, note response.
      (b) Rotate contrast control, note response.
      (c) Rotate volume control, note response.
      (d) Rotate automatic gain control (agc), note response.
      (e) Conclusions from above checks as to probable cause/most logical next check.
    Note: Use one or more logic-tree charts to illustrate logic of observing and analyzing visual/aural symptoms.

The difference between these two outlines should be apparent. The first outline is only the most general guide for your writing, does not identify your specific points or subordinate objectives, nor preconceive the illustrations and aids which you can easily foresee the need for. In short, such an outline is of limited usefulness to you and represents inadequate planning, especially if you must rely on research for your data.

You cannot usually draw up a detailed outline before doing your research unless you are already thoroughly expert in the subject and anticipate that little research will be needed. In that case you should be able to draw up your detailed type 2 outline as part of your initial planning. Otherwise, it is likely that you will draw up the type 1 outline first and refine it gradually as you carry out your research and are able to decide what points you must make, what objectives you must reach, and what you must write to do so. With a type 2 outline fully developed—and good type 2 outlines usually go into even more detail than the sample shown here—the actual writing becomes enormously easier than it would otherwise have been, and the amount of revision and rewriting you will have to do are almost certainly reduced. Make it an article of faith, if you plan to write, that the more planning you do, the less writing you will have to do to produce your final product in its finished form. It is almost always true that the more extensive and detailed your planning is, the better your final product will be. Writing is far more a matter of planning and organization than it is a matter of grammar and punctuation.

ORGANIZATION

Most material falls into certain natural groupings, according to the subject itself and your purpose or goal in writing it. In the sample outline used here, the purpose was to teach someone the rudiments of TV trouble-symptom observation and diagnosis. If this were intended for the home owner as a kind of do-it-yourself first aid before calling the TV repair shop, its natural division of topics would be along the following lines:

1. Simplified explanation of how a typical TV receiver functions; text and block diagram, explaining high voltage and raster, color, scanning/sweep circuits, video, audio, sync, agc, power supply
2. Front-panel controls, what they do or should do; rear-panel controls, what they do or should do
3. Major components, tubes and solid state, rectifiers, circuit protectors, picture tube
4. Typical failures, most frequent, least frequent, symptoms exhibited
5. Observing symptoms, chain of logic directing succeeding checks, drawing conclusions, verifying conclusions, what can be done by home owner without getting into TV cabinet, cautions and warnings

The same subject, if directed toward the electronics student, would take an entirely different course since it would be reasonable to assume that the reader understood TV circuits and their functioning, and the purpose of this writing would be to teach troubleshooting procedures and logic.

As an aid to organizing your material, you may find the functional flowchart methods and the *why-how* guideline useful. In the outline just presented we started out with the goal of guiding the TV-set owner in how to do preliminary trouble diagnosis so that he might carry out some of the simpler repairs such as replacing a protective fusible device or resetting the circuit breaker that many TV sets carry to protect the easily damaged silicon power rectifiers. At the least, this material will provide the TV owner a general understanding of how his TV works and enable him to discuss his problems intelligently with the TV repair shop operator. In any case, we can work backward from our overall goal of enabling the TV owner to understand his set and do simple repairs. If we apply the chain of functional/logical reasoning, we can develop the main points and objectives, as in Figure 12:

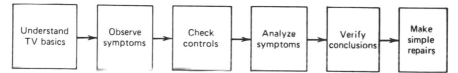

FIGURE 12. Using the flowchart to develop main points/objectives.

This method simply identifies the several main points you must make or objectives your writing must achieve, and in so doing establishes the natural groupings of content. From this you must develop the outline by elaborating on this synoptic analysis. In so doing you may very well wish to return to this flowchart and develop it further, perhaps decide that there are still more points to be made and areas of presentation. Even when you are finally writing, reviewing, or editing your material you may discover a need for further revision of what you have written or plan to write. Good writers have open minds about their own work, always ready to modify or revise if the work can be materially improved thereby; only novices believe that their first drafts are beyond reproach.

The organization also depends on the end-product you plan. If it is to be a book, you will almost surely divide it into chapters or sections. In such case, the example shown here would be entirely too brief, although it might provide a guideline for a single chapter. The content must justify a full-length book, although a book may vary in size from something as small as a dozen pages to as large as several hundred or even several thousand pages. The criterion of what constitutes a book, therefore, is not size but something else. A book is a piece of writing and/or illustrating produced as an independent publication under its own covers. Some such publications are divided into parts which the author refers to as "Book 1, Book 2," and so forth. However, when we use the word *book* we usually refer to a separately bound work of several hundred pages, more or less, and it is in that sense that I use the term here.

RESEARCH AND DATA GATHERING

To select the best three eggs out of a dozen, you must examine the entire dozen and then exercise your judgment. Researching data for a book or article is somewhat similar in that good research and data gathering generally mean discovering, reviewing, and evaluating far more information than you can or will use. The research should have as its objective the review of everything worth looking at on the subject. The idea is to select the best data. But what does "best" mean? Here are a few criteria to use in deciding what information is best for your writing effort:

The information most germane to your overall goal and the objectives you have set up as the itinerary for reaching the goal

That information which appears to be most complete and most accurate or most dependable

That information which appears to be most recent or most up-to-date

That information which provides you, as a writer, with the greatest opportunity for drama, excitement, or other interest-arousing aspects

You are likely to find redundancy and anomalies or contradictions between sources. You will have to make the best determination you can as to which is the most reliable information. It's a writer's occupational hazard.

SOURCES OF INFORMATION

The biggest problem usually is not how to find information, but how to assimilate it; we live in an age of great masses of information. Here are just a few sources generally available:

Public libraries

Newspapers (Many make files of back issues available to the public.)

Government agencies (The federal government is a rich lode of information. See the last chapter, "The Reference File," for guidance to many of these sources.)

Local Chambers of Commerce

Business, professional, and general-interest magazines

Colleges and universities

Advertisements

Associations and societies

Go to the public library and ask the librarian for help. You can also try the libraries of any large government agencies near you. Many government agencies maintain large libraries and keep on file there many specialized newspapers, newsletters, magazines, and other periodicals as well as books. Call on the Small Business Administration.

Manufacturers are often a great help in your research. In preparing technical articles, I have often requested and have been given a wide variety of information, brochures, photographs, drawings, and sundry other materials, with permission to use them. Permission to use is generally easy to get if you specify that you will identify the source of the photo or other material. This represents publicity, a form of free advertising for the manufacturer.

WRITING THE DRAFT

Expect to write a rough draft first. Even the most experienced professional writers expect to do at least two drafts, a first draft and a rewrite, to achieve a final product. At the same time, don't succumb to the trap some do of skimming the subject carelessly in the first draft, assuring yourself that "it's only the first draft" and you'll take care of the problems in the rewrite. What happens all too often in such cases is that the writer overlooks or forgets that there was a problem in the development of the first draft and the problem resurfaces when the work has been finally published and it's too late to do anything about this now-embarrassing matter. Even though you know that you will almost surely do a rewrite and produce a second draft, or at least do very heavy editing of your first draft, treat all your writing as though it is the only chance you will ever have to write it, as though it were in fact your final draft. You will discover this to be the soundest practice.

This is not the proper place for lessons in usage—grammar, spelling, punctuation, and other such matters. These are the tools of writing and have nothing to do with the art of writing, any more than skill in using a hammer and saw has to do with the art of cabinet making. However, it is worthwhile to spend just a few minutes recalling and explaining some of the basics of using our language well. (You should keep a good grammar text at hand when you write, along with a good dictionary and a style guide. See the last chapter for some suggestions along this line.)

You should always bear in mind that every subject must be introduced. As any piece of writing, whether it is a brief article or a complete book, must have a beginning, a middle, and an end, so must the various component elements, the chapters, subsections, paragraphs, and sentences. A paragraph must begin with what is referred to formally as a *topic sentence*. That means nothing more or less than that the first sentence of a paragraph must telegraph to the reader what the paragraph is to be about. Look back at the first sentence of this paragraph to see the principle in practice.

The middle of the paragraph—everything between the first and last sentences of the paragraph—is the body of the paragraph, presenting what that introductory topic sentence promised to present. And the end of the paragraph, the last sentence, sums up the message of the paragraph and provides a transition or bridge to the next paragraph, which is particularly needed when the next paragraph is to take up an entirely new subject.

This paragraph does just that. Instead of discussing introductions and the parts of a paragraph, this paragraph is going to discuss transitions or bridges, and the last sentence of the previous paragraph provided a bridge between it and this paragraph. It prepared you, the reader, for this paragraph, so you could follow the author's train of thought instead of being puzzled, dismayed, or confused by an abrupt change of subject. That is the purpose of a transition—to avoid confusing the reader with an abrupt change of topic, which tends then to be a type of *non sequitur*, something which prompts the reader to think: Why bring that up here? What's the point? What's the connection with what I've been reading? For that is exactly the point of a transition—to make a logical connection with the discussion just concluded.

Smooth transitions are one of the hallmarks of professional writing, and the lack of transitions are the hallmark of inexpert, clumsy writing. It's something of an art to perceive the material from a reader's viewpoint and so judge the quality or the lack of a good transition, but a writer soon develops the sensitivity to this.

Sentences do not necessarily have to be short to constitute an easy-to-read style, but they do have to be uncomplicated, flow smoothly, and have stops of some sort. A lengthy sentence with several stops is just as easy to read as is a series of short sentences if the information or thoughts flow logically and smoothly. Study some of the sentences used here, and you will see that many are quite long, but the long ones have stops—colons, semicolons, and dashes. Be sure that each sentence deals with only one main thought or idea, use words which are familiar to most people, and keep the statements short, either with separate sentences or stops within a sentence, and you will have an easy-to-read style.

As in speaking, once you have made your point, go on to the next one or, if you have made them all, stop. Most writers overwrite rather than underwrite.

One common mistake even professional writers make is the probably unconscious assumption that a writer deals primarily, if not entirely, in words. Because of that fallacy, a great many writers fail to make good use of illustrations. Many writers attempt all explanations and presentations in words, and when they do use illustrations of some sort, the illustrations tend to be an afterthought. Unfortunately, this is glaringly apparent in too many writings where the illustrations appear to have been pasted on at the last moment before printing the work.

The fact is that a writer's mission is to present information, and the information ought to be presented by the most effective and efficient means available. There are some things which can be best presented by words, but there are many other things which can be best presented by or with the direct aid of some graphic device—a photo, diagram, chart, plot, drawing, or other graphic device. Let's take a quick look at different kinds of information or ideas which must be presented, and see what we can deduce.

Descriptions of specific physical objects

Concepts which are more or less concrete, such as ideas about architectural design

Ideas which are relatively abstract, such as principles of organization or management

Complete abstractions, such as vectors or probability statistics

The significance of these examples is that they are on an ascending level of abstraction, which is also to say that they are on an ascending level of difficulty in bringing about understanding by your reader. That means that you must resort to one or more aids to understanding in presenting the more abstract of these. Don't be misled by this into believing that it is only the abstract idea which needs the aid of something other than direct description; sometimes it is the completely concrete that needs it.

Take the case, for example, of describing a chair to your reader. Since the chair is a fairly early invention of man, we have an almost limitless variety—metal, wood, plastic, curved, plain, upholstered, painted, upright, reclining, and others. If you wish to convey the *idea* of chair, the word *chair* will do. Even if you wish to convey the idea of upholstered chair, the two words will do the job. But suppose that for your purposes it is essential that your reader have the *exact* image of the chair you have in mind. It is nearly impossible to find words that can be depended upon to evoke exactly the same image of chair in every reader's mind. But there is a way to bring this about—a drawing or photograph. In fact, even if it were possible to do the job with word descriptions alone, an illustration would do it far more efficiently and far more surely.

This is again the problem of *referents:* The word *chair* itself evokes a different image for you than it does for me because each of us has a different referent for the word. Even such a word as *orange* may give us problems if the precise image is important, because there are several varieties of orange, and that inevitably means a variety of referents. So there are two considerations, when the problem is one of referring to a familiar object:

1. Is it important that the reader have the exact image, or is the mere *idea* of the object enough?

2. If the exact image is important, how many referents, or varieties of the object exist?

Answering those questions tells you whether you need an illustration of some sort and, if so, how detailed and precise it must be. Presenting more abstract information is an entirely different kind of problem. Those ideas which are at a relatively low level of abstraction, such as architectural-design considerations, lend themselves readily to graphic illustration. The writer can easily show design variants and would be dealing with drawings to a large extent, both artist's views and engineering drawings. As the level of abstraction increases, so does the problem of communicating the information or ideas.

A medium level of abstraction, such as management theory, has a range of abstraction. If the writing deals with organization, several types of chart are suitable—the typical organization chart, for one, but also functional flowcharts. When the writer gets into the more abstract areas of the subject, illustration becomes a bit more difficult, more sophisticated, and begins to become more abstract of itself. For example, describing an organization may require more than one organization chart because the hierarchy of management in terms of reporting order or order of authority may very well be entirely different from the hierarchy of function. It is not unknown for a manager with special skills to be assigned to give at least some of his or her time to a subordinate who is in total command of a given project and who gives orders to the manager as far as that project is concerned. Such a situation is far more clearly explained to a reader by using two charts to show the organization.

When we get to high levels of abstraction, such as what a vector means and how it is derived, the illustration itself becomes largely symbolic and is often only an analogy or an example of an application. For example, the Pythagorean Theorem might be exemplified by showing how one could measure the height of a tree without climbing the tree. That's an example to show application. On the other hand, showing a haystack with a needle buried somewhere in it to show how difficult it is to find and extract heavy water from ordinary sea water is an analogy.

EVALUATING ILLUSTRATIONS

Evaluating the effectiveness of an illustration of any kind—photograph, line drawing, chart, or whatever—is simply an application of the principle that an illustration is often far better at conveying the information than are words alone; it consists of asking this question of the illustration: How much explanation does it need? A good illustration needs little or no explanation. The more explanation (words) an illustration needs, the weaker it is. Always seek to provide illustrations that explain themselves. This does not mean that text passages cannot be based on illustrations, but that the whole idea is to make text passages easier to follow and understand.

OTHER "ILLUSTRATIONS"

Not all illustrations are graphic. That is, not all are photographs or drawings. Verbal illustrations are often the most efficient way of bringing about communication and understanding, and verbal illustrations are also direct descriptions of applications or examples and analogies. Such verbal illustrations will often do the job of presentation quite effectively and are far less expensive than graphic illustrations. Such material is referred to as "imagery" and includes metaphors, similes, and other figures of speech. Many writers use various figures of speech for purely stylistic reasons, to lend their writing some characteristic flavor. The purpose of using such imagery in writing for business and professional reasons, however, is entirely one of practical need and efficiency, of using the most effective and efficient means possible of accomplishing absolutely clear and unambiguous communication. It is, for example, far more efficient to use the verbal expression, "As hard as finding a needle in a haystack," than it is to actually draw a haystack and indicate a needle buried somewhere in it. Graphic material should be used when it is the only effective means or the most efficient means, but never when it is not truly needed. Graphic illustrations should never be an afterthought added after the writing is completed because it seems as though it might be nice to have a few illustrations. The writer must plan to convey certain specific ideas, images, concepts, or other information, and consider the difficulties and most effective means, trying to foresee in advance the need for photographs and artwork. Decisions should be made within the constraints of what is necessary and what is effective or efficient, but within those constraints the writer should consider what to use in this ascending order:

1.   Straight verbal descriptions and explanations
2.   Verbal examples, illustrations, analogies, figures of speech, and so forth
3.   Graphics—photos, artist's renderings, charts, graphs, plots

DO-IT-YOURSELF ARTWORK

When you find it necessary to use graphic illustrations, consider what kind you will use, for there is a vast difference in convenience and cost among the many alternatives open to you. Costs of graphic illustrations are in this ascending order:

1.   Photography
2.   Line drawings
3.   Artist's concepts or renderings

If you are a pretty good photographer and if you are willing to do the simpler line drawings yourself, these two alternatives are even less expensive, although photography has one drawback for the consultant: If the document is to be duplicated by office copier, the reproduction of photographs will be poor in quality even if the photos are screened. To get better quality for a short run (e.g., 25–50 copies), the relatively expensive alternative is to make actual glossy copies of all photos and bind these into the document.

However, with today's artists' aids available in any well-stocked artists' supply store, you need not be an artist to do an almost professional job of simple charts, graphs, plots, and other such line drawings. Today you can buy a wide variety of templates, transfer lettering and symbols, paste-up material, and sundry other aids which enable you to turn out near-professional quality line drawings. Explain your needs to the counter personnel in such an establishment, and you'll get lots of help.

LEVEL OF DETAIL

In technical writing there appears to be a continuous contention between writers and editors on the one hand and engineers and scientists on the other hand, about the level of detail that should go into the publications. The writers and editors generally tend to want to provide a great deal more detail than do the engineering/scientific staffs, who appear to be convinced, about every point of reader needs in dispute, that "they'll know that."

The problem is simply this: The engineers and other professionals who are not writers often have trouble adjusting their thinking to the idea that they are not writing to themselves. They appear to have become accustomed to writing only during their college days and in contributing to professional journals and technical reports since, all of which material has been addressed to their technical/professional peers.

You must have some clear idea of who your reader is and what he or she needs to know to follow what you are saying. That is not to suggest that you write down, either, for it is never writing down to be absolutely specific and clear about your meaning. Nor will it annoy or be offensive to your technical/professional peers to have technical terms explained if you do it tactfully. There is more than one way to provide definition of a term or concept if you have the slightest doubt that any of your readers will understand the term or concept immediately. Here is a convenient way that should give no one offense:

> The interface is multiplexed, permitting the equipment to carry on concurrent exchanges of information with several dozen sources.

This furnishes a functional definition of "multiplexed," although not a technical explanation, without being condescending to any reader who is well aware of what multiplexing is. If the material was part of a detailed technical publication, it would be carried down to that level too:

> The interface is multiplexed, sampling each of several dozen inputs at 50-microsecond intervals in turn, so that for practical purposes, several dozen transmissions are received concurrently.

There are other ways, too, of providing definitions diplomatically. One way, a variant of the way just illustrated, is this:

> The interface is characterized by multiplexing or ability to handle a number of inputs and outputs in such rapid succession that it is virtually simultaneous.

Still another way is to put the definition in brackets, a signal to the reader that it is provided for those who are not familiar with the term or concept:

> The interface has a multiplex characteristic (ability to handle a number of inputs and outputs in such rapid succession as to appear to be simultaneous).

There are still other ways to handle the problem. If you believe that some but not all of your readers will need some amplification or explanation, you can do either or both of these things: Provide a glossary of terms and/or provide one or more appendices in which detailed explanations are given. The text should guide the reader to these as appropriate. In many cases this is the best solution, since it enables those who do not need detailed explanation to proceed without delay, while still providing the necessary details for those who do need or want them.

In general, beware that handy little rhyme so many are fond of—"when in doubt, leave it out." The opposite advice is more suitable, and, if you need a rhyme to help you remember, try this: "It's never a sin to leave it in."

HOW TO MAKE SLIDES AND TRANSPARENCIES

It is apparently not well known to many people that transparencies or "vugraphs"—those 8 × 10-inch acetates that can be projected onto a large screen by using the device known as an *overhead projector*—can be made quite easily on an ordinary office copier. Most office copiers sold today are of the type often referred to as "plain-paper copiers," which means that any ordinary paper may be used in them. These are xerographic copiers, all using the same basic electrostatic process with only minor differences among them. In any case, any plain-paper copier can make the copy on a blank transparency or acetate of the proper thickness in precisely the same manner it makes that copy on paper. If you place your original material on the copy board and load the paper tray of the copier with the acetates, the image will be transferred to that acetate, producing a transparency you can use with an overhead projector.

You can prepare the original any way you wish to—typing, lettering, pasting up from some source, drawing free hand, or whatever. If it will transfer to plain paper, it will transfer to the acetate.

Many neighborhood copy shops keep the acetates in stock and will make transparencies for you at quite a low cost. If your local copy shop does not stock such acetates, you can get them at any well-stocked art-supply or even a good office-supply dealership and take them to the copy shop along with your original. The acetates are available in colors, also, and you can use colored acetates with your presentation if you like.

Slides are a different proposition. If you can use a good 35mm camera, you may wish to make your own slides. For best results you should have a special apparatus that permits you to make slides conveniently, although many individuals manage quite well without the special apparatus. If you can make your own slides in this manner, they will be quite inexpensive. However, if you have them made in a graphic-arts shop, they can run as high as $10 for each master, not including the original artwork if you choose to have that done in a shop also.

The pros and cons between slides and transparencies are several. Here are some of them:

Subjectively—as far as their effectiveness in presenting information is concerned—there is not much difference, although slides tend to project more vividly.

If the material you wish to present is photographic in nature, transparencies are impractical; slides are definitely indicated.

Transparencies are in many ways more convenient, especially if you want to make only a few of them and need them immediately. They can be made in minutes, once your originals are ready.

You can write on transparencies with a grease pencil while the transparency is on the projector and showing on the screen. Or you can use a pointer or marker to indicate things directly on the transparency rather than on the projected image. You can't do that with a slide.

Slides can be more convenient to use because they can be mounted in a carousel, changed automatically, or changed remotely, whereas presenting transparencies is a somewhat awkward manual operation.

Overhead projectors are more commonly available in clients' facilities than are slide projectors; few clients expect a lecturer to bring an overhead projector, but many expect the lecturer to provide the slide projector.

All in all, transparencies for overhead projectors are probably more convenient and practical than slides for most occasions.

13

Additional Profit Centers for Your Consulting Practice

The truly well-rounded consultant, and generally the most successful one, functions well in many professional capacities: Consultant, lecturer, writer, teacher, leader, and mentor. Consulting itself is only the beginning.

"CONSULTING" IS DIFFERENT THINGS
TO DIFFERENT CONSULTANTS

As you develop your consulting practice, even if you do not make a deliberate effort to expand your activities, you will find yourself doing so. While these expanded activities will help you greatly in achieving those material benefits we all regard as success, it will not be entirely because you seek more profits that you will expand your base of activity. Your basic success as a consultant leads you, almost compels you, to enter into many activities other than direct consulting services. Your consulting practice tends to assume a life of its own, as does any growing business, and pushes you in certain directions. It begins to dictate your moves, much to your amazement.

Several of the larger and more successful management consulting firms did not start out to be management consultants or consultants at all. Some of them began as Certified Public Accountants. At least one of the leaders in the field was initially an engineering firm, another intended to be nothing more or less than a developer of custom training programs.

One successful independent consultant of my acquaintance is today devoting most of his time and energies to publishing specialized books, while another is publishing a newsletter, and still another is marketing his own proprietary computer programs. In each case their original practices led them in the directions they finally pursued.

There are other consultants who divide their time among a great many activities; in addition to selling their customary consulting services, they write, lecture, and teach. Some do some or all these other things for clients on a fee basis, while others do them as independent entrepreneurial efforts. In this chapter we are going to explore these other profit centers so readily available to most consultants as well as the several ways the consultant can utilize the opportunities.

WHAT ARE "PROFIT CENTERS"?

A large corporation is usually made up of a number of divisions or companies, each operating on an at least semi-autonomous basis. The General Electric Company, for example, has several divisions doing government work. One specializes in "light" weapons while another concentrates on "heavy" weapons, and still another handles missile and space projects. There is a division that manufactures jet engines for aircraft, and several commercial-products divisions for consumers such as you and me. Because each of these fields requires different talents and different facilities to operate it successfully, each is separately organized and managed.

You don't have to be a super-corporation, however, to have more than one income-producing activity or enterprise. Even the self-employed, independent entrepreneur can have more than one income-producing activity operated more or less independently of other such activities. Instead of being divisions or separate companies, they are usually treated simply as "profit centers." (Although some entrepreneurs do choose to organize other activities as separate companies and even as separate corporations.)

A profit center is really nothing more than an income-producing activity which you keep track of separately, either by setting up a separate set of books for it or by putting it on your books in such a way that you can keep a close check on all costs and income resulting from that activity. For example, as an individual you may choose to publish a newsletter or produce seminars as profit-targeted activities, each with its own marketing goals, budget, and other characteristics of an independent enterprise. Even if you conduct these other activities as part of your consulting practice, each may be deemed a profit center, and it is probably good business to keep records in such a manner that you can determine exactly what each activity contributes to your overall enterprise in gross income, costs, net income, and profits, if any.

There are other considerations, and there is no particularly compelling reason to consider these other activities to be separate enterprises. In one sense, they are all part of the consulting service you offer. If you publish newsletters or books, you are providing technical/professional information on a general basis rather than on a custom basis, but it is simply an extension of your service, the provision of specialized information, skills, and counsel. The same may be said for seminars and lectures. However, under certain circumstances, these activities come even closer to being extensions of your consulting services, as you will see presently.

WHY OTHER PROFIT CENTERS

There are at least three reasons, any or all of which may underlie your decision to enter into the related activities referred to here as other profit centers:

1. You are more or less forced into these other activities by such factors as demand, opportunity, and chance circumstances.
2. You deliberately choose to expand your successful consulting practice in this manner rather than by hiring staff and seeking more or larger consulting projects.

3. Consulting assignments are not numerous enough or lucrative enough to support your expenses and produce an adequate personal income. You must diversify to produce enough gross income for your needs.

A fourth reason, which is related to the first two reasons, is this: Many consultants decide that they prefer lecturing and/or writing to consulting, and begin to deliberately build up these other activities so that they can reduce the amount of time they spend on consulting and possibly discontinue consulting work eventually. You may discover that you really enjoy the seminar business or the publishing business, while there is something about consulting—perhaps the travel requirements or perhaps the continuous pressure to market—that you do not like. Or you may find that a full menu of consulting is boring. You may be one of those individuals who much prefers to be on an impossibly busy and diversified schedule, doing it all yourself. If so, you will not lack for opportunities to stick your finger into a great many pies.

THE COMMON DENOMINATOR IS SPECIALIZED KNOWLEDGE

If there is any common denominator among all the technical/professional specialties upon which consultant practices have been founded, it is specialized knowledge. Some consultants base their services upon actually *performing* their specific skills while others base their services strictly upon counseling, analyzing situations and offering advice. Many do both, but in every case the sine qua non of the practice is some field of special knowledge. The chief difference among consultants is principally one of how each chooses to market that knowledge. There are three general methods for providing that knowledge to clients:

1. Direct contact on a custom basis, giving full time and attention to the client's specific needs
2. Writing
3. Lecturing

The first method is what most of us think of as basic consulting service; it is the basis for the consulting practice and, therefore, not one of those other profit centers which are the subject of this chapter. Those other profit centers all derive in one way or another from those other two major activities, writing and lecturing. Each of these offers a variety of opportunities or ways of using the activity, as a consultant specialist, to produce income and profit.

HOW WRITING PRODUCES INCOME

There are two ways to earn money as a writer: 1) by writing for others, and 2) by publishing your own writing. Which you choose to do depends in part on *what* you choose to write, in part on how skilled a writer you are, and in part on your personal preferences. Let's consider some of the factors.

It is possible to sell articles and books to publishers of periodicals and books, respectively. Most periodicals, except for daily newspapers, buy a great deal of their material from contributors who sell their writing in this manner. Many periodicals buy almost everything from free-lance contributors. Book publishers also buy all their book manuscripts from contributors, and a great many of them from authors who are entirely unknown to the publisher before the offer of a book manuscript by the author.

There are also a number of syndicates that sell the work of freelancers to periodicals, principally to newspapers. Syndicates are middlemen or brokers. They market the freelancer's writing (and other specialty things such as cartoons and crossword puzzles), keeping a percentage (usually on the order of 40–60 percent) as their fee for the service. (Literary agents, who sell book manuscripts for authors, usually charge 10 percent for their services, although many are beginning now to ask for 15 percent in light of increased costs.) Most major newspaper columnists, such as Jack Anderson and Art Buchwald, sell their columns through such syndicates. Syndicates, it should be noted in fairness, do much more work than do literary agents in the sense that they do extensive mailing to market a writer's work to a large number of newspapers, and they handle duplicating the manuscript and sending it out to the various customers. The literary agent, on the other hand, does relatively little work after the sale is made, but continues to collect 10 or 15 percent of the author's earnings as long as the book produces royalty payments. (Most books are published on a royalty basis.)

It is possible to publish your own work, in which case you will have to make whatever investment is necessary and do your own marketing, taking the risk of losses but also enjoying the possibility of great profits. For some kinds of publications you have little choice, however; the circumstances dictate that you must be your own publisher. Publishing a newsletter is such a case. While it is possible to write a complete newsletter published by someone else, it would be a rare set of circumstances that made that possible. If you choose to write a newsletter, you will almost certainly have to be the publisher of the newsletter.

Very much the same thing may be said for those pieces that are generally called reports or monographs. These are usually too short, too specialized, and/or too narrow in their interest to merit publication as books, and are also usually unsuitable for publication in any periodical. Frequently the only way to market these profitably is to publish them yourself, and that means marketing them yourself.

Books and articles are not the only products of the pen that you might generate as income producers, however; there are some specialty items that can also produce income. One enormous field of written products is training materials. There is an active and hungry market for training manuals, lecture guides, lesson plans, instructor guides, curriculum plans, audiovisuals (slides, filmstrips, transparencies, videotapes, audiotapes, films and perhaps even a few other items), posters, learning aids, and anything else that is useful for training purposes. There are publishers of such materials just as there are publishers of books of all kinds.

There are also a great many producers of industrial films, and they are in the market almost continuously for new material.

There are also clients who need writing in specialized areas on a custom basis. I am often retained to help a client write a proposal, a capability brochure, an annual report, or a marketing brochure. Sometimes I am retained because I can provide certain writing competence and publications knowledge, sometimes because I can provide certain specialized technical knowledge. Whatever the reason, I am paid as a consultant to provide writing and publications services on a custom basis. Am I a writer or a consultant when I undertake such projects? Is there any point in even trying to make such a distinction? The main point is that the assignment calls for more than one skill, but is essentially a writing chore on a custom basis. There is a market for that, too, and it is one of the exceptions, a case where you may be able to write a newsletter for a client on a fee basis. Some organizations do contract with specialists to write and produce their newsletter or in-house magazines, but they may also contract with a specially qualified consultant/writer to produce any of several other kinds of written products.

Let's consider several of these areas/products and what is involved in making them profit centers.

FREE-LANCE ARTICLES

Every field—industrial, professional, technical, and commercial—has its special publications, often referred to as "trade journals" or "trade papers." Here is a small assortment of such publications:

Aviation Travel & Times	*House Beautiful*
Commercial Car Journal	*Forecast for Home Economics*
Electrical Contractor	*The New Physician*
Computer Consultant	*Training*

There are also those magazines which appear regularly on newsstands, generally referred to as general interest publications, such as *Reader's Digest, Money,* and *Sports Illustrated.* They are "general interest" because they appeal to enough people to be offered on newsstands to the general public rather than by mail to people in a special occupational field or having a special interest. The name is something of a misnomer because some of the magazines that appear on newsstands are really special-interest publications, too. For example, a newsstand publication may deal entirely with numismatics or investment and be bought only by those with such interests. But there are enough people having that special interest to justify newsstand distribution and make it economically practical, so such publications are lumped with those which are truly of general interest.

There are several ways such publications produce their content each week or each month: In many cases some of the material is written by staff writers or by contributing writers and editors. These are usually free-lance writers who are located almost anywhere around the country and who write regularly for the publication. Sometimes they are local representatives who cover their geographical area for the publication. A great many publications have a Washington, DC, representative because they want coverage of events in the capital. These regional representatives may be assigned to cover some special area for the publication. A business magazine may assign its Washington representative to cover all the Congressional hearings on business matters that are held on Capitol Hill, as well as providing general coverage of the Small Business Administration, the Department of Commerce, and other federal agencies closely tied to the interests of business generally.

Depending on your own field and other considerations, you may want to seek such an arrangement, possibly with some special publication with interests that require coverage in your own area. It is more likely that you will want to begin by trying to write and sell an occasional special article to some suitable publication.

Be aware that rates of payment vary quite widely among the various publications, and even within a given publication. The article you write may be of great value to some given publication, which would encourage the editor to make a better offer for it than if your article were of only passing interest. There are other factors, too, one of which is how well you are regarded as a contributor to the publication. Obviously, that cannot be considered until you have been a more or less frequent contributor, so you can't expect much of a price the first time when you're still an unknown quantity.

In general, trade publications pay less well than do general-interest publications. But even that doesn't say very much, for there are many exceptions to that rule. Some general-interest publications do not pay well at all, and some trade publications do pay rather well. But regardless of what kind of publication you sell to, payment may be on any of these bases:

1. By the word. Total number of words, which you should estimate by counting some representative sample and multiplying by total number of manuscript pages, is multiplied by a given word rate. This may range from as low as 3-4 cents per word to as high as 40-50 cents per word or even higher, depending on various factors.

2. By the printed page. Many trade journals, especially those slick-paper professional journals, pay this way, and rates may vary widely here too, from as little as $25 per page to as much as $150 per page.

3. By negotiation. This really means that the author is made an offer, and he may or may not be able to truly negotiate, depending on how much the editor wants the article.

There is also such a thing as "space rates," which is a variant of paying by the page, except that it is payment by the column-inch. Newspapers often pay in this manner.

Every publication has its own special "slant" or orientation. Even publications in the same general field all have their special slants according to what the editor believes will appeal to the readers. Take, for example, two journals on selling computers, *Computer Dealer* and *Computer Retailing*. The former wants articles covering a wide variety of sales/marketing information for dealers in computer hardware, software, and services. The latter wants emphasis on microcomputers and prefers interviews with dealers. One has a circulation of only 10,000 and pays only on publication (which can mean a long wait for payment); the other pays on acceptance, has 8,500 circulation (trade journals tend to have relatively small circulation). One reports that it pays $50 per page minimum and 8 cents per word maximum; the other reports that it pays $100 to $200 for articles of from 750 to 2,000 words.

Reading such reports on publications in the *Writer's Market* and other publications reporting such information will give you a pretty good idea of what publications exist in fields related to your professional interests, what they want, how much they pay, and what their slants are, but most editors insist that you can't really understand their slants well enough to write for them successfully unless you read sample copies of their publications. Certainly it helps to know what the editor wants if you're to have any hope of selling what you write.

There are two ways of going at free-lance writing of articles: One is to study the markets by reading appropriate publications (see the last chapter, "The Reference File," for listings) and prepare articles especially for certain ones. Another way is to write what you believe ought to be written and then study the markets to decide where it has the best chance of being accepted. Of the two methods, the first one makes a great deal more sense for at least these reasons:

You have a much better chance of selling your articles by slanting them to carefully selected markets.

You can select only those markets whose terms of payment are acceptable to you.

You can query the editor first and probably avoid wasting time on something you may never sell. (More on this subject in a moment.)

The market study itself often provokes good ideas for articles.

COLD TURKEY VERSUS QUERIES

If you read the market reports referred to, you'll find that some editors of periodicals prefer a query first, while others are entirely willing or even prefer that you send them a completed manuscript to examine. A query is, in its simplest form, a letter to the editor describing the article you propose to write and your qualifications for writing it, and asking whether he is interested in seeing it. If the editor expresses interest, you've a much better chance of selling him than if you've sent it in "cold turkey," with no advance communication. You also run the risk that your query will be a great deal less interesting than the article would have been and so you get a turndown when he might have bought the article. (Everything is a trade-off.) Some writers prefer to work with queries. (I usually do.) Others prefer to write the piece, usually with a given publication in mind, because they are confident that every article they write is salable inventory, and if the first editor does not buy it another one will. (They are careful to write only articles for which they know several possible markets.) Both methods work, and whatever works is right.

You need not confine your article writing to a professional or trade journal. Many technical fields concern things of interest to the general public. The computer specialist, for example, may write a general-interest piece on computers that a general-interest magazine will be pleased to publish. It cannot be a highly technical piece, but must be an interpretation of the technical to the lay level. It might, for example, be a "gee whiz" kind of article, explaining just how fast modern computers really are and how they get that way. Or it might explain that the computer really *is* a moron, as Peter Drucker has denounced it, performing its miracles only because of its extreme speed and despite the primitive way it handles mathematical operations. (Repetitive addition and subtraction to perform multiplication and division, for example.) Or it might report on computers for the home or pocket-sized computers about to become available.

The same ideas are valid in many special fields—medicine, medical equipment, aircraft, space systems, social programs, and others. The opportunities for articles so based are growing rapidly because the public wants explanations of modern miracles, and because general free-lance writers are less and less able to cope with increasingly complex subjects. There are, therefore, few fields in which the technical/professional specialist could not report interestingly to the general public on what is happening in his or her field.

The heart of the successful query lies in convincing the editor to whom it is addressed that 1) his or her readers will be interested in what you propose to write and 2) you are well qualified to write it and can deliver what you promise. The query must therefore explain *why* you believe the editor ought to consider the idea favorably, and offer as much information as possible about what the proposed article will cover and how it will cover it. If you can come up with a dynamite lead for the article, including that lead in your query letter will help enormously to sell the idea to the editor. That brings up still another point about query letters: They are called *queries*, but they ought to be called and ought to be *proposals*. They should not query as much as they should *sell*, for that is really the proper objective of the so-called query letter. (More on this when we discuss the writing and selling of a book.)

The most difficult time is when you are still new and have published little or nothing. An editor who does not know of you expects you to enclose some clips of your previously published work. Save copies of everything you have ever published, even if it was without payment in some association newsletter or magazine. Don't ever send originals unless you have a large supply of them. Make copies and, when you enclose samples with a query, try to select samples most relevant to what you are proposing to write. Describe your technical/professional qualifications as well as your writing qualifications, especially if the subject is a highly technical one. (Read earlier sections of this book dealing with marketing and selling and adapt those principles to selling editors with query letters.)

Especially with slick-paper publications, photographs help enormously to sell articles. If the subject lends itself to photography, by all means try to supply good photographs, and mention in your query that you will do so. Editors often buy a story they don't care a great deal about because they want the photos. They also pay extra for photos or pay more for an article which includes good photos.

Truly professional writers often manage to earn a substantial living at their trade despite low rates of pay from trade journals by taking advantage of the fact that each publication has its own slant. The true professional writer of trade-journal articles takes advantage of that by using the basic data-gathering research several times over, writing several versions of the article for different trade journals. That is, a single task of gathering materials—information, drawings, photographs, and perhaps other material—supports the writing of as many as a half-dozen articles based on that material. Writing goes fast when articles don't have to be researched independently of each other.

I once decided that not nearly enough had ever been published on transducers. I queried an engineering magazine about it and got a go-ahead. I then wrote to a number of manufacturers and soon had a large store of technical reports, brochures, manuals, drawings, and photographs, with permission to use them freely with attribution (credit lines acknowledging the source and identifying the products).

I did a first article on transducers and sold it readily to the magazine which had given me the go-ahead. But I still had lots of material, so I did a piece for another magazine on one type of transducer, strain gauges. I discovered among the materials good information and good photos on an ultrasonic type of burglar alarm, so I wrote and sold an article about that device. I also found material which enabled me to write an article about a power sequencer. This gave me four articles based on one research job. None of the journals paid particularly well, but the four together produced a sum worth the total effort.

Sometimes the several articles are even more similar than these were but are written simply for different audiences. Take a simple project such as a garage-door opener, for example. One article might explain how such devices work. Another could be on how to install such devices, another on how to troubleshoot them when they malfunction, and still another on how to choose the one best suited to your own needs. You can get the technical information, drawings, and photographs free as a rule, with permission to identify them in your article. After studying the bundles of information sent to you by manufacturers, you would probably get a few other ideas for still more articles about them.

The idea is adaptable to many fields. If you are a social scientist of some sort, you can do articles about the technologies in your field, about existing programs, how they work, case histories, government activity and interest, private foundations and their programs, forecasts of future developments, and probably many other aspects. Simply gathering a set of reports on some major project or set of projects would probably provide ample raw data for such articles.

THE LEAD

It was suggested a few paragraphs ago that one great aid to selling your article idea in your query letter is to incorporate a dynamite lead for the proposed article. That term *lead* is a special term, writer's jargon encountered frequently among newspaper reporters, which means introduction, in general terms, and yet means a great deal more than the word "introduction" covers. It is somewhat difficult to define briefly because the connotation of the term is far more wide-ranging than is its mere denotation, and it is necessary to understand fully what the term means to a writer.

An introduction generally telegraphs what the article is going to present and what the main point is to be. For example, if an article begins with the statement that cigarettes have been shown to be bad for one's health, you can expect to be offered evidence along that line which should make a case for the premise that smoking cigarettes is harmful. What most professional writers refer to as a lead, however, goes beyond that to accomplish at least three things:

1. Telegraph what, in general, the piece is about and where it will wind up, what main points or premises are to be pursued.
2. Prepare the way for the general strategy or approach the piece will follow in making the presentation. It will, in fact, lay the groundwork of the piece for the writer, pointing him in the right direction to follow in writing the piece.
3. Arouse the reader's interest by piquing curiosity or providing some reason for getting interested immediately.

Of these three objectives and characteristics of a good lead, the first is easy to accomplish if the writer has planned and thought out what the article is to say.

The second item, the need for the writer to be satisfied with the strategy, groundwork, and direction of the piece, is the reason even the best of writers often write a dozen or more leads and throw them in the wastebasket before proceeding further. There is a relationship between the quality of the writer and the number of leads drafted, because good professional writers refuse to go on until the lead is right, so that the whole piece feels right. (There is more art than science in writing, even in writing factual reports.)

Many writers—and I confess to being one of them—are thinking out loud on paper when they draft leads, and that is largely why they find it necessary to draft a large number of leads before finding the right one. A great many writers simply are unable to continue writing if their leads do not feel right, and they are actually compelled to discard everything they have written and start over when the lead proves to be awkward. It means that the writer has made a false start; there is no alternative to starting over. In my own case—and I believe that I am typical of a large number of writers who appear to be in agreement on this—I find myself in something of a quandary as to which of several possible ways I should state or explain something. I find it necessary, therefore, to try each way on paper until I find the one that works best for me. Once I find that, I recognize it quickly enough, and I proceed then with greatest confidence to follow my original plan. I am now pointed in the right direction and my strategy is right for me.

At least part of that strategy is called out by the third item on the list of things the lead must do—hook the reader with something that gets attention and generates interest. It is when that is accomplished with great success that the lead is "dynamite," because if it is right to hook the reader, it is likely to hook the editor as well.

WHAT YOU SELL

When you sell an article, you are selling the publisher *rights*, and there are several kinds of rights. What most publishers of periodicals really have direct need of and use for are the *first rights*, which are the rights to publish the material first. But there are also *secondary rights* of several kinds, for reprinting or republishing, movies and TV, and other possible uses of the material, and sometimes the secondary rights prove to be quite valuable. Therefore, it is advisable to try to sell first rights only to magazine publishers and reserve all other rights to yourself.

Some periodical publishers will insist on buying all rights but will give you back all secondary rights after the original publication. This is a move to protect those first rights and is a fairly common practice. Whether you agree to this or not is up to you, but most publishers are quite reliable; if they pledge to return secondary rights, they will generally do so without trouble. If you are dealing with a publisher who operates on this basis, make it quite clear that you will want the secondary rights returned to you after publication.

There are at least two possible ways for you to earn additional profits from those secondary rights. There are other periodicals willing to reprint previously published material, and they will pay something for that privilege. There is also the possibility of collecting a number of your articles and making a book of them. Some such anthologies are quite successful, and you may have a valuable literary property in the form of a collection of previously published articles to which you still have secondary rights.

ETHICS OF FREE-LANCE WRITING

At one time it was considered highly unethical by publishers for a writer to offer the same piece of work to more than one publisher at a time. If a publisher learned that a writer was offering work to him which he had simultaneously offered to other publishers, he would promptly return the work and never consent to even look at anything that writer sent him in the future. This despite the fact that the publisher might take many weeks, even months, to decide about the piece and then reject it. If the writer needed to offer the piece to several publishers before selling it, and each publisher took a few months to look it over before rejecting it, the writer might have to circulate it for a year or more before selling it or deciding that it was unsalable. This was true for any kind of writing—articles, essays, poems, books, or whatever.

Somewhere in recent years—I'm not sure when it happened—the ethic began to change, and publishers generally began to accept the writer's right to make simultaneous submissions. There are today still some publishers who insist that they will not look at anything you are simultaneously offering elsewhere, but they are a vanishing breed. However, most publishers still insist that you must advise them that you are making simultaneous submissions if you want consideration.

Probably the advent of modern copy machines has had something to do with this change. Prior to the existence of such machines, you had only one original unless you were willing to retype the piece, and of course a publisher recognized a carbon copy as such, accepting this as evidence of simultaneous submissions. Now it is much more difficult to tell a copy from an original produced on an electric typewriter, and it is quite easy for a writer to make a number of submissions simultaneously.

I see nothing wrong with simultaneous submissions, in light of the time you otherwise lose while waiting for a decision from a publisher. I think that if it is a free market for publishers, it ought to be an equally free market for writers. One basis for objection to the practice is that many publishers object to being put into the position of being forced to bid; they object to what is called an *auction technique*. (Although book publishers will use auction techniques sometimes to sell paperback rights to the highest bidder!)

In any case, if you want to be entirely ethical according to the standards of most publishers, you will either not make simultaneous submissions or you will advise each publisher to whom you make such a submission that you are doing so.

There are some other ethical considerations, but these are virtually the same standards you would use in any business relationship. They are as follows:

Keep your promises. If you have agreed to do a piece for someone at some agreed-upon price, live up to your bargain even if someone comes along with a better offer or you find the article more difficult to do than you anticipated.

Stick to your schedule. This is another case of keeping a promise. If you have promised delivery by a certain date, make that a firm deadline and deliver on time. Editors in general, but especially those who have tight deadlines for getting their publications out, aren't going to have much faith in you in the future if you let them down in this regard.

Exercise common courtesy. Most editors are quite busy, so don't drop in on them unexpectedly. Make appointments in advance. For the same reason, make your queries by letter rather than telephone. (You can invite the editor to call you collect, if he or she wishes, with a response. Some writers say that this has increased their acceptance percentage.)

ESSAYS

Essays—sometimes called "think pieces" because they are often pure opinion—are hard to sell unless you are a noted authority whose name and reputation alone will command readership. Save your essays for Letters to the Editor columns and some other uses we'll come to presently. Don't try to sell them to editors of periodicals as articles. They won't sell, at least not to periodicals. Sometimes a collection of essays may be made into a salable book, but even that is not the most frequent of occurrences.

COLUMNS

Many syndicated columnists are essayists in that their columns are actually little more than essays. It is possible that this may be the exception to the above—that someone may want you to do a regular column.

Be aware that it is extremely unlikely that any syndicate will even attempt to market you as a general columnist or commentator; it is difficult to market even a noted newspaperman or woman as a columnist. Unless you have some quite novel and interesting idea for a column, you are almost surely wasting your time even attempting to get a syndicate interested.

On the other hand, it is entirely possible that an association to which you belong or some local periodicals may be interested in having you do a regular column, either gratis or for some modest sum. They are not likely to be able to pay very much, but you may wish to do it anyway. This is one chance to do a regular essay and see it published.

BOOKS

Books offer the consultant a magnificent opportunity to profit both directly and indirectly from writing. Being the author of a "serious" book is itself a prestigious accomplishment that will enhance your professional image immediately. Even a modestly successful book also enhances your bank account, and there is always the possibility that your book may be more than modestly successful. More than one technical/professional specialist who was most definitely not a professional writer has succeeded in producing enormously successful books. Here are a few examples:

Lancelot Hogben was an engineer confined at home by illness for quite a long time in his native England during the mid-1930s. To amuse himself he began to write a manuscript about the origin of mathematics. (Engineers must master a rather prodigious amount of mathematics in learning their professions.) Friends who saw his manuscript urged him to offer it for publication, and he finally did so. The resulting book, *Mathematics for the Million*, has been through numerous editions in both hardcover and paperback since 1937 and is still selling well.

Carl Sagan, the noted physicist-astronomer, has written more than one best seller about science. *Broca's Brain* and *Cosmos* are two such works.

Robert Townsend wrote about his experiences as chief executive officer of Avis, the car rental firm, in what became a best seller, *Up the Organization!*

Don Dible, another engineer, wrote a book about how to start your own business, borrowing from and paraphrasing Townsend by calling his book, *Up Your OWN Organization!* It too has been highly successful and has been through several editions in both hardcover and paperback.

Isaac Asimov wrote science fiction stories while he was earning his degrees in chemistry, but it was only later that he began to put his academic/scientific knowledge to work, writing non-fiction on scientific subjects, popularized for general-interest readers. He has his name on well over 250 published books and long ago became a full-time writer, principally of non-fiction. He is one of the most successful of contemporary writers due to his enormous productivity and versatility.

Several successful books have been written by such financial/ investment counselors as Howard Ruff, Douglas Casey, and Tyler Hicks, some of them even managing to ring the best-seller bell.

Many people are awed by the thought of writing a book; it seems to the uninitiated to be such a monumental task. All those pages and all those words . . . Oddly enough, in many ways it is easier to write a book than it is to write an article, and it often proves far easier to sell a book than to sell an article. Here's why:

Data research inevitably requires examining a greater mass of material than you are likely to be able to use in whatever you are writing. One major problem you always face in writing an article is that of sifting that mass of information and material, trying to decide what is truly germane and must be covered in your writing, while still containing the writing to some specific maximum length. This can be a real problem in writing an article, especially when the editor has specified in advance that you are limited to two or three thousand words. To some degree this problem also exists when you write a book, but to a far lesser degree because the book is much longer and because the author of a book generally has far more freedom in required size and coverage of the final product. In addition to that, there is relatively little problem of any particular slant when you are writing a book; book publishers may specialize in subject-matter areas or types of book, but they do not usually have any particular slant requirements. For example, a publisher may publish text books and may even confine his efforts to college-level texts or even to college-level engineering texts, but that is as far as his slant goes, and it is not really a slant at all.

A book, then, typically gives you far greater freedom in all respects—allowable length, range of coverage, treatment, style, and other matters. A book is also easier to find a publisher for. Because your book will probably not require any particular slant (with the possible exception of that case where your editor believes some slanting may help the book in the marketplace), you have a much wider range of prospective publishers than you do when you offer an article for sale. Also, in the case of selling an article to an established periodical, the editor is already completely aware of the market (known readers' preferences). However, book publishers welcome marketing suggestions from authors, and good marketing ideas and information may be instrumental in selling a manuscript to a book publisher.

MARKETING YOUR MANUSCRIPT

As in the case of the article, your book manuscript has a far better chance of being accepted for publication by an established book publisher if its marketability, or "publishability" to coin a term, is one of the major considerations in planning. There are at least two ways to approach this sensibly:

1. Conceive one or more book ideas and immediately examine each one for its marketing prospects before deciding which to adopt for your book-writing project.
2. Study market needs, list a few, select one you believe you can handle well.

You should never go beyond that first step of conceiving one or more book ideas before you study the probable market for such a book. There are a great many book manuscripts languishing today in various places. (An executive of the National Press Club in Washington, DC once told me that she was convinced that nearly everyone had a book manuscript hidden under the mattress. At least, most of the people she knew were working on a book.) One reason that many of them will never see public print is simply that the authors did not consider the market before expending all the labor.

Some of these never-to-be-published manuscripts are well written; their lack of marketability has nothing to do with the literary quality of the writing. Many successful books are not at all well written as far as literary craftsmanship and style are concerned. These qualities do help a salable manuscript, but they cannot rescue an unsalable one. Weaknesses in writing craftsmanship will not keep a manuscript from finding publication if it has an apparent appeal to a large enough number of prospective book buyers.

At one time, publishing was a "gentleman's occupation," indulged in principally by those wealthy enough to treat publishing as a hobby and lose money at it. Such publishers claimed often enough to publish those books which "ought to be published"—those books, that is, which the publisher thought to have great literary worth—whether the books earned back their costs or not. Some people believe that modern-day publishers (many are now owned by conglomerates such as Gulf & Western, Columbia Broadcasting System, and RCA) are still publishing some books that they believe to be losers in the marketplace, but which are literary treasures. Even if this is true, and I rather doubt that any publisher today chooses deliberately to publish a book that appears unlikely to recover its investment, it is not a truth to depend on in marketing your own manuscript. For all practical purposes, you must assume that you will be able to interest a publisher in your manuscript only if it appears to be a commercially attractive prospect, one with a reasonable probability of earning a profit. That must be the prime consideration, far outweighing any considerations of literary merit.

The typical publishing firm does not maintain a total book-production and manufacturing capability, but contracts for all or nearly all typesetting, printing and binding. The publisher has an in-house editorial staff, but may also use some free-lance editors, probably uses free-lance indexers (unless the author does the indexing), may even use contracted services to store and ship books and even market them through distributors. Among the factors a publisher must consider in reviewing your manuscript are these:

Does this fit our marketing capability?

Does this fill some conceived gap in our line of books? Complement others we have? Or is it redundant with one we already have, either in print or in process for publication?

What and how big is the potential market for this?

What will it cost to produce? How much editorial work do we have to do on it? Are we looking at other manuscripts similar to this? If so, how do they compare with this one for quality, appeal, amount of work required?

What is the competition? Is there any? How strong is it? How do competitive books, if there are any, compare with this?

Can/will the author help us promote this—personal appearances, perhaps? A foreword by some well-known authority? Reviews and comments for publication by well-known authorities?

What are the author's credentials? Does he have "a name" that will help sell the book?

How much can we ask for this without killing sales? How many can we expect to sell? What's the probable shelf-life of the book?

These and other factors enter into the final decision about your manuscript, and the decision is not made by the editor alone. Most publishers have some sort of committee or story conference meetings, and consider the recommendations of various editors. The marketing people are heard from; they offer their estimates on marketability. Numbers are projected—costs, prices, and profit. Risk is evaluated.

In short, a manuscript may be accepted or rejected for reasons having little or nothing to do with the intrinsic merit of the manuscript. The manuscript that is rejected in March might have been eagerly accepted in January; circumstances may kill the sale. Or the reverse may be true; sometimes timing is everything.

Once it was common practice for an unknown author to simply mail a manuscript to a selected publisher with a letter verifying that the manuscript was offered for publication, usually with a few words about the author's qualifications, background, dreams and hopes, and whatever else the author thought might interest the editor and improve the chances of acceptance.

These were all "unsolicited manuscripts" in the jargon of the trade (although public pronouncements by publishers in various market reports did and still do invite authors to submit their work for appraisal). Unsolicited manuscripts were said to come in "over- the transom" and were deposited in what some called a "slush pile." Publishers employed "first readers," usually young people with some qualifications for evaluating book manuscripts (often graduate students working part-time). The job of the first reader was to sort out the slush pile, send back the hopelessly unsuitable manuscripts, pass on those thought to be possible candidates for acceptance, with their comments. (Most manuscripts were returned, but a few were passed on, and a few of those even were finally accepted.)

Today it has become too expensive to employ platoons of first readers to cope with the enormous flow of unsolicited manuscripts, and the majority of publishers refuse to accept unsolicited manuscripts. Instead, publishers want query letters sent and the editor will decide whether he or she is interested in seeing the manuscript. Even then few editors want the whole manuscript, but ask for two or three chapters as a sample. (In some cases, publishers will accept or prefer to get sample chapters with the original query.) It is therefore usually a waste of time to send book manuscripts unsolicited to any publisher unless that publisher is one of the exceptions to the rule.

It may occur to you to ask yourself this: If the publisher does not want to see the whole manuscript, why not send him a query or a query and sample chapters before I finish the book? Will I not save a lot of time and possibly have a better chance of selling my manuscript this way?

The answer to these questions is affirmative. If you are a well-known authority or have already published one or more successful books, it is possible that you will be offered a firm contract before you write the book, perhaps even before you write the first chapter on the strength of a query and detailed outline or description. That is how most professional book authors work, some even getting cash advances when signing contracts if they have become well-established as authors.

TYPICAL CONTRACT TERMS

There is such a thing as a standard contract in book publishing. That dosen't mean that every publisher uses the same contract form and terms, but that most publishers have their own standard contracts, and that the terms are roughly similar to each other. Here are some typical terms and considerations:

Advance.   This can vary quite widely according to the author's name and reputation, but is predicated largely on anticipated sale. The new and unknown author is not likely to get an advance on his or her first book, and sometimes willingness to sell a book manuscript without an advance is an aid to selling the manuscript, whereas insistence on an advance may prevent its sale.

Royalty Payments.   It is fairly typical for royalties to be paid on this basis: 10 percent of net receipts on the first 5,000 copies; 12.5 percent on the next 5,000 copies sold; and 15 percent on all copies thereafter. Or royalties may be based on the book's cover price, in which case the percentage will usually be somewhat lower.

Author's Copies.   The author generally gets from 10 to 25 copies of the published book and may buy additional copies at dealer discount.

Secondary Rights.   Most standard contracts call for an equal division between publisher and author of receipts from the sale of secondary rights, such as sale of rights to publish a paperback edition or sale of rights to publish a foreign edition. This means one half the royalties on such editions. Another secondary right is the right to a book-club edition, and that may or may not mean additional payments.

There are several other clauses in book contracts, but these are the principal points covered and are typical arrangements for the new author. The author with a record of one or more successful books may be able to negotiate somewhat better terms, but they will be along these general lines.

AGENTS

There is little point in seeking a literary agent for a single book, nor is any agent likely to be interested in a one-book author. An agent is a definite asset for most authors if they produce books more or less regularly. A good agent will usually get you the best contract terms possible, more than earning the traditional 10 percent commission or even the 15 percent many agents require today. Agents know the market far better than most authors do and have better entree to publishing houses. With an agent you operate under a different set of rules, and many publishers even specify that they don't want to see the work of unrepresented writers.

Writing and getting an agent is a chicken-and-egg kind of quandary. It is difficult to sell without an agent, but it is difficult to get an agent until you have proved that you can write salable material. Or so goes a common belief about the situation. But let me relate my own situation as an example.

Although experienced in technical writing and other activities, primarily as a staff writer, I had never sold a book to a commercial book publisher. But one day circumstances threw me together with the vice president of a publishing house which had had great success with a book on government grants. He was interested, therefore, in discovering that I was a writer and heavily experienced in government contracting. We had little difficulty in arranging a contract for doing a book on the subject.

After I had completed that book I discussed other book ideas with that vice president, but he obviously wanted to wait until he saw how my first effort had turned out, and that was a long way off. (It appears to take 10-12 months for the typical book publisher to turn your manuscript into printed books on the shelf, and then it is another year or even two before you can judge how well the book is doing or will do in the marketplace.) That's a rather typical situation, I believe, although it's not entirely logical. An author's first book may be successful or it may be a failure economically, but that has no logical relationship to how a next book might do.

I therefore sent out query letters to several publishers and got back several thanks-but-no-thanks rejections, a few interesting-idea-but-not-right-for-us rejections, a couple of maybe-but-I'll-let-you-know responses, and one tentative acceptance which was later withdrawn.

I then devised a book proposal, which I thought much better than a query letter, and tried again. This time I got two acceptances, one from a publisher I had serious misgivings about (later confirmed as being well-founded), and one from a well-known publisher who offered no advance.

I corresponded with the latter and persuaded them to offer a small advance, but I was not yet satisfied. Since I intended to write a great many books, I decided it was time to seek an agent, who would know far better than I how to cope with the contract and negotiation side of the effort. I therefore wrote a number of agents whose names I got from advertisements in the monthly magazine, *Writer's Digest*, and from that magazine's annual hardcover book, *Writer's Market*. I found only one of the 12 agents I wrote to suitable for me, and she has represented me since. Had I found none, I would have written to 12 more. The main points of interest here are the reasons I either rejected some of the other agents or they rejected me as a client:

In a number of cases the agent responded with a lukewarm acceptance, which I interpreted as meaning that the agent did not see a great deal of potential profit in me, since the kinds of books I write are not likely ever to become best sellers or be sold to Hollywood or TV. I did not want an agent who was not enthused to handle me and who did not perceive any great potential in me.

Some agents simply failed to respond at all despite the fact that they spent money to advertise and solicit clients and despite the promises they make in their advertisements.

One agent took over a month to respond, apologized and made an excuse for the delay, expressed great interest, and then failed to respond to my follow-up letter.

Several agents asked me to pay reading fees despite my explanation that I was an experienced writer, had sold a book and many magazine articles, and neither sought nor wanted editorial assistance, but was interested in marketing and contract negotiation services.

One agent who does a great deal of expensive advertising insisted on misunderstanding my letter (which no one else appeared to have trouble understanding), became quite hostile when I wrote to point out his misinterpretation of my original letter, and we wound up exchanging acrimonious barbs.

In light of this, at least as far as writing the specialized kind of books consultants are most likely to write, an agent is not an essential for making sales to publishers, but it is possible to get a good agent interested if you approach the problem properly. However, to sell your book manuscript yourself, you must take the time and make the effort to study the market, and to get an agent to represent you if you plan to continue writing books, you must do likewise. I do believe that it is a distinct advantage to have an agent if you plan to write books continuously, but that you must select that agent with great care. Agents, like publishers, tend to be specialists, and you need one who is right for the kinds of books you write. I know, for example, which markets my own agent is most familiar with, and I often do my own market research and suggest publishers to her.

TIPS ON WRITING BOOK PROPOSALS

A proposal outline in the style I generally employ is included in the final chapter of this book. The rationale is presented here, and its basis is the same as that recommended earlier for the article query—don't query; *sell!*

One item that often becomes a casualty before my book manuscript is finally typeset and printed as a book is the title. Rarely does the book title finally emerge as I have originally suggested. Sometimes the editor is entirely right, and the title which finally emerges is far better than the one I suggested originally. There are times when I am less than completely happy over the change, perhaps because I have fallen in love with a title I originally intended strictly as a "working title." Most books begin with a working title which is primarily descriptive and is not intended to be the final title. But in writing a book proposal, the working title should be an advertising headline. It should sell the editor by helping the editor perceive the market and the appeal of the book. On my shelf is a book called *Washington IV*. It is the fourth edition of a book listing various associations and organizations in and around Washington, DC. You could never deduce that from the title. A far better title, in my opinion, would be something such as *Washington, DC, Organizations*, possibly preceded by "Directory of." *How to Prosper During the Coming Bad Years* was an excellent book title with great appeal to prospective buyers. *Crisis Investing*, on the other hand, was a cryptic title; what casual bookstore browser would guess what it was about?

A book title, especially that working title you use in your book proposal, ought to *sell* the book idea. It should reveal as much as possible about what the book deals with, its objective, its intended reader, the benefits to be derived from reading it, and the reason for buying it. Study the titles of books on your own shelves and see how close they come to doing any of these things.

Bear in mind clearly that when you deal with specialized fields, as I did in writing about government markets and you are likely to do when you write about your own field, the chances are that the publisher's people are not especially familiar with the field and must depend on you for information about market size, how to reach the market, and other such information. You must, therefore, not only supply some concrete information about this, but also be credible as an expert. It is essential that your credentials cover not only your capability for writing the book, but also your capability for guiding the publisher accurately to the market.

Statistics are important. It helped to be able to tell my publisher how big the market was (over 13 million logical prospects) as well as how big the subject was (federal procurement running in excess of $100 billion annually at that time).

A hook in the proposal helps hook the editor as it should later hook a reader, and sometimes the same hook can be used. It proved an effective hook to headline that the federal government paid me $6,000 to answer their mail. It got attention and aroused interest.

I frequently submit a brief preface with my proposal, as 1) an expansion of the rationale underlying the proposed book and explained briefly in the proposal, and 2) a small sample of my writing style. I believe that it helps greatly.

I try to make my outlines as definitive and detailed as possible, and I try to put additional hooks in there, also. I try also to demonstrate that I write well enough and grammatically enough so that editing my work is not a difficult (and expensive) task. I believe that that helps, too. (Samples of published work and titles of books published do not reveal how much work editors had to do on my manuscripts.)

SELF-PUBLISHING YOUR BOOK

Some controversy rages over selling your work to established commercial publishers versus publishing your own books and other material. There are those who self-publish because they can't sell their work to established publishers or, at least, have so far not succeeded in doing so. There are those who have never even tried to sell their work to established publishers, but simply assumed that they could not or were unwilling to make the effort. There are those who are convinced, not entirely without justification, that it is more profitable to publish their own work. Don Dible (*Up Your OWN Organization!*) and Robert Ringer (*Winning Through Intimidation*) found it so, apparently, although they might have done as well without publishing their own books.

There are two ways you can pursue self-publishing. One is to resort to what is generally described as the "vanity press." The other is to attend to all the details yourself. Here is a brief explanation of each method:

Vanity Press

There are several organizations who will publish your book for you on a subsidy basis. For a fee of several thousand dollars, paid by the author, the organization will edit, typeset, print, and bind a quantity of the books. The author gets a number of these, and the organization promises to advertise and market (publish) the rest. In only a rare and exceptional case is one of these books a commercial success, and there is a stigma attached to such a book in that being subsidized in that manner suggests that the book was not good enough for commercial publication. Therefore, the author had to pay to have it published, and therefore the term "vanity press."

The system is patently unfair to the author in at least one other way. Having already paid for the services, the author must pay still more if he or she wishes to take title to the remaining unsold books. (The organization represents that the author has not paid the whole cost, but only part of it, a claim about which most people are quite skeptical.)

True Self-Publishing

There are today some printing firms who will edit, typeset, and manufacture finished books for you for a price and turn them over to you for marketing. This is an entirely legitimate way to get your book produced. You may be able to have the books manufactured a bit more cheaply by shopping around for each service—editing, typesetting, printing, and binding—but it is a lot of work and takes a lot of time.

However you do it, you have the problem of marketing the books. That is also time-consuming and can be costly if you wish to use direct mail for it or run space advertising in periodicals.

One way to reduce costs is to cut a few corners. For example, type may be set by electric trypewriter. Modern electric typewriter copy is quite acceptable today, and with modern offset printing methods, any clean typed copy is suitable as camera-ready, reproducible copy.

Perfect binding—the way mass market paperback books are bound, with a glued back—is relatively inexpensive, and you can produce your book that way. However, many self-publishers use the plastic spiral binders, side-stitching (stapling), and, if the book is not too large, saddle stitching (folded and stapled in the center).

There is one way you may be able to market your own book successfully without major investment. Persuade publishers of periodicals to run "P.O." or "P.I" advertisements. These are per-order or per-inquiry advertisements, with the publisher's address used. If there are orders for the book, the publisher keeps a commission—from 40 to 65 percent, usually—and sends you the rest. You then fill the order. If it is per-inquiry, the publisher sends you the inquiries, and you pay him some fixed fee for each inquiry, while you mail a sales solicitation to each inquirer. Many self-publishers have done quite well with this method.

REPORT PUBLISHING

Although there is no definition as to what constitutes a book—a book can be just about any size you want it to be—smaller written products of a few thousand words can be marketed as reports. Even much larger products can be so marketed. There are certain benefits in doing so: One is that the customer does not expect anything resembling a book binding, and it is far easier and less expensive to assemble a quantity of typed pages and use a corner staple if there are only a few pages, or two side staples if there are many pages. (Or even an inexpensive plastic or paper report binder if you prefer.) The customer who buys a report is buying information, not a book, and does not expect to get a handsome addition to his bookshelves.

I experienced no difficulty or resistance whatsoever to a price of approximately 50 cents per page for reports of only a few pages, and that was a number of years ago. A 10,000-word report—about 20 pages—will bring between $5 and $10 without complaint if it is well written and the information is truly useful. A most successful self-published book I know of is slightly over 150 pages, but is actually only about 25,000 words long since it is double-spaced and many of the pages are title pages and divider pages. But it is handsomely bound, well written, and the content is useful and pleasing to readers, so the author-publisher has had no difficulty in selling many thousands of these at a cover price of $20 each.

You should strive for a cover price of at least three times your manufacturing cost and preferably five times, for these products are relatively expensive to market, and you need that margin if you are going to market them effectively.

In many ways I found reports to be more profitable as a self-publishing enterprise than books. Once I had built up a large number of related reports, customers ordered several at a time, so that the order size began to average more than that of a book.

NEWSLETTER PUBLISHING

Newsletter publishing, a growth industry in the United States for a great many years, is inherently a self-publishing enterprise, and it is a natural for many consultants because the entire rationale underlying newsletters is a parallel or analogy of the consulting concept. The consulting idea is founded on the concept of a need for highly specialized knowledge and skills, and newsletters were founded on exactly that same concept; they provided specialized information not to be found anywhere else in a single source and sometimes not to be found anywhere else at all. The concept has been broadened considerably since then, but many newsletters are still of that description. One deals entirely with electric cells and batteries, there are several dealing with consumer product safety, others dealing with some aspect of computer usage, and still others dealing with a variety of specialized subjects. (There are now three or more dealing with consulting.)

Some newsletters are distillations of what has appeared in many other periodicals. Their value is that they save the reader an impossible reading job because the newsletter publisher has extracted and condensed the information. Others are purely news items, the latest happenings/developments in the field of interest, and still others are interpretive or advisory, such as investment newsletters.

To create your own newsletter is simple enough. It can be four or more pages; published daily, weekly, monthly, bi-monthly, or quarterly; need not be typeset—in fact, it is considered by many to be an asset or even de rigeur to have it typed; it is printed easily and quickly in any offset printing shop; and it is easy and relatively inexpensive to mail. Pricing is generally such that it requires only a few hundred subscribers to be profitable, and solicitation of subscriptions appears to produce satisfactory results only when conducted by mail.

The downside is that it is a stern master. Each issue's deadline appears sooner than you would have suspected and always when you have so many other, more important things to do. Subscribers write with questions, complaints, comments, suggestions. You have some obligation to answer them, and you soon find that you can't answer them all in the newsletter itself, nor should you even if it were possible. The printer's equipment breaks down or he has some other excuse for not getting your job done on time, and before you know it you are getting angry calls and letters from subscribers for whom your newsletter has become a fix.

Even if the newsletter is not especially profitable, it is an excellent medium for selling your reports. Build up a sizable circulation—you might want to keep your price way down for that purpose—and keep producing new reports, and the reports may produce far more income than the newsletter could. One newsletter publisher I know produces a new, self-published hardcover book on a relafed subject every year, and sells thousands of copies of the book through the newsletter. The annual book is far more profitable than the newsletter. Some consultants create the newsletter strictly as marketing tools for whatever else they sell.

HOW LECTURING PRODUCES INCOME

Lecturing is similar to writing in at least one sense; it can be performed as a fee-paid service for a client or it can be packaged and sold, very much in the manner of self-publishing your written products.

It is well known that such public luminaries as Art Buchwald, Norman Vincent Peale, and Gerald Ford command fees running to thousands of dollars for each appearance as a speaker. There are thousands of others not known to the public at large and not commanding such many-zeroed fees for their appearances. It is not unusual for such little-known specialists as you and me to command from $500 to $1,000 for a speaking engagement, and that is a modest range of fees even for a not-the-best-known speaker, as long as he or she is a good speaker.

For many consultants public speaking is an adjunct, one of their several profit centers, although some tend to make it a main function. If you wish to pursue fee-paid speaking engagements, you will have to subject yourself to much travel and many motel rooms as well as many chicken-and-peas dinners. (Some veterans of public speaking refer to it as the chicken-and-peas circuit or the rubber-chicken circuit, because chicken a la king and chicken in other disguises so often appear on the banquet tables at after-dinner-speaking engagements.) If you wish to pursue it seriously, some preparation and marketing are necessary:

You need to make up a brochure of some kind in which you describe yourself and the several presentations you offer to make. (If your presentation is of universal interest, such as Norman Vincent Peale's "power of positive thinking," you may need only one.)

You should have an audition tape as well, so that you can send on a sample of your voice and presentation style. It need not be a full presentation, of course, but only a few minutes.

You must make yourself known in some manner, such as sending out a sales letter and copy of your brochure to colleges and universities, to the program chairman or chairwoman of associations, to business clubs such as the Rotary and Lions, and to other such prospects. You send a copy of the audition tape to those who express an active interest in possibly engaging you.

You try to get yourself listed with one or more speakers' bureaus. (These are analogous to literary agents in that they book speakers, although they usually get about one third of the fee rather than 10 or 15 percent.)

If you do sign with a speakers' bureau, do not agree to exclusive booking through them. It is a rare speakers' bureau that can keep you busy unless you happen to be Henry Kissinger or a living ex-president, in which case you hardly need the bureau. You will have to make many of your engagements through your own efforts, and it helps to be listed with more than one bureau.

Most such speaking engagements require you to speak from about one-half hour to one hour. Speaking for longer periods than that begins to verge on seminars rather than speeches, and a seminar or training session can go for several hours to several days in length. I have presented many three- to four-hour or half-day seminars and some two-day seminars, but most of my seminar presentations are one-day sessions requiring me to be on the dais for a total of about six hours.

Depending on your field, you may be able to do such seminars on a fee basis for organizations, companies, government agencies, associations, unions, and others. Since I do this, my marketing aid is principally a brochure which presents an outline of my usual coverage and information about myself and my qualifications, with as much discreet sales appeal as I can crowd into my small brochure. (It is a standard typewriter-sheet-sized paper, folded twice, to provide a six-panel brochure that fits easily into a number 10 business envelope.) I send along a sales letter explaining my terms and providing several references so the prospect can verify that my presentation has been well received elsewhere. If I wished to pursue this work more vigorously, I would have more literature for the mail package, with my photo, and I would have audition tapes available. Properly presented, these sales are not especially difficult to make.

Many consultants and professional speakers combine their speaking engagements with their writing and publishing activities. They bring a supply of their books, manuals, reports, or whatever they write and publish to their speaking engagements and arrange to have someone sell them at the back of the room, or they handle the sales themselves after concluding their presentation. Many speakers report good results, with the book sales equaling their speaking fees.

OPEN-REGISTRATION SEMINARS

You need not wait to be asked to speak for fees if you prefer to take matters into your own hands and make things happen. You can produce and present your own seminars if you choose to, with less work and probably less investment and risk than most enterprises require. You present your seminar in public facilities, with open registration; anyone may pay the fee and attend.

Clearly, such an enterprise requires preparation and advertising. The correct advertising method depends on the type of prospects you must reach, which in turn depends on the subject matter and nature of the seminar coverage. There are two kinds of prospects:

1. The individual, acting as an individual and paying for attendance out of his or her own pocket
2. The representative of a business, with the employer paying for attendance

Now it is fairly obvious that if the seminar is on how to write a resume and handle other problems of finding a job, it is unlikely that an employer will be sending employees and paying for their attendance. (There are exceptions, however, even in such cases as this example.) In general, it may be assumed that attendees will be individuals seeking jobs and paying for their own attendance.

However, employers may well be sending employees to a seminar on how to be more effective salespeople, write better business letters, be more efficient generally, or otherwise learn things that will aid the employer's business.

There are some areas where the distinction is not clear-cut, where attendees may include both people whose employers are paying for their attendance and individuals who are paying for their own attendance. My seminars on proposal writing are an example of this. Although most of my attendees had been sent by their companies, a few were small, independent entrepreneurs or individuals seeking to launch an enterprise.

That the last were in a minority was demonstrated graphically and at great cost when I experimented with my advertising, using a method and media useful primarily to draw individuals rather than people sent by their companies. On that unhappy occasion I managed to draw only four people!

MARKETING THE SEMINAR

If you watch the business/financial pages of your daily newspaper, you will find seminars advertised there occasionally. Generally these are seminars to which you must attract individuals paying for their own attendance or, at least, operators of very small businesses.

On the other hand, if you are presenting a seminar to which it is likely that companies will send employees, space advertisements on business/financial pages rarely reach those in the companies who are likely to order employees to attend and will send you their registrations. Those may be the marketing directors, personnel managers, comptrollers, or any other functionary, or it may be the employees, who will bring the information to their superiors with a request for approval to attend.

Experience shows rather clearly—and I speak of others' experience, as well as of my own—that direct-mail solicitation is usually most effective in drawing registration for seminars. When appealing to companies to send employees, the best marketing method is an effective direct-mail package and a good mailing list. While it is usually possible to get any mailing list of companies that you want, it is all but impossible to find a just-right list of individuals; they would have to be local residents or people who live a not-unreasonable distance from your lecture hall and have some directly related interest. Therefore, the only practical expedient is using space advertising or a combination of space advertising and direct mail. (Space advertising to draw inquiries, direct mail to follow up and close.) Those who offer seminars which appeal primarily to individuals as individual consumers generally operate in exactly that manner, with primary reliance on space advertising. If you present your seminar repeatedly and accumulate the names of those who attend and those who inquire, you will ultimately develop a good mailing list, and that will begin to produce a significant part of your response.

THE DIRECT-MAIL PACKAGE

The traditional direct-mail package includes three or four items: a sales letter, a brochure, an order form, and a return envelope. Some packages contain a great deal more than this, some less. Those that contain less generally do so by omitting the return envelope (my experience casts some doubt on its usefulness) and incorporating the order form in the brochure. For some reason, direct mail for seminars appears to be universally a single large brochure or broadside, mailed as a self-mailer (without envelope, with an address box on its outside surface), using bulk mail. (As far as I have been able to determine, I have been the only one using the more traditional direct-mail package to solicit attendance at seminars.) Most often, this is a large sheet that is folded down to present four or six business-letter-size panels, the last of which includes an order form. Your name appears on a sticker on one of the outer surfaces, and the piece is mailed flat without an envelope.

I have just received one of the numerous seminar brochures that are addressed to me. This is a *broadside;* it's about 17×22 inches, and has been folded in such a manner that it presents an overall dimension of approximately 9×12 inches. This one offers a seminar in direct-mail techniques by a presenter who is lauded for his outstanding qualities as a direct-mail expert and dynamic speaker. The broadside is quite "busy," with every possible inch of space used to urge the reader to sign up. (Presumably, this is an example of the speaker's skill at creating direct-mail literature.) There are numerous testimonials from former attendees scattered throughout the broadside in convenient corners or left-over spaces. Studying these carefully turns up only one who claims specifically to have made money as a direct result of the seminar. All others are testimonials to a great presentation and lots of good ideas. No doubt such testimonials help persuade many to register for the seminar, but they would be far more motivating if they testified to specific *results* of having attended.

These kinds of testimonials are generally gathered by distributing an evaluation form at the conclusion of the seminar and asking the attendees for permission to quote their remarks. (Then you use only the laudatory remarks, of course.) It would be far more effective if you were to send attendees a follow-up form 30 to 90 days after the seminar, and ask specifically what benefits they could report.

WHEN TO HOLD SEMINARS

Every now and then I note someone new to the seminar business making the mistake of scheduling seminars illogically. For example, if you are soliciting individuals to attend as individuals, Saturday is the best day of the week (although some speakers have also used Sunday successfully) because most of your attendees have regular jobs and Saturday is almost invariably more convenient for them than work days are. On the other hand, Saturday is usually a bad day for those sent by their companies because either the company would have to pay them overtime or the employee would have to give up a day off for company business. A normal work day is far better in this situation.

There are two days to avoid, even when you schedule a seminar for a work day—Monday and Friday. Those coming from out of town will be reluctant to travel on Sunday, usually necessary when coming from out of town to attend an event that begins on Monday morning, and almost equally reluctant to travel home on Friday evening, a bad time for travel. When I had the misfortune to be scheduled as the presenter of a half-day seminar on Friday afternoon in New York City, I lost most of my audience long before the afternoon ended, as they quietly departed for the airport and home.

I have found Tuesday and Wednesday to be the best days for seminars held in the city or in ordinary locations, but there are exceptions to the rule. If you hold a seminar in some resort or vacation area—Atlantic City; Williamsburg, Virginia; Las Vegas; or other such location—Monday and Friday scheduling becomes an advantage because attendees can then combine their seminar attendance with a holiday weekend. Some seminar producers take advantage of that to make their seminars even more attractive.

WHAT TO CHARGE

Seminar fees vary widely, from lows of about $65 to $100 per day to highs of $200 to $300 per day. There is no evidence that fee has any direct relationship to attendance. It seems that if the appeal is strong enough, those who want to attend will not be greatly influenced by the size of the fee—a high fee will not discourage those who want to attend, and a low fee will not draw attendance from someone who isn't greatly interested. One seminar presenter in the Washington, DC, area several years ago started charging $65 and drawing his attendance from a six-inch display advertisement in the *Washington Post*, on the *Post's* financial/business pages. Over the years, he gradually increased his fee until it is now $175 per attendee, without noticing any significant drop in appeal or attendance. Over approximately four years, his attendance fee has gone up nearly threefold, and he hasn't lost any significant amount of business thereby, as far as he can determine. He tells me that he plans to continue raising his fee as long as it does not appear to discourage those who wish to attend.

SALES/ADVERTISING COPY FOR SEMINARS

Whether you use space advertising or direct mail to advertise and promote attendance at your seminar, the methodology is based on the same principles enunciated earlier:

   The promise (of beneficial results)
   The logical evidence (rationale)
   The dependable supplier (credibility and confidence)

It helps to make the promised benefit as specific and concrete as possible. Promising a reader that you can show him or her how to earn up to $500 a day has much stronger appeal than promising to show the reader how to earn more money. Consider the following pairs of headlines and compare their appeal and pulling power:

EARN UP TO $500 AND EVEN MORE EVERY DAY!

DOUBLE YOUR INCOME!

HERE'S HOW TO BECOME A HIGH-PAID CONSULTANT

HERE'S HOW TO BECOME SELF-EMPLOYED

The more general benefit promise requires the reader to interpret and translate that promise into something concrete, which makes it a much weaker appeal. "Double your income" is almost an abstract idea, as is the idea of being self-employed, while $500 a day is quite concrete, and being a consultant is a more concrete and specific concept than the broader idea of being self-employed.

Even if your seminar is on a rather broad and relatively abstract concept, it is usually possible to structure your advertising and sales material to focus on a concrete idea by selecting something from your coverage or hypothesizing an application. Let us suppose that you teach positive thinking, a fairly popular seminar subject. Certainly you must use some examples of specific applications in your presentation. You can use one or more of these as the subject of your headline and theme. If, for example, your presentation is aimed at sales representatives, to help them improve their sales performance through positive thinking, make the positive thinking a secondary subject and the improvement in selling ability foremost, possibly as in the following:

Sell One Third More Every Day

Past participants in this program report

immediate increases in their sales of one

third to two thirds of their previous

record months.

The copy can then go on to explain more of what the seminar content will be and to extol the virtues of positive thinking. The sales appeal works best when one or more specific benefits are promised. It is best to promise only one specific benefit if that is of great enough appeal. While some people evidently think that promising an array of benefits will capture the interest of a greater number of readers, it rarely works out that way. Instead, the overall impact is greatly diluted by too many claims or too extravagant a claim. Even if you thought you could legitimately claim that some past participants had more than tripled their sales as a result of their attendance at your seminar, it might be a mistake to so state—not because it is not true, but because it is not credible. (Remember, it is *customer perception* that counts in a sales presentation.) It is far more persuasive to scale the claim down to what most readers will have no great trouble accepting.

Once the basic promise is made, it is necessary to furnish the rationale and the evidence as to why and how the presentation achieves the promised result. The chief factor in persuading prospects to register for a seminar is the speaker's credentials. You must sell the speaker, so it is absolutely necessary to work on the speaker's bio. It's almost an exact duplicate of the requirement to sell the consultant's credentials; in attending a seminar, the participant is buying the speaker's time and capabilities. Testimonials and other copy features help, but the whole thing fails if the reader is not thoroughly convinced of the speaker's credentials to teach what he promises to teach.

Figure 13 presents the brochure I have used to advertise open-registration seminars in the Washington, DC, area. The brochure was printed on letter-sized paper and folded twice. It was mailed in a business envelope, first class, with a covering letter. The letter urged attendance and carried a box in the corner to encourage routing the letter and brochure to others in the company. See Figure 14 for an example of such a letter.

COSTS

A typical meeting room may cost you anywhere from about $25 to $100 per day, depending on many factors—day of the week, location, season, and, in some cases, how good a negotiator you are. On the other hand, if your session includes a luncheon, or if you manage to get enough out of town participants to register at the hotel, you may be able to get the meeting room at no charge; it's commonly done that way.

There is no law that says you must use a hotel meeting room. You may be able to arrange a far better meeting room elsewhere, and some seminar producers do arrange for the use of meeting rooms in public buildings and other facilities, such as the local Chamber of Commerce building. (In one case I produced a series of "mini-seminars" and held them in my own offices every Saturday.)

How To Obtain Government Contracts

UBI

UNITED BUSINESS INSTITUTE

presents
A Professional Seminar

How To Obtain Government Contracts

THE TRUTH ABOUT WINNING GOVERNMENT CONTRACTS!

Come prepared to get the inside story—priceless tips and techniques known only to the experts, presented by an experienced marketeer who has won over $100 million in Government business.

Saturday, June 28 and July 26, 1980,
9:00 a.m. to 4:30 p.m.

WESTPARK HOTEL
Tysons Corner
8401 Westpark Dr., McLean, VA
(I-495 Exit 10W off VA Rte. 7)

Attend the most convenient session.

You'll learn not only how the Government buys, but how to SELL to the Government—NOT THE SAME THING AT ALL!

Telephone: 423-3200

UNITED BUSINESS INSTITUTE
OXON HILL CENTER, BOX 10448
OXON HILL, MD 20021

This exclusive book included as seminar material.

You are especially invited to attend a seminar on:
How To Obtain Government Contracts
The Truth About Winning Government Contracts!

The truth about winning government contracts!

If you want a share of over $100 billion in Government business—especially if you happen to also be a small business, minority- or woman-owned—this relevation seminar is a must for you.

Every attendee will get a copy of the exclusive, just-released book *The $100 Billion Market: How To Do Business With The U.S. Government,* published by AMACOM, NYC, 1980. The author is Herman Holtz, well-known government-marketing consultant and lecturer, who presents this entire seminar in person.

This is a "how-to" seminar. You'll get a wealth of *inside tips and strategies,* drawn from Mr. Holtz's personal experiences in winning over $100 million of government business. You'll learn, for example, how to *appear* to be the low bidder (even when you are not), how to use the Freedom of Information Act effectively in marketing and bidding, all about discounts and when to use them (or not to use them), and more, much more, in this no-nonsense, all-business session.

The Federal Government is a multi-billion dollar buyer of goods and services. A set percentage of all government contracts MUST be awarded to small businesses and minority-owned businesses. Women-owned businesses are in line for tremendous new benefits in Government contracting. You will learn how to take advantage of these tremendous opportunities. You will learn how to effectively and efficiently obtain government contracts.

FIGURE 13. (a) Outside panels of seminar brochure.

WHO SHOULD ATTEND: Every man and woman seeking government contracts; especially small business owners and representatives, women and minority business owners/representatives, including salespersons, customer service representatives, marketing representatives, consultants, lawyers, accountants, contract specialists, trainers, manufacturers, service companies, etc.

SEMINAR OUTLINE

8:30-8:55 a.m.   Final Registration (Coffee and Danish)

9:00   Introduction

I. What is "The Government"
Explanation of the bureaucracy, its needs, how it functions, the major agencies, which ones do most of the buying.

II. What/How the Government Buys
Scope of government needs in goods and services; size of the market; how procurements are initiated, how bids and proposals are solicited—IFBs, RFPs, and RFQs; annual supply agreements—e.g., federal supply schedules; centralized procurement and supply services; FSS, DLA, VA, Postal Service.

III. Types of Contracts
Basic types: Fixed price and cost reimbursement, variations and hybrids; purchase orders, letter contracts; T&M, BOAs, BPAs, CPFF, CPAF; advertised versus negotiated procurement; pertinent regulations: ASPR, FPR, NASPR, DAR, FAR.

IV. Special Programs
Socioeconomic programs for small business, minority business, woman-owned business; the SBA and the 8(a) program; MBDA and its programs.

V. Marketing—Finding the Sales Leads
The Commerce Business Daily, Form 129 and bidders lists, bid rooms and bid boards; how to use all these most effectively; freedom of information and how to use it to support marketing.

VI. How to Make Bids
The typical bid set in formal advertising; the public opening; tips and techniques for appearing to be the low bidder; discounts—when they count and when they don't; the "laundry list" contract and how to bid it; at least three major considerations in pricing your bid.

VII. How to Prepare Proposals
What "negotiated" procurement means; why proposals are wanted; how to write a proposal, and how to write a winning proposal; the proposal elements, and the importance of each; the letter of transmittal; a dozen or more tips and techniques.

VIII. Summary of Key Points and Q&A
Final questions invited for discussion. (Questions may be asked at any time during day.)

FACULTY
Herman Holtz, publisher of Government Marketing News, is the author of over $100 million worth of successful-winning—proposals, in a variety of fields—electronics and weapons systems, training and human resource development, publications, safety, computer software development, and others. He spent a number of years as an electronics engineer, writer, director of marketing, and general manager, before becoming a small, independent government contractor and, later, a publisher/consultant/lecturer. He is also the author of several books on the subject. He consults regularly with a number of highly successful companies and lecturers widely. He is also called on frequently by government agencies to conduct seminars and training sessions in federal procurement and government marketing. In his seminar presentations, Mr. Holtz reveals many strategies and techniques of his own, which he developed over the years, in learning how to win against the odds.
Books authored by Mr. Holtz include these:

Government Contracts: Proposalmanship and Winning Strategies, Plenum Publishing Corporation, NYC, 1979.

The $100 Billion Market, AMACOM (publishing division of American Management Association), NYC, 1980.

The Winning Proposal: How to Write it, McGraw-Hill, NYC, 1980 (scheduled).

Anyone Can do Business With the Government, Government Marketing News, Washington, DC, 1976.

MATERIAL
Each seminar attendee will receive a valuable package of materials immediately useful as aids in obtaining government contracts, PLUS a personal copy (autographed by request) of The $100 Billion Dollar Market.
Here is just some of the coverage in this great new book: Understanding the System, Get Help from the Government to Sell to the Government, How to Make Bids, Special Buying Arrangements and Opportunities, Government Freebies You Can Use, and The Proposal Game, plus 8 appendices of valuable reference data.
One reviewer called this book "An impressively ready reference," and described "a wealth of tips on making the government offers it can't refuse."

REGISTRATION FORM   DETACH AND MAIL   **UNITED BUSINESS INSTITUTE**
Oxon Hill Center, Box 1048, Oxon Hill, MD 20021
(301) 423-3200

How To Obtain Government Contracts
THE TRUTH ABOUT WINNING GOVERNMENT CONTRACTS!

To ensure participation in this exclusive seminar we urge you to register in advance. You may register by telephone or by returning the form below. List your name and other data in the space below and enclose remittance or call 423-3200 with credit data.

Additional Registrants from same organization:

NAME

COMPANY/ORGANIZATION   NAME

ADDRESS   NAME

CITY   STATE   NAME

ZIP   PHONE

Remittance: $125.00 advance; $150.00 at door.
□ Check □ Money Order □ VISA □ Master Charge
Card No.
Expiration Date
Planned Date of Attendance:

*Discount: additional registrants pay only $95 advance or $115 at door.

FIGURE 13. (b) Inside panels of seminar brochure.

Herman R. Holtz
President

Dear fellow marketer:

15,000 Government agencies are spending $170 <u>billion</u> a year for goods and servic- es of (literally) every kind. Yet, 98.1% of businesses are not sharing in this huge market. And many who do are getting far less than their fair share of the market.

You can change that. You can get into this market or get more of it, if you are already in it. Our seminars have already helped many do so. Minority enterprises and other small businesses have already benefited, and even the large corporations have eagerly sought the help we offer--Genasys, Sikorski Aircraft, Dun & Bradstreet, Pitney Bowes, Memorex, Alcoa Aluminum, and Bethlehem Steel are only a few of the great comp- anies who have registered for these sessions.

It's not an ordinary seminar. It's a <u>revelation</u> session. You'll learn many eye- opening facts: what and how the government buys (many things in many ways); about Fed- eral Supply Schedules and other almost-guaranteed ways of winning contracts; how to <u>use</u> the CBD, as well as read it; how to <u>appear</u> to be a low bidder, when you are not; and many, many other insider tips and strategies.

Most important, you'll learn about proposalmanship, the art of writing winning proposals. You'll get a sensational, new manual on the subject, too, which offers you a complete <u>system</u> for writing winners! (Yes, it's an art <u>and</u> a methodology.)

Space is always limited at seminars, by their nature. Register now to assure yourself of a seat at this most important event. Join us and learn how the experts win millions of dollars every year.

Sincerely,

Herman R. Holtz

Herman R. Holtz

Proposalmanship:

The art of winning government contracts!

Don't be <u>just</u> a proposal writer. Become a contract winner!
Now! A program in Proposalmanship designed for your
entire staff!

Government Marketing News, Inc.

FIGURE 14.   Cover letter with routing box to accompany seminar brochure.

facilities, such as the local Chamber of Commerce building. (In one case, I produced a series of "mini-seminars" and held them in my own offices every Saturday.)

Coffee—and it is a rare seminar that does not furnish coffee—will generally cost you from $10 to $30 per gallon, according to the circumstances. Some hotels charge rather high prices; others are quite modest. (I have found some hotels high on room rates but low on food and coffee, while other hotels were exactly the opposite.)

Printing and mailing costs vary widely. If you choose to print and mail those large brochures, sent out without envelopes and by bulk mail, you can expect a slim response rate because the piece is immediately evident as advertising matter. It advertises itself as junk mail at first sight, and much of it finds its way to the wastebasket without so much as a glance. In fact, the mail rooms of some companies have standing instructions to discard all such mail immediately. Those who use such solicitations usually find that they must print and mail upwards of 50,000—and often several times that number—to produce a viable number of registrations. The printing and postage bill on such a mailing can easily run to $10,000 or more, a substantial investment.

Using first-class mail, sent out in a business envelope, ensures that the envelope will be at least opened, and I found that the first time I did such a mailing I had good results (54 registrations) from a mailing of only 1,000 brochures and letters. That was unusual, and was the result of my being able to select my addressees most carefully; I screened my mailing lists and mailed to the cream of them. Even later, when a great many of my best prospects had attended sessions and I was not screening my lists, I never mailed more than 5,000 pieces to get an acceptable number of registrants (usually 30 to 40), and the only time I ever lost money on one of these sessions was the occasion when I tried to get my registrations via space advertising.

My typical mailing, then, was 2,000 to 3,000 brochures at a cost of approximately $600 for printing, postage, and labor, and my typical revenue from a given seminar session was on the order of $3,000, producing a quite acceptable profit for the day.

SOME MISCELLANEOUS IDEAS, TIPS, AND OPPORTUNITIES

Every area has colleges, universities, and institutions of learning, and a great many of these conduct adult-education classes and special courses. In my area, for example, most of the nearby counties have junior colleges, and there are also a number of universities. Almost all have programs of special adult-education courses and seminars on a remarkably wide range of subjects. Here are just a few of the subjects on which courses are offered:

Mail order business	Dancing
Writing and editing	Illustrating
Computer programming	Association management
Consulting	Advertising
Music	Choreography
Drama and acting	Office skills
Public speaking	Family counseling

Most of these courses are taught by local specialists, many of whom are consultants themselves. The fees paid are modest, but many consultants and other entrepreneurs choose to conduct these courses because the marketing exposure helps them. I have found that the officials responsible for these courses are not only eager to find good instructors, but are highly receptive to ideas for courses they do not offer at present. The reason many courses are not offered is simply that the institution does not have an instructor for the course, and they would offer it immediately if they could get an instructor.

There is the same opportunity for "back of the room" sales of your books, reports, and newsletter subscriptions at your own open-registration seminars as there is at occasions when you are a fee-paid lecturer or are lecturing at a local adult-education course. It is precisely because of this opportunity that many consultants who publish newsletters and books volunteer to conduct seminars and speak without charge. One consultant I know has been able to sell several thousand dollars' worth of his books at such occasions, earning him considerably more than any fees he could command.

Running inquiry advertisements is only one way of compiling mailing lists; there are several others. One of these is to use membership directories of associations whose members appear to be good prospects for you. Some associations will not permit their membership lists to be made available to anyone not part of their organization, but others will, and many organizations sell their membership lists for nominal sums. There are also such sources as the U.S. Small Business Administration, local Chambers of Commerce and other business organizations, and various directories. (Some of these are listed in the final chapter.)

Many newsletter publishers will run free announcements of your seminars if you send them a press release, and in some cities the daily newspapers will list your seminar as one of the events coming up. Such sources as these have helped me to solicit registrations.

One useful source for my purposes was the government's own *Commerce Business Daily*, in which they list contract awards among other things, usually listing the addresses of the awardees as well as their names. I compiled many productive mailing lists from these listings.

As your mailing lists begin to grow, you can double their size swiftly by swapping lists with others whose mailing lists are of people or companies who appear to be good prospects for you, while your offer is not directly competitive with the other fellow's. Mailing lists grow swiftly in this manner.

If you publish a newsletter, it is usually easy to swap complimentary subscriptions with other newsletter publishers, and of course it is relatively easy to agree with the others to cooperate in running each other's press releases. This alone can give you an opportunity to reach many thousands of readers at virtually no extra cost to yourself.

If you do publish anything—newsletter, books, reports, or other things—here is a method I used that reduced my front-end costs for seminars to virtually nothing and even showed me some extra profits. When mailing brochures and letters soliciting seminar attendance, I enclosed literature offering my various publications. Sometimes I sold publications to people who also registered for the seminar, more often to those not registering for the seminar. I usually did enough business to pay for the printing and mailing, and often realized even more than those costs. Such a return ensures a profit on the seminar because all costs have been covered in advance.

14

Business Ethics
in Consulting

Ethical conduct is always important. The consultant is placed in positions which may make the very existence and continuance of the consultant's practice dependent on conduct beyond the slightest hint of impropriety

CONFLICTS OF INTEREST

Because a consultant is often privy to highly confidential information about a client's business and even personal affairs, discretion is absolutely essential. Any reason to doubt that the consultant may be trusted to be not only honest but also absolutely scrupulous about keeping his client's confidential affairs confidential can destroy the practice. Consultants must manage to avoid even the appearance of being loose-lipped or less than absolutely trustworthy.

The reason for this is simply the nature of consulting work. For example, I am retained to assist people who are each other's competitors. Each trusts me to do work for his competitors without revealing anything I know about one company to another company. If I am helping a firm pursue a contract, and another firm tries to retain me to help them pursue that same contract, I am honor-bound to advise the second firm that I cannot help them since that would create a conflict of interest for me. It is partly because I have often turned down assignments for this reason that my clients know that I am to be trusted.

That is not the only situation you may find yourself in which will involve questions of ethics. You must also be careful that you do not tell a client anything you know about a competitor which you have learned while working for that competitor. That does not mean that you can't reveal knowledge about a competitor gained in some other manner, such as by reading an article in a business journal, or by any other means which does not place you under an obligation to treat the information in strictest confidence. This may bring up situations in which you have some doubts as to what is ethical and what is not. Let's take this case as an example:

You are attending a convention, and you fall into conversation with someone who is an executive of a firm which could conceivably be your client. You talk to the executive, seeking to persuade him to consider retaining you in your consulting capacity to help him. He discusses his situation, telling you things which you can easily see are confidential matters, although he doesn't exact from you a promise to treat this information as confidential. He obviously assumes that you can be trusted to understand that the information is proprietary and is told you in confidence. As things turn out, you do not succeed in winning a contract with this man's firm. Are you bound to keep this information in strictest confidence?

The answer is yes, you should, if you are completely ethical; respect the confidence, despite the fact that you did not win any work from this man and despite the fact that he never actually said that he was passing on confidential information or asked you to promise confidentiality. Aside from what your own moral scruples dictate to you, there is the practical side. If you do use that information to help win a contract elsewhere, perhaps from a competitor, it may or may not ultimately be known that you did so, but there is an excellent possibility that it will be. There is also the effect on the people to whom you leak this information; will they not decide that you are not to be trusted? If you revealed inside information about a competitor, can you be trusted not to leak similar information about them if they allow you to gain such information?

Here is another situation:

A company has paid you an annual retainer—perhaps a few hundred dollars every month—to ensure your availability when they have a need for your services. One day they call and ask you to help them in pursuing a contract opportunity. You have meanwhile begun to help a competitor pursue that same contract because, as far as you knew, your regular, retainer-paying client had shown no interest in that contract and had not yet ever used your services. What is your proper position in this situation?

You are now in a bad situation. You have committed yourself to a competitor, perhaps already been paid something, but you certainly owe something to the client who has kept you on retainer all this time.

The fact is that you should not have permitted yourself to get into this situation at all. As soon as the new client asked you for help, you should have called your retainer-paying client and explained your situation, asking them whether they intended to pursue the contract and whether they objected to your taking on this assignment. It's either accept the need to do such things, or do not accept annual retainers. They put you under certain obligations.

There is a variant of the problem of what you must keep confidential. In some situations, information you have about a former employer, rather than another client, may be useful in helping a client or in helping you win a contract for yourself. Is what you know about a former employer—information gained while on a private payroll—also to be treated as given you in confidence?

A great many consultants appear to think that this is an entirely different situation, and that information acquired while on a payroll need not be treated as information given in confidence. Here again it is my opinion that the question revolves entirely around the nature of the information, not the manner in which it was learned. You know whether the information is information your former employer would like to have kept in confidence. For example, your former employer does not wish competitors to know anything about his own costs, financial condition, backlog of business, plans for the future, problems, special contacts, technical and business methodologies, and a host of other things bearing directly on his business. If you have any doubts as to whether a particular piece of information is confidential or proprietary, the safe and ethical course of action is to assume that it is and treat it accordingly.

Information you have about your former employer's business should be treated the same way you treat information about a client's business. Aside from the moral considerations, there are practical ones. First of all, a former employer may become a consulting client; many consultants do business with former employers. Secondly, if you reveal confidential information about a former employer to a client or prospective client, it is the same indication mentioned earlier that you are not totally trustworthy.

On the other hand, if you can use such information to help yourself win assignments without revealing the information itself, I see no ethical breaches in so doing. The unethical action is revealing such information to others or using it to help a competitor unfairly. There is nothing wrong with using it to help yourself if it does not aid a client's or former employer's competitor or work against the interests of the client or former employer in any way.

FEES AND FEE-RELATED ETHICAL CONSIDERATIONS

Earlier in this book the subject of fees was discussed, and the point was made there that some might consider it unethical or less than completely honest to charge different fees to different clients and in different circumstances. There is nothing inherently unethical in customizing your fees for each individual situation, although some consultants find the practice of doing so to be unprofessional. There are a number of considerations which affect fee-setting. Overhead costs—marketing, especially—are much higher on short-term assignments than they are on long-term projects, and therefore it is perhaps even more ethical to charge a reduced fee on long-term projects.

What does appear to be unethical and may do your professional image serious damage is a failure to be honest about how you set fees. You would do well to define a specific policy for fee-setting and make the policy known to your clients or at least have it formally drawn up in a brochure or rate card, so that you can always demonstrate that you do have an established policy regarding fees and are not improvising spontaneously. No one can quarrel with your right to set fees according to any pattern or formula you wish to use. In some situations a variable scale according to circumstances may actually enhance your image and produce more business.

I have never found anyone resentful of my conducting myself and my dealings in a businesslike manner, especially when I can readily explain a sensible rationale for my business policies and practices. When I explain calmly to a client or prospective client how I do business and why I do things as I do, objections fade rapidly.

There is the problem of verifying the time devoted to the work when the work is done on the consultant's premises rather than on the client's premises. For example, let us suppose that you have estimated five days maximum for a given project at a rate of $500 per day, but you are doing most of the work in your own offices. Let us suppose that you manage to complete the project in four and one-half days. The client will pay for five days, you know, because you have so stipulated. What should you charge the client?

The temptation is great to charge for the full five days, and the matter is entirely between you and your conscience. The honest and ethical thing to do is render your bill for four and one-half days and, aside from the moral question, it will probably be good business to do so; you'll have a delighted client who will now perceive that 1) you know your business and can estimate the effort accurately, and 2) you are honest and ethical and are to be trusted with future projects.

The opposite situation may and probably will occur, in which that estimated five days turns out to be five and one-half days. Since you have committed yourself to a five-day maximum, what should you do?

You have three possible courses you can follow:

1. Simply submit your invoice for five and one-half days.
2. Explain that you ran a little over your time estimate and discuss with the customer whether there is a problem in billing the extra half day.
3. Submit an invoice for five days, and write off your extra half day of work.

The first course is likely to lead to an angry confrontation with your client. The probability is that you will be paid your full amount, but it is also highly likely that your client will consider the extra charge unjustified and your action in billing it and insisting on payment for it to be unethical. At the least, the client is likely to take the position that you should have checked with him or her before expending that last half day, in light of a five-day commitment.

The second course of action is far better, especially if you are willing to write the extra half day off and make that clear to the client, who may then insist on paying you. To some degree, this will depend on how firm your commitment to a five-day maximum was.

The third course of action is the one I generally pursue in such circumstances, under the policy I generally pursue of guaranteeing my clients a
maximum or "not-to-exceed" figure. I consider any time overruns resulting from my own failure to estimate accurately to be overhead costs,
and my daily rate is designed to cover *all* overhead costs, as it ought to be.
In many cases it is because I do guarantee a maximum figure that I am
able to close the sale and win the contract.

There are two exceptions to all of this:

1.   If you have been asked to furnish a fixed-price figure, you have the
moral right to bill every penny of it even if the work has consumed far less
time than you had originally estimated. You are bound to bill that figure
even if the job takes far more time than you originally estimated. It is well
accepted that your fees and/or profit margins are or should be higher
when you run the risk of a fixed-price job.

2.   You are only bound to your maximum or not-to-exceed figure if
there are no changes. If the client changes the nature, scope, or anything
else about the work after you've started, you are no longer bound by the
original agreement. You are now morally and ethically justified in
renegotiating your agreement and, in fact, are unwise if you do not do so
immediately. There is still another circumstance that entitles you to
renegotiate: If the original work description or specifications furnished
you by the client prove to be in error, your estimate is automatically invali-
dated, and you have the right (and the obligation to yourself) to reopen
negotiations.

In short, business ethics is a two-way street. It is your concern to conduct
yourself in an ethical manner, but you have a right to expect and insist
that your client also do business ethically. Being ethical does not mean
that you must be unfair to yourself and damage your own business
interests.

USING CLIENTS' NAMES IN ADVERTISING

One of the more influential devices you can use in your advertising and
sales promotion is listing your important and prestigious clients. It is a
help to be able to point out that your consulting services were used by
large and important corporations and, especially, the more prestigious
corporations in your field. There is no legal reason why you should not tell
readers of your brochure or other promotional literature that you have
been a consultant to General Motors or Smith, Kline, and French, if you

have been. Many, however, consider it unethical to do so without first asking the former client's permission to list them in your literature. Most who want you to ask permission usually wish to see the literature in which their name is to appear, because they fear the possibility of usage that will embarrass them or compromise their image in some way.

I tend to agree with that position, and I think you would do well to supply the client a draft of the literature and what you intend to say about them and your relations or former relations with them. At the least, it is a courtesy that makes good sense to observe, and if the client or former client does object, the objection may be well-founded and in your own interest to consider seriously. There is also the possibility of legal action if you have miscalculated in some manner and the client or former client can prove that your act was damaging to them. On the other hand, if they are merely to be listed as a client or former client in a tasteful and dignified brochure, the probability is that you will have no difficulty whatever, and you may even get a testimonial letter from them.

ADVERTISING AND SALES ETHICS

Perhaps customers and customer prospects expect those hawking goods in highly competitive markets to make inflated claims, misleading statements, and banal arguments. Certainly many successful businesses do use such advertising and sales-promotion materials. Not only is much of such material and many such presentations undignified and even idiotic, but much of it is insulting because it suggests strongly utter contempt for the reader's or viewer's intelligence.

Professional people must somehow remain aloof from such travesties on advertising and selling. Doctors, dentists, lawyers, and other professionals have long had ethical codes forbidding all blatant advertising, and permitting only the most discreet and dignified indirect approaches, such as announcement cards and, if possible, highly dignified publicity, such as professional appearances on TV or at some public affair. Recently, lawyers have been given the green light on advertising their services, and a few have gone to some of the extremes of bad taste in advertising. Perhaps for some it is acceptable because they appeal to people who are not sensitive to such things. Most lawyers are not using their new freedom to advertise, purely out of considerations of ethics and dignity.

As a consultant, you, too, are a professional, and it is likely that most, if not all, of your clients and prospective clients are people who will be "turned off" by bad taste in advertising. This is not to say that you cannot or should not advertise; there is absolutely no tradition which dictates that, as it does in the case of lawyers and medical specialists. But you must exercise good taste in your advertising and sales promotion, with tasteful brochures and sales letters, and dignity in everything you do in the name of sales promotion.

Set, as your ethical standards for advertising and sales promotion, at least these benchmarks:

No extravagant promises or claims that you would not be willing to be held to strict account for.

No weasel-wording, in which you deliberately mislead through such choices of words that you appear to be saying something other than that which you are really saying. (A favored advertising device, unfortunately.)

No "come ons" or loss leaders, enticing prospects with worthless bargains with the intention of trading up later in the traditional "bait and switch" swindle.

The ethical problem arises here quite often when the consultant begins to expand and diversify into producing and selling other products, such as newsletters, books, reports, audiotape cassettes, and other such items. The temptation to "hype" such items is much greater than it is in the case of pure consulting services, because physical products lend themselves better to such unethical sales methods.

This is not to say that you cannot or should not offer specials, such as free books or special reports with newsletter subscriptions, or special prices on tie-in packages of products. It is perfectly legitimate and ethical to do so, provided you are offering sincere and honest propositions. (It has always amazed me how rarely some entrepreneurs try honesty, and how surprised they are to find that it works when they finally do try it either by accident or as a desperate last resort.)

Whether you confine yourself entirely to selling consulting services or diversify into lecturing, seminars, newsletters, and other such fields and extra profit centers, your ultimate success still depends almost entirely on your personal reputation. Destroy that with unethical and dishonest practices, and you destroy your practice.

15

The Reference File

As Henry Ford pointed out in a courtroom one day, knowing where and how to get the information when you want it makes a great deal more sense than trying to memorize all of it.

I have made a serious effort in these pages to bring you as complete a collection of information and ideas on the subject of consulting as can be fitted into an average-size book. One thing you must have observed as you read is that consulting is a profession that calls for and lends itself to a most diverse set of skills and activities. The truly able consultant is a man or woman for all seasons—technical specialist, practicing professional, lecturer, writer, executive, and probably several other things as well. It is almost inescapable that the serious consultant must maintain a reference library. This final chapter is a beginning, if you have not already begun to accumulate such a library. In this chapter you will find various lists, but you will also find a number of recommendations of other books and periodicals that this consultant has found helpful. However, instead of an almost endless string of titles, as you often find bibliographies offered, these lists of books and other items of reference information are grouped functionally, as, for example, information useful for writing, information useful for selling to the government, and so forth.

A FEW BOOKS ON WRITING AND PUBLISHING

Following are some of the books and periodicals I have found helpful in understanding commercial publishing and useful in my writing activities.

A Writer's Guide to Book Publishing, Richard Balkin, Hawthorn Books, New York, 1977. Balkin is a literary agent, knows the book publishing industry.

How You Can Make $20,000 a Year Writing, Nancy Edmonds Hanson, Writer's Digest Books, Cincinnati, 1980.

How to Get Happily Published, Judith Appelbaum and Nancy Evans, Harper & Row, New York, 1978. An extremely successful and popular book.

Law and the Writer, edited by Kirk Polking and Leonard S. Meranus, Writer's Digest Books, Cincinnati, 1981.

How to Write Articles That Sell, L. Perry Wilbur, John Wiley & Sons, New York, 1981. By a man who has sold many articles.

How to Write Books That Sell, L. Perry Wilbur, Contemporary Books, Chicago, 1979. By a man who has sold many books.

The Publish It Yourself Handbook, edited by Bill Henderson, Pushcart Press, Yonkers, 1973. Has become something of a classic of its own kind.

The Writer's Market, Writer's Digest Books, Cincinnati, published annually, generally edited and contributed to by the editorial staff of *Writer's Digest* magazine. An ever-larger and indispensable directory for serious freelancers.

How to Self-Publish Your Own Book & Make it a Best Seller, Ted Nicholas, Enterprise Publishing Company, Wilmington, 1975. Head of his own publishing company, the author has done just what his book title promises to reveal.

Book Publishing: What It Is, What It Does, 2nd ed., John Dessauer, R. R. Bowker, New York, 1980.

How to Publish, Promote and Sell Your Book, Joseph Goodman, Adams Press, Chicago, 1980.

The Book Market: How to Write, Publish, and Market Your Book, Aron Mathieu, Andover Press, New York, 1981.

The Writer-Publisher, Charles N. Aronson, Arcade, NY
  1976 (Self-published.)

The Self-Publishing Manual, Dan Poynter, Parachuting Publications, Santa Barbara, 1979.

BOOK WHOLESALERS/DISTRIBUTORS

The following are book wholesalers or distributors who will place your selfpublished book in bookstores and libraries if it is a viable book for the market.

ACP Distributors, 105 Pine Rd, Sewickley, PA 15143.

Atlantis Distributors, 1725 Carondelet, New Orleans, LA 70130.

Book Bus, Visual Studies Institute, 4 Elton Street, Rochester, NY 14607.

Bookpeople, 2940 7th Avenue, Berkeley, CA 94710.

Bookslinger, 2163 Ford Pkwy, St. Paul, MN 55116.

COSMEP/South, Box 209, Carrboro, NC 27510.

Distributors, 702 S. Michigan, South Bend, IN 46618.

Liberation Book Service, 16 E. 18th Street, New York, NY 10003.

New England Small Press Association, 45 Hillcrest Pl., Amherst, MA 01002.

New York State Small Press Association, Box 1264, Radio City Station, New York, NY 10001.

Plains Distribution Service, Box 3112, Rm 500, Block 6, 620 Main St, Fargo, ND 58102.

SBD, 1636 Ocean View Ave., Kensington, CA 94707.

Skylo Distribution, 1502 E. Olive Way, Seattle, WA 98112.

Small Press Traffic, 3841-B 24th Street, San Francisco, CA 94141.

Southwest Literary Express, 901 Pinon, Las Cruces, NM 77004.

Spring Church Book Co., Box 127, Spring Church, PA 15686.

Some established book publishers will distribute books supplied by the writer-publisher which they consider marketable. Hawthorn Books, Inc., of New York; Stein and Day, of Briarcliff Manor, NY; and Harper & Row, of New York are three publishers known to have done so (Hawthorn Books often distributes books produced by others), but there are other established publishers who will also do so.

WRITING RESEARCH: SOURCES OF INFORMATION

Until you begin to do research for the first time, you have no idea of how many information sources there are. Just the information on where the information is and how to get at it would fill a substantial bookshelf. An enterprising fellow named Matthew Lesko founded a successful firm named Washington Researchers in downtown Washington, DC, after he came to the realization that most people did not know how to go about searching out what they wanted to know in Washington, the greatest information center in the world. Now Washington Researchers helps others find their way around the Washington information maze through books and seminars on the subject. The following is just a small starter kit on how to find the information you want, with Lesko's address for a beginning: Washington Researchers, 918 16th Street, NW, Washington, DC 20006. *The United States Government Manual* is published every year, runs to hundreds of pages, lists all government agencies, legislative, executive, and judicial, along with much other information. It's published by the National Archives and Records Service (NARS) of the General Services Administration (GSA), printed and sold by the Government Printing Office (GPO) at its various book stores. If your local telephone directory does not list a GPO book store near you, you can order whichever copy is current from the following:

Government Printing Office, Washington, DC 20402. Like everything else, the price is not stable, but is usually a bit higher every year. It's probably on the order of $8-$10 now.

A particularly rich source of information is the Bureau of the Census, the U.S. Department of Commerce, Washington, DC 20233. Address your request to the Data User Services Division, ask for information along the lines of your need, and you should soon find your mailbox stuffed full with pamphlets and brochures describing what's available. (My recent request for information for my next book brought a 272-page book in the mail, and that was only to list and explain what was available along the lines of my expressed interest!)

For information on diseases, poisons, and a variety of other such subjects, write the Director of Information, Center for Disease Control, 1600

Clifton Road, NE, Atlanta, GA 30333. (It's part of the Public Health Service, Department of Health and Human Services.)

Copyright is a function of the Copyright Office, Office of Information and Publications, Library of Congress, Washington, DC 20559. Write for information, and you'll get the information and forms to be used if you wish to copyright something.

A general compendium of sources, including such things as airlines, government agencies, corporations, newsworthy people, and dozens of others is *Names and Numbers*, Rod Nordland, John Wiley & Sons, New York, 1978.

Another such compendium is the *National Directory of Addresses and Telephone Numbers*, published annually by W.C.C. Directories, 850 Third Avenue, New York 10022. It lists financial institutions, firms of many kinds, consultants, media and information sources, government agencies, hotels and travel facilities, and thousands of corporations. I have found it indispensable.

The Writer's Resource Guide, edited by William Brohaugh, Writer's Digest Books, Cincinnati, 1979, is another treasure trove of guidance to thousands of information sources.

Ulrich's International Periodicals Directory, an annual, R.R. Bowker, New York, is the last word in directories of periodicals, probably far exceeds the needs of most writers. It is expensive, but you may find it in your public library where it won't cost you anything to consult it.

For a complete list of publishers and related matters such as agents and editorial services, try the *Literary Market Place*, commonly referred to as LMP, also published by R.R. Bowker, and practically the bible of the book-publishing industry.

For a reasonably complete directory of newsletters, try *The Newsletter Yearbook Directory*, published periodically by Howard Penn Hudson, The Newsletter Clearinghouse, 44 West Market Street, Rhinebeck, NY 12572.

PERIODICALS YOU SHOULD KNOW ABOUT

As a consultant, you may be interested in seeing a copy of the *Business Opportunities Digest*, 301 Plymouth Drive, NE, Dalton, GA 30720. Editor J.F. (Jim) Straw will be glad to hear from you. It's a monthly newsletter, typeset and packed with news items and business leads every month.

If you write or plan to write, you should be reading the *Writer's Digest* every month. It's on well-stocked newsstands and in better bookstores. It's written and read by practicing writers, mostly freelancers.

If you plan to pursue government contracts seriously, you should be reading the *Commerce Business Daily*. It's published five days a week, lists federal needs with information on how to get the bid or proposal solicitation, costs $80 a year or $45 for 6 months. You can order it from the Government Printing Office, Washington, DC 20402.

PUBLICATIONS ABOUT CONSULTING

There are now several publications written especially about, by, and for consultants. The newest periodical is a bimonthly tabloid which generally runs 24 to 32 pages of news, information, tips, leads, and ideas, and has been extremely well received. I have the honor of serving as its editor, but for subscription information write the publisher's business offices: *Consulting Opportunities Journal*, P.O. Box 17674, Washington, DC 20041. on,

Probably the oldest periodical in the consulting field is that of Jim Kennedy, the *Consultants News*, a monthly newsletter. Address Kennedy & Kennedy, Inc., Templeton Road, Fitzwilliam, NH 03447.

The consultant's Library is a growing collection of books about consulting, published by Bermont Books, 815 15th Street, NW, Washington, DC 20005. Among the titles are these: *How to Become a Successful Consultant in Your Own Field, How to Win With Information or Lose Without It, How to Create and Market a Successful Seminar or Workshop*, and more than a dozen more at this writing. A request to the address above will bring you a descriptive catalog.

All the foregoing publications are directed at consultants generally. *The NAFCO Letter* is designed especially for financial consultants. It's a monthly newsletter of Ivy Publishing Co, Box 1, Ischua, NY 14746; editor: Dick Brisky.

Sharing Ideas! Among Professional Speakers is a bimonthly publication of Dottie Walters, 600 West Foothill Blvd, Glendora, CA 91740, aimed at professional speakers but read enthusiastically by many consultants and others who spend part of their time on speaking engagements. It generally runs about 24 pages, in a letter-sized format, virtually bubbles over with the positive thinking of its publisher and readers.

PUBLICATIONS ABOUT GOVERNMENT CONTRACTING

The following books deal with contracting with the federal government, but unlike the government's own handout brochures, these are from the contractor's viewpoint—how to *sell* to the government, rather than how the government *buys*.

The $100 Billion Market: How to Do Business with the U.S. Government, Herman Holtz, AMACOM, New York, 1980.

The Winning Proposal: How to Write It, Herman Holtz and Terry Schmidt, McGraw-Hill, New York, 1981.

Directory of Federal Purchasing Offices: Where, What, How to Sell to the U.S. Government, Herman Holtz, John Wiley & Sons, New York, 1981

How to Sell to the Government, W.A. Cohen, John Wiley & Sons, New York, 1981.

Government Contracts: Proposalmanship and Winning Strategies, Herman R. Holtz, Plenum Publishing Corp., New York, 1979.

SPEAKERS BUREAUS

The Dottie Walters Speakers Bureau, 600 West Foothill Blvd, Glendora, CA 91740.

American Program Bureau, 850 Boylston Street, Chestnut Hill, MA 02617.

Keedick Lecture Bureau, 475 5th Avenue, New York, NY 10017.

Leigh Lecture Bureau, Inc., 1185 Avenue of the Americas, New York, NY 10036.

National Speakers Bureau, Inc., 222 Wisconsin Ave., Suite 309, Lake Forest, IL 60045.

New York Management Center, Inc., 360 Lexington Ave., New York, NY 10017.

Gateways Speakers Bureau, 221 N. Kirkwood, St. Louis, MO 63122.

Speakeasy, Inc., 400 Colony Square, Suite 1130, Atlanta, GA 30361.

The Speakers Bureau, 1930 E. Pacific Street, Philadelphia, PA 19134.

Speakers Bureau International, Box 19442, Las Vegas, NV 89119.

Success Leaders Speakers Service, 3121 Maple Drive, NE, Suite 1, Atlanta, GA 30305.

Aimee Entertainment Associates, 14241 Ventura Blvd, Sherman Oaks, CA 91423.

American Society of Association Executives, 1101 16th Street, NW, Washington, DC 20036

AMR International, Inc., 1370 Avenue of the Americas, New York, NY 10019

Bestconventions, Inc., 24118 Woodway Road, Cleveland, OH 44122

Conference Management Corporation, 17 Washington Street, Norwalk, CT 06854

Ray Bloch Productions, Inc., 1500 Broadway, New York, NY 10036

Ray Bloch Productions, Inc., 230 Peachtree Street, NW, Atlanta, GA 30303

Jack Blue Agency, 1554 Fairfax Street, Denver, CO 80220

Bostrom Management Corporation, 435 N. Michigan Blvd, Chicago, IL 60611

Kathleen Brenner, 460 Mission Valley Center West, San Diego, CA 92108

George Carlson & Associates, 1319 2nd Avenue, Seattle, WA 98101

Colorado Conventions & Reservations, 1665 Grant Street, Denver, CO 80203

George Colouris Productions, 1782 W. Lincoln, Anaheim, CA 92801

Conference and Exposition Management Co., Box 844, Greenwich, CT 06830

Contemporary Programs, Inc., 3136 Lafayette, Houston, TX 77005

The Speaker's Guild, Inc., 11607 Stonewood Lane, Rockville, MD 20850

Freeds Speakers Bureau, 927 15th Street, NW, Washington, DC 20006

Program Corp. of America, 595 West Hartsdale Avenue, White Plains, NY

The Washington Speakers Bureau, 10106 Cornwall Rd, Fairfax, VA 22041

Schwab's Convention and Special Events, 3122 M Street, NW, Washington, DC 20007

American Talent Agency, 305 Taylor Avenue, Rockville, MD 20850

CCD, 1004 Rhode Island Avenue, NW, Washington, DC 20001

Convention Masters, Inc., 1430 K Street, NW, Washington, DC 20005

Marketing Coordinators Int'l, 1001 Conneticut Avenue, NW, Washington, DC 20036

National News Speakers Bureau, National Press Bldg, Washington, DC 20045

National Speakers Forum, 1629 K Street, NW, Washington, DC 20006

Convention and Conference Consultants, Box 313, Deerfield, IL 60015

Convention Services Int'l, 494 Lake Shore Lane, Grosse Pointe, MI 48236

Adelle Cox Convention Service & Consultants, 321 NW 186th Street, Miami, FL 33169

Custom Conventions, 1739 Julia Street, New Orleans, LA 70113

Southwest Speakers, Box 13606, Savannah, GA 31406

The Forum Corporation, 84 State Street, Boston, MA 02109

People Potential Speakers Bureau, 3560 Lancaster Drive, NE, Salem OR 97303

Al Heydrick Associates, 2830 NE 29th Avenue, Lighthouse Point, FL 33064

Success Seminars, 1539 Monrovia Avenue, Newport Beach, CA 92663

Marketing Concepts, Inc., Two Pennsylvania Plaza, New York, NY 10001

Penton Learning Systems, 420 Lexington Avenue, New York, NY 10017

The Ruffles Co., Box 47, Bushkill, PA 18324

SCL Group and Convention Services, 10521 S. Post Oak, Houston, TX 77035

Dorothy Sarnoff's Speech Dynamics, 111 W. 57th Street, New York, NY 10019

Sherman Exposition Management, 1330 Boylston Street, Boston, MA 02167

Showcase Associates, Inc., 173 Fernbrook Avenue, Wyncote, PA 19095

People Plus, 5701 51st Street, Lubbock, TX 79424

Unconventional Conventions, 8 Park Road, Paterson, NJ 07514

Verbal Communications, Inc., 7241 Midbury, Dallas, TX 75230

Harry Walker Agency, Inc., Empire State Bldg, 350 5th Avenue, New York, NY 10016

Success Systems, Inc., 1600 East 25th Street, Chattanooga, TN 37407

Talbot, Talbot & Berlin, Inc., 9441 Common Street, Baton Rouge, LA 70809

Wayne Short Lecture Management, 1736 Stockton Street, San Francisco, CA 94133

The Handley Management, 51 Church Street, Boston, MA 02116

Booking Sun West, Seminars, Inc., 4023 E. Grant Rd, Tucson, AZ 85712

Contemporary Programs, Inc., 3136 Lafayette, Houston, TX 77005

Eastern U.S. Show Productions, Inc., 121 Chestnut Street, Philadelphia, PA 19106

California Speakers Bureau, 1517 Andreas Avenue, San Jose, CA 95118

PROPOSAL-WRITING REMINDERS

A recommended format for small-to average-size proposals is this:

1. INTRODUCTION
   Introduce yourself (organization) and your understanding or appraisal of the requirement in brief terms.

2. DISCUSSION

Continue understanding of requirement by exploring, analyzing (thinking out loud), leading logically to selected approach.

3. PROPOSAL PROJECT/PROGRAM

Implement approach selected now with specific plans and commitments, including staffing, organization, management, schedule, deliverables.

4. ORGANIZATION'S QUALIFICATIONS

Demonstrate capability and experience of your organization as such, with descriptions of facilities, resources, track record of successful past projects. Include references, letters of commendation, other testimonials.

For larger proposals more chapters or sections may be needed, especially separate section on management and contract administration, possibly separate section on understanding of requirement.

PROPOSAL DO'S AND DON'TS

Do be as specific as possible.

Do make specific commitments.

Do quantify, as well as qualify, all specific items.

Don't use hyperbole, superlatives, adjectives and adverbs generally. Stick to the most impressive nouns and verbs you can command.

Be sure that if the client has failed to furnish specifications, you furnish (propose) them, both for your own protection and because it strengthens your technical proposal.

Do remember that the client really wants to buy some result or set of results. Promise those results and then prove that you can and will deliver.

Do check carefully to see that your cost proposal (a separate document) agrees in all respects with (and is totally compatible with) your technical proposal.

Do remember that all of these points apply as much to a 2-or 3-page letter proposal as they do to a 100-or 200-page formal proposal; it's a matter of degree, but not of kind.

Do take the trouble to customize each proposal in all respects for each project you pursue. Using standardized boiler plate material is an almost sure route to failure in the proposal game. Don't cut corners.

Do remember that there is ordinarily only one winner in a proposal contest; "close" may count in pitching horseshoes, but it does not count here.

Do analyze the client's problem most carefully and at length before beginning to write. Beginning to write before doing a careful analysis is the same as racing your tongue before putting your brain in gear.

Do try to get someone to play Devil's Advocate with your proposal before submitting it. If you wrote the proposal, you're prejudiced, so don't trust your own judgment.

UNDERSTANDING COSTS

The single most confusing point about profit and costs for many self-employed individuals is their own draw or salary. Many have a strong tendency to regard their salaries as profits. Not so; all salaries and wages are *costs*. Profit is what is left over, if anything, after all costs have been recovered. Here is an example to illustrate why that is true:

Suppose that you have several slow weeks when you do absolutely no business. But you do have cash reserves and you go on drawing $500 every week as a weekly salary. Can you call that $500 profit? Obviously not; it is cost. It is still cost when you have taken in $2,000 every week. Your salary, like the salaries of anyone else employed by you, is always cost. If you draw $100,000 a year from your practice, pay all bills as they come due, but have not taken in more than enough to pay all expenses and your handsome salary, you have made zero profit that year. Perhaps you banked part of your salary and have saved $20,000. That's your personal gain; your business still shows zero profit. And even if you take that $20,000 you saved and put it back into your business, the business still shows no profit; you have merely capitalized it further by lending the business money. The business is an entity and should be regarded as a separate entity. It's a businesslike attitude.

There are other factors to consider about costs. If you diversify into publications and possibly audio cassettes, you will also begin to carry an inventory, and that represents cost, the cost of money tied up (money costs money) and the cost of storage space and handling. In some cases you have inventory shrinkage or spoilage; books can become damaged from mildew, moisture, and other conditions.

If you are going to do business with government agencies, you need to understand something of the terms, but even if you are going to get no closer to the jargon of accounting than talking to your own accountant, you need to understand some of the terms in common use and what they usually mean. ("Usually" because some accountants and others have somewhat different understandings of many of the commonly used terms.)

A Handful of Terms You'll Run into and What They Mean

Asset:	Any property with an intrinsic value, including patents, inventory, proprietary knowledge, and special contacts.
Bid:	Quotation or offer, price only ordinarily; may be written and sealed.
Bid set:	Jargon for solicitation package with bidding instructions.
Burden:	Indirect costs, especially fixed costs.
Burden rate:	Percentage of selling price or percentage rate attached to direct cost to cover a pro rata portion of your indirect costs.
Bottom line:	According to what kind of document is in question, the bottom line is the final price a customer must pay, including all costs and fees, or is the profit or loss appearing as the bottom line of a financial report. In more general use, it refers to the essence of the matter or the basic question.
Cost, direct:	Costs incurred specifically and wholly for the project or transaction in question.
Cost, indirect:	Cost of being open for business whether you are making sales or not, and including such closely related costs as taxes and insurance.
Debit:	Bill or debt, something on the "minus" side of the ledger.
Entry:	Any item entered into the accounting ledgers.
Gross:	Figures before adjustment, as in gross sales, meaning total sales before deducting cancellations; or in gross dollars represented by sales; or in gross profit, meaning difference between direct cost handling price, before adjusting for other costs.
Liability:	A negative factor which may be debts owed, a bad investment, something that is going to force a loss, limit profits, or otherwise operate against your best interests.
Loss leader:	Sale item or "special" on which you will lose money but which you think will produce more business and ultimate profit.

Markup:	Amount by which you increase cost of an item to cover all your costs and produce a profit. Also used to designate rate of increase.
Overhead:	General cost of doing business, including such items as rent, heat, light, telephone, postage, advertising, printing, taxes, and insurance.
ROI:	Stands for return on investment, which is a means for determining if an investment is worthwhile, producing a profit commensurate with the risk and the money tied up. (Especially as compared with ROI if money were invested at low-risk, as in government bonds.)

Abbreviations

Following are the abbreviations used in this book, plus a few others you are likely to run across:

AAA:	Highest credit rating possible (see also "Triple-A")
ADP:	Automatic data processing
A&E:	Architect & engineer (also A/E and A-E)
ARC:	American Red Cross
ASPR:	Armed Services Procurement Regulations
B/L:	Bill of lading
BMEWS:	Ballistic Missile Early Warning System
BOA:	Basic ordering agreement
BPA:	Blanket purchase agreement
CBD:	*Commerce Business Daily*
CEO:	Chief executive officer
CFR:	Code of Federal Regulations
CO:	Contracting officer
COB:	Close of business
COR:	Contracting officer's representative (see also COTR and GTR)
COTR:	Contracting officer's technical representative (see also COR and GTR)
CPAF:	Cost Plus award fee
CPFF:	Cost plus fixed
CPM:	Critical path method
CVS:	Certified value specialist
DACA:	Days after contract award

DAR:	Defense Acquisition Regulations
DLA:	Defense Logistics Agency
DOD:	Department of Defense
DOT:	Department of Transportation
EPA:	Environmental Protection Agency
FAR:	Federal Acquisition Regulations
FOB:	Free on board
FPR:	Federal Procurement Regulations
FSC:	Federal Supply Classification
FSS:	Federal Supply Service
FTC:	Federal Trade Commission
G&A:	General & Administrative (costs)
GAO:	General Accounting Office
GE:	General Electric Company
GFE:	Government-furnished equipment (also GFM, Government-furnished material, and GFP, government-furnished property)
GNP:	Gross national product
GPO:	Government Printing Office
GSA:	General Services Administration
GTR:	Government technical representative (see also COR and COTR)
HVAC:	Heating, ventilation, and air conditioning
IBM:	International Business Machines
IFB:	Information for bid (solicitation form 33)
IG:	Industrial Group (supply classification, but also Inspector General)
indef. qty.	Indefinite quantity (bidding stipulation)
ITT:	International Telephone and Telegraph
MBDA:	Minority Business Development Agency
MBO:	Management by objectives
NAB:	National Alliance of Business
NARS:	National Archives and Records Service
NASA:	National Aviation and Space Administration
NASPR:	NASA Procurement Regulations
NSN:	National stock number

NTIS:	National Technical Information Service
OEO:	Office of Economic Opportunity (now defunct)
OFPP:	Office of Federal Procurement Policy
OMB:	Office Management and Budget
OMBE:	Office of Minority Business Enterprise (now MBDA)
OSHA:	Occupational Safety and Health Administration
PERT:	Program review and evaluation technique
PO:	Purchase order
PR:	Public relations (also purchase request)
RCA:	Radio Corporation of America
R&D:	Research and development
RFP:	Request for proposals
RFQ:	Request for quotations
ROI:	Return on investment
SAVE:	Society of American Value Engineers
SBA:	Small Business Administration
SOW:	Statement of work
T&M:	Time and materials

AVERAGE CONSULTING RATES

The chief difficulty in establishing average consulting rates is that it has been exceedingly difficult to determine exactly what *consulting* means and doesn't mean; there has long been controversy over it. There are several factors which affect the rates you may or should charge:

A relative rank in terms of experience and training—for example, *senior, mid-grade, junior.*

Scarcity of the skills or law of supply and demand—for example, financial experts are presumably scarcer than technical writers, hence should be able to command more.

Local conditions—a given consultant living in New York City is likely to price daily fees higher than one living in Phoenix.

These factors show why some consultants can command fees of $1,000 per day and even more while others have difficulty getting $200 per day. As a general guideline, here are the ranges most commonly encountered:

Engineering or other high technology specialist:	$300–$650
Sales and marketing specialist:	300–500
Management specialist:	300–500
Executive recruiter (search) specialist:	400–600
Communications specialist, public relations:	200–400
Instructor/lecturer:	200–400
Planning, office systems specialist:	200–400

Even these are only the most general of guidelines. Most consultants begin asking for low rates and gradually raise them until they believe their rates are about right. Some do it the other way, asking for high rates at first, and lowering them until they begin to close sales.

SEMINAR GUIDELINES

Here are the important things to remember and do when you wish to begin producing seminars:

Decide whether individuals will pay to attend or whether it is possible to get employers to send staff people and pay for them. Accordingly, advertise in newspapers or by direct mail, respectively, and schedule for Saturday or work day, respectively.

If you use direct mail to solicit, remember that using bulk mail and self-mailers (flat brochures that require no envelope) means that you must mail large numbers of brochures to get results. You can reduce quantity needed and make mailing package more sophisticated (and presumably more effective) by using envelopes and first class mail.

Engage meeting room at local hotel/motel or other facility, arrange to serve coffee in morning. Good schedule for one-day seminar is as follows:

8:00 am: Coffee and registration or registration verification (if advance registrations taken by mail)

9:00 am–12:00 noon: Presentation; 10-minute coffee break mid-morning

12:00 noon–1:30 pm: Lunch break

1:30–4:30 pm: Presentations; 10-minute coffee break mid-afternoon

4:30 pm until? Questions and answers, sale of back-of-the-room materials. (May also be sold during lunch break and during coffee breaks)

Although you sell books, newsletters, and/or reports, you should have some kind of handout to give attendees. It need not be elaborate, but a seminar attendee wishes to leave with something in hand to show for the expense and experience.

Lunch may be included as part of the seminar—it is a feature that helps greatly to attract attendance, but it is also expensive—or you may simply tell all attendees where nearby eating places are located.

Try to use visuals—charts, posters, transparencies, slides, or other—in your presentations. It helps make points and hold attention.

Change your pace as often as possible, to hold attention: lecture, show a visual, involve attendees in a group discussion, have them do a workshop exercise, and otherwise relieve the tedium of straight lecturing unless you happen to be an exceptional lecturer.

Show your enthusiasm. Don't be reluctant to wave your arms, raise your voice, grin, laugh out loud, gesture, make faces, tell humorous stories about your own misadventures. Nothing is as contagious as enthusiasm, but you have to *show* it.

Don't try to be Bob Hope. You're a consultant, and you may even be a good lecturer, but Bob Hope you're not. Don't strain to be funny, and if you must tell a funny story, be sure that it's not ethnic, sexy, or in questionable taste: you've absolutely no way to predict the attitudes of your listeners, so play it safe. Best of all, don't tell jokes at all; just stick to your subject.

Best not to ask people to hold their questions until later. It's better to answer the question while the individual remembers it and can get any confusion straightened out. Otherwise, that individual may miss out on much of what you are saying. Take questions as indicators that you have either not been as clear as you think you are or not as complete in covering the subject as you think. It is likely that others in the room have the same confusion about the matter.

If an attendee gets a bit hostile or tries to have fun at your expense, be good natured about it and hold your temper. Don't exchange barbs; it is almost sure to backfire on you, even when you win a battle of wits with a heckler. If it gets to be a serious interference, offer to meet privately with the individual at the end of the session, as a courtesy to others who want to proceed.

SEMINAR IDEAS

Seminars are training sessions. Most are specific how-to presentations, and the more sharply focused the how-to-do-it objective is, the easier it is to get prospects interested. But always be sure that you know exactly to whom your seminar is directed if you want to get results. Here is an example: After I had been interviewed on a local TV program as a consultant on marketing to the federal government, I was swamped with telephone calls and letters for several weeks. I soon learned that these calls were coming from individuals and self-employed entrepreneurs (during my interview, I had made it clear that many government contracts go out to individuals), many of whom could not afford my full-day seminar, nor were they interested in everything I presented in that seminar. I therefore hit on the idea of $25 mini-seminar of about 3 hours, to be held on Saturdays in my own offices for a group of not more than 15–20 people. During that session I would make a 1-hour general presentation of opportunities in the federal market for small contracts and small contractors, and then answer questions and offer individual counseling to questioners. (One reason for limiting the size of the group.)

The experiment was highly successful. The profit was not great even at that time. (Today I would have to charge considerably more than $25 were I to repeat the experiment.) But it was satisfactory, compensated me for my time, and gave me a good feeling because I was helping people. (I had been frustrated by all those calls when I could not offer much help to callers; this plan was the result of my thinking hard and long about how to help those who had called.)

A gentleman from California who gives seminars on consulting and claims pre-eminence as the leading authority on the subject of consulting and related matters is pursuing a somewhat similar idea. For several years he has been traveling the country offering all-day seminars on the fine art of becoming a consultant, but he has changed his pattern in that he now offers two 3½-hour seminars: a morning session on consulting, and an afternoon session on how to produce successful seminars and workshops. At the moment, he charges $65 for each session, $120 for both sessions. The fact that he sells his books, reports, and newsletter subscriptions, too, at each of his seminars, is one of the reasons he has them priced rather modestly.

REGISTRATION

Although many seminar presenters register attendees at the door a few minutes before the seminar begins, there are benefits in advance registration, and it is in this manner that I have generally arranged my own seminars. For one thing, advance registration provides ample time to clear personal checks and verify credit-card payments. For another, it gives you a pretty good idea ahead of time as to how many attendees you will have. It is also a great help to the perennial cash-flow problem that most small businesses and a great many big businesses have.

This is not to say that you should not accept spontaneous registrations at the door. To encourage advance registration, however, many seminar producers have a reduced fee for advance registration, and that almost invariably results in few at-the-door registrations. There is one drawback: Many people are reluctant to pay several weeks ahead for fear that they will not be able to attend due to some last-minute problem, and that they will then lose the money. To combat this, you must have some kind of protective guarantee, but many seminar producers offer a rather unsatisfactory guarantee in that they demand an unreasonably long advance notice of inability to attend and request for refund. Many also exact a penalty payment, a la university or college registration, and refund only 75 or 80 percent of the fee.

I have used this plan with satisfactory results: Any registrant unable to attend may send a last-minute substitute without advance notice. Anyone who can't attend has an automatic rain check for any of the next three times the seminar is held in the same city, regardless of how late the notice of inability to attend is given. The rain check may be used by anyone designated by the original registrant. This has produced registrant satisfaction and fewer problems than any other system I have tried.

GROUP CONSULTATION IDEAS AND POSSIBILITIES

The mini-seminar idea is useful in another way. Yours may be one of those fields where your clients really do not require a great deal of your time, but need only some general orientation and guidance. You may be able to adapt the mini-seminar idea and combine it with the group-therapy concept to produce group-consultation sessions. This may even be of a nature that lends itself to a series of sessions stretching over a period of time. That is, you may wish to enroll a group for a once-a-week or twice-a-week series of mini-seminars at which you will make a general presentation at the first session, and then conduct discussions and question-and-answer exchanges at a series of future sessions at some modest cost per attendee.

This begins to take on something of the coloration of a school or training class, and in a sense it is. The distinguishing feature is that you are customizing the information for each attendee, by soliciting his or her problems and offering direct counsel. Each attendee is entitled to bring his or her specific problems to the sessions and get your personal analysis and advice, as though each had contracted individually for 10, 20, or 30 minutes of your time.

Such a plan would lend itself to consultation in such fields as writing, public speaking, office systems, weight loss, and many other areas.

CUSTOM IN-HOUSE SEMINARS FOR EXTRA PROFITS

One very neglected idea is that of doing seminars in-house for clients on a custom basis. Without actively seeking such contracts, I find myself receiving a steadily increasing number of inquiries and subsequent requests to present seminars on this basis. Early in my seminar-pesentation efforts, when I was favored with such a request I thought in terms of government contracts and developed a proposal which called for an effort to design a seminar program and then present it, with a required budget of several thousand dollars. The cost was largely for the effort to develop the custom seminar.

I discovered quite quickly that this idea was impractical. I had had such inquiries from some rather large companies, such as Westinghouse in Baltimore, Maryland, and Emerson in St. Louis, Missouri. I thought that surely these companies, who so often spent several thousand dollars to send only two or three of their people to a seminar, would welcome the opportunity to present a seminar to perhaps 20 or more of their people for the same cost. I was wrong. I failed to close a single one of these prospects, although I tried many times. The situation was the same one I had learned earlier as an executive with a training developer—the federal government is almost the only customer for expensive custom development of training; almost everyone else wants to buy training off the shelf.

Accordingly, I set about deciding how I would do this in the future. I decided that I would make my response to such inquiries in the future along these lines:

1. I would offer any of my standard seminars on government marketing and/or proposal writing.

2. If the client would furnish me suitable information about interests and needs, I would customize my presentation to the extent that I could do so without special preparation.

3. I would charge my regular consulting fee (plus expenses if travel was required).

4. I would furnish my standard handout manual at a modest per-copy cost. (I later changed this when I found little profit and lots of trouble involved in doing this. I now furnish the client one reproducible copy in advance, with permission to duplicate enough copies to hand out to the attendees.)

Since adopting this method, I have not failed to close a single prospect. I do not realize the kind of profits from such a seminar that I have from organizing and producing my open-registration seminars, but neither do I run any risk nor go to any trouble and extra work. I simply present myself and make my day's presentation, collecting a day's consulting fee therefore, and sometimes winning subsequent consulting work to assist the client with a specific project.

I have also found that it is not really necessary for me to pursue clients directly. In a number of cases others in the area have acted as brokers or booking agents for me, selling the day's seminar presentation to one of their own clients and marking up what I charge the agent, which is my standard consulting fee for the day. That demonstrates that I could undoubtedly raise my price, since my booking agents are charging at least a 50-percent markup on my fee, but I prefer to maintain the same fee, whether dealing with the client directly or with someone in a middleman position.

I have no doubt that this is a viable idea for anyone who has one or more standard presentations. To assist you in pursuing such prospects, I have listed elsewhere in this chapter approximately 65 speakers' booking agents, many of whom specialize in convention and conference support. These are only a sampling, and a search under the headings "Lecture Bureaus" and "Convention Management" in the Yellow Pages of any large city telephone directory will produce many more of these.

CANNED SEMINARS

Many seminar producers tape record their seminars and then have a professional sound studio do suitable editing and make a master tape (although some seminar presenters have also used the raw, unedited tape successfully). They then sell the tapes to those who have attended and to those who cannot attend, and command as much or almost as much for the cassettes as they do for the personal attendance at the seminars.

A FEW NAMES THE CONSULTANT OUGHT TO KNOW

Among those who specialize in consulting by lecturing, writing, and otherwise dealing in the subject of consulting itself are the following, in alphabetical order:

Berliner, Stan: The Consultant's Network, 57 W. 89th Street, New York, NY 10024.
   The Consultant's Network is an organization of consultants in various disciplines. The mission of the organization is to enable all members to gain by an exchange of referrals.

Bermont, Hubert: The Consultant's Library, Bermont Books, Inc., 815 15th Street, NW, Washington, DC 20005.

Hubert Bermont is a consultant specializing in the book-publishing field and is himself the author of a number of books, some of which were published by his own firm with great success. He is also a publisher, an activity which now commands much of his attention. He publishes only those books which are of direct interest to consultants in the pursuit of their profession.

Kennedy, James H., Consultants News, Kennedy & Kennedy, Inc., Templeton Road, Fitzwilliam, NH 03447.

James Kennedy publishes the monthly newsletter *Consultants News,* which reports on doings and ideas about consulting and consultants, and is regarded as one of the better informed authorities on the subject. He also stocks and sells a variety of books on the subject of consulting and on related subjects through his "Consultants Bookstore," for which he has a catalog available. He is not a complete stranger to the seminar platform.

Hartman, Charles, Hartman Consulting Services, 11437 Cherry Hill Road, Beltsville, MD 20705.

Charles Hartman is a practicing consultant who occasionally guest-lectures at seminars, and has often presented seminars on consulting and related activity in adult-education programs in the Washington, DC, area. He provides his services primarily to high-technology firms.

Lanning, J. Stephen. Consulting Opportunities Journal, P.O. Box 17674, Washington, DC 20041.

Steve Lanning is himself a consultant in developing and marketing mail-order publications, is founder and publisher of the *Consulting Opportunities Journal,* a 24- to 32-page tabloid which is the most ambitious periodical in the consulting field, having counted its subscribers in the thousands before the fourth edition was printed.

Shenson, Howard, L., Howard L. Shenson, Inc., 20121 Ventura Blvd, Suite 245, Woodland Hills, CA 91364.

Howard Shenson devotes most of his time to travelling the country giving seminars on consulting and related activities, but he has found the time to produce a few small books and a newsletter on the subject.

Tennant, Frank B. Jr., The Frank Tennant Consultancy, 1301 Forestwood Drive, McLean, VA 22101.

Frank Tennant is a retired Army officer, formerly an instructor at West Point, a fluent speaker and expert in specialized instructional techniques and publications. Tennant offers his own seminars frequently on how to develop and operate a successful consulting practice.

NEWSLETTER IDEAS AND TIPS FOR THE CONSULTANT

Newsletters and consultants go together like ham and cheese; they are a natural combination. One reason is that just as the basis for many consultancies is some highly specialized area of skills and knowledge, the basis for many newsletters is some highly specialized area of information and guidance—written consultancy, in a very real sense.

There are three basic types of newsletters; the newsletter deals in and offers one of the following, along with information that might be called news, although it is difficult to call what you offer *news* if you publish only once a month or once a week:

Distillation of items abstracted from many other publications, often as many as a hundred

Minute details about some highly specialized subject which gets scant coverage elsewhere in the business or professional press

Advice and counsel, possibly along with some insider tips

An example of the first type is any of many newsletters dealing with sales and marketing. The publishers draw from dozens of business magazines and other publications. The value of such a newsletter is that the reader gets the distillation of far more publications than he or she has time to read. The success—and to a large degree the subscription price it may command—depends largely on how accurately the editor/publisher gauges the readers' areas of interest.

The second type of newsletter is often a technological one, dealing with specialized batteries or electronic miniaturization, medical subjects, or any of literally thousands of highly specialized areas. Such a newsletter generally can be written only by a highly trained technical specialist.

The third type of newsletter is typified by the investment-advisory newsletters, of which there are a good number, some of them extraordinarily successful. This kind of newsletter, because of its main reason for existence and the main reason subscribers pay the high prices most of these command, is almost another kind of group consulting. The interest and motivation of the subscribers is to get the insider tips most publishers of such letters offer, but their chief motivation generally is to receive good advice from an expert. If the expert who publishes such a newsletter is right often enough, he or she becomes almost sanctified as a guru, a prognosticator, a sage, perhaps a modern-day Nostradamus.

The logical newsletter for the consultant is either the second or third variety or a combination of the two. The easiest type of newsletter to write is the first type becaue it is nothing more than a rehash of what has already appeared elsewhere. The chief skills required are reading rapidly and identifying what is of interest and abstracting efficiently so that a great deal of information is packed into a few pages every month.

The second and third types are somewhat difficult. For one thing, they require disciplined and faithful reading of very dull material regularly and painstaking consideration of what is worthy of abstracting. For another, they require following up leads to get "the story behind the story." (More on this in a moment.)

WHERE/HOW TO GET INFORMATION INPUT

Getting useful information—and for some types of newsletters, this means getting information that no one else has—can be an arduous job; don't underestimate what it takes to produce a good newsletter every month. (Unless you can put lots of your time into it, don't try to publish more often than once a month—at least not when you begin.) Before you put out your first edition, try to have at least some of your copy for a second and third editon on hand or know where you are going to get it, and, above all, have your information-supply pipelines established and open. Here are some of the ways of doing that:

Get a form letter drawn up announcing that you are a newsletter publisher (no need to mention how new you are!) and wish to be "put on distribution" for any releases and other information of interest. (You will already have identified the nature of your newsletter and the kinds of information you want.)

Make up a mailing list for this form letter. Send it to PR firms, manufacturers, legislators, non-profit organizations, and anyone else you consider might be a source of information. (Because I write a newsletter on government marketing, I am on distribution for release from a great many legislators and government agencies.)

You'll soon start receiving news releases. Many will be worthless. (Perhaps because those who received your form letter can't read, or perhaps because they don't care.) But many will be helpful. You'll also soon begin to receive releases from people you didn't write to; somehow your name gets on lots of mailing lists. You'll be amazed at what else you'll get—advertising mail (don't be too quick to discard it; some of it contains useful information and ideas), books, pamphlets, brochures, broadsides, samples, other people's newsletters, and many other things.

Now you'll discover why your release ought to have a name on it as a contact—once in a while you'll get an intriguing release and want to know more. That's when you call that listed contact, begin to ask questions, perhaps get the story behind the story.

Before long you'll be swapping complimentary subscriptions with others, and then you'll begin swapping information. Your telephone will start ringing with items others want to pass on or leads they give you on stories.

Properly handled, the newsletter can be a great asset in at least the following ways:

A successful newsletter is a profit center in itself, producing substantial income.

A newsletter with a good circulation produces sales of other things you produce—books, reports, seminars, tape cassettes, consultations.

A well-done newsletter enhances your professional image, lends you added prestige, gives you a bigger voice.

A successful newsletter is a powerful marketing tool in other ways than as a direct medium for selling services and products to your subscribers; if it is circulated widely enough, it aids you in becoming better known, which is one major key to success in the consulting profession generally. Some of the marketing ideas about to be described are aimed at achieving that, as well as at producing enough paid subscriptions to make the publication economically viable.

MARKETING YOUR NEWSLETTER

It has become virtually an article of faith that newsletters must be sold by direct mail. Other methods of marketing newsletter subscriptions have proved to be far less successful.

Many newsletter publishers hit on what they believe is the original idea of sending complimentary copies to prospects. This method not only does not work well but is actually to be shunned. (There have been notable exceptions, but mark well that they were exceptions.) For some reason, the sample newsletter appears to come as a disappointment to the recipient, possibly because few newsletters are truly impressive in appearance and they are, by their very nature, quite brief as compared with a magazine or daily newspaper. Yet they generally cost considerably more than a magazine or daily newsletter.

One scheme that has been tried by a few publishers and which appears to work well is the trial subscription. There are at least two ways to offer a trial subscription, and one way works far more effectively than the other.

1. Call anything less than 1 year a trial subscription—offer either 3- or 6-month subscriptions. Trouble with this is that it is too much like the sample newsletter; the renewal rate is often quite dismal.

2. Offer a year's subscription, with the first issue free—on trial—and advise the subscriber that he or she needs only to write *cancel* across the invoice if he or she doesn't like the newsletter. Send the invoice for a 1-year subscription with the first issue, and if it is not returned marked *cancel*, keep on sending issues. It works pretty well in most cases, better than many other methods.

Other newsletter publishers offer special discount prices, free books, free special reports not available elsewhere, and other inducements. My experience suggests that discounts work better than any bonus books. On one occasion with a newsletter I was promoting, I offered this special: I would increase anyone's subscription by one-half again, free of charge. A 6-month subscription at the 6-month price would bring 9 months of issues; a 1-year subscription would bring 18 months of issues. It worked out well and was a successful subscription drive.

In another drive I offered three special manuals as well as special reduced price on the 1-year subscription. (The campaign offered only 1-year subscriptions.) There were four separate items, each priced separately and available separately, but a subscriber could order the entire package at a substantial saving for $100, and this campaign was most satisfactory in the results it produced. The prospect of a bargain seems never to lose its appeal, and always to be more persuasive than any "free gifts" are.

OTHER READILY AVAILABLE SOURCES

Lists of Small Business Administration and General Services Administration offices throughout the United States are to be found in the *Directory of Federal Purchasing Offices*, already listed earlier in this chapter, or may be requested from the following headquarters offices:

The Small Business Administration, 1441 L Street, NW, Washington, DC 20416, (202) 653-6365

The General Services Administration, 18th and F Streets, NW, Washington, DC 20405, (202) 655-4000

For information on state governments and their procurement and special programs offices, request the *Directory of State Small Business Programs* from the Office of Chief Counsel for Advocacy, the Small Business Administration, at the address listed here.

CHAMBERS OF COMMERCE

Chambers of Commerce for several of the largest cities in the United States are listed here. Information on others may be requested from the United States Chamber of Commerce, 1615 H Street, NW, Washington, DC 20062, (202) 659-6207.

NEW YORK, NY 10005, 65 Liberty Street, (212) 766-1300

ATLANTA, GA 30335, N. Omni International, (404) 521-0845

CHICAGO, IL 60628, 11145 S. Michigan Ave., (312) 928-3200

LOS ANGELES, CA 90051, 404 S. Bixel, (213) 629-0711

BOSTON, MA 02111, 125 High Street, (617) 426-1250

SAN FRANCISCO, CA 94104, 465 California Street, (415) 392-4511

Index